RURAL ECONOMY AND SOCIETY
IN THE DUCHY OF CORNWALL
1300–1500

RURAL ECONOMY
AND SOCIETY IN
THE DUCHY OF
CORNWALL
1300 – 1500

JOHN HATCHER

Lecturer in History, University of Kent
at Canterbury

CAMBRIDGE
AT THE UNIVERSITY PRESS
1970

Published by the Syndics of the Cambridge University Press
Bentley House, 200 Euston Road, London N.W.1
American Branch: 32 East 57th Street, New York, N.Y.10022

© Cambridge University Press 1970

Library of Congress Catalogue Card Number: 74-10 5495
Standard Book Number: 521 07660 9

Printed in Great Britain by
Alden & Mowbray Ltd
at the Alden Press, Oxford

CONTENTS

Contents

FIGURES

vii

Figures

MAPS

TABLES

Tables

PREFACE

This study is based largely upon records stored in the Public Record Office and the Duchy of Cornwall Office, and I thank the staff of both offices for kindly allowing me access to the contents of their muniment rooms; I am particularly grateful to Sir Patrick Kingsley, Secretary and Keeper of the Records of the Duchy of Cornwall, and to Mr Stanley Opie who assisted my studies at the Duchy of Cornwall Office by efficiently furnishing me with manuscripts and freely giving me the benefit of his wide knowledge of Cornwall and its history. I am indebted to Dr A. R. Bridbury and Miss Olive Coleman for much help and guidance during and since my undergraduate days, to my friend Dr Ian Blanchard for the stimulus of many conversations on economic history in general and Cornish medieval evidence in particular, and to Mr Peter L. Hull and Mr Harold Fox for discussions on place-names and field-systems respectively. Professor Gordon Mingay kindly read and commented on a draft of Chapter I. My indebtedness to Professor Postan is two-fold: firstly, in common with all students of the medieval economy, my studies have benefited immeasurably from the framework provided by his writings; and secondly, on a personal level, he kindly read two complete drafts of this work and provided me with many expert and perceptive criticisms and suggestions. In conclusion it is a pleasure to record, albeit inadequately, my deep gratitude to Professor Eleanora Carus-Wilson whose inspiration, guidance and assistance has at all times far exceeded that which any post-graduate could hope to receive from his supervisor. She has selflessly and skilfully worked through innumerable drafts and improved them out of all recognition, with a multitude of suggestions ranging from corrections of grammar and style to the clarification and justification of argument; it is no mere platitude to state that without her help and friendship this book would be much the poorer.

The editors of the *Economic History Review* and the *Agricultural*

History Review have kindly given permission for material previously published in those journals to be reproduced here. This book, which is based upon my London Ph.D. thesis, submitted in 1967, has been published with the assistance of a generous grant from the late Miss Isobel Thornley's Bequest to the University of London; some money towards the cost of publication was also granted by the Duchy of Cornwall.

AUTHOR'S NOTES

Place-names: owing to the uncertainty which at present surrounds the study of Cornish place-names the majority of spellings used in the book follow the most common form found in the documents.

Rent: the peculiar system of tenure by which the bulk of the lands of the Cornish manors of the Duchy of Cornwall were held required tenants to make two distinct money payments: a rent and an assession fine. The rent was payable annually and the assession fine in instalments six years in every seven. Thus there exists the possibility of confusion between *rent* meaning the aggregate money payment the tenant made for the land he held (including both assession fine and the annual payments of rent), and *rent* meaning only the annual payments of rent. To avoid this confusion, throughout this study the annual payment of rent alone has been referred to as annual rent, and rent, rent receipts, rent levels etc. refer to the more important aggregate cost of land comprising both annual rents and assession fines.

Canterbury, March 1970   JOHN HATCHER

ABBREVIATIONS

Ag. Hist. Rev.	*Agricultural History Review*
B.M.	*British Museum*
B.P.R.	*Registers of the Black Prince*
C. Ch. R.	*Calendar of Charter Rolls*
C.C.R.	*Calendar of Close Rolls*
C.F.R.	*Calendar of Fine Rolls*
Cal. Inq. Misc.	*Calendar of Inquisitions Miscellaneous*
Cal. Inq. P.M.	*Calendar of Inquisitions Post Mortem*
C.P.R.	*Calendar of Patent Rolls*
D.C.O.	Duchy of Cornwall Office
D.N.B.	*Dictionary of National Biography*
Ec. H.R.	*Economic History Review*
J.E.B.H.	*Journal of Economic and Business History*
J.R.I.C.	*Journal of the Royal Institution of Cornwall*
P.R.O.	Public Record Office
Reg.	*Episcopal Register*
Rot. Parl.	*Rotuli Parliamentorum*
T.R.H.S.	*Transactions of the Royal Historical Society*
V.C.H.	*Victoria County History*

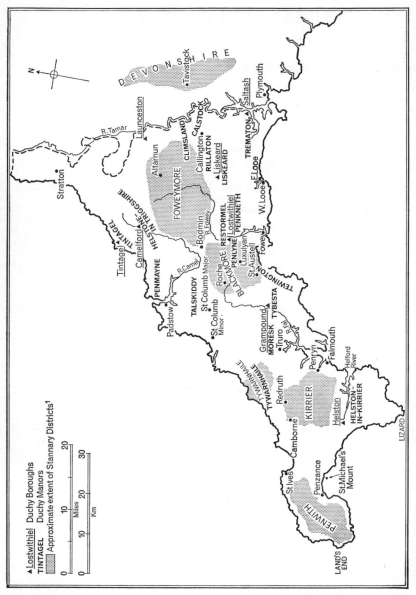

1. Sketch-map of late medieval Cornwall.

The extent of the stannary districts of Cornwall was never defined in the middle ages, and only a very approximate guide to tin-working areas can be gained from the records. Furthermore, the centres of mining activity shifted constantly throughout the period. It should be noted that the area of a stannary cannot be equated with its productivity; for example Foweymore, which covered perhaps the largest area, was the least productive Cornish stannary.

INTRODUCTION

THE SUBJECT AND THE SOURCES

Writing forty years ago Mary Coate expressed herself bewildered by the neglect of the history of the Duchy of Cornwall shown by serious historians.[1] But Miss Coate's words fell on deaf ears, and the fruits of her excellent but incidental work on the Duchy in the Civil War period[2] and some stimulating but brief mentions by A. L. Rowse[3] comprise virtually the only scholarly writings on its history produced in modern times.[4] The Duchy of Cornwall formed in the middle ages, as it still does today, a body of royal estates of the first importance and, being centred on Cornwall, its records have much to tell of the history of an area of Britain about which very little has so far been written.

Cornwall was a remote and somewhat forbidding county to most Englishmen in the middle ages. Adjoining the rest of England only by its eastern boundary, Cornwall must have seemed barely accessible by land and, inhabited by 'a strange unfriendly folk' who spoke an alien tongue, it could have offered little attraction to the visitor. John de Grandisson, soon after his appointment as Bishop of Exeter in 1327, wrote despairingly to his friends at Avignon describing the south-west peninsula as 'not only the ends of the earth, but the very end of the ends thereof',[5] and Adam de Carleton in a pathetic letter tendering his resignation as Archdeacon of Cornwall in 1342, after more than 35 years in office, confessed himself unable to communicate with the Cornish, but it was not just a

---

[1] M. Coate, 'The Duchy of Cornwall: its history and administration, 1640–1660', *T.R.H.S.*, 4th ser., X (1927), 135.

[2] *Ibid.* and *Cornwall in the Great Civil War* (Oxford, 1933).

[3] 'The Duchy of Cornwall', *The Gentleman's Magazine* (January 1937) and *Tudor Cornwall, Portrait of a Society* (1941), especially pp. 77–83.

[4] For an interesting account of the Duchy written in the seventeenth century see: Sir John Doddridge, *The History of the Ancient and Modern Estate of the Principality of Wales, Duchy of Cornwall and Earldom of Chester* (1630).

[5] 'Et ecce, Pater dulcissme, dum nedum in mundi finibus, set—ut ita dicam—in finium finibus consisto' (*Reg. Grandisson*, I, 97–8).

Introduction

question of language difficulties for he plainly stated that 'the folk of these parts are quite extraordinary, being of a rebellious temper, and obdurate in the face of attempts to teach and correct'.[1] Yet personal opinions and reminiscences, however eloquent, make poor history, and we can counter the charges of Adam de Carleton with the commendation of Richard Germyn, who wrote to his employer Sir William Stonor in 1481: 'And as to your tenaunts in Cornwale, thei be as trew unto you as y can understond as any tenauntes that ye have.'[2] Furthermore, an examination of the records of the Cornish estates of the Duchy of Cornwall reveals that the manors in this remote county, with its notoriously recalcitrant population, were managed with efficiency and equanimity throughout the later middle ages. The relations between the Duchy and its tenants were remarkably cordial, and no examples of serious or concerted opposition are recorded; the absence of compulsion from large areas of manorial life combined with a prompt and apparently fair hearing for most grievances created a most satisfactory working atmosphere.[3] The higher branches of the administration, which were based in London, kept in close and constant touch with affairs in Cornwall, thereby achieving an exceptional standard of management and solvency.

This present study of the seventeen Cornish demesne manors of the Duchy in the fourteenth and fifteenth centuries is based upon a magnificent range of documents, probably unrivalled for lay estates. Almost one hundred years of enrolled manorial accounts survive in the Public Record Office and the Duchy of Cornwall Office for the period between the foundation of the Duchy in 1337 and the accession of Henry VII in 1485, and in addition some 27 accounts exist of the estates under the Earls of Cornwall, from 1287–1336.[4] Furthermore, there are more than eighty receivers' accounts dealing in part with the assessionable manors. But perhaps most valuable of

[1] 'Item populus in illis Partibus est valde mirabilis, rebellis et difficillis ad informandum et corrigendum' (*Reg. Grandisson*, II, 958).
[2] *The Stonor Letters and Papers, 1290–1483*, ed. C. L. Kingsford, 2 vols, Camden Society, 3rd ser., XXIX and XXX (1919), II, 120
[3] It must be borne in mind, however, that almost all extant records were drawn up by Duchy officials.
[4] For details of these accounts see below, pp. 298–9.

Introduction

all is the series of assession rolls. These rolls, the product of the leasehold (conventionary) system by which the bulk of Duchy lands in Cornwall were held, were compiled, with few exceptions, every seven years and they contain the names of all tenants, as well as the size, location, and rent of each holding, omitting only the freeholdings. Although bearing some resemblance to ordinary manorial rentals, the assession rolls far surpass them in value to the historian as they exist in an almost continuous sequence for the whole of the fourteenth and fifteenth centuries. Within the separate categories of free conventionary, unfree conventionary and *nativi de stipite* the holdings of each vill were grouped together. The rolls provide a unique source of information on the Duchy tenantry and on demand for land. They enable the fluctuating rents of each individual holding to be catalogued, as well as the aggregate rental of each manor. The size of landholdings acquired by tenants at different periods in the fourteenth and fifteenth centuries can be seen at a glance, and the listing of the names of Duchy tenants enables some study to be undertaken concerning the interrelation of agriculture with other branches of the Cornish economy.

THE DUCHY OF CORNWALL IN THE MIDDLE AGES

The Duchy of Cornwall was created by Edward III in full Parliament at Westminster in March 1337 for the maintenance of his eldest son who was then seven years of age.[1] Although many of the features of this creation were novel the core of the estates of the new Duchy was the old Earldom of Cornwall as it had existed during the tenure of Earl Edmund (1272–1300), with possessions in almost a score of counties after extensive purchases and exchanges had been made by his father Richard. Under Edmund the estates of the Earldom in Cornwall contained seventeen demesne manors, the same seventeen manors that were later to become the assessionable manors of the Duchy of Cornwall.[2] These manors, which form

---

[1] Edward of Woodstock was probably created Duke on 3 March. The Great Charter of the Duchy of Cornwall is dated 17 March (P.R.O. Charter Rolls, 124, 11 Edward III, no. 60, m. 28; *Reports touching the Dignity of a Peer of the Realm*, v (1829), 35).

[2] For a full description of the life and estates of Edmund see L. M. Midgley, *Ministers' Accounts of the Earldom of Cornwall, 1296–1297*, Camden Society, 3rd ser., LXVI and

Introduction

the subject of this study, were well distributed throughout the county.[1] In the south-east lay Trematon, Calstock, Climsland, Rillaton and Liskeard; in the north-east Tintagel, Helstone-in-Triggshire and Penmayne; in central Cornwall Talskiddy, Restormel, Penlyne, Penkneth, Tewington and Tybesta; and in the west Tywarnhaile, Moresk and Helston-in-Kirrier.

Edmund's unhappy marriage left him childless, so on his death in September 1300 the Earldom of Cornwall passed to Edward I, his cousin and next heir.[2] For the remaining years of Edward's reign the Earldom stayed in the hands of the Crown, sometimes helping to provide for Thomas of Brotherton and Edmund of Woodstock, sons of the king by his second marriage. But the death of Edward in 1307 heralded a most turbulent period in the history of the Cornish estates, in which they left and returned to the hands of the Crown with bewildering and disruptive frequency. Soon after his accession Edward II used the Earldom to heap favour upon the feckless Gaveston,[3] but opposition to the favourite limited both his tenure of the estates and his life to five years from the time of the grant, and he was executed in 1312. Ignoring the claims to the Earldom of Margaret, widow of Gaveston, and Sir Hugh de Audley, whom she had subsequently married,[4] Edward granted the Cornish lands in 1317 to his wife, Isabella of France.[5] Once again, however, the tenure of the grant was short-lived and in 1324, as a result of a dramatic reversal of favour, Isabella was deprived of her lands in Cornwall, as well as her other estates scattered over many parts of the realm, on the pretext of their vulnerability in view of the threat of invasion from France.[6] The modest alternative sources of revenue provided by Edward II for the maintenance of her household did little to placate Isabella,[7] and she conspired to engineer the downfall of

LXVII (1942–5), and 'Edmund Earl of Cornwall and his Place in History' (Manchester M.A. thesis, 1930). The article on Edmund in the *D.N.B.* is apparently inaccurate in details.

[1] See map, p. xiv. [2] *Cal. Inq. P.M.* III, 456. [3] *C. Ch. R. 1300–1326*, p. 108.
[4] The claims of Margaret and Sir Hugh were finally settled in 1318 by a grant of lands to the value of 2,000 marks whilst Margaret lived. If she died before Sir Hugh the grant was to be reduced to 1,200 marks (*C.P.R. 1317–1321*, p. 251).
[5] *C.P.R. 1317–1321*, pp. 5, 8, 9, 268. [6] *C.F.R. 1319–1327*, pp. 300, 302, 308.
[7] For an account of the financial arrangements made for Isabella by Edward II see T. F. Tout, *Chapters in the Administrative History of Medieval England* (6 vols, Manchester, 1920–33), V, 274–5.

4

her husband. This was successfully accomplished with the help of Mortimer and an invasion from France in the autumn of 1326, and within a few months of the accession of her son as Edward III, Isabella's old estates were restored in full, and as a token of gratitude her total dower was almost tripled in value.[1] But Isabella failed to maintain her influence for long over her strong-willed son, and in December 1330 Edward with a show of strength successfully asserted his independence, to the detriment of both his mother and the Mortimer faction, and once again she was deprived of her lands.[2]

John of Eltham, the brother of Edward III, had been created Earl of Cornwall in 1328, but the title remained an empty one until 10 October 1331 when he was finally granted the Cornish lands traditionally associated with the Earldom.[3] John, who was to be the last Earl of Cornwall, did not live to enjoy the estates for long, and he died at Perth in the autumn of 1336.[4] As he left no heirs, by the terms of the original grant the estates of the Earldom once more returned to the Crown.[5]

Possibly influenced by the unsettled history of the Earldom of Cornwall in the previous generation, Edward III contrived to create from it an unchanging, indeed a virtually unchangeable institution, the tenure of which should never be in dispute. By the Great Charter of 1337 Prince Edward was made Duke of Cornwall and granted the seventeen assessionable manors and a number of boroughs and towns in Cornwall, which had also been part of the estates of the Earldom, namely Trematon, Saltash, Tintagel (sometimes called Bossiney), Grampound, Helston, Camelford, Lostwithiel, Launceston and Liskeard. Among the more important privileges also made part of the Duchy of Cornwall were the right to appoint the sheriff of the county, the profits of the county courts and eight and one third of the nine hundred courts, the rights of prisage and custom of wine, the profits of all the ports and havens of Cornwall including 'Ancient and New Customs', wrecks and royal fishes;[6] and the profits of the stannaries, which included the most

---

[1] *C.P.R. 1324–1327*, p. 346; Tout, *op. cit.* pp. 247, 275–6. [2] *C.P.R. 1330–1334*, p. 23.
[3] *C. Ch. R. 1327–1341*, p. 233. [4] *D.N.B.* [5] *C.P.R. 1334–1338*, p. 447.
[6] For a fuller description of the rights of the Duchy of these fields see Stella M. Campbell, 'Haveners of the Medieval Dukes of Cornwall', *J.R.I.C.*, new ser., IV (1962). It should be noted, however, that the profits of the assessionable manors were

valuable single perquisite of all, namely the right to take a duty of 40s. on each thousandweight of tin mined within the county.¹ In addition the Duke was to have 'advowsons of all churches, abbeys, priories etc., free warren, all knights fees, wards, escheats, reliefs, and services, and all profits liberties and advantages whatsoever appertaining to the aforesaid lands, manors, parks etc.' And it should be remembered that Cornish possessions formed only a part of the estates, and the rights and properties of the Duchy spread far beyond south-west England.

According to the express words of the charter of creation, none of the estates of the Duchy of Cornwall were ever to be dismembered, nor granted other than to the Duke of Cornwall. The Dukedom was to pertain to the eldest son of the reigning monarch, and in the absence of such a rightful Duke it was to remain in the hands of the Crown until such time as a Duke was born. Unlike the Principality of Wales and the Earldom of Chester, which also accrued to the eldest son of the reigning monarch, no investiture to the Dukedom was necessary, for the title devolved upon the first-born son from the moment of his birth, although it has subsequently become customary for the estates to be granted at any period up to his becoming of age.

Thus, the Duchy was created with many built-in bulwarks against change to exist within strictly defined limits, but it did not augur well for its future stability that even the constancy of Edward III towards his own brain-child waned. The Black Prince was allowed to grant various manors and appurtenances of the Duchy to retainers and veterans of his Continental campaigns for the duration of their lives,² and on his death in 1376 Edward III created his

consistently many times greater than those of the havenry, and on occasion the profits of the hundred courts also exceeded those of the havenry.

¹ The 'profits of the stannaries' also included revenues from the four stannary courts, the farms of the bailiwicks of the stannaries, revenues from a poll-tax on tinners working with shovels within Blackmore and Penwith-and-Kirrier districts, 'fine of tin', 'dublet', and occasional sums realised from the sale of forfeited tin (see G. R. Lewis, *The Stannaries* (Harvard Economic Studies, III, 1906), especially chapters IV and V). Some lists of the Duchy revenues are contained in Lewis' Appendixes O, R and S, but they are incomplete and contain many inaccuracies. For more complete statistics of the production of tin in Cornwall see below, Appendix C.

² For grants made to Walter de Wodeland, Nigel Loheryng and William Lenche, see below, pp. 111, 130, 193.

grandson Richard Duke of Cornwall, giving him two thirds of the estates of the Duchy,[1] whilst the remaining third by value was granted to Princess Joan, widow of the Black Prince, in dower.[2] On becoming king, Richard showed no desire to retain any of the assessionable manors in his possession and, with the exception of a number of deer-parks and castles, the manorial estates were dispersed far and wide in gross neglect of the terms of the Great Charter, effecting the most serious disruption of the Duchy ever made without legal sanction.[3]

With the accession of Henry IV, however, many of the assessionable manors were restored once more to the Duchy, and with the assistance of a Parliament anxious to keep down royal expenses it was established that in the future only life interests could be granted out of the estates of the Duchy.[4] Nevertheless, it was not until Edward of Westminster, son of Henry VI, was made Duke of Cornwall that the complete manorial estates lay once more in the hands of the Duchy administration, where they were to remain for the rest of the medieval period.[5]

The Medieval Dukes of Cornwall[6]

3 March 1337–8 June 1376	Edward the Black Prince
20 November 1376– 29 September 1399	Richard 'of Bordeaux', as Duke until 22 June 1377 and subsequently as King
15 October 1399	Henry 'of Monmouth', as Duke until 21 March 1413 and then as King
6 December 1421	Henry 'of Windsor', as Duke until 1 September 1422 and then as King
13 October 1453	Edward 'of Westminster', son of Henry VI
4 March 1461	Edward IV (Henry VI restored 3 October 1470, deposed 11 April 1471)
17 July 1471	Edward Plantagenet, later Edward V
26 June 1483–9 April 1484	Edward, son of Richard III

[1] *C.C.R. 1374–1377*, p. 421.   [2] *Ibid.* pp. 407–8; below, pp. 136–7.
[3] Below, pp. 137–8.   [4] *Rot. Parl.* III, 531–2.
[5] Below, pp. 159–60.
[6] This table is for the most part based upon the lists of Dukes of Cornwall contained in the *Handbook of British Chronology*, ed. Sir M. Powicke and E. B. Fryde (1961), p. 423.

I

THE CORNISH ECONOMY
AND THE DUCHY MANORS

The economic and social history of Cornwall in the middle ages has been sadly neglected, and our knowledge of her rural economy in particular is extremely limited, being largely confined to an examination of early field-patterns. The necessity to say something of the structure and efficiency of Cornish agriculture in works of a general nature has driven historians into making a series of misleading generalisations. We are told, for example, that Cornish farming techniques were 'rough and primitive',[1] and possibly 'of that backward type which ploughs vast tracts for a poor return';[2] consequently 'Cornish manors were not rich',[3] their lands 'yielded a poorer harvest', and the mass of Cornishmen were so poor that they 'provided no large market for imports'.[4] Tin has been seen as the major source of wealth, and agriculture relegated to playing a minor role in the economy, and what is more, to playing it badly.[5]

This dismal picture is perpetuated by comparative analyses of the population and wealth of English counties, based upon subsidy rolls, which have contrived to reveal Cornwall as a very backward region with only a smattering of persons and a very low level of wealth to each acre.[6] But it is readily apparent that for a county such as Cornwall where the topography leads to a markedly uneven settlement, computations of the average density of population and wealth can be extremely misleading. In the middle ages a large part of the county, perhaps as much as one third, was almost completely

[1] Sir John Clapham, *A Concise Economic History of Britain from the Earliest Times to 1750* (Cambridge, 1949), p. 88.
[2] F. W. Maitland, *Domesday Book and Beyond* (Cambridge, 2nd edn, 1907), p. 425.
[3] Clapham, *op. cit.* p. 138.
[4] M. W. Beresford and J. K. St Joseph, *Medieval England: An Aerial Survey* (Cambridge, 1958), p. 190.
[5] N. S. B. Gras, *Evolution of the English Corn Market* (Cambridge, Mass., 1915), p. 52.
[6] See, for example, E. J. Buckatzsch, 'The Geographical Distribution of Wealth in England, 1086–1843', *Ec. H.R.*, 2nd ser., III (1950); R. S. Schofield, 'The Geographical Distribution of Wealth in England, 1334–1649', *Ec. H.R.*, 2nd ser., XVIII (1965).

devoid of agricultural resources and scarcely inhabited.[1] Furthermore, the tin-mining population of Cornwall was exempt from all forms of royal taxation, and therefore its wealth is not registered on the subsidy rolls[2] and, what is more, it is evident that many affluent persons managed to evade payment by claiming to have mining interests.[3] A more subtle analysis than has so far been possible on a national scale must be undertaken before the distribution of the population and wealth of medieval Cornwall can be accurately portrayed.

TOPOGRAPHY AND FARMING

Cornwall is, of course, far from ideally suited for the practice of agriculture, and lands of the best quality are rarely found. Much of the inner part of the county is composed of four great granite masses which, owing to a daunting combination of height, exposure and infertile soil, were condemned to be bleak moorland rather than farmland. Upon these and other moorlands one finds only a blackish heath at higher levels and a cotton grass at lower levels; the less wild of such lands in the middle ages were used primarily as rough summer pasture. In contrast, a large part of the remainder of the county, in particular those regions bordering on the sea, could be successfully cultivated; for there the rock structures had frequently broken down into a light well-drained soil of moderate richness which, despite the high level of acidity common in the Devonian soils of south-west England, could prove suitable for the practice of both arable and pastoral husbandry. Nevertheless, many parts are so hilly as to have rendered cultivation extremely arduous, and in some fields upon the steeper slopes draught animals could scarcely have been able to take sure footing. Another hindrance to successful crop-growing was the presence of many rocks and boulders, and it was sometimes necessary to dig over by hand those places which could not satisfactorily be ploughed.[4] A small annual range of

---

[1] *The Domesday Geography of South-West England*, ed. H. C. Darby and R. Welldon Finn (Cambridge, 1967), p. 304.

[2] J. F. Willard, *Parliamentary Taxes on Personal Property, 1290–1334* (Cambridge, Mass., 1934), pp. 118–20; Lewis, *Stannaries*, pp. 164–6.

[3] For attempts at evasion of taxation in both Cornwall and Devon see, for example, *Rot. Parl.* II, 343; *C.P.R. 1338–1340*, p. 71; *ibid. 1343–1345*, pp. 73, 165.

[4] P.R.O. SC.6.1094/14, Helstone-in-Triggshire.

temperatures is a feature of the Cornish climate, and this gives mild winters and relatively cool summers which, coupled with a high annual rainfall, makes a good land for animal husbandry, since grass can grow throughout most of the year; but for arable cultivation the familiar succession of wet days and high winds can bring difficulties, and sudden violent storms can seriously damage harvests.

It would be injudicious to draw any firm general conclusions of the nature of Cornish agriculture in the later middle ages from Duchy records alone, especially as the information they contain is necessarily limited by the almost complete absence of demesne exploitation.[1] Nevertheless our knowledge of medieval agriculture in Cornwall is so sparse as to justify a detailed analysis of the farming methods practised on Duchy manors, as far as they can be discovered, in order to assist in establishing the main outlines for the county as a whole.

The testing environment within which Cornish farmers had to work fostered the evolution of a highly individual system of farming, which sought to compensate for deficiencies and exploit advantages. No trace of classical open-field agriculture can be found on any Duchy manor from the start of records in the late thirteenth century,[2] and throughout the county physical and cultural conditions appear to have combined to ensure that this form of rural organisation was never of more than peripheral importance. Almost without exception the open-fields whose existence has been firmly established in medieval Cornwall were the result of combinations of untypical conditions, amongst which the open-fields of the run-rig type must be counted.[3] Frequently encountered also are the open-fields of a number of boroughs,[4] although even these appear to have been

---

[1] Some small-scale arable demesne cultivation is in evidence on the earliest manorial account of 1287/8 on the manors of Helstone-in-Triggshire and Calstock, but by the time of the next available account some 9 years later it had ceased (cf. P.R.O. SC.6.816/9 and P.R.O. E.119/1). A final ill-fated attempt to cultivate a demesne, using the Old Deer Park of Helstone-in-Triggshire, was made in 1335/6, but high winds and torrential rains ruined the harvest (P.R.O. SC.6.1094/14).

[2] Before the Duchy was created in 1337 these manors formed part of the Earldom of Cornwall.

[3] H. L. Gray, *English Field Systems* (Cambridge, Mass., 1915), pp. 412–14; N. J. G. Pounds, 'Lanhydrock Atlas', *Antiquity*, XIX (1945).

[4] Charles Henderson, *Essays in Cornish History*, ed. A. L. Rowse and M. I. Henderson, (Oxford, 1935), p. 67; W. G. V. Balchin, *The Making of the English Landscape, 2 : Cornwall* (1954), pp. 46–7; Gray, *op. cit.* pp. 263–6; R. R. Rawson, 'The Open-Field in Flintshire, Devonshire and Cornwall', *Ec. H.R.*, 2nd ser., VI (1953).

small and to have had little in common with the classical Midland open-field. The absence of demesne farming meant that all lands, except for a number of deer-parks, were in the hands of Duchy tenants. The bulk of all land was termed either *terra* or *terra vasta*, according to quality. Within each manor lay a number of different hamlets or vills, and within these vills the *terra* was divided into plots of varying size, but generally of less than 30 acres, which were demised by the Duchy as individual holdings, usually with a dwelling-house and farm buildings upon them. Many of these individual holdings were completely enclosed, but alternatively, a number of holdings within a vill might be enclosed together. The enclosures consisted in the main of ditches and hedges; the soil was thrown up from the ditch to form a mound upon which a quickset hedge was planted.[1] Such hedges, thick with hawthorn, hazel, oak, ash and other coppice wood remain a distinctive feature of the Cornish landscape, and apart from facilitating the use of improved methods of husbandry they also acted as shelter from the high winds for animals, and invaluable sources of fuel supply in a county deficient in wood and timber. Moorlands and waste lay open for the most part, although small enclosures nibbling at the perimeters were made from time to time.[2] These enclosures were most likely to have consisted of stone walls, as they had in Iron Age times, rocks being easily gathered and the soil generally being too poor to allow the easy growth of hedges.[3]

Mixed farming appears to have predominated on Duchy manors in the later middle ages. The main sources of information on farming practices—manorial court rolls and inventories of the possessions of unfree tenants ceded to the Duchy on death—[4] indicate that the vast majority of tenants divided their resources between arable and pastoral husbandry. Within the holdings of *terra* a form of convertible husbandry or ley farming was practised.

---

[1] Details of the methods of enclosure are found in fifteenth-century manorial records, when the Duchy frequently made grants for repairs and extensions. See, for example, P.R.O. SC.6.822/1, Tybesta; D.C.O. 59, Moresk.

[2] For example, in 1463, 5s. was granted by the Duchy towards the cost of enclosing a piece of waste on Helstone-in-Triggshire manor (P.R.O. SC.6.822/1).

[3] O. G. S. Crawford, 'The Work of Giants', *Antiquity*, x (1936).

[4] For this custom see below, p. 63; for a list of the contents of some inventories see below, pp. 254-6.

Holdings were divided into interchangeable units, each unit bearing corn for a number of years, probably experiencing a rotation of crops, and then lying fallow whilst providing good quality pasture. Such a system of rotation was likely to have brought substantial improvements to both corn yields and the quality of pasture.[1] Unfortunately, sufficient evidence does not exist to support firm conclusions on the average length of the ley and the period of cropping respectively; but although the soil, relief and climate of Cornwall would lead one to expect an overwhelming preponderance of pastoral husbandry, it appears that a number of factors, amongst them the persistence of a high level of demand for foodstuffs from the important non-agrarian sectors of the regional economy, encouraged arable farming.[2]

The medieval Cornish husbandman used a wide range of techniques to improve the quality of the soil, in addition to the application of manure. On the first occasion that land was to be used for arable after serving as pasture it was customary, and evidently essential, to prepare it most thoroughly by a process called beat-burning.[3] In the late spring the grass would be cut up into turves, which would then be raised up so that the sun and wind might dry them—this was called beating. When dry the turves were piled into small heaps and burnt, and just prior to ploughing the ashes were spread over the ground.[4] The process of beat-burning produces potash and causes significant biochemical processes to take place in the soil which, if it is not repeated too frequently, result in very

[1] E. Kerridge, *The Agricultural Revolution* (1967), Chapter III. It was well known in the middle ages that the periodic ploughing of grassland greatly improved its quality; this occurred through a reduction in the acidity of the soil. See, for example, *B.P.R.* II, 27.

[2] Professor Finberg has found that arable farming often surpassed pastoral farming in importance on Tavistock Abbey manors in west Devon in the fourteenth and fifteenth centuries (H. P. R. Finberg, *Tavistock Abbey—A Study in the Social and Economic History of Devon* (Cambridge, 1951), pp. 155–8). Richard Carew, writing in the late sixteenth century, states that after preparing the land for use as arable, the farmer could normally raise two crops of wheat and two of oats and then would leave the land fallow for at least seven or eight years (*Survey of Cornwall* (ed. 1769), p. 20).

[3] Detailed examples of what beat-burning actually entailed on the assessionable manors are difficult to find, but the terms of a lease of Carrybullock park stated that the tenant should 'faciet totam terra in parco predicto, ubi bosc' et petre non impedunt fossat', adhustam ac zabulat' voc Bete arat' et seminat'' (D.C.O. 480).

[4] For discussions of the early farming practices of the south-west see Carew, *Survey of Cornwall*, pp. 19–20; Finberg, *Tavistock Abbey*, pp. 91–4.

favourable conditions for grain-growing.[1] Acidity in the soil is sharply reduced, and the value of the phosphoric nutrients increased; furthermore a pronounced mineralisation of the organic nitrogen compounds is effected, which facilitates the exploitation of the nitrogen reserves in the soil by the grain. Over-zealous beat-burning can be most deleterious, however, as it destroys the humus in the soil. The application of sea-sand to the soil also has beneficial results; if the sand is rich in calcium carbonate it helps to negate acidity and floculates heavy soils. The ancient practice of sanding can be traced as part of the regular system of cultivation on assessionable manors as far apart as Calstock and Trematon in the extreme east[2] and Helston-in-Kirrier in the far west,[3] and sand was used in such quantities that a considerable traffic of barges and packhorses was organised to satisfy the demand.[4] Carew, writing in the late sixteenth century, estimated that most husbandmen used 120 sacks of sand to the acre, although he notes that some sowed it as thinly as the grain itself.[5] Of the application of seaweed, fish, and salt to the land, widely practised in later centuries, no trace can be found in Duchy records.

It was by the expenditure of much skill, effort and money, that the resourceful Cornish farmer was able to conquer the many obstacles that stood in the way of the successful cultivation of grain. The cost of labour alone in beat-burning one acre, namely paring, burning and scattering, amounted to more than 3s. at the turn of the fourteenth century,[6] whilst two centuries later Carew estimated that the total cost involved in 'Beating, Burning, Scoding and Sanding' usually amounted to no less than 20s. per acre.[7] The existence of compact holdings, frequently enclosed, and discriminate use of beating, burning, sanding and manuring, combined with the alternation of land use, could well have produced impressive yields of grain

[1] A. M. Söininen, 'Burn-beating as the Technical Basis of Colonisation in Finland in the 16th and 17th centuries', *Scandinavian Ec. Hist. Rev.*, VII, 1959.
[2] P.R.O. SC.8, file 333, petition E.1092.   [3] *B.P.R.* II, 130–1.
[4] Traces of the trade in sand can be found in the records of Duchy manors. At Trematon barges carrying sand in the Tamar paid 1s. each as toll, and the Abbot of Tavistock's barges paid regularly. A similar due was exacted at Calstock, whilst at Tywarnhaile horses carrying sand across Duchy land paid ½d. each.
[5] Carew, *Survey of Cornwall*, pp. 19–20.
[6] Finberg, *Tavistock Abbey*, p. 93.   [7] Carew, *Survey of Cornwall*, p. 20.

and high-quality grazing land. Unfortunately no indication of yields on Duchy manors is obtainable, but Professor Finberg has discovered that corn yields on the demesnes of Tavistock Abbey manors in Devon, some situated only a few miles from Duchy manors in south-east Cornwall, were 'little short of miraculous', being greater than those set up as standards by Walter of Henley and substantially in excess of those obtained on soils apparently far more amenable to arable cultivation in southern England.[1]

Some confusion surrounds certain aspects of arable farming in medieval Cornwall, and in particular the importance of the 'infield-outfield' or 'run-rig' system. From the records of the seventeen manors of the Duchy of Cornwall in the fourteenth and fifteenth centuries it is quite plain that arable farming was almost exclusive to the holdings of *terra*, and that the cultivation of waste and moorland never constituted more than a tiny fraction of the total acreage under crops.[2] It is apparent that the waste was ploughed and sown only when prevailing conditions justified such a costly process. It was in the decades immediately preceding the Black Death of 1348/9, a time of mounting pressure on the land in Cornwall, that the cultivation of the waste was most common, but even at this time it was never regular nor of more than minor importance.[3] Changed economic conditions after the Black Death, and in particular the steep rise in labour costs, meant that even intermittent small-scale cultivation of waste land aimed at producing crops profitably, rather than improving the quality of the pasture, was uneconomic.

The average Duchy conventionary tenant or villein appears to have possessed a larger number of animals than his counterpart in many other regions of England,[4] and tenants dying and bequeath-

---

[1] *Tavistock Abbey*, pp. 106–7, 110–15. In order to render his findings comparable with other parts of England and also to avoid inaccuracies consequent upon variations in the size of local acres and bushels, Professor Finberg has expressed the yield as a multiple of the grain sown. For a more detailed comparison of the yields of some of these Devon manors with those of manors in other counties see P. D. A. Harvey, *A Medieval Oxfordshire Village: Cuxham 1240–1400* (Oxford, 1965), p. 58.

[2] Professor Finberg comes to a similar conclusion based upon the evidence of manors practising demesne farming in medieval Devon (*Tavistock Abbey*, pp. 105–7).

[3] Below, pp. 82–4.

[4] Compare the lists of tenants' possessions given in: Harvey, *Medieval Oxfordshire Village*, Appendix VI; and R. K. Field, 'Worcestershire Peasant Buildings in the Later Middle Ages', *Med. Arch.* IX, 1965.

The Cornish Economy and the Duchy Manors

ing 10 or more *averii* were not uncommon. Heriots paid in cash were rare, whilst substantial numbers of animals were often impounded by manorial officials for arrears, or as strays. Some tenants accumulated considerable wealth in livestock, and from the limited number of court rolls available many examples could be given of herds of 20 or more *averii* and of flocks of 60 or more sheep.[1] The tenants of most manors had access to areas of waste and moorland which served as rough pasture, and in addition the Duchy sold pasture rights in its deer-parks. There was, however, no common pasture on Duchy manors, all land not held by freehold or villein tenure was subject to assessions, that is to periodic leasing on competitive terms, and although the tenants of a certain vill might lease a waste or pasture in common they had to lease it in competition with others, and they could be dispossessed when their leases expired.[2]

Cornwall has never contained much meadow, and the middle ages were no exception. Many Duchy manors possessed no meadow at all, whilst others had only a few acres each. But the lack of meadow presented no serious handicap to pastoral farming, for the long growing season for grass and the mild winters enabled animals to remain out in the fields for most of the year; and in the sixteenth century, if not earlier, fine quality hay was produced in the dry uplands which were specially prepared for the purpose.[3]

From the evidence in the records of the Duchy of Cornwall manors and elsewhere it is apparent that there was little pronounced regional specialisation in agriculture; a wide range of crops and animals can be found in most regions.[4] Despite the considerable difficulties of cultivation wheat appears to have been grown and traded throughout the county, and oats, which were admirably suited to the damp climate, were also a very popular crop.[5] Barley, rye and peas appear

---

[1] Below, pp. 171n, 254.
[2] The system of tenures found on Duchy manors is described in Chapter 3 below.
[3] John Norden, *Description of Cornwall*, p. 20.
[4] Information concerning the distribution of crops and livestock has been gleaned from manorial and stannary court rolls and inventories of the possessions of unfree tenants; but see also *Reg. Stapledon*, pp. 570–5.
[5] Large quantities of oats were frequently purchased in Cornwall for the campaigns of the fourteenth century. See, for example: P.R.O. E.101/554/1, 603/2; C.145/111/1; *B.P.R.* II, 105; *C.P.R. 1321–1324*, p. 93; *C.C.R. 1330–1333*, p. 16.

to have been the next most frequently cultivated grains. Pastoral husbandry was, of course, of great importance and sheep, cattle, oxen, horses, pigs and goats can be traced on all the assessionable manors. Sheep had been particularly numerous in Cornwall at the time of Domesday,[1] and they continued to be kept in large numbers, with perhaps an added stimulus provided by the rapid growth of textile manufacture in the south-west from the later fourteenth century onwards.[2] Horses were remarkably common, perhaps many of them being small 'rounceys', essential for transport in a rough and hilly country where carts were often at a disadvantage. As for the keeping of cattle, little can be said beyond remarking upon the frequency with which they appear in manorial records.

Some indication of the pattern and density of population settlement on Duchy manors can be gained from the assession rolls which list the names of customary tenants, and the size and location of their holdings.[3] But these documents can only provide an approximate guide, for they do not list all the inhabitants of a vill, and indeed they usually provide only a partial list even of the manorial tenantry, as free tenants are only rarely given. And of course, as with all manorial surveys, no indication is given of the extent to which sub-letting was practised; from other sources it appears to have been prevalent amongst all classes of tenants.[4] Good lands frequently interspersed with lands of poorer quality is the typical topography of Cornwall, and this was bound to lead to wide variations in the density of settlement. The size of holdings on Duchy manors in all parts of the county appears to have been closely tied to the fertility of the soil, with fertile soil encouraging smaller holdings, though local conditions might also play their part. For example, in 1347 on Tewington manor, which lay close to the stannary of Blackmore on a particularly fertile belt of land,[5] the vill of Tyngaran containing only 76 acres was divided into 13 separate holdings; and the vill of Pensenten comprising 47½ acres was divided

---

[1] Darby, *Domesday Geography of South-West England*, p. 339.
[2] Below, pp. 169–71.
[3] Professor Beresford has undertaken some research into settlement on Duchy manors in the first half of the fourteenth century; see his 'Dispersed and Grouped Settlement in Medieval Cornwall', *Ag. Hist. Rev.*, XII (1964).
[4] Below, pp. 232–5. [5] Henderson, *Essays in Cornish History*, p. 110.

into 9 holdings.[1] At the other extreme on Helston-in-Kirrier, the most westerly of all Duchy manors and one containing much infertile land,[2] holdings comprising a single messuage and over 100 acres were not uncommon.

There is no conclusive evidence in Duchy documents to determine whether the farmsteads of the holdings in each vill were grouped together into 'little communities',[3] or each one situated at some convenient point within its enclosure. Perhaps archaeological investigation will one day tell us more.

THE SEVENTEEN ASSESSIONABLE MANORS

The seventeen assessionable manors of the Duchy of Cornwall being well dispersed throughout Cornwall provide a good insight into rural conditions in all parts of the county in the later middle ages. The earliest detailed survey of all the manors is the Caption of Seisin of 1337[4] which, when combined with the assession rolls of 1333, 1340 and 1347[5] make it possible to construct a full picture of the manors as they were in the decades before the Black Death struck Cornwall.

The Cornish manors of the Duchy fall conveniently into four geographical groups.[6] The first group lay to the south-east in fertile but hilly land, an appreciable distance from the main tin-producing regions of Cornwall, and comprised the manors of Trematon, Calstock, Climsland, Rillaton and Liskeard. The eastern boundary of the first three of these manors was the River Tamar, the county boundary with Devon. Trematon, situated in St Stephen's parish at the mouth of the Tamar almost opposite Plymouth, was the most southerly of the manors in this region and was bounded by water on three sides. It was a manor of medium size for Cornwall, with a

[1] D.C.O. 472.
[2] *The Report of the Land Utilisation Survey of Britain*, ed. L. Dudley Stamp (1937–41), vol. IX, part 91, pp. 438–9.
[3] The conclusion reached by Professor Beresford ('Dispersed and Grouped Settlement in Medieval Cornwall', p. 26).
[4] P.R.O. E.120/1.
[5] D.C.O. 471; P.R.O. S.C.11/Roll 153; D.C.O. 472.
[6] See map on p. xiv.

little over 1,000 acres of land[1] by English measure[2] in the hands of some 60 conventionary and villein tenants, and 5 or 6 Cornish acres, perhaps 250 standard English acres, in the hands of free tenants. Unlike most Cornish manors Trematon contained no waste lands and very little land that was specifically designated pasture, although the small deer-park adjacent to the castle of Trematon provided some additional grazing for the livestock of the tenants.[3] Within the boundaries of this manor there were two boroughs: Trematon and Saltash. Trematon borough was very small and, contained wholly within the walls of the castle with no more than a handful of burgesses, it resembled medieval Welsh castle boroughs. Saltash, on the other hand, was an important Cornish port, with over 100 burgesses at the start of the fourteenth century.[4] A valuable and important ferry, which connected Saltash with Devon, was appended to the manor of Trematon; it landed at Little Ash where 35 acres of land divided into two holdings also belonged to the Duchy.

The manors of Calstock and Climsland were centred on the fertile and well-wooded Tamar Valley, with its landscape of rounded hills sloping down to rivers. Calstock, conterminous with the parish of the same name, lay less than 10 miles from the Devon borough of Tavistock and was bounded by the Tamar to the east and north. To the north-west of Calstock lay Climsland manor and the parish of Callington, and to the south the parish of St Domonic. Calstock was an extensive manor with more than 80 conventionary and villein tenants holding approximately 1,500 acres of land; whilst 9 Cornish acres lay in the hands of free tenants. The area of waste and pasture within this manor is difficult to assess exactly, but it was in excess of 200 acres and must have provided adequate rough grazing for the needs of tenants. Calstock was a well-wooded manor and contained

---

[1] 'Land' throughout this study refers to the *terra* of Duchy documents, *terra vasta* and pasture are always distinguished from *terra*.
[2] In Cornwall land was measured in either English or Cornish acres. The lands of the free tenants were always given in Cornish acres, a measure of indeterminate extent but which can be taken in most cases to be equal to approximately 40 to 60 English acres, depending on the fertility of the soil; whilst the lands held by conventionaries and villeins were measured in English acres.
[3] The Duchy usually sold pasture in the deer-parks to the tenants after allowing for the needs of the deer (below, pp. 179–84).
[4] P.R.O. E.152/8, Trematon.

three separate woods called Herewood, Northwood, and Crins-combe. The Tamar was a favourite haunt of salmon in the middle ages, as it still is today, and appended to Calstock manor were the rights to a large and valuable fish weir which spanned the river.[1] In the late thirteenth and early fourteenth centuries a number of mines in this region of the Tamar Valley had provided quantities of lead and silver for the Crown, but they were soon exhausted.[2]

Climsland manor stretched upwards from the north-western edge of Calstock to the River Inny, which lay less than 10 miles from the important Cornish borough of Launceston. Covering the whole of the parish of Stoke Climsland, it was the second largest Duchy manor in Cornwall, and almost 100 conventionary and villein tenants held approximately 2,500 acres of land and more than 500 acres of waste, including the extensive wastes of Hengesdoun and Northdoun. In addition, free tenants held about 10 Cornish acres, possibly more than 500 English acres. A large deer-park called Carrybullock, still a Duchy farm today (measuring three leagues in circumference and containing 150 head of deer in 1337), was situated within the manor, and this provided tenants with considerable amounts of additional pasture.

To the west of Climsland lay the once extensive manor of Rillaton, located in the parish of Linkinhorne.[3] On the creation of the Duchy, however, less than 300 acres of land and 100 acres of waste remained in the hands of conventionary and villein tenants. But the holdings of the free tenants of the manor were vast and two tenants held between them land amounting to half the area of the manor.

The remaining Duchy manor in south-east Cornwall was Lis-keard. Centred on the Duchy borough of the same name and lying south of Bodmin moor, Liskeard was a large manor with over 2,000 acres of land in the hands of more than 80 conventionary and villein tenants, seven Cornish acres were in the hands of free tenants. Extensive pastures and wastes verged on the moors, and additional pasture was also frequently made available to tenants in the manorial deer-park. Liskeard was the most thickly wooded of all Duchy

[1] Below, p. 191.   [2] P.R.O. E.101/260/22 ff.
[3] Henderson, *Essays in Cornish History*, p. 125.

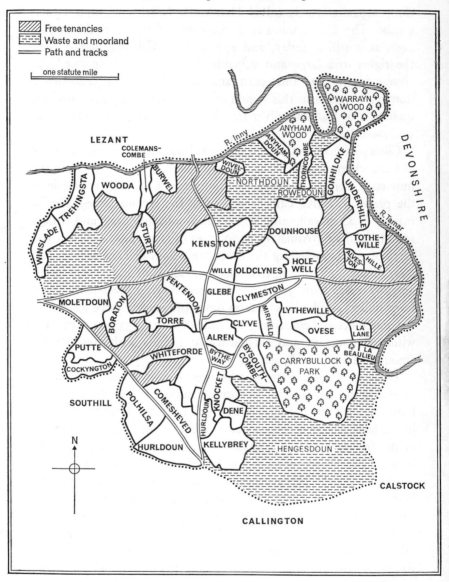

2. Reconstruction of Climsland manor (based on a map by R. L. Clowes, 1930).
This reconstruction of the topography of Climsland manor in the later middle ages is by
no means representative of all Duchy manors in Cornwall, as settlement patterns
varied substantially from place to place. Professor Beresford has constructed outline
maps of a number of Duchy manors in Cornwall ('Dispersed and Grouped Settlement
in Medieval Cornwall', *Ag. Hist. Rev.*, XII, 1964).

The Cornish Economy and the Duchy Manors

manors in Cornwall and contained four woods which together formed an extremely valuable asset.[1] The borough of Liskeard was an important Cornish borough in the later middle ages, and in the subsidy of 1334 it was assessed to pay £6 14s. 0d., the fifth highest amount of all the Cornish boroughs;[2] though of course most Cornish boroughs were small by national standards.

Both Rillaton and Liskeard manors were situated close to Bodmin moor upon which the tin-workings of the stannary district of Foweymore were located, and the courts of this stannary were often held at Liskeard borough.[3] Liskeard was also nominated as a tin-coinage town in the early fourteenth century, but it rarely performed this function.[4] Although the stannary of Foweymore covered a very wide area of the moors between Bodmin and Launceston it was of relatively minor importance, and in 1307 the assessment on tinners of this region was less than 5 per cent of the total tax levied on all Cornish tinners.[5]

Despite variations in the size of conventionary holdings from vill to vill, and even within the same vill, a holding of between 20 and 30 acres may be taken as typical of the south-eastern manors of the Duchy, although at Trematon and Calstock there was a significant number of smaller holdings, and at Liskeard some holdings were larger than 30 acres. Similarly the rents[6] of conventionary lands varied considerably within the individual manors,[7] but nevertheless it would be useful to estimate an average rental for the decade before the Black Death. On Rillaton and Climsland manors the rent of an acre of land (*terra*), as opposed to waste and pasture (*terra vasta*), was usually between 3d. and 4d.; rents were frequently higher at Calstock and Liskeard and the range was greater at 3d. to 6d. The highest rents in this region were to be found on Trematon manor, where they averaged from 6d. to 8d. an acre, which might be

[1] Below, p. 185. [2] P.R.O. E.179/87/9.
[3] Court rolls of Foweymore stannary, *passim*.
[4] The famous tinners' charter of 1305 calls for Helston, Lostwithiel, Bodmin, Liskeard and Truro to be made coinage towns (P.R.O. Charter Rolls, 33 Edward I, no. 40, m. 8: transcribed Lewis, *Stannaries*, Appendix D, pp. 239–41).
[5] P.R.O. E.372/161, m. 41; below, pp. 31–2.
[6] 'Rent' here and elsewhere in this study refers to the total sum paid by the tenant, including both assession fine and annual rent.
[7] See the examples given in Appendix B below.

explained in part by the presence of the flourishing ports of Saltash and Plymouth, and the greater proportion of relatively flat lands, which were easier to farm than most others in the region.

The five assessionable manors of south-east Cornwall, although distant from the most productive tin-mining regions of the county were favourably sited for supplying agricultural produce to a number of important markets. The ports of Plymouth, Sutton, Saltash, Fowey, and East and West Looe, which needed supplies both for their native populations and for the victualling of ships which visited them, were all within easy reach; and substantial demands from Devon were to exert a great influence on these manors after the Black Death.

In the north-east of Cornwall lay three assessionable manors— Tintagel, Helstone-in-Triggshire and Penmayne. Tintagel manor lay on the Atlantic coast in the parish of Tintagel and abutted southwards on to Helstone-in-Triggshire manor. Of modest dimensions, Tintagel manor contained 800 acres of land and some areas of waste and pasture, held by some 50 conventionary and villein tenants in 1337. A further 9 Cornish acres were held by free tenants. Both a castle and a borough lay within the manorial boundaries. The castle is now famous for its reputed, though probably mythical, connections with King Arthur, but the borough of Tintagel, later called 'Boscyny', which contained almost 90 burgesses when the Caption of Seisin was taken in 1337, is now no more than a small fishing village.

Helstone-in-Triggshire was a large inland manor, centred on the Camel valley and extending over the parishes of Lanteglos, Michaelstow, and Advent. More than 100 conventionary and villein tenants held over 1,500 acres of land and 500 acres of waste and pasture, with perhaps as much again in the hands of free tenants.[1] Once again, like so many other Cornish manors, Helstone-in-Triggshire contained a borough—Camelford borough which lay where the main road from Launceston crossed the Camel; it had 62 burgesses in 1300.[2] A large deer-park also lay within the manor, as well as the site of an old park which had been demised to conventionary tenants.

1 The free tenants held 35 Cornish acres.
2 P.R.O. E.152/8; C.133, file 95.

The tiny manor of Penmayne which lay in the parish of St Minver opposite Padstow on the Camel estuary was appended to Helstone-in-Triggshire.[1] It comprised only 150 acres of land in the hands of conventionary and villein tenants. The Duchy ferry of Blacktorre provided the essential link with Padstow on the western side of the water.

The coastal regions of north-east Cornwall generally contain much good land, but father inland towards the fringes of the moors the quality rapidly deteriorates. For example, the coastal parts of Advent parish were included in the regular holdings of *terra*, whilst the inland regions of the same parish comprised much of the waste of Helstone-in-Triggshire manor and the valuable turbary of Goosehill. Nevertheless the moorlands of north-east Cornwall provide cattle-pastures of fine quality, renowned throughout the south-west of England; and in the sixteenth century, and possibly much earlier, graziers from Devon and Somerset as well as from other parts of Cornwall pastured 'great droves' of cattle upon them.[2] Indeed these pastures were so highly thought of that it was said that they 'will keep fatt oxen all the wynter, and in as good case as in some places they can be kepte with haye'.[3]

Waste and moorland (*terra vasta*) was, of course, considerably cheaper to lease than holdings of *terra*, and after the Black Death the differential widened in most parts of Cornwall. The higher quality of waste and moorland in the north-east was reflected in the rents it commanded, for whilst on Tintagel and Helstone-in-Triggshire such land was leased for 2d. or 3d. per acre before the Black Death it was far cheaper in the south-east, where its rental ranged downwards from about 2d. per acre at Liskeard to as little as 1d. or even less at Climsland and Rillaton when a tenant took a large area.

The vast majority of holdings on Duchy manors in north-east Cornwall were less than 20 acres in extent, and on Tintagel manor many holdings were as small as 10 acres or even less. Most noticeable was the relatively wide variation in the rents of conventionary lands

[1] It was not until Penmayne was granted to Walter de Wodeland in 1350 that Helstone-in-Triggshire was accounted for separately (below, p. 111).
[2] Carew, *Survey of Cornwall*, p. 23.
[3] Norden, *Description of Cornwall*, pp. 72–3.

within each manor. On Helstone-in-Triggshire they ranged from 5d. an acre in the vills of Trethin and Helstone to as much as 9d. in the vills of Michaelstow, Trevelek and Tregreenwell in Michaelstow parish; whilst on Tintagel, although the average rent was 7d. to 8d. per acre, some of the smaller holdings in the coastal vills of Tregatta, Trenal and Trenan were leased at rents of a shilling an acre.

The six Duchy manors in central Cornwall were, with the exception of Talskiddy which comprised only 96 acres of land, all situated in the southern coastal regions. Three of the smallest manors, Penlyne, Penkneth and Restormel, lay on the banks of the Fowey in Lanlivery parish, grouped around the important Duchy borough of Lostwithiel. Lostwithiel was the administrative centre of the Duchy in Cornwall, and also the leading tin-coinage town in the middle ages.[1] In 1300, 305 burgages were occupied,[2] and by 1337 almost 400.[3] In the subsidy of 1334 the inhabitants of Lostwithiel were assessed to pay £8 13s. 4d., a sum which was exceeded only by the boroughs of Bodmin and Truro.[4] Lying to the south of Bodmin moors and to the east of the granite masses which formed the stannary district of Blackmore, Penlyne, Penkneth and Restormel together had less than 400 acres of land in the hands of conventionary and villein tenants. Restormel, centred on the castle of Restormel two miles north of Lostwithiel, was the largest of the group with a little over 150 acres of customary land. The castle of Restormel, within two miles of Lostwithiel, was often used by Dukes of Cornwall and visiting dignitaries, and was almost the only Duchy castle in Cornwall that was kept in a reasonable state of repair in the later middle ages. The largest of the Duchy deer-parks and a substantial fishery in the Fowey River were also part of this manor. The manor of Penkneth was situated to the west of Lostwithiel and in the taxation records of the early fourteenth century the 'borough of Penkneth' and Lostwithiel were assessed separately, but they were

---

[1] Throughout the fourteenth and fifteenth centuries, Lostwithiel and Truro were the only two regular coinage towns, and for long periods in the fifteenth century Lostwithiel operated alone. Even when both towns were in use Lostwithiel was invariably responsible for the coinage of far more tin than Truro (receivers' accounts and coinage rolls, *passim*).

[2] *Cal. Inq. P.M.* III, 457.   [3] P.R.O. E.120/1.   [4] P.R.O. E.179/87/9.

soon merged.[1] The holdings of the conventionary tenants of these small manors were themselves small, with none more than 16 acres and the majority less than 10 acres. Nevertheless, despite the nearness of the borough of Lostwithiel the average rent of *terra* in the decade before the Black Death was only 6d. an acre.

To the west of Lostwithiel lay the manor of Tewington which together with some of the southern portion of Tybesta manor was situated on one of the most fertile belts of land in the county.[2] Tewington was a very extensive manor and it spread over the parishes of St Austell, St Blazey, and Roche in a region which was intimately connected with tin-mining in the Blackmore stannary district, and large quantities of tin were frequently dug within the boundaries of the manor. The free tenants of Tewington held 50 Cornish acres, possibly amounting to more than 2,000 English acres. In contrast only 500 English acres of *terra* and 200 acres of waste were held by more than 60 conventionary and villein tenants. The customary lands of this manor were situated in admirable farming country for Cornwall and centred on the vill of Towan on the western side of the bay of St Austell. They were divided for the most part into tiny holdings of 5 acres or less; and in the decade before the Black Death it was not uncommon for two or even three tenants to share a 5-acre holding.[3] Rents were consistently as high as any on the assessionable manors, and in the first half of the fourteenth century *terra* was leased for 1s. 3d. or 1s. 4d. per acre throughout the manor. Tewington was also endowed with extensive wastes and pastures, primarily to the north of the manor on the moors of Gwallan, Porthmelyn and Towan, and even these realised rents of 3d. per acre. The high rents prevailing on this manor can be partly explained by the exceptional fertility of the soils for this part of England, and the sea giving ease of communications. But probably most important of all was the proximity of the stannary of Blackmore, which in 1307 accounted for fully half of the total number of tinners who were taxed in Cornwall and over 40 per cent of the total tax assessment.[4]

[1] Henderson, *Essays in Cornish History*, pp. 46–7. [2] *Ibid.* p. 110.
[3] See, for example, D.C.O. 472 Tewington.
[4] P.R.O. E.372/161 m. 41. For the stimulus given to farming by tin-mining see below.

The Cornish Economy and the Duchy Manors

The manor of Tybesta lay to the west of Tewington almost wholly within the parish of Creed on the east bank of the Fal, and was centred on the vill of Tybesta. Some 50 conventionary and villein tenants held almost 1,000 acres of land, and 37 Cornish acres lay in the hands of the free tenants of the manor. The small Duchy borough of Grampound or *Ponsmur*, which had only 30 burgesses in 1300, lay within the manor straddling the Fal at the point where the main road running eastwards from Truro crossed by the *grandis pons*. The lands of Tybesta manor lay farther from the tin-workings of Blackmore than those of Tewington and on the whole were not so fertile. Holdings on Tybesta manor were generally larger than on Tewington, with the majority of them composed of more than 10 acres and many of more than 20 acres. There were, however, vills in which the holdings were considerably smaller, in Pennans and Caruur for example they were all 10 acres or less in size. Rents throughout the manor were substantially lower than those prevailing at Tewington and generally averaged from 7d. to 9d. an acre, although some were as low as 6d. Rents of the wastes and pastures of Tybesta manor varied from as little as 1d. to as much as 3d. an acre.

The three remaining Duchy manors, Moresk, Tywarnhaile and Helston-in-Kirrier, form the western group. Moresk lay to the north and east of Truro, almost exclusively in the parish of St Clements, and was bounded to the east, west and south by the Truro and Tresilian rivers. The borough of Truro was one of the largest and wealthiest of all Cornish boroughs in the first half of the fourteenth century, and as such was assessed to pay a subsidy of £22 in 1334.[1] Moresk manor was intimately connected with tin-mining, having the three most important Cornish stannary districts of Tywarnhaile, Penwith-and-Kirrier and Blackmore within easy reach, although only small quantities of tin were actually mined within the manor in the later middle ages. Barely ten miles from the western edge of Moresk lay Redruth, perhaps the most significant centre of mining in the stannary district of Kirrier, whilst another ten miles from the eastern edge of the manor lay the

[1] P.R.O. E.179/87/9.

26

fringes of Blackmore stannary. Moresk manor consisted of approximately 800 acres of land divided amongst some 50 conventionary and villein tenants, with considerable expanses of waste and pasture, and 20 Cornish acres in the hands of free tenants. Holdings varied greatly in size, ranging from less than 10 acres to more than 30 acres each, with the majority consisting of more than 15 acres. The average rent for an acre of conventionary land in the decade before the Black Death was between 8d. and 10d.

On the other extremity of the stannary district of Tywarnhaile lay the manor of Tywarnhaile. Situated in the parishes of St Agnes and Perranzabuloe in the heart of mining country on the Atlantic coast, Tywarnhaile manor formed an enclave of good land amongst a profusion of barren and indifferent soils. Although there were more than 25 conventionary and villein tenants in the decade before the Black Death, Tywarnhaile was small in area consisting of only 300 acres of land in customary tenancies and some 17 Cornish acres in the hands of free tenants. The pressure on these lands was so great in the years before the Great Plague of 1348/9 that both agriculture and mining were practised right down to the sea shores. Many lands were cultivated which were constantly threatened with sand blown from the beaches, and in the Caption of Seisin of 1337 the greater part of a number of holdings in the vills of Pennans and Stawen were described as being completely covered by sand. The encroachment of sand was to be a problem throughout the fourteenth and fifteenth centuries.[1] In structure and in its relation to mining, Tywarnhaile had many similarities with Tewington manor; its holdings were small with very few exceptions under 10 acres in extent, and its rents were high with some as much as 1s. 6d. per acre and the vast majority over one shilling.

The most westerly of the assessionable manors, Helston-in-Kirrier, was also the largest and it spread over the whole of the great parish of Wendron and overflowed into Stithians, Breage, Cury, and Mawgan. Before the Black Death at the time of peak demand for land in this part of Cornwall, approximately 5,000 acres were leased to the tenants of the manor, with perhaps an additional 2,500 acres in free tenancies. And some of the holdings on this

---

[1] Below, p. 151.

manor were so large that it is quite possible the acreages given on the assession rolls were considerable underestimations of their true areas. The structure of Helston-in-Kirrier differed from that of other Duchy manors owing to the vast areas of waste and pasture which completely overshadowed the land that could support continuous arable cultivation. From the variations in size and rent per acre of the various holdings which made up the conventionary lands of the manor some of the enormous differences in the quality of the soils become apparent. For example, in the vill of Crostang a messuage and 16 acres were leased for 26s. a year in 1337, whilst at the other extreme a messuage and 30 acres in the waste of Polmargh were leased for 2s. The more fertile land, suitable for intensive and continuous farming, such as that found around the borough of Helston, where the burgesses had their own fields, and in the wooded regions stretching down towards Gweek, was divided into relatively small holdings of 20 acres or less and, in a region where comparatively rich lands were scarce, realised rents of from 8d. to 1s. or even more for an acre before the Black Death struck. At the opposite extreme to the sparse fertile areas came the vast tracts of barren land which dominated the landscape of much of the manor and which were suitable only for use as rough pasture. The bleak uplands verging on Carmenellis were leased for barely ½d. per acre, and large amounts of waste could not be leased at all in separate parcels, but were leased *en bloc* in the 'farm of the Chace' on very reasonable terms.

But the moors of Helston-in-Kirrier manor were not only of value as pasture, for they realised substantial sums for the Duchy from the sale of tin exacted as toll[1] and from the sale of turbary.[2] In the later fourteenth century considerable quantities of peat charcoal were also mined on Redmoor.[3]

In 1307 the stannary of Tywarnhaile accounted for 10 per cent of the total tax assessment on tinners within the county, and the stannary of Penwith-and-Kirrier for fully 40 per cent.[4] Between them these mining regions exerted a dominating influence on the demand for

[1] Toll-tin was the right of the lord to a certain proportion of the tin mined on his land (below, pp. 188–91).
[2] Below, pp. 187–8. [3] D.C.O. 13 ff, [4] P.R.O. E.372/161, m. 41.

28

The Cornish Economy and the Duchy Manors

the land of the western Duchy manors, and a close correlation between rent receipts from conventionary lands and the output of tin can be traced throughout the fourteenth and fifteenth centuries. These manors were relatively isolated from alternative markets, and Moresk and Helston-in-Kirrier contained much poor land which would only be leased in response to exceptional demand for foodstuffs and land, such as that created by extensive mining activity.

THE REGIONAL ECONOMY

In any under-developed economy based firmly on the land, such as that of England in the middle ages, the size of the population is most often the primary determinant of the gross product of that economy, and of the demand for land and the products of the land. In certain regions of late medieval England, however, economic activities alternative to agriculture assumed an importance great enough to compromise this basic tenet. Cornwall was one such region. Within Cornwall agriculture was only a part of a diversified economic structure which featured mining, fishing, and shipping, as well as textile manufacture, quarrying, and shipbuilding, which all assumed some importance in the fifteenth century. To some extent these non-agrarian activities competed with agriculture, especially for labour and capital investment; but almost certainly of greater importance was the stimulus they gave to demand for land and the development of agriculture, by providing a market for its produce.

Mining was by far the most important of the various non-agrarian activities in medieval Cornwall, and the mines were overwhelmingly concerned with the extraction of tin, although there were a number of lead and silver mines within the county. An overall impression of the significance of tin-mining to the economy at large can be gained from the amounts of tin presented each year for the payment of duty, called coinage. All tin produced in Cornwall was subject to a duty of 40s. per thousandweight (1,000 lbs)[1]

[1] G. R. Lewis was mistaken (*Stannaries*, Appendix J) in stating that the Cornish thousandweight contained 1,200 and not 1,000 lbs; see L. F. Salzman, 'Mines and Stannaries', *The English Government at Work, 1327–1336*, ed. J. F. Willard, W. A. Morris, W. H. Dunham, III (Cambridge, Mass., 1950), p. 92.

before it could be sold.[1] Wide fluctuations occurred in the output of the tin mines during the course of the fourteenth and fifteenth centuries and these are reflected in the amounts of tin presented for coinage contained in Appendix C, pp. 286–7.[2] Even taking decennial averages, and excluding the thirteen-fifties when production was at a catastrophically low ebb, the amount of tin presented for coinage varied from as little as 500,000 lbs annually to as much as 1,500,000 lbs. From 1390 to 1410 an average of more than 1,250,000 lbs was presented for coinage each year which, assuming a selling price of £10–12 per thousandweight in Cornwall at this time,[3] was worth more than £12,500.[4] The true value of all tin actually produced in Cornwall at this time may well have been considerably in excess of this figure, for a tax amounting to some 20 per cent of the final selling price was a great incentive to evasion.

The accuracy of any attempt to assess the numbers and wealth of those engaged in Cornish mining in the later middle ages must be impaired by the lack of evidence, caused primarily by the exemption of the mining population from most forms of taxation from the early fourteenth century onwards.[5] Nevertheless there are two main sources of information; the most comprehensive being records of a subsidy levied on tinners in 1307, despite the immunity to such taxes apparently granted by the charter of 1305.[6] This subsidy, a twentieth in urban areas and a fifteenth in rural, was imposed on all Cornish tinners, but only a few decayed fragments of the original lists survive.[7] Fortunately, however, there is a full list of all tinners who had not paid this disputed subsidy by 1316.[8] Originally assessed to pay £127 10s. od., all that the tinners had paid by 1316 was £47

---

[1] Lewis, *Stannaries*, pp. 149–56.
[2] The amounts of tin presented for coinage are not synonymous with production, for there was widespread evasion of duty throughout the middle ages (*V.C.H. Cornwall*, II, 538). Nevertheless the rate of duty remained stable and there is no reason to assume that the incidence of smuggling fluctuated significantly in the course of the fourteenth and fifteenth centuries.
[3] Tin was being purchased by the Duchy of Cornwall at this time for use in repair work at 2½d. per pound.
[4] This figure includes coinage duty of £2,500.
[5] Above, p. 9.
[6] Printed in Lewis, *Stannaries*, Appendix D.
[7] P.R.O. E.179/87/5.
[8] P.R.O. E.372/161, m. 41.

3s. o$\frac{1}{2}$d., leaving £80 6s. 11$\frac{1}{2}$d. outstanding.[1] Altogether the names of some 1,300 persons are listed as owing tax in 1316, which suggests that a total of approximately 2,000 persons were taxed in 1307, when an average of 800,000 lbs of tin were being presented for coinage annually; and this figure must constitute only a fraction of the total numbers employed in tin-mining at this time, for many miners must have either evaded the tax or gained exemption from it.[2]

The only other source of information on the size of the mining population of medieval Cornwall is the tribulage accounts. Tribulage was a poll-tax imposed on all 'who worked with a shovel' within the limits of the stannaries of Penwith-and-Kirrier and Blackmore.[3] This tax would thus not have fallen upon many stannary workers such as smelters, charcoal-burners, carters, carpenters, pumpmen, foremen, and so on; and of course any number of migrant and casual workers must have managed to avoid payment when it fell due at Michaelmas. A measure of the incompleteness of the tribulage accounts as a record of the whole mining population is furnished by a comparison of the numbers of tinners still owing tax in 1316, with the numbers paying tribulage in 1307, when the original tax assess-ment was made. On Penwith-and-Kirrier stannary, for example, approximately 450 persons are recorded as owing tax, yet only 240 had paid tribulage, and whilst some 650 persons from Blackmore stannary owed tax only 265 had paid tribulage.[4] Therefore when the tribulage dues of Penwith-and-Kirrier were farmed to the stannary bailiff for £13 6s. 8d. per annum from 1404 to 1420, a sum equiva-lent to 1,600 persons paying tax at 2d. per head,[5] the enormous significance of mining to the Cornish economy once again becomes apparent.[6] It would hardly be an over-estimation to double the figure of 1,600 to arrive at an approximation of the total numbers

---

[1] The Pipe Roll entry is confusing; apparently £47 3s. o$\frac{1}{2}$d. had been contracted to be accounted for separately. The placing of the letter 'T' against many names on the Roll in a different coloured ink may well signify they had since paid, i.e. after 1316.

[2] Large numbers of labouring tinners were migrant and may have avoided payment. Others must have possessed less than the requisite amount of movables.

[3] Both Lewis's description of the tax (*Stannaries*, pp. 140–1) and the statistics of receipts from it that he published (*ibid.* Appendix O) contain many inaccuracies.

[4] P.R.O. SC.6.811/9, tribulage was paid at the rate of $\frac{1}{2}$d. per head.

[5] The rate of tax was raised from $\frac{1}{2}$d. to 2d. per head on Penwith-and-Kirrier stannary in 1349/50 (D.C.O. 5).

[6] P.R.O. SC.6.819/15 ff.; D.C.O. 35 ff.

The Cornish Economy and the Duchy Manors

directly connected with mining on this stannary in the first decades of the fifteenth century—taking into account the manifold exemptions and evasions, and the margin of profit for the farmer. Thus with probably more than 3,000 workers employed in a single stannary, albeit the most productive of the four Cornish stannaries at this time, it would be reasonable to assume that in this period of peak production, when approximately 1,250,000 lbs of tin were being presented for coinage each year, more than one person in ten of the adult population of Cornwall was engaged in work directly connected with mining.[1]

The sea was a crucial element in the regional economy, and its importance as a source of wealth and employment can scarcely be over-emphasized. Cornwall derived great benefit from rich local fishing grounds, and from lying on the sea route to the Mediterranean and the wine-producing regions of France. Cornwall was provided with ample opportunities for profiting from trade and victualling, as well as from smuggling, piracy, ship-wrecks and wrecking. No production figures or estimates of the total numbers employed are possible for the Cornish fishing industry which after agriculture came second in importance only to mining in the economy. Nevertheless, the widespread significance of sea-fishing is attested by a multitude of documents, and not least by the magnitude of the exports of fish and the imports of salt.[2] Perhaps the best indication of the scale of the Cornish fishing industry in the later middle ages can be gained from the Particulars of Customs (P.R.O. E.122) which become available in their detailed form in the reign of Henry VI. From these accounts fish appear to have been by far the most important single commodity exported from Cornwall, with the exclusion of tin. For example, in 1438 fish valued by customs officials at almost £1,000 was exported,[3] and much more doubtless went coastwise to other parts of England. London, Bristol,

[1] 34,274 persons paid the Poll Tax of 1377 in Cornwall (J. C. Russell, *British Medieval Population* (Alburquerque, 1948), p. 132); a number which almost certainly did not include workers in the stannaries.
[2] In the accounts of the Duchy havener, often to be found at the rear of the enrolled ministers' accounts, salt is consistently the most valuable commodity brought to Cornwall by alien merchants. See also A. R. Bridbury, *England and the Salt Trade in the Later Middle Ages* (Oxford, 1955), Appendix F, p. 171.
[3] P.R.O. E.122/113/55.

32

Southampton, and Exeter for instance, regularly received large quantities of Cornish fish, which was distributed thence far into the interior.[1]

The sea around Cornwall had 'greate store and manie kindes of verie excellent fishe, whose perticuler names are infinite'.[2] By far the most valuable and numerous of all the fish despatched from Cornwall were *dentricii*, almost certainly hake;[3] which were valued in the later fifteenth century at 26s. 8d. or 30s. per pipe, compared with 8s. 8d. or 10s. for most other fish, and only 6s. 8d. per pipe of pilchards, which were not then exported in great quantities. By the later sixteenth century pilchards were a source of great wealth to the county,[4] but hake were no longer found in great abundance.[5] Amongst other kinds of fish regularly despatched from Cornish ports in the fifteenth century we find herring, cod, haddock, whiting, congers, rays, ling and plaice. In addition oysters, salmon and trout were caught in great numbers in certain parts of the county.[6] It is impossible even to attempt to assess the numbers employed in the fishing industry, but apart from fishermen many hundreds must have worked on shore preparing the catch for its ultimate destination, each fish being cleaned, salted and pressed, and then either dried, pickled or smoked.

The affection felt by many Cornishmen for the sea expressed itself in an extensive participation in overseas trade as well as in fishing

---

[1] For London see, for example, P.R.O. E.122/113/55 ff.; for Bristol, E. M. Carus-Wilson, *Medieval Merchant Venturers* (1954), pp. 7–8; for Southampton, H. S. Cobb (ed.), *The Local Port Book of Southampton, 1439–40*, Southampton Record Series, v (1961), 32, 44 *et. al.*; for Exeter, Henri Touchard, 'Les Douanes municipales d'Exeter (Devon): publication des rôles de 1381 à 1433', doctoral thesis, University of Paris, Faculté des Lettres et Sciences Humaines (1967).

[2] Norden, *Description of Cornwall*, p. 22.

[3] The common translation of *dentrix* is pike, but this is clearly unacceptable. A. L. Rowse (*Tudor Cornwall* (1914), p. 72) takes *dentrix* to be congers, but this seems just as unlikely. Both hake and pike have a similar etymology deriving from their distinctive hook-shaped under-jaws. *Hacod* is Old English for pike (W. W. Skeat, *An Etymological Dictionary of the English Language*, 4th edn, Oxford, 1924).

[4] Norden, *Description of Cornwall*, pp. 22–4; Carew, *Survey of Cornwall*, pp. 32–4.

[5] Carew, writing at the turn of the sixteenth century, states that hake 'not long since, haunted the coast in great abundance, but now, . . . are much diminished' (*op. cit.* p. 34).

[6] A toll was levied on oysters caught at Trematon in the early fourteenth century (P.R.O. SC.6.811/1 ff.). Salmon frequented rivers east of Fowey and were especially common in the Tamar.

and coastal trade. The scale and scope of Cornish overseas trade in the fourteenth and fifteenth centuries were to a large extent determined by long periods of hostilities and consequent embargoes,[1] but at one time or another it flourished with Portugal, Spain, the Low Countries, Ireland, the Channel Islands, and many regions of France. The leading Cornish ports were Fowey, Falmouth, Padstow and Mounts Bay, but a substantial amount of Cornish trade was also pursued through Saltash and Plymouth.[2] The accounts of the havener of the Duchy of Cornwall and of royal customs officials show that a considerable proportion of the overseas trade of the county was carried by Cornishmen in Cornish ships. Regularly each year, when hostilities permitted, large fleets of local vessels set sail for France and the Iberian peninsula in late autumn and in spring for the wine harvest, with some ships making as many as three separate voyages in a single season.[3]

By the early fifteenth century a number of industries of some antiquity rose to new prominence within Cornwall and the Devon border regions. Of particular note was the rapid growth of textile manufacturing,[4] and the detailed customs accounts preserved in the Particulars of Customs class at the Public Record Office which, unlike the Enrolled Customs Accounts, distinguish between cloth exported from Plymouth and cloth exported from Cornish ports, suggest that Cornwall shared to a greater extent than has yet been realised in the industrial expansion of south-west England. Between 1418 and 1438 exports from Cornish ports accounted for almost 40 per cent of the exports of cloth both from Plymouth and Cornwall, although these were never great by national standards and the proportion appears to have declined in ensuing years.[5] The quarry-

---

[1] *V.C.H. Cornwall*, I, 477–84.
[2] For a brief review of some of the features of Cornish ports in the middle ages see: R. Pearse, *The Ports and Harbours of Cornwall* (St Austell, 1963). For an account of the office of Duchy havener see Stella M. Campbell, 'The Haveners of the Medieval Dukes of Cornwall and the Organisation of the Duchy Ports', *J.R.I.C.*, new ser., IV (1962).
[3] See, for example, P.R.O. SC.6.817/8.
[4] Cornish textile manufacturing on a commercial scale was of great antiquity. Cornish burel cloth was purchased by the Royal Almoner in Henry II's reign ('Great Roll of the Pipe, 1180–81', *Pipe Roll Society*, xxx, 33). The expansion of the industry in the later middle ages is examined in greater detail below, pp. 169–71.
[5] Below, p. 170.

ing and exporting of slates and stones called 'hellyngstones' also flourished in the fifteenth century, and the north-eastern Duchy manors of Helstone-in-Triggshire and Tintagel, close to where the famous Delabole quarries are now situated, shared in this activity.[1] In the later fifteenth century shipbuilding for export first becomes apparent, and in 1462 vessels of the combined value of almost £100 were made for export; including small crayers costing less than £6 each, *scaffs* selling for as much as £12 each, and carvels (*karvellas*), largest of all, selling for as much as £20 each.[2] Although, of course, the lack of suitable timber prevented the industry becoming of more than limited significance.

To this long list of industries we must add the small but ubiquitous rural industries indispensable to every agrarian society. The many small towns and boroughs of medieval Cornwall also helped to create a unique context for the agriculture of the county, by providing a market for its produce. To the great internal market for agricultural products must be added the very substantial quantity of foodstuffs needed to re-victual ships trading in Cornish ports, stopping before proceeding to London, Southampton or Sandwich, as was the practice of some Mediterranean vessels, or driven involuntarily into Cornish havens by bad weather.[3]

Thus it can be seen that the structure of the Cornish economy was fundamentally different from the economies of many other English counties; it was complex and diverse, with a high industrial and commercial content. But what follows will attempt to show that the picture of Cornish agriculture in the middle ages as the Cinderella of the county, under-capitalised and under-developed at the expense of industry, and in particular of tin-mining, cannot be substantiated. Indeed the primary effect of non-agrarian activities upon agriculture was to stimulate demand for land, an upward movement in rents and agricultural prices, and often an expansion in the area

---

[1] See, for example, P.R.O. E.122/113/55. Stones from Tintagel and Helstone-in-Triggshire were frequently used in Duchy building projects (P.R.O. E.101/461/15 ff.). See also L. F. Salzman, *Building in England down to 1540* (Oxford, 1952), p. 233.

[2] P.R.O. E.122/114/1.

[3] In Carew's exquisite prose (*Survey of Cornwall*, p. 3): 'the lying in the way bringeth forraine ships to claime succour at their harbours, when, either outward, or homeward bound, they are checked by an East, South, or South-east wind: and where the Horse walloweth, some haires will still remaine'.

under cultivation; efficiency rather than neglect was encouraged. Miners sometimes sought land, they invariably purchased some foodstuffs; textile industries required wool and many of their workers also purchased foodstuffs. There is abundant evidence in stannary court rolls to show that miners frequently engaged part-time in some form of agrarian activity, mostly by keeping a few animals and occasionally by growing crops, but such activity could have served only to cushion these miners against the more violent fluctuations in the supply of foodstuffs and was rarely on a scale large enough to have rendered them completely independent of the market.

The documentation of the manors of the Duchy of Cornwall lends itself to an analysis of the effects of industrial activity on agriculture; and such evidence as it has produced suggests that in some parts of Cornwall, particularly the south-east, it was possible for a growing demand for agrarian produce from centres of industry and trade to negate completely the depressive effects upon rents of substantial population decline.[1] Furthermore, although within Cornwall the level of population may well have influenced the amount of tin produced, the very close correlation between trends in the rent yields of western Cornish manors and the output of tin is most striking.[2]

[1] Below, Appendix A, Figs 1–3.
[2] Below, Appendix A, Figs 6–9 and Appendix C, Fig. 1.

2

ESTATE MANAGEMENT

Apart from the civil services of Church and State, medieval bureaucracies were confined almost exclusively to the management of large estates. The administrative machinery required to control a leading baronial inheritance, with perhaps well over a hundred manors in a score or more English counties and frequently lands in Wales and France also, was of necessity vast and complex with its own codes of rigid procedure and intricate systems of checks and balances. The present study is concerned with the administration of the seventeen assessionable manors, a single twig on the branch of one such institution; for the estates of the Black Prince included the Earldom of Chester and the Principalities of Wales and Aquitaine as well as the Duchy of Cornwall, and when the Duchy was in the hands of the King it was of comparatively less importance still. Furthermore, the Duchy of Cornwall itself in 1337 comprised more than 50 demesne manors in a score of counties, as well as many boroughs, the stannaries of Devon and Cornwall, and the shrievalty and the havenership of Cornwall.

The adminstrative hierarchy of the estates of a medieval Duke of Cornwall divided into three distinct tiers. The bottom tier comprised the purely local officials, generally reeves and bailiffs, concerned solely with a single unit: a manor, a stannary, a hundred and so on. The second tier consisted of officials who supervised the management of a number of units within a specific region, such as the stewards and receivers who were responsible for estates in Devon and Cornwall. At the apex of the administration was the council, the receiver-general, the steward-in-chief, and the auditors, who controlled and co-ordinated the regional administrations.

MANORIAL ADMINISTRATION

Although demesne farming was not practised on any of the assessionable manors after the creation of the Duchy in 1337, there was a

37

multitude of important executive and administrative functions to be performed. The rents and assession fines payable for the lands, mills, fisheries and other properties of the manors had to be collected and accounted for, as had the fines imposed in the manorial courts, with all the consequent difficulties involved in distraining for debts.[1] The most profitable use had to be made of lands left *in manu domini*, and numerous manorial properties such as turbary, pannage, and pasture had to be sold from year to year. Death duties had to be exacted, valued and disposed of, and heirs had to be found. Repairs to capital equipment had to be initiated and supervised—a task which assumed added significance if a castle or deer-park were attached to the manor. Finally the discipline of the manor had to be enforced and the rights of the Duke preserved.

The bulk of these tasks and a general responsibility for the smooth running of the manorial economy on behalf of the Duchy devolved upon the reeve. All the Cornish manors of the Duchy, except one, had reeves who were elected annually from within the ranks of the free and unfree conventionaries and the *nativi de stipite* at the first meeting of the manorial court after Michaelmas;[2] the sole exception was Helston-in-Kirrier manor which, owing to increasing administrative difficulties in the decade before the Black Death, it was found necessary to entrust permanently to a salaried bailiff.[3] The right to elect reeves appears to have resided exclusively in the homage, and no traces of any intervention by the Duchy can be found.[4] From the first records of the assessionable manors dating from the late thirteenth centry, the office of reeve appears to have been widely regarded as a particularly onerous burden, and tenants were often

---

[1] Livestock was usually distrained upon for outstanding debts both to the Duchy and to individuals. After confiscation animals had to be fed, and protected from theft and possible attempts by their owners to regain possession (manorial court rolls, *passim*).

[2] It is perhaps surprising that free conventionaries were liable to serve as reeve, for this office was closely connected with villeinage in many parts of England (H. S. Bennett, *Life on the English Manor*) (Cambridge, 3rd edn, 1948), p. 169; N. Neilson, 'Customary Rents', *Oxford Studies in Social and Legal History*, ed. P. Vinogradoff, II (Oxford, 1910), 101 ff. [3] Below, pp. 95–7.

[4] The conditions of tenure of the customary tenants of Duchy manors state: '*et prepositus . . . cum electus fuerit*' and not '*et erit prepositus ad voluntatem domini*', which was a common condition on many English manors at this time (Bennett, *op. cit.* pp. 169–71). At Mitchell in Cornwall the lord nominated who was to serve as reeve (P.R.O. Anc. Deeds A.8639).

willing to pay substantial fines to avoid service when elected.[1] For example in 1301 at Moresk three tenants paid fines totalling 14s. to be excused serving as reeve,[2] and in 1302 at Tewington Christopher de Tewynyn paid 6s. 8d. and another tenant 2s. for the same privilege.[3] At Moresk in 1297 Ipolito de Polhusek' was fined 10s. *pro contemptu quando electus fuit prepositus*;[4] whilst at Liskeard in the late fifteenth century John Hogge was fined £4 for a similar offence.[5] Under the Duchy the normal procedure appears to have been that the homage would elect two or three tenants to the office, and leave it to those elected to decide which of them was to serve.[6] Probably the fines to be excused from service were then bid up until one of them elected to take the office rather than pay the fine. Unlike conditions prevailing on many manors elsewhere in England at this time the reeves of the Cornish manors of the Duchy generally held office for only a single year;[7] which says much for their native ability as significant arrears in their payments to the receiver of the Duchy were rarely encountered except in periods of severe and widespread depression.[8]

The majority of persons who served as reeve possessed above-average size landholdings, poorer tenants seem rarely to have been chosen.[9] Tenants of the largest holdings or groups of holdings can nearly always be traced serving as reeve, and frequently for periods longer than a single year. For example, Nicholas Kernek, who leased extensive pastures on Helstone-in-Triggshire manor for approximately 46s. rent annually,[10] was reeve in 1350/1, 1351/2, and from

---

[1] For similar practices see: Bennett, *op. cit.* p. 171; Finberg, *Tavistock Abbey*, p. 254; R. Somerville, *History of the Duchy of Lancaster, Vol. 1: 1265–1603* (1953), pp. 96–7.

[2] P.R.O. SC.6.811/2. [3] P.R.O. SC.6.811/3.

[4] P.R.O. E.119/1.

[5] D.C.O. 58.

[6] For examples of this procedure see P.R.O. SC.2.160/27, court held at Liskeard, 18 October, 2 Henry V; P.R.O. SC.2.158/12, court held at Calstock, 10 October, 10 Edward IV. See also Finberg, *Tavistock Abbey*, p. 254.

[7] Bennett (*Life on the English Manor*, p. 167 f.) concludes after a wide search amongst the records of many counties that the reeve was often as permanent an officer as the serjeant or bailiff.

[8] Below, pp. 196–217.

[9] It was common in many parts of England for substantial tenants to be preferred (Bennett, *Life on the English Manor*, p. 169; Neilson, 'Customary Rents', pp. 101–2).

[10] Below, p. 249.

Estate Management

1358 to 1362.[1] Richard Juyl, a prominent burgess of Saltash and holder of extensive lands on Trematon manor,[2] was reeve in 1350/1, 1352/3 and 1355/6;[3] whilst at Tybesta manor John Walla, who leased two separate holdings for almost 20s. rent annually,[4] was reeve from 1359 to 1362.[5] John Wyllyot, who in the assessions of 1462 and 1469 held on Helstone-in-Triggshire manor leased one of the largest and most valuable groups of holdings,[6] was reeve to our knowledge in 1466/7, 1467/8 and for three years from 1478 to 1480.[7]

It was natural that tenants of some standing, with large landholdings and probably some experience of management, should have been preferred.[8] Furthermore, although the responsibilities and risks involved in being reeve were likely to have appeared daunting to the inexperienced tenant of limited resources, the same office may well have appealed to more substantial tenants as an attractive opportunity for personal gain and the exercise of power. The office of reeve brought with it many perquisites and abundant occasions upon which to swindle a penny or two.[9] Certainly the small customary allowances paid to reeves, ranging from 5s. on Calstock and Tewington manors down to only 2s. on Helston-in-Kirrier, Moresk, and Rillaton, offered little enough inducement by themselves.[10]

Reeves were assisted in the running of their manors by other local officials, some elected and some hired. On a number of manors jurymen, beadles, and tithingmen were elected each year. Beadles and tithingmen were concerned mainly with the maintenance of

[1] P.R.O. SC.6.817/1, 817/3, 817/6, 817/7, 817/8; D.C.O. 13.
[2] Below, p. 248.
[3] P.R.O. SC.6.817/1, 817/3; D.C.O. Library, Transcript of 19/20 Edward III account.
[4] D.C.O. 472ᵃ.
[5] P.R.O. SC.6.817/7, 817/8; D.C.O. 13.
[6] D.C.O. 479, 480.
[7] D.C.O. 59, 60, 69, 70 and 71, 73.
[8] Bennett, *Life on the English Manor*, p. 169; Neilson, 'Customary Rents', pp. 101–2.
[9] Bennett, *op. cit.* p. 174 f.; Harvey, *Medieval Oxfordshire Village*, p. 69 f. It was widely recognised that manorial officials had many perquisites; cf. the description of the office of bailiff of Helston-in-Kirrier manor: *Vad', feod', profit', et commoditat'* (D.C.O. 59).
[10] These allowances remained unchanged from the late thirteenth century to the accession of Henry VII; furthermore Duchy reeves, unlike those upon many other manors, were required to pay the full rent for their holdings.

Estate Management

law and order, and the enforcement of manorial discipline, and they can be seen in the court rolls presenting offenders at court and levying for distresses. Juries, consisting of twelve annually elected jurymen, played an important part in both the legal and economic functioning of manors. It was part of the duties of the jury, or at least of a quorum selected from it, to assess the cash value of all goods forfeited to the lord; and the reeve was charged to deliver this amount to the Duchy receiver, not the amount they actually realised when sold. Juries also held enquiries into the possessions left by unfree tenants upon death and valued them;[1] they also formed commissions of enquiry, such as those set up in Edward IV's reign upon Climsland and Calstock manors to report on the state of repair of the buildings and enclosures of tenants' holdings.[2]

Those Duchy manors with extensive woodlands elected woodwards annually from within the ranks of the customary tenants, whose duties were largely connected with the maintenance of the rights of the Duke; they were to see that no animals were allowed to trespass, that no trees were felled illegally, and that no brushwood or acorns were stolen.[3] Liskeard, the most heavily wooded of all Duchy manors in Cornwall, elected 6 woodwards each year, one for each of the manorial woods.

Assistance was usually given to reeves in the collection of rents, and unpaid collectors appear to have been elected on most manors.[4] Usually the reeve retained ultimate responsibility for moneys collected, but at Helston-in-Kirrier before the appointment of a permanent bailiff a group of tenants were personally responsible for all that they collected.[5] At Climsland the holder of a free tenement called Beales' paid no rent but owed the services of collecting rent

[1] The possessions of unfree tenants were ceded to the Duchy upon death (below, p. 63).
[2] P.R.O. SC.2.159/32, court held at Stoke, 17 December, 6 Edward IV. P.R.O. SC.2.158/12, court held at Calstock, 4 February, 11 Edward IV.
[3] Below, p. 185.
[4] For such an election at Calstock see: P.R.O. SC.2.158/12, court held 20 March, 14 Edward IV; for Climsland P.R.O. SC.2.159/32, court held at Stoke, 17 December, 6 Edward IV, and D.C.O. 60; for Liskeard P.R.O. SC.2.160/26, court held the *die Lune prox. ante fest. St. Matthias*, 2 Henry IV.
[5] The debts they accumulated from 1341 to 1344 are listed in D.C.O. 3.

from free and conventionary tenants, but the *nativi de stipite* fell outside his jurisdiction.[1]

There is a great deal of evidence in fifteenth-century accounts to suggest that the Duchy had by this time become more appreciative of their reeves, and a considerable amount of paid assistance was given to them. Regular payments were made, for example, to Jacob Chidley for the help he gave to the reeve of Tewington manor,[2] and to John Carmarthen for his labours in surveying woods and appraising lands left *in manu domini* on Tybesta manor.[3] The bailiff of Helston-in-Kirrier was allowed to claim expenses for an assistant collector of rents and fines, and for extra labour involved in the sale of turbary and the collection of toll-tin.[4] Reeves also appear to have been more liberally rewarded than hitherto for efficiency and for the performance of tasks beyond their normal range of duties, as for example in 1460 when John Webbe, reeve of Calstock, was granted 13s. 4d. by the auditors for selling wood worth £7 13s. 8d. on behalf of the Duchy.[5]

DUCHY OFFICIALS

The material throwing light on the administrative organisation of the Duchy of Cornwall estates in the later middle ages is considerable, and during the tenure of the Black Prince in particular the procedures by which the estates were governed can be studied in exceptional detail owing to the fortunate survival of a series of council registers covering the years 1348 to 1365. For this reason it will be most satisfactory to attempt an outline of the administrative machinery governing the Cornish manors in the first forty years of the Duchy's history, and to note subsequently the more important changes which occurred in the ensuing decades of the later middle ages.

The receiver and the steward of the Cornish estates stood at the head of the regional administrative hierarchy, and they spent most of the year attending locally to duties within their bailiwicks. As there

[1] P.R.O. E.120/1. [2] D.C.O. 57 ff. [3] D.C.O. 48.
[4] D.C.O. 33, 36, 37, 58; P.R.O. SC.6.821/11, 822/1. [5] D.C.O. 58.

was no separate organisation to deal with manors, these bailiwicks also included ultimate responsibility for all Duchy estates within Cornwall, namely: the stannaries, boroughs, havenry, county and hundred courts, feodary, and the host of duties stemming from the Duke's position as a great feudal lord.

A marked differentiation between the basic functions of the receiver and those of the steward can be readily distinguished in the records, but it is also apparent that some duties were not strictly reserved to one or the other. The council of the Prince was the supreme policy-making body and, together with the chief-steward and receiver-general of the estates of the Prince throughout England, they directed the local steward and receiver within closely defined limits which offered little scope for the exercise of any significant personal initiative or autonomous action; both officers were used locally to implement decisions reached centrally.[1] Only in the execution of relatively minor matters were the steward and receiver allowed to act independently and without close supervision, and although in their relationships with lesser officials they appear to have acted with a great deal of authority they were in reality often acting with an authority that had been pre-determined for them and they were constantly being asked to account for their actions. Nevertheless, despite lacking the power to initiate new policy directly, the counsel of the local receiver and steward was valued, trusted, and sought after by higher officials less in touch with conditions prevailing locally in Cornwall.[2] Tenants of the Duke could also seek to influence Duchy policy by petitioning the council, which they did with great frequency,[3] and often in opposition to

[1] For general surveys of aspects of the central administrative system of the Black Prince see T. F. Tout, *Chapters in the Administrative History of Medieval England* (6 vols, Manchester, 1920–33), v, Chapter XVIII, Section II; M. Sharp, 'The Administrative Chancery of the Black Prince before 1362', in *Essays in Medieval History presented to T. F. Tout*, eds. A. G. Little and F. F. Powicke (Manchester, 1925). See also M. Sharp, 'Contributions to the History of the Earldom and County of Chester, 1237–1399' (Manchester Ph.D. thesis, 1926).

[2] *B.P.R.* II, 14, 39, 40, 51, *et al.*

[3] Many of these petitions are contained in the council registers of the Black Prince—for Cornwall see *B.P.R.* II. Others are contained in P.R.O. Anc. Pet. SC.8—in particular see file 333 which contains 106 petitions dated 1375/6 from Cornwall and England alone (i.e. not including Wales and Chester).

decisions made by local officials,[1] even on such matters as the conduct of assessions.[2]

The cardinal duty of the receiver with respect to the assessionable manors was to receive and account for the money due from reeves and bailiffs, both from the charge of the current financial year and from the arrears of previous years.[3] From the money in his possession the receiver was also responsible for the payment of certain fees and salaries. In the absence of any specially instituted official he was answerable for the supervision of the capital equipment of the Duchy in Cornwall, which comprised parks, castles, and other buildings, ensuring that it was maintained in reasonable condition, that repairs were carried out efficiently and economically, and that repair costs claimed by lesser officials were not exorbitant.[4] Occasionally the receiver would be instructed to initiate and pay for large-scale building works, although these were often inspected afterwards to check on his honesty and efficiency.[5]

The duties of the steward were concerned only indirectly with finance and were mainly executive and judicial in nature. On the judicial side he was in theory liable to preside over all manorial courts, but the sheer physical impossibility of holding thirteen courts annually on each of the seventeen Cornish manors, to say nothing of other Duchy courts in Cornwall, induced him to delegate the bulk of this work to others. But the steward almost certainly visited most manors during the course of each year, probably for the more important views of frankpledge which were held twice annually. The foremost executive functions of the steward were to ensure the efficient working of the estates and to obtain the most economic use of the resources of his lord, but he also attended to the rights of the tenants. On instructions from the council the steward frequently headed commissions of enquiry in Cornwall dealing with matters

---

[1] See, for example, P.R.O. SC.8, file 102, no. 5080 and file 333, no. E. 1046; *B.P.R.* II, 22, 90, 96–7, 108 *et al.*

[2] *B.P.R.* II, 117–18. This petition was favourably received (below, pp. 126–7).

[3] The receivers' accounts were usually enrolled with the manorial accounts in Edward III's reign, but were subsequently separated from them.

[4] The special responsibilities of the receiver in this field can be seen in the council registers; most directives concerning buildings were addressed to the receiver.

[5] See, for example, *B.P.R.* II, 76, 175. An elaborate system of controls and checks on both income and expenditure existed within the Prince's administration.

arising from the administration of the estates, many of which were set up in response to petitions presented to the council.[1] Many of the more important and valuable conventionary leases, such as those concerned with mills and fisheries, were made by the steward or the auditors rather than the reeves,[2] and lands left *in manu domini* after the seven-yearly assessions had been held were the subject of special attention by the steward when he visited the manors.[3]

Tasks of particular importance or urgency often concerned both the receiver and the steward; in any case the Duchy sought the services of both to expedite matters when the occasion demanded. A number of directives from the council were addressed to both officials jointly, as was that of 12 July 1357 when they were ordered to investigate alleged defects and malpractices in the assession held the previous year;[4] and a directive of 21 November 1359 ordered both officials to survey all the Prince's castles in Cornwall for the protection of the county as the Prince planned to venture abroad.[5]

Thus it can be seen that the duties and responsibilities of the receiver and steward with respect to the assessionable manors alone were considerable, and within the Cornish estates as a whole they were prodigious. In addition, many of the persons who held these offices also contrived to hold other responsible and burdensome positions at the same time.[6] For the efficient performance of their duties, therefore, a large measure of responsible assistance was essential. A permanent bailiff-errant was appointed and paid by the Duchy to assist in the administration of the Cornish estates—his primary function being to aid the receiver in the collection of money.[7] But in addition both the receiver and the steward appointed and

---

[1] *B.P.R.* II, *passim.*

[2] For example, D.C.O. 1, Moresk; P.R.O. SC.6.816/12, Calstock; P.R.O. SC.6.818/9, Helston-in-Kirrier.

[3] For example, D.C.O. 46, Liskeard; P.R.O. SC.6.818/9, Tewington; P.R.O. SC.6.819/10, Tywarnhaile (below, pp. 112, 128).

[4] *B.P.R.* II, 117. See also below, pp. 126–7.

[5] *Ibid.* p. 166.

[6] For example, John Dabernoun managed to hold, within the estates of the Duchy of Cornwall, the offices of steward of Cornwall and of Devon, sheriff of Cornwall, keeper of the Prince's fees of Cornwall and Devon, keeper of the game of Dartmoor chase, keeper of the stannaries of Devon, and keeper and constable of the castles of Trematon, Tintagel, and Exeter (*B.P.R.* II, *passim*).

[7] *B.P.R.* I, 11; II, 4, 8, 171.

paid for deputies, attorneys, and general aids out of the profits of their offices.[1] The Duchy accepted these unofficial aids and generally allowed them to act in the names of their overlords within the estates, but the steward and the receiver remained fully responsible for all that was executed by them, with only the official bailiff-errant being himself accountable directly to the Duchy. Many persons were also hired from time to time by the Duchy to perform specific tasks, such as acting as messengers or assisting at the assessions.[2] On occasion the tenants of the Duchy of Cornwall protested at the great numbers of people who 'meddle in the prince's name', and action had to be taken to restrict them.[3]

Keepers of Duchy deer-parks and constables of castles were also connected with the administration of the assessionable manors. Retainers and yeomen of the Prince frequently held these offices on salaries of 2d. to 3d. per day, with the receiver and the steward invariably possessing a number of them. At times a 'surveyor of all the game in Cornwall' was appointed, whose responsibilities included the supervision of the individual parkers;[4] and in Edward IV's reign there was a Controller of Works within Cornwall, who was primarily concerned with the maintenance of Duchy buildings.[5]

An important part in the functioning of the local administration was also played by the auditors of accounts, who on their visits to Cornwall did much more than hear and determine the accounts of local ministers. The duties of a 'court' of auditors sent to Cornwall in 1350 in the wake of the Black Death, give a good idea of the scope of the power entrusted to these officials.[6] They were instructed by the full council of the Black Prince to perform no less than twenty-seven specific tasks, which included amongst others: 'arrent and assess all lands in the lord's hands'; 'examine the number of officers and ministers . . . remove those that are not profitable to the lord, put others in their places, . . . remove unnecessary officers';

---

[1] Council directives were frequently addressed to the steward or the receiver 'or their deputies or lieutenants' (*B.P.R.* I, 92; II, 57, 74, 80).
[2] *B.P.R.* II, 60, 107, 116.
[3] See, for example, *B.P.R.* I, 151; transcript of the Mt Edgecumbe White Book (preserved in the County Museum, Truro), p. 15.
[4] *B.P.R.* II, 14.   [5] P.R.O. E.101/461/20 ff.
[6] Transcript of the Mt Edgecumbe White Book, pp. 15–17.

'hear the complaints of all the lord's subjects in these parts . . . and try them of such business as is not as needs the advice of the lord and his grand council'; 'find the cause of the arrears of £62 9s. od. on Helston-in-Kirrier manor'; and finally 'survey and examine and do all things that can be done to the profit of the lord and the better government of his lordship'.

The administrative structure which had been built up to manage the estates of the Black Prince was based upon a widely practised pattern, and it was to persist virtually unchanged in essentials for the remainder of the middle ages.[1] Even when the first Duke died in 1376 and his estates were divided between his son, Richard, and his widow, Joan, there were few notable modifications, for the two sectors although run as completely separate entities, each having its own receiver, steward, and auditors of Cornish estates, both followed closely the patterns of the previous administration.[2] Furthermore, the households of Joan and Richard employed many who had been servants of the Black Prince.[3]

In the course of the fifteenth century firm moves were made towards the creation of a wholly separate administrative system for the Duchy of Cornwall. A receiver-general of the Duchy, who had deputies in Cornwall, Devon, and England, was appointed in Henry VI's reign in place of the local receivers who had previously been responsible directly to the receiver-general of all the estates of the prince or monarch. As the fifteenth century progressed so the receiver-generalship of the Duchy and the stewardship of Cornwall were held by successively more important political personages. Indeed the power and profit afforded by the stewardship of the Cornish estates was so prized that a full-scale private war flared up between Sir William Bonville and Thomas Courtenay, Earl of Devon, as to who was to hold the office. Each produced a royal patent in support of his claim and it was not until 1442, after prolonged hostilities in which 'many men were hurt and many

---

[1] The desire for continuity is exemplified by the enquiries made in Edward IV's reign as to the salaries paid to officials in Edward III's reign so that they might be justly adopted (P.R.O. C.47/55/56; SC.6.1291/3).

[2] For the administrative structure of Richard's Cornish estates see P.R.O. SC.6.818/6; for Joan's see P.R.O. SC.6.818/9.

[3] Tout, *Chapters*, II, 329–31; IV, 190–1.

slain', that the Earl of Devon was finally installed as steward.[1]

The contrast between the respective holders of the stewardship and receivership in the fourteenth century with those of the fifteenth became even more pronounced after the accession of Edward IV in 1461, with figures such as William Lord Hastings, brother-in-law of Richard Earl of Warwick, and Anthony Woodville, Lord Scales and second Earl Rivers, holding the receiver-generalship. Obviously such men did not execute the duties of their offices locally in Cornwall as their predecessors in the time of the Black Prince had done. It was not uncommon in the second half of the fifteenth century for the receiver-general and steward to be members of the council of the Duke, and the authority they possessed must have accrued more to their persons than to the offices they occupied. Often the receiver-general and steward held a formidable number of important offices at the same time in other administrative hierarchies[2] and the executive duties in Cornwall must have been performed by a veritable army of deputies and underlings.[3]

Nevertheless, despite pluralities and great political upheavals the efficiency with which the assessionable manors were governed did not suffer to any considerable extent, indeed throughout the fourteenth and fifteenth centuries they were managed with great skill and flexibility.

FINANCIAL ORGANISATION

Lostwithiel, with its impressive range of buildings constructed in the time of Earl Edmund,[4] was quickly adopted by the Duchy as its administrative headquarters in Cornwall, and it became standard procedure for the accounts of Cornish ministers to be presented

---

[1] *Proceedings and Ordinances of the Privy Council of England*, ed. Sir Harris Nicolas (6 vols, 1834–7), v, 158, 165, 173–5; *Rot. Parl.* v, 284, 332.

[2] For a list of the posts held by William Lord Hastings in royal administration see A. R. Myers, *The Household of Edward IV* (Manchester, 1959), p. 239 f.; for posts held within the Duchy of Lancaster estates see Somerville, *History of the Duchy of Lancaster*, 'List of Officers', *passim*. Anthony Woodville was a member of the Duke of Norfolk's council (A. E. Levett, *Studies in Manorial History* (Oxford, 1938), pp. 26, 38).

[3] For the comparable position within the Duchy of Lancaster estates, see Somerville, *op. cit.* pp. 193, 197–8.

[4] Henderson, *Essays in Cornish History*, p. 47.

there for audit a few months after Michaelmas, the close of each financial year.[1]

The annual visit of the auditors to Cornwall was an important event, and a special summons might be sent by the council to the steward instructing him to warn local ministers and bailiffs to prepare for the audit.[2] Auditors of local ministers' accounts, although inferior in status to auditors of the accounts of officials of the household, were trusted servants of the Duchy possessing wide discretionary powers with which to deal with the accounts, and their decision was invariably final. Reeves had to explain and justify each failure to deliver the expected revenue, each sum expended. Unfortunately we can learn little of the fascinating negotiations between reeves and auditors for only the final decisions survive; the extant accounts are fair copies drawn up by scribes after the audit.[3]

Lacking the complications of demesne exploitation, inter-manorial liveries, and frequent 'foreign' receipts and expenses, the Cornish manors of the Duchy were possessed of a relatively simple method of accounting. The first part of the manorial account consisted of a list of the various sums the reeve was charged to deliver, commencing with 'Rents of Assize' and 'Rents and Fines of the Conventionary Tenants', proceeding to 'Profits of the Manor', which included revenues from such items as sales of pannage, pasture and wood, profits of turbaries and toll-tin and so on, and closing with 'Yields of the Manorial Court'. The moneys thus itemised were then added together to give a *summa totalis*. Arrears, if any, were not included in this charge. The second part of the account consisted of allowances made against the first part. The first heading, '*Allocaciones*', could include the small customary payments made to reeves and tithes given to local churches. Then 'Expenses' were listed, and these were often heavy upon manors where parks and castles necessitated frequent and costly repairs.

---

[1] Only rarely was the audit delayed, as for example when that held in July 1374 served to hear the accounts of both 1371/2 and 1372/3 (P.R.O. SC.6.818/4, 818/5); in most years it was held within six months of the close of the financial year. An attempt to audit the accounts of the ministers of Richard of Bordeaux in London was soon abandoned.

[2] For example, *B.P.R.* II, 5.

[3] Two or sometimes even three copies were made of the manorial accounts after the audit (*B.P.R.* II, 38; P.R.O. SC.6.813/22; D.C.O. 207).

Finally in this part of the account came the claims for allowances against the charges recorded in the first half, which in some periods included such items as rents lost because lands or mills were *in manu domini*, fines uncollected from tenants who were too poor to pay, and so on. The grand total of the second part of the account was then subtracted from that of the first to produce the amount that the reeve was charged to deliver to the receiver. Separately inscribed at the foot of the account might be moneys paid over by the reeve before the annual audit, and the arrears of previous reeves and accounts.

In the course of Henry V's reign the format of the account was changed, probably to bring it more into line with established procedure in other parts of the royal estates. As a result all outstanding arrears began to be entered at the head of the account and included in the charge, whilst any payments made by the reeve before the audit were listed in the second part of the account and subtracted from the charge. These changes were not in the interests of clarity, for the new accounts gave no ready sight of the 'yield' of manors, and the burdening of the reeves' accounts with arrears for which they were not personally responsible nor held liable to repay served only to confuse.[1]

The receiver, or his deputy, accounted for all payments collected from reeves and other local officials in the course of the financial year, allowing them against the charge of the current year, or on the rare occasions when arrears persisted deducting them from the outstanding debts of previous years. Whenever a payment was made two receipts were written, one copy given by the receiver's clerk to the minister concerned, and the other retained by the receiver's office. Many of these receipts or tallies survive and it is possible to follow in some detail the system of book-keeping used by the receiver.[2] The tallies of each manor were sewn together and a note of the amounts received duplicated on the dorse so that the totals paid by each minister could be readily calculated. At the annual audit the tallies in the receiver's hands were matched with those in the hands of ministers, and outstanding debits calculated.

[1] Compare the account of 12–13 Henry IV (D.C.O. 41) with the next available account 3–4 Henry V (D.C.O. 42).
[2] P.R.O. SC.6.1290/1ff.

Estate Management

The annual Receivers' Account was presented after the accounts of local ministers had been audited and moneys paid over, it listed all the sums paid from the start of the financial year to the close of the audit, and credited the appropriate persons. Moneys received in payment against the charges of the current year were kept separate from those paying off arrears. The receiver also prepared, after the Receivers' Account was closed, a further account called the Great Roll of Debtors, which listed outstanding arrears.[1] All arrears were carefully ascribed to the individuals who had contracted them, each newly elected reeve taking office completely free of debt.[2] The absence of any prolonged general accumulation of arrears in the later middle ages usually rendered it unnecessary for the receiver to resort to extreme measures to secure payment. Occasionally, however, it was necessary to seize the property of defaulting reeves;[3] and in the early years of the Duchy and again in Richard II's reign some recourse was made to imprisonment for debtors, but most debtors were quickly released, either upon payment of their debts or upon finding adequate security for them,[4] but throughout the later middle ages the persistently healthy financial position of the majority of manors at all times rendered such measures largely superfluous.

[1] See for example the Great Roll of 1355/6 (P.R.O. SC.6.812/7) which lists all arrears from the first year of the Duchy, 1337/8.
[2] Often persons leasing valuable manorial properties, such as ferries, fisheries, and mills, were made personally responsible for their own debts.
[3] For example, in 1341/2 the goods of Richard de Fentenwausaut, reeve of Helstone-in-Triggshire were seized; they are listed in the account of that year (D.C.O. 1).
[4] For a similar procedure in South Wales, see T. B. Pugh, *The Marcher Lordships of South Wales, 1415–1536* (Cardiff, 1963), p. 158.

3

THE OBLIGATIONS AND LEGAL STATUS OF TENANTS

The seventeen Cornish demesne manors of the Duchy of Cornwall differed so markedly in structure from manors in most other parts of England, and in particular had so little in common with manors in the 'classical' or 'champion' regions, that it is questionable whether they can be called manorialised at all. Any definition of the elements essential to manorialism and their relative importance must be extremely flexible, nevertheless, however loose a definition one accepts, as long as it remains at all meaningful, the structure of the seventeen assessionable manors is likely to contravene more than one of its premises. At the turn of the thirteenth century, when records of these manors commence, there was, as we have seen, no direct exploitation of demesnes, no open-fields, no common pastures, and settlement was scattered. On the tenurial side the manors were no less unusual, and instead of the customary division of tenants into free, villein, and cottar, Duchy tenants were free, conventionary, or villein: indeed the bulk of the tenantry held land in conventionary tenure, the basic conditions of which were not hereditary security of tenure with rents and obligations regulated by custom, but a seven-year lease at a free market rent with negligible services and no renewal as of right.

TENURE BY CONTRACT

Conventionarii were by no means limited to Duchy manors. A glance through the collections of Cornish manorial documents in the Public Record Office and the Cornwall County Record Office is sufficient to impress how widespread tenure *per conventionam* was throughout the county in the later middle ages; it even existed in some regions of Devon.[1] Nevertheless, it would be premature to suggest that the detailed conditions of tenure on Duchy manors were paralleled elsewhere.

[1] Finberg, *Tavistock Abbey*, pp. 249–52; W. G. Hoskins, *Devon* (1954), p. 90.

The Obligations and the Legal Status of Tenants

When the Duchy was founded in 1337 there were approximately 800 conventionaries on the seventeen manors, three times as many as the number of free tenants and more than ten times the number of villeins; furthermore, conventionary rents at this time were in aggregate more than six times as great as the combined free and villein rents. Thus, we can see that the *conventionarii* were not merely a small group of *adventitii* or the farmers of parcels of demesne,[1] but by far the most important category of tenants on the Cornish manors of the Duchy in the later middle ages.

Conventionary tenure, as it existed after its revision in 1333,[2] could be either free or unfree in status, and in many respects it resembled ordinary leasehold tenure. The basis was a contract made between the Duchy and the tenant; the Duchy agreeing to demise, for example, a holding of land or a mill, and the tenant agreeing to pay a sum of money and be liable to perform certain specified services. It was the normal practice of the Duchy to make leases *en bloc* at a court of assession, held on each of the manors every seven years a few months before the leases then in force were due to expire.[3] The price of the lease was made up primarily of an annual rent and a fine, called an assession fine; both of which were in theory freely variable according to what officials of the Duchy and potential tenants thought the property being leased was worth.[4] In practice, annual rents invariably remained fixed whilst adjustments to the fines reflected changes in demand.[5] But the fines themselves very much resembled rents as they were payable in

---

[1] Leasehold was, of course, a common form of tenure in medieval England, and most *compoti* contain details of assorted lands, of meadows and pastures, perhaps also of portions of demesnes, and almost certainly of mills, water-courses, fisheries and other manorial properties. But leases of customary holdings before the late fourteenth century were much less common, though of some importance (R. H. Hilton, 'Gloucester Abbey Leases of the Late Thirteenth Century', *University of Birmingham Historical Journal*, IV (1953–4); E. Miller, *The Abbey and Bishopric of Ely* (Cambridge, 1951), pp. 93–4).

[2] Below, pp. 74–7.

[3] In the mid-fifteenth century many leases were made for fourteen- and twenty-one-year periods, but by the accession of Henry VII the seven-year lease was once again made the only term.

[4] Of course when a holding or mill was not burdened with a fine, as sometimes was the case, then annual rents had to be adjusted.

[5] Throughout this study 'rent' means the total monetary charge upon the land, and its component parts are referred to as 'assession fines' and 'annual rents'.

instalments over the first six years of the seven-year *conventio*.[1] The customary conditions of the conventionary contract, unlike the financial terms, were not negotiable and they were only altered in a small minority of cases, usually as the result of exceptional circumstances surrounding a particular lease.

Conventionary leases ran from Michaelmas to Michaelmas, and a few months before the Michaelmas in which they were due to expire, a commission of assessioners would be appointed to create new leases. The assessioners, usually four or five in number, frequently included the receiver and the steward of the Cornish estates of the Duchy, the auditors of the ministers' accounts, and a senior official such as the receiver-general or the steward-in-chief of all the Prince's estates.[2] Permission was generally given for a quorum to be formed from within those appointed, but it was invariably stipulated that one or other of the more senior officials should always be present. Each manor was visited in turn and all persons wishing to take leases had to attend the court of assession held on their manor in person. If a tenant did not attend to renew his lease he could lose his holding by default.[3] But if a tenant had a good excuse for failing to appear at the court of assession, such as sickness, then another might be given authority to act as an attorney in his absence.[4] Leases were sometimes taken up by women, who were often the widows of previous tenants,[5] and leases taken jointly by two, three or even more persons were not uncommon.[6]

---

[1] This is true for all except the first two assessions of 1333 and 1340, when assession fines were made payable over three years and four years respectively.

[2] Many commissions are contained in the preambles of the assession rolls themselves, but see also: *B.P.R.* I, 64; *B.P.R.* II, 91, 205; *C.P.R. 1422–1429*, p. 423.

[3] The assession rolls do not usually record the reason for holdings changing hands, but we are told that Henry of Tywarnhaile lost his holding on the manor of Tywarnhaile in 1333 for failing to attend the court of assession (D.C.O. 471).

[4] For example, William Geel of Calstock took lands for Edward Lowys in 1333 and 1340 because Edward was infirm (D.C.O. 471; P.R.O. SC.11/153); and Sarah, wife of Milo de Tregorra, took the lands of her husband as he was ill at the time of the assession in 1333 (D.C.O. 471, Moresk).

[5] Many examples of female lessees could be given. Women often held lands for a considerable length of time, renewing leases when they fell due. The lands they leased were not always of modest dimensions, and Alice Stere held one of the most significant groupings of conventionary land on Helstone-in-Triggshire manor in 1504 (D.C.O. 483).

[6] Waste land was often leased and shared by a group of tenants, but similar arrangements for holdings of *terra* were by no means uncommon.

The Obligations and the Legal Status of Tenants

To ensure the suitability and credit-worthiness of persons wishing to take up a conventionary lease for the first time, each potential tenant was subjected to careful scrutiny, for the assessioners were frequently reminded that they should grant leases only to 'proper and sufficient persons'. How many potential lessees were refused by Duchy officials we cannot know, but we are told for example that John Harebeare was refused a lease on Calstock manor in 1333 because not enough was known about him.[1] It was common practice for two tenants to pledge themselves as security for each conventionary tenant before a lease was granted, and they were responsible for debts of that tenant if he was unable to pay them himself or if he fled owing money to the Duchy. If the payments due from a tenant were in arrear for more than a month and 'sufficient distress' could not be found, then the Duchy could evict the tenant from his holding and lease it to another. In the period before the Black Death, whilst the regular assession system was in its infancy, a major part in the acceptance of new tenants appears to have been played by the homage of the manor, and a number of holdings at this time were filled by persons elected to them by the homage.[2] On occasion the officials of the Duchy refused to grant renewals of leases on the grounds of the misbehaviour or incapacity of tenants. For example, at Climsland in 1333 John Lobeck was granted a lease to a holding which Walter de Leye *minus sufficiens adhuc tenet*, and John Byle took a holding which Richard Putte had held *impotens*.[3]

It is evident that the rights of conventionary tenants did not extend beyond the life of their leases, and that sitting tenants could not demand a renewal of their leases as of right. Generally, however, a first option was given to the tenant in possession to renew his lease at a rent and assession fine as great as any other potential tenant was willing to offer, but such an option depended upon the sufferance of the Duchy assessioners and not upon any customary right, as was to be frequently demonstrated in the later middle ages. The right of the Duchy to grant leases to whom it wished is constantly stressed, and the exercise of this power is conveniently

---

[1] D.C.O. 471, Calstock.
[2] See, for example: D.C.O. 471, Tintagel, Moresk; P.R.O. SC.11/153, Climsland.
[3] D.C.O. 471, Climsland.

illustrated in an instruction sent to the auditors of the ministers' accounts of the Cornish estates by the council of the Black Prince in 1357, which directed them to let William Romsey atte Dunrewe have at the next assession the lands at present held by Roger Vicaire in conventionary tenure.[1] Nevertheless, whilst this grant categorically denies Roger Vicaire any renewal of his lease it also emphasises the strength of his existing contract, for he could not be evicted within its term despite the fact that the auditors had not needed a similar directive made on William Romsey's behalf before the 1356 assession.[2]

At assessions the inhabitants of the Duchy manors were free to take conventionary lands or leave them as they desired,[3] and this resulted in as near a free market in land as existed on such a large scale anywhere in England at this time, with assessions resembling auctions. During the first hundred years of the Duchy the prices of leases were readily adjusted to meet fluctuation in demand, with each assession bringing some change in the levels of assession fines.[4] The refusal to pay the current market price for a conventionary holding normally meant eviction, and a large number of holdings must have changed hands at the assessions because sitting tenants were unable or unwilling to match the values put upon their holdings by rivals. Of such occurrences that which took place at the assession of 1364 on Tewington manor may be taken as typical: John de Nansmelyn went to this assession to renew his lease on a messuage and 11 acres in Nansmelyn, for which he had paid a fine of 20s. in the previous assession; but John Jordan also came to the assession and offered a fine of 33s. 4d. for this holding, which John de Nansmelyn refused to equal, and so lost possession.[5]

This feature of conventionary tenure contrasts most strongly with the attitudes and practices concerning landholding prevailing

[1] *B.P.R.* II, 113–14.
[2] *Ibid.* p. 65; for a further example see also p. 67.
[3] There are a few isolated references from Climsland manor to compulsion being used to force tenants to hold conventionary land in the years immediately following the Black Death (see for example, D.C.O. 472a; and P.R.O. SC.6.817/2, in which the reeve records only 8d. chevage 'because others, when able, have been compelled to hold land'), but these were wholly exceptional.
[4] Below, pp. 278–87.
[5] D.C.O. 473, Tewington.

The Obligations and the Legal Status of Tenants

in most regions of medieval England, where invariably the holders of customary land were secure in their tenure and holdings descended to heirs within the same family, usually intact and via the eldest son; and furthermore, there was usually a strong sentiment against alienation of land and in favour of continuity in manorial relationships, despite alienation by villeins which has been shown to have been much more common than historians once thought,[1] and the ability of lords to evict tenants who were unable or refused to pay their rents or perform their services. On Duchy manors, by contrast, a very high proportion of holdings changed hands every seven years in the fourteenth century; for example less than half the conventionary holdings on western and central manors remained in the hands of the same tenants from 1337 to 1348, whilst on eastern manors more than a third changed hands. Such a rapid turnover may well have had some deleterious effects upon the state of repair of holdings and the care with which they were farmed, and no doubt the Duchy were generally anxious that tenants should renew their leases, as long as there was no financial loss.

Although the rents of conventionary leases were freely variable according to the interplay of market forces, and as a general rule tenants had to pay the full market rate or forfeit their lands, the Duchy on occasion made allowances for the disabilities of certain of its tenants and acted with compassion towards them, reducing their assession fines or allowing them to remain stable whilst others were rising, on account of their tenants' old age, sickness, or poverty.[2] But it was an exception when Richard Russell of Tintagel in 1371 successfully contrived to obtain a reduction in the annual rent of his holding from 11s. to 10s. by claiming that it had been only 5s. at the time of Queen Isabella some 40 years before.[3]

All demises and transfers of conventionary lands and properties by tenants within the life of their leases from the Duchy had to be licensed by the manorial courts, a stipulation which was continually

[1] *Carte Nativorum: A Peterborough Abbey Cartulary of the Fourteenth Century*, C. N. L. Brooke and M. M. Postan (eds.), Northamptonshire Record Society, xx (1960).
[2] For example, D.C.O. 473, Climsland; in which Nicholas Midwinter did not have the fine on his holding increased, 'because of his age, poverty and infirmity'.
[3] P.R.O. E.306/2/2, D.C.O. 475, Tintagel. The earliest record we have of this holding (1331: P.R.O. E.142/41) gives the annual rent as 6s. 6d. plus 3s. 6d. new increment.

stressed in the commissions to the assessioners throughout the middle ages.[1] If a tenant wished to surrender his holding before his lease expired he had first to find another person who would undertake to lease it for the rest of the assessional period upon the same terms as it had previously been leased; and this person had to be acceptable to the Duchy. Upon the licensed transfer of such a holding a small fine, usually 8d. or 12d., was payable by the incoming tenant and the transfer was duly recorded in the manorial court. Tenants did not always wish to relinquish complete holdings, and many instances of half or even quarter holdings changing hands are recorded. Often tenants wanted to grant short-term leases of portions of the lands they held from the Duchy to other persons; these transactions also required a licence, although complete responsibility for the payment of rents and fines to the Duchy still remained with the original tenant. A nominal fine of 2d. or 3d. was usually charged of the conventionary tenant for such licences. Certain tenants, by virtue of the large amounts of land they leased from the Duchy, obtained special dispensation to sub-let without recourse to the manorial court, though even they could not dispose of complete holdings without having first obtained permission.[2]

The extreme flexibility of conventionary tenure meant that the relative numbers of free and unfree conventionaries could fluctuate considerably from one assession to another. Land invariably assumed the status of its tenant, and by the close of the fourteenth century most holdings had been held in both free and unfree conventionary tenure; but the holdings of the *nativi de stipite* were kept distinct from conventionary holdings.

FREE TENURE

Free tenants were numerous on Duchy manors in Cornwall, and freehold land probably constituted more than a third of all land,[3]

---

[1] For a fuller discussion of sub-leasing on the assessionable manors see pp. 232–5 below.

[2] See for example, the terms of the leases granted to William Jagow of Tybesta manor: D.C.O. 467; Henry Gartha of Liskeard manor: D.C.O. 478; and John Trewyk of Helston-in-Kirrier manor: P.R.O. E.306/2/3.

[3] Free tenancies appear to have been prolific in south-west England (Finberg, *Tavistock Abbey*, p. 69). For extents of freehold lands on Duchy manors see above, pp. 17–19.

whilst on some manors, such as Tewington and Helstone-in-Trigg-shire, freeholdings were more extensive than customary lands. As a class of tenants, freeholders comprised a wide range of persons of differing wealth and social status, ranging from humble peasant farmers up to members of the lesser nobility. But the poorer classes of peasant, perhaps equivalent to the cottars of more traditionally manorialised regions, were not in evidence, for the vast majority of freeholdings were large, comprising between 50 and 100 acres with some as extensive as 600 acres or more. Rents were far from uniform, but in general extremely low, with often as little as 2s. or 3s. payable annually for a holding of perhaps 60 acres. In addition some tenants held massive amounts of land from the Duchy for negligible rents. For example, in 1337 on Tewington manor William Bodrigan was in possession of seven Cornish acres for which he paid 18s. 6d. annually, and William Denysek held twelve Cornish acres, possibly more than 700 English acres, for an annual rent of 37s. 7d.[1] In addition to land, mills, both corn[2] and fulling,[3] water-courses and mill-ponds,[4] ferries,[5] fisheries,[6] and bird snares[7] were held in freehold.

The basic conditions of freehold tenure on the assessionable manors were a money rent, suit to court, fealty to the Duke, and a relief payable on death of 12s. 6d. for each Cornish acre held.[8] Money rents were usually payable at the four principal terms of the year in fixed proportions,[9] and 'suit to court' generally meant attendance every three weeks, similar to the obligations of customary tenants. Many free tenants obtained relaxation of suit to court upon

---

[1] P.R.O. E.120/1.
[2] In 1337 the manorial corn-mills of Helstone-in-Triggshire and Moresk were held in freehold (*loc. cit.*).
[3] Half the fulling mill of Moresk was held in freehold for 2d. or 2 capons (*loc. cit.*).
[4] For example: Helstone-in-Triggshire, Liskeard and Rillaton (*loc. cit.*).
[5] The ferry across the Tamar at Calstock was held in freehold for 2s. 6d. annually (below, p. 193).
[6] Freehold fisheries existed on Liskeard and Tybesta manors (below p. 192).
[7] P.R.O. E.120/1, Moresk.
[8] This sum appears to have been uniform throughout Cornwall (Henderson, *Essays in Cornish History*, p. 56).
[9] See, for example, P.R.O. E.120/1, Tybesta, wherein the amounts of rent payable at each of the four terms are given.

payment of a fine of approximately 12d.[1] On the death of a free tenant the amount of relief payable and the next heir were determined by the homage of the manor concerned, and the heir paid a small sum for 'acknowledgement', and swore fealty to the Duke before entering into the tenancy.[2] If there were no heir or the heir was not yet of age the holding escheated to the Duchy.

Although the above-mentioned conditions of tenure were common to the majority of freeholders, there were exceptions. On some manors freeholders were liable for customary money payments or even light labour services,[3] whilst certain tenants, such as Stephen Rede of Penlyne and Ivo de la Hona of Moresk, paid a pound of pepper to the Duchy each year instead of a money rent. Others such as Richard de Roskymmer of Helston-in-Kirrier and Roger le Veel of Tybesta paid no rent at all, owing only suit of court and fealty; whilst some, such as John de Cresy of Helston-in-Kirrier, paid a money rent but were not liable to attend the manorial court. On Calstock manor, and for many free tenants of Helston-in-Kirrier, suit to court was limited to two attendances each year. Finally there were those freeholders who held their lands free of all rents and services except for the performance of a single specific duty; examples of such tenants were Thomas Bile of Climsland who collected the rents of all the tenants of the manor each year, and John de Kellygrey of Helstone-in-Triggshire and John de Landewarent of Liskeard were liable to meet the Duke on his coming to Cornwall at 'Poulestonbrigge' and, wearing a grey cape, accompany him throughout the county for forty days at the Duke's expense.[4]

VILLEIN TENURE

The *nativi de stipite*, villeins by descent, formed a category quite distinct from the conventionary and free tenants of the assessionable manors, and they resembled in many respects the typical English

---

[1] Court rolls, *passim*.
[2] For an example of the procedure adopted see P.R.O. SC.2.159/32, court held at Climsland 20 May, 17 Edward IV.
[3] See pp. 66–9 below.
[4] When the Black Prince visited Cornwall in 1354 John Dabernoun, late keeper of the Prince's fees of Cornwall and Devonshire, purchased a grey cape for John de Kellygrey to carry for 3s. 4d. (*B.P.R.* II, 69).

villeins of this time. They were tied to their lands, which they held hereditarily, were not subject to the periodic assessions of the conventionary tenants, and their rents were fixed. Under the Duchy the *nativi de stipite* were never numerous and their distribution throughout Cornwall was uneven; being found in great numbers on the eastern manors. As their rents were fixed a period of rising demand for land which led to increases in the prices of conventionary lands, such as that which occurred in the decades before the Black Death, could create marked differences in the relative rent levels of conventionary and villein land. The sole means of effecting some adjustment to the price of villein lands rested in the right of the lord to tallage the *nativi de stipite* at will, a right which, with the advent of the regular system of assesssions in 1333, resolved itself into the imposition of a certain sum for tallage every seven years. With each assession after 1347, regardless of movements in demand for land, the amounts of tallage levied on villein lands were slowly but steadily increased, until by the beginning of the fifteenth century the differences in the prices of comparable villein and conventionary lands had become much less marked.

The numbers of *nativi de stipite* were bound to decline in the course of time as families died out, since it was the policy of the Duchy not to create new tenancies of this type. The Black Death of 1348/9 gave a great boost to this inevitable process, as the unprecedented mortality caused whole lines of succession to be wiped out within the space of a few months. The results of the plague are plain to see: for example on Climsland manor in 1347 there were 19 *nativi de stipite*,[1] by 1356 this total had fallen to 13,[2] and by 1364 to 12 and one of these, Desiderata Alren, daughter and heir of Reynald Alren, had a note placed against her name on the assession roll stating that the 'issue of blood' would cease on her death as she had no progeny except by a free husband.[3] But lack of heirs was not the only reason for the decline in the numbers of the *nativi de stipite* and many examples can be found of *nativi* being upgraded into unfree conventionaries and even into free conventionaries.[4] At the assession of 1364, for example, all the *nativi de stipite* of Restormel

[1] D.C.O. 472, Climsland.   [2] D.C.O. 472a, Climsland.
[3] D.C.O. 473, Restormel.   [4] See below, pp. 134–5.

manor except one, were made unfree conventionaries without increase to their rents or tallage.[1] This action was probably the result of a personal favour bestowed on them by the Black Prince who had spent the early spring of 1363 at Restormel castle.[2]

The ministers' account of 1355/6 was the last to include the rents of the *nativi de stipite* under 'Rents of Assize', and from this time on they were included under 'Rents and Farms of Conventionaries'.[3] By the fifteenth century there was very little difference between the price of a villein holding and that of a comparable conventionary holding, and the assession roll of 1406 is the last extant roll which adheres to a distinction between conventionaries and villeins.[4] It appears that tenure *de stipite* was abolished and that villein holdings became subject to the same conditions as unfree conventionary holdings.[5]

CUSTOMARY RENTS AND OBLIGATIONS

All conventionary tenants and the *nativi de stipite* had certain conditions of tenure in common with each other.[6] They paid their rents at the four principal terms of the year and their instalments of assession fines or tallage at Michaelmas in each of the first six years of the seven-year assessional term. They swore fealty to the Duke, owed suit to the manorial court from three weeks to three weeks, were liable to serve as reeve, tithingman or beadle when elected, and

---

[1] D.C.O. 473, Restormel.

[2] The Prince stayed at Restormel from 24 February to Easter 1363 while an expedition to Gascony was being prepared at Plymouth (*B.P.R.* II, 203–4).

[3] Cf. the account for 1355/6 (transcript in D.C.O. Library), with that for 1356/7 (P.R.O. SC.6.817/5 or D.C.O. 11).

[4] The next assession roll (P.R.O. E.306.2/10), dated 1420 contains no distinctions between conventionaries and villeins of stock.

[5] But unfree conventionary tenure persisted until the seventeenth century (below, p. 79).

[6] Some conditions of tenure specified in the early assession rolls and in the Caption of Seisin of 1337 are misleading and ambiguous. At the time these rolls were compiled the assession system had not been in existence for long and certain discrepancies appear as the result of misunderstandings which were clarified in later documents. For example, in 1333 most unfree conventionaries are stated to be holding *ad voluntatem domini* (D.C.O. 471); and in 1337, for example, the unfree conventionaries of Tintagel were held liable to be tallaged at the will of the lord, although being conventionary tenants their conditions of tenure should have been specified and secure.

were required to manure their lands and maintain their holdings in good repair.

A cardinal difference between the conditions of tenure of the free conventionaries and those of the unfree conventionaries and *nativi de stipite* lay in the death duties with which estates were burdened. Estates of free conventionaries were liable to a heriot of the best animal for each holding the deceased tenant held, but no other goods.[1] On the other hand all the goods and chattels of unfree conventionaries and villeins were forfeited to the lord on death,[2] with the sole exception of the unfree tenants of Rillaton manor, who for some reason were liable only for heriots. The forfeiture of all possessions was a particularly oppressive burden on the unfree and although in law most English villeins remained the property of their lords and thus could not in theory possess anything, in practice estates usually passed intact to heirs after heriot and mortuary had been paid. It should be mentioned, however, that on some estates it was customary for the lord to seize part of his deceased villeins' estates, commonly one third.[3] In practice the customary right of the Duchy to all the goods of the unfree tenants was not exercised: on the death of an unfree tenant his movable estate was valued by six manorial jurymen, with a third part allowed to pass to his widow or next heir without charge, and the expenses of the burial and wake were usually deducted from this valuation. Furthermore the estate was usually re-sold cheaply to the heir.[4] Nevertheless this custom was onerous enough to provoke separate petitions from the unfree tenants of both Climsland and Liskeard to the council governing the Duchy in 1382. These petitions, which asked that the custom prevailing on Rillaton manor and on certain other Cornish estates, notably those of the Bishop of Exeter and the Earls of Stafford and Warwick (i.e. a heriot only), should be adopted on all Duchy manors, met with no success.[5]

---

[1] 'Unum averium quod maioris pretii fuerit, et nichil percipiet de aliis catallis suis.'
[2] 'Et cum obierit dominus habebit omnia catalla sua.'
[3] Bennett, *Life on the English Manor*, pp. 145–6; Finberg, *Tavistock Abbey*, pp. 76–7; W. F. Mumford, 'Terciars on the Estates of Wenlock Priory', *Transactions of the Shropshire Archaeological Society*, LVIII (1965).
[4] For examples of the process at work see: P.R.O. SC.2.160/2, court held at Liskeard, 22 January, 7 Henry V; P.R.O. SC.2.158/12, court held at Calstock, 20 January, 10 Edward IV.   [5] *B.P.R.* II, 215–16; *Cal. Inq. Misc.*, IV, 190.

The Obligations and the Legal Status of Tenants

Impartible inheritance was the rule for all holdings on Duchy manors in Cornwall. Inheritance customs were not a crucial element with conventionary holdings, as heirs retained possession only for the remainder of the lease. Holdings of the *nativi de stipite* descended to the youngest sons—ultimogeniture or Borough English. Conventionary and free holdings descended to eldest sons—primogeniture.

Unfree conventionaries and *nativi de stipite* were subjected to a number of further restrictions common to English villeinage with which free conventionaries were not burdened. They were unable to give away their daughters in marriage without first obtaining licence from the manorial court, a privilege which could cost from 12d. to 6s. 8d., and they could not send their sons to school or allow them to enter the Church without permission, though this could frequently be obtained by petition to the Duke.[1] Unfree tenants could also be fined for fornication.[2]

In addition to these general conditions of tenure the tenants of many Duchy manors were liable to specific services and customary rents, which had apparently evolved to suit the structures of the particular manors upon which they were to be found. The assession rolls and the Caption of Seisin alone do not provide a comprehensive source for these services and rents, and at best they give only a summary of some of the more important; whilst at other times they present information in a misleading manner, thus rendering a study of all available documents imperative. References to labour services on a number of Duchy manors can be found, but in all cases they were extremely light and had probably never been onerous and by the early fourteenth century they had, almost without exception, been rendered obsolete. Furthermore, it is obvious that by the time the Duchy was created in 1337, many customary rents and services had lost much of what significance they had once possessed, and were included in the rents of tenancies, permanently commuted, or even ignored.

Customary tenants of Duchy manors that had deer-parks appended to them were invariably liable to perform specific services concerned

---

[1] See for example, *B.P.R.*, II, 118, 193; *C.P.R. 1413–1416*, p. 138.
[2] The fine for fornication was 5s. 1d. It was not imposed in the fifteenth century.

The Obligations and the Legal Status of Tenants

with these parks. Generally conventionary and villein tenants were required to assist when the lord, or someone else in his name, wished to hunt.[1] On Restormel manor fifteen conventionary and villein tenants were required to assist in the hunt or pay a 1d. in lieu of such assistance; this payment was termed *stabulagium* or *huntyngsylver*.[2] Ten works mentioned on some accounts of Penlyne manor and permanently commuted for 10d. were probably of similar origin.[3] The performance of these services was rarely necessary as Dukes visited Cornwall most infrequently. The conventionary and villein tenants of Helstone-in-Triggshire manor were liable to perform nominal ploughing and reaping services whenever the Old Deer Park was broken up and used as arable, with each of them owing the ploughing of half an acre of land by English measure for each half acre of land by Cornish measure that was held.[4] As the average holding was less than half a Cornish acre most tenants would have been liable to plough only a half statute acre each year, and for this ploughing they would receive ½d. in wages and 1d. for sustenance.[5] The only other mention of ploughing services relates to the manor of Climsland, which contained the deer-park of Carrybullock: in the assession roll of 1364 it is stated rather abruptly that the customary tenants should plough for the lord when necessary.[6] As no further attempt was made to practise demesne farming on any of the assessionable manors after the catastrophic failure of the project to re-introduce it on Helstone-in-Triggshire in 1336[7] these labour services were rendered irrelevant and merely ignored. A duty which was exacted from the conventionary and villein tenants of all manors with parks was that they should assist in the maintenance of the enclosures, but as they received payment of 1¾d. or 1½d. per

[1] See, for example, P.R.O. E.120/1, Helstone-in-Triggshire, Penkneth, Restormel, and Liskeard.

[2] For similar dues elsewhere in England see N. Neilson, 'Customary Rents', *Oxford Studies in Social and Legal History*, ed. P. Vinogradoff, II (Oxford, 1910), 19 f.

[3] The liability to perform these works can be seen as a condition of the leases of certain holdings in 1337 (P.R.O. E.120/1).

[4] The size of a Cornish acre appears to have varied according to the fertility of the soil, but usually contained from 40 to 60 English acres.

[5] Some mention of these services is made in P.R.O. E.120/1, but see D.C.O. 473 for a fuller description.

[6] D.C.O. 473, Climsland.

[7] P.R.O. SC.6.1094/14.

perch, this work may well have provided a welcome source of employment in the slack periods of the farming year.[1] Only once is this service mentioned on an assession roll, however, and then with reference to the unfree conventionaries of Liskeard manor alone.[2]

A number of other services can be found which had evolved to suit specific tasks, all of which were extremely light. Calstock manor, for example, had a very large weir located on the banks of the Tamar called the *Hacche*, and certain of the free tenants and all the customary tenants of the manor owed works of one or two days each year to maintain it in a good state of repair. After the creation of the Duchy the works were only exacted once, and this was in 1338/9 when the whole of the 150 works owed by tenants were expended in repairs.[3] For almost the whole of the fourteenth and fifteenth centuries the weir was farmed to the Abbey of Tavistock without the labour services which the Duchy commuted for 1d. each. Upon Rillaton manor, which had the beadleship of the hundred of East appended to it, customary tenants were liable to assist in the driving of animals impounded by the beadle for distresses.[4] The *nativi de stipite* of Climsland were liable to carry wood from the woods of the manor up to the borough of Launceston, some ten miles away. If their lord was in residence at Launceston they had to carry wood whenever he wanted it at their own cost; if the justices were in session they were liable to carry a single cart-load each at their own cost; and finally if the steward required wood then for the carrying of it to Launceston they would receive ½d. per load.[5] The *nativi de stipite* of Calstock manor had to carry mill-stones to the manorial mills when necessary and assist in the maintenance of the *grond-briche*.[6] At Liskeard manor a regular payment amounting to 2s. 2d. annually was made by the tenants in commutation of services involving the carriage of wine, though further details of what this service had originally entailed are now lost to us.[7] There also appears to have been a service involving the carriage of letters on Liskeard manor, for William Drem was fined for refusing to perform it in

---

[1] Ministers' accounts, *passim*.   [2] D.C.O. 476, Liskeard.

[3] P.R.O. SC.6.816/11, Calstock. They were once again commuted for 1d. each in the account of the following year (P.R.O. SC.816/12).

[4] For example, P.R.O. E.120/1.   [5] P.R.O. E.120/1, Climsland.

[6] P.R.O. E. 120/1, Calstock.   [7] See, for example, P.R.O. SC.6.816/11.

The Obligations and the Legal Status of Tenants

1298.[1] The free, conventionary and villein tenants of Tewington and Penlyne paid 23s. 11¾d. and 8s. 3d. respectively each year for the relaxation of works, the nature of which it is no longer possible to determine.[2]

Omissions from the lists of services included on the assession rolls and the Caption of Seisin are striking. A glance at a number of consecutive assession rolls will show that there was no consistency in the incidents of tenure that were included or omitted, some were enrolled on one roll and not on the next as the assessioners and their clerks saw fit. It is also readily apparent that the conditions covering conventionary and villein tenure on Duchy manors did not depend upon what was enrolled upon the assession rolls but upon the ancient customs of the manors, and as far as is known these were never comprehensively listed. No mention is ever made in the assession rolls of labour services on Trematon manor, and yet the account of 1338/9 shows the customary tenants performing services consisting of the reaping and carrying of hay.[3] Only once on an assession roll is any mention made of tenants owing suit to manorial mills, and then with reference to the unfree conventionaries of Rillaton manor alone,[4] yet it is probable that conventionary and villein tenants of all manors owed suit of mill just as they all owed suit of court; fines of evasion of suit to mill are not uncommon in the court rolls of the first half of the fourteenth century.[5] Similarly no mention is made of the carrying services to the mills of Tewington manor which some tenants apparently owed.[6]

The general conditions of tenure invariably applied in full only to tenants who leased landholdings and not to tenants who took conventionary leases of mills, fisheries and other similar properties, for these were most frequently free conventionary leases and liable only to a small money heriot. Similarly a person leasing only a small

[1] P.R.O. SC.6.811/1.
[2] These are mentioned in P.R.O. SC.6.811/1. The free tenants of Tewington are also mentioned as owing money in commutation of works in the Inquisition *Post Mortem*, made on the death of Earl Edmund in 1300 (P.R.O. E.152/8 and C.133, file 95).
[3] P.R.O. SC.6.816/1, Trematon.
[4] D.C.O. 478, Rillaton.
[5] P.R.O. SC.6.811/1 ff. See also the dispute concerning the liability of the tenants of Moresk to suit of mill in the seventeenth century (B.M. Add. MS. 36, 644).
[6] These are mentioned in a petition of Reynold Trenansaustel (*B.P.R.* II, 104).

piece of waste land was not burdened with the full services of a complete conventionary or villein landholding. But even the conditions attaching to conventionary holdings of land were not inflexible. Although the vast majority of leases were made without varying any of the manorial customs, a number were granted which changed or nullified particular clauses. For example, a few leases were granted which stipulated that a money heriot, usually half a mark, was payable on the death of the tenant within the term of his lease instead of an animal heriot.[1] In 1364 the estate of a tenant who leased two holdings on Tewington manor was specifically made liable for only one heriot if he died before the lease expired, as the holdings he took had been 'in the hands of the lord'.[2] Clerics invariably obtained special dispensation from being liable to serve as reeve, tithingman or beadle without extra payment,[3] but laymen could pay for the same privilege.[4] We have already noted that some tenants with substantial landholdings were granted leave to sub-let their lands at will without reference to the manorial court.

In addition to payments of rents, assession fines or tallage, and commuted labour services, there were a number of customary payments in evidence on Duchy manors. The merging of these payments indistinguishably with the rents of tenancies and 'Rents of Assize' was a process which had been taking place ever since they had been instituted, and their absence from records after 1288 is no proof they had never existed.

One of the most interesting customary dues was *berbiagium*, and it can be traced upon Climsland, Calstock, Liskeard, Tintagel, Tewington, Tybesta, and Helston-in-Kirrier manors. The amounts of *berbiagium* payable varied from 74s. 10½d. annually on Climsland manor, owed by the conventionaries and *nativi de stipite*, down to 5s. owed by the free tenants of Helston-in-Kirrier. But *berbiagium*

---

[1] See, for example, the leases of: John Baigga of Helstone-in-Triggshire and the Rector of St Hermit of Tywarnhaile, D.C.O. 472; Thomas, son of Adam Drinker, of Liskeard, D.C.O. 473; Michael Gerneys of Helston-in-Kirrier was excused being liable for any heriot as his holding had been *in manu domini*, D.C.O. 473.

[2] Philip Symon, D.C.O. 473, Tewington.

[3] See, for example, the lease of the vicar of St Wendron on Helston-in-Kirrier manor, D.C.O. 473: Climsland 1364.

[4] For instance, William Dobyn of Liskeard paid 20d. for such exemption in 1364 (D.C.O. 473).

was not a payment restricted to Duchy manors, Cornwall, or even England.[1] From Duchy records it is quite plain that it was a money payment in lieu of a payment in sheep.[2] Why it was imposed is less clear, but it seems to have originated as a poll-tax upon the numbers of sheep kept by tenants. By the late thirteenth century the amounts paid had become inflexible. Another unusual customary due shrouded in mystery was the 'fine of tin' payable on Tewington manor alone. Situated in close proximity to the stannary district of Blackmore, Tewington was intimately connected with mining throughout the middle ages. Each year 'fine of tin' totalling 35s. 6½d. was collected, 14s. 7d. from certain free tenements, 20s. from conventionaries and *nativi de stipite*, and 11½d. from lands not actually within the manor.[3] One possible explanation of the payment is that it gave those who paid it exemption from the lord's right to take a toll on all tin dug up on the lands they held, although the reeves of the manor continued to account for considerable sums derived from toll-tin throughout the later middle ages.[4] No connection can be found between this payment and the 'fine of tin' amounting to £5 8s. od. payable through the bailiffs of the four Cornish stannaries, apparently for 'enjoying the liberty of the stannaries'.[5]

The remaining customary due was *auxilium*, and it was paid on Helstone-in-Triggshire, Liskeard, Tybesta and Tintagel manors by free, conventionary and villein tenants alike. By the time of the creation of the Duchy in 1337 the sums payable in *auxilium* by the tenants of Helstone-in-Triggshire, Tybesta and Tintagel, namely 56s., 27s. 8d. and 66s. 8d. respectively, had been combined with the annual rents of the holdings from which they were due. On Liskeard manor, however, the 50s. paid annually in *auxilium* remained separate from the rents and was paid by free tenants, conventionaries and villeins at Michaelmas.

---

[1] *Berbiagium* was a common payment in Devon, and can also be traced in Wales and France (E. Smirke, *Arch. Journ.*, v (1848), 273–7).

[2] In 1337 an unusually detailed entry was made in the Caption of Seisin (P.R.O. E.120/1) of payments by the free tenants of Helston-in-Kirrier.

[3] Much of this information is contained in the Caption of Seisin of 1337 (P.R.O. E.120/1, Tewington).

[4] Below, pp. 188–91.

[5] Lewis, *Stannaries*, p. 139. He is wrong about the first record of 'fine of tin' as it can be found on the earliest available account of 1287/8 (P.R.O. SC.6.816/9, *Stagnaria*).

The Obligations and the Legal Status of Tenants

LIFE TENURE

Tenure for life or lives was the remaining method by which the customary lands of Duchy manors in Cornwall could be held. Many of the conditions governing the life tenancy were very similar to those governing free conventionary tenure, indeed tenants holding for life were often described as 'holding for life in free conventionary tenure'.[1] But although based upon free conventionary tenure the terms governing life tenancies were frequently varied to suit each individual grant, being regulated primarily by the letters patent of the Duke's council under which they were instituted, rather than manorial custom. Tenants holding for life were not usually liable to serve as reeve, beadle or tithingman, and sometimes were required to attend the manorial court only twice a year.[2] In addition the rents of life tenancies were often allowed to be in arrear for two months before the holding was rendered liable to re-possession, instead of the single month allowed to conventionary tenants.

Life tenancies can be found for the first time in the manorial surveys made between 1327 and 1332.[3] The commissions to the assessioners of John of Eltham in 1333 gave authority for conventionary leases to be granted for life or lives,[4] as did most other commissions issued to assessioners in the fourteenth century.[5] Nevertheless, the life tenancy was never at any time responsible for more than a tiny proportion of the total conventionary lands; and the reason lay more in the reluctance of the Duchy to grant such tenancies rather than the dearth of tenants to enter into them. Before the Black Death life tenancies were extremely rare and generally only granted as rewards or favours to servants or retainers of John of Eltham or the Black Prince. The first life tenancy granted by the Duchy was in favour of Richard Bakhampton, a retired steward of the estates of the Earldom of Cornwall.[6] He held approximately 400 acres of *terra* and *terra vasta* in four different manors for the

[1] For example, *B.P.R.* II, 61.
[2] For example, *B.P.R.* II, 99–101, 125–7, 176.
[3] P.R.O. E.142/41.
[4] D.C.O. 471.
[5] For example, *B.P.R.* I, 64, *B.P.R.* II, 91, 205; assession rolls, *passim*.
[6] Below, pp. 236–8.

term of his life, with successive remainders for the lives of his two sons William and Alner.[1] Amongst other life tenancies granted before the Black Death were those of John de Kendale, parker and constable at Restormel,[2] and John Dabernon, an outstanding Duchy official who held a multitude of posts in the administration.[3] Even after the Great Plague of 1348/9 the Duchy continued the same policy towards life tenancies; whereas it was quite willing to grant them for lands that were difficult or impossible to lease on seven-year contracts, it was never part of general policy to proliferate them on lands that were in demand. Life tenancies might be granted as a result of petitions to the council,[4] but the overall reluctance is strikingly illustrated by the case of the nine conventionaries of Trematon who declined to renew their leases at the assession held in the spring of 1364, and as a consequence their holdings were listed as being in the hands of the lord.[5] These holdings must have remained without takers for a short while, for the Duchy subsequently relented and offered the nine tenants the option of leasing them for life. They accepted and commenced their new tenancies when their seven-year leases expired at Michaelmas 1364.[6]

After reaching a small peak of importance in the thirteen-sixties the life tenancy entered a period of decline. By the first decade of the fifteenth century only three of the nine manors then in the hands of the Duchy had life tenancies upon them,[7] by 1413 Climsland alone had a tenant holding for life,[8] and no more were granted in the fifteenth century.

THE HISTORY OF THE ASSESSION SYSTEM

The assession system as it existed at the founding of the Duchy of Cornwall in 1337 was very much in its infancy. From the earliest record in 1288 until the early years of Edward III's reign the tenants of the assessionable manors had been divided into only three

---

[1] *C.P.R. 1340–1343*, p. 13.
[2] D.C.O. 1, Penlyne.
[3] D.C.O. 472, Trematon.
[4] *B.P.R.* II, 121, 125–7.
[5] D.C.O. 473, Trematon.
[6] Their new leases were subsequently enrolled on the assession roll.
[7] P.R.O. E.306/2/7, 8, Helston-in-Kirrier, Climsland, Tybesta.
[8] D.C.O. 42.

categories: *liberi tenantes*, *conventionarii*, and *villani*. It was not until the regular system of assessions was instituted in 1333 that conventionary tenants could be either free or unfree. From the rather unsatisfactory documentation of the period before 1333 it is possible to glean only a few details of the prevailing conditions of tenure. It appears that the *villani* held on very similar terms to the *nativi de stipite* of the post-assession period, having hereditary titles to their lands at fixed rents, owing all their goods and chattels to their lord on death, and paying an entry fine on inheritance.[1] The conventionaries were all free and held their lands by leases of apparently indeterminate length[2] which were renewed on a rather haphazard basis for nominal fines; only when a conventionary holding changed hands was a fine of any consequence charged. Upon the death of a conventionary tenant his estate appears to have been charged with either a heriot or a relief, with the incoming tenant paying a fine for the right to enter into the holding.

The earliest surviving document giving an account of the numbers and distribution of the tenants of the seventeen manors is the Inquisition *Post Mortem* made on the death of Earl Edmund in 1300.[3] Out of 766 customary tenants on the manors at this time 393 were villeins and 373 conventionaries.[4] The average villein appears to have held approximately 10 per cent more land than the average conventionary tenant, but he paid on average 40 per cent less rent for it;[5] although nothing can be said of the relative fertility of villein and conventionary holdings at this time.

There is no trace of conventionary tenure in Domesday Book,

---

[1] The main source of information on conditions of tenure prevailing in the pre-Duchy period is the abbreviated record of court proceedings contained in the ministers' accounts (P.R.O. SC.6.811/1 ff.).

[2] The demise of land to Paschasio de Nansmelyn for a ten-year term in 1296/7 appears to have been exceptional (P.R.O. E.119/1, Tewington; Midgley, *Ministers' Accounts*, II, 244.)

[3] The original enrolments are contained in P.R.O. E.152/8 and C.133, file 95, but both documents are in very poor condition. For a reliable sixteenth-century transcript see B.M. Add. MS. 41,661.

[4] These figures do not correspond with a similar analysis made by Mary Coate ('Duchy of Cornwall', p. 141). The discrepancy appears to lie in the number of tenants on Liskeard manor which Miss Coate has taken as 47, comprising 41 conventionaries and 6 villeins, but which I take to be 67, comprising 41 conventionaries and 26 villeins.

[5] Approximate figures only can be given as the extents are in Cornish acres of indeterminate size.

The Obligations and the Legal Status of Tenants

indeed the 40 *cervisarii* of Helston-in-Kirrier are the only unusual class of tenant listed in Cornwall;[1] although the main categories into which tenants were put, namely *servi*, *bordarii*, and *villani*, may well conceal marked variations in tenure.

The south-west of England, and Cornwall in particular, is shown in Domesday Book to have had a much higher proportion of unfree persons than most other areas in England. Of special note are the large numbers of *servi* and *bordarii*, the lowest categories in the survey, which together comprised two thirds of the Cornish population, compared with a proportion of only two fifths in the rest of England, as can be seen from Table 1.

TABLE 1   *The proportions of unfree tenants in Domesday Book*

	Cornwall	Assessionable manors[a]	Rest of England[b]
Servi	21%	26%	9%
Bordarii	45%	39%	32%
Villani	32%	35%	38%
Total Unfree	98%	100%	79%

[a] Figures from eleven manors mentioned in Domesday and later to become part of the Duchy of Cornwall.
[b] F. Seebohm, *The English Village Community* (4th edn, 1890), p. 86.

In the two hundred years from Domesday to the earliest available extent of the assessionable manors of 1300, a revolution in the status of customary tenants had taken place; and in 1300 on the eleven manors mentioned in Domesday, 53 per cent of customary tenants were conventionaries and only 47 per cent *villani*. No doubt the upsurge in both colonisation and tin-mining in twelfth- and thirteenth-century Cornwall were major influences working in the tenants' favour, and the purchase of free status by many villeins during the tenure of the Earldom of Cornwall by Edmund (1272–1300) also did much to redress the preponderance of unfree tenants.

[1] *V.C.H. Cornwall*, II, pt 8.

The manorial accounts of 1287/8[1] and 1296–8[2] record many inquisitions into the status of tenants, instigated by the tenants themselves and at their own expense. Such inquisitions usually resulted in the sale of charters of freedom. From the abbreviated proceedings of the manorial court of Tybesta of 1296/7 it is possible to see the procedure that was followed: Matilla le Sorn instigated an inquisition into her own status and that of her two sons, and Mariota de Treweledyk' did the same for herself and her four children, for which they paid 26s. 8d. and 40s. respectively; later in the same year Matilla and Mariota paid 33s. 4d. and 40s. each respectively for charters of freedom. Often in these years we find men purchasing their own freedom, and free men purchasing freedom for their wives, as did three tenants of Tywarnhaile in 1296/7 who paid sums ranging from 20s. to 40s. for this concession. The revenues obtained from inquisitions and charters were considerable, for example the profits of the manorial court of Moresk manor in 1297/8 were swollen to £12 9s. 4d., more than four times the average receipts of this court at this time.

The first indication of a major reorganisation in the systems of tenure on the assessionable manors came in the early years of the reign of Edward III, coinciding with an upward re-assessment of the rents of conventionary lands, mills and other properties.[3] Conventionary tenures had apparently existed for many years previous to our first record of them in 1287/8, yet the failure to effect any significant reassessment in their rents to bring them into line with changes in their value for at least 40 years before the estates of the Earldom passed into the hands of Edward III in 1330, belied their true nature. Finally, however, in response to intense and mounting pressure on the land in the generation before the Black Death it was decided to turn the potentially flexible qualities of these tenures to the lord's advantage, by creating short-term leases subject to frequent revision of rents. The preamble of the first assession roll, made in 1333 during the tenure of the manors by John of Eltham, sheds much light on the economic background to this period and

[1] P.R.O. SC.6.816/9.
[2] P.R.O. E.119/1; SC.6.811/1.
[3] For a discussion of the economic background to the increases see below, pp. 92–3.

upon the minds of those who were commissioned to create new conventionary leases.[1] We are told that the leases in force in the spring of 1333 were all to expire the following Michaelmas, and that the Earl 'without doing wrong to anyone was free to take the lands into his own hands again and make his profit thereof, which might perhaps turn to the injury and damage of the said tenants', and yet 'if the tenants are willing to pay according to the true valuation of the lands then the Earl is prepared that new contracts might be enacted upon such terms as might be agreed between the tenants and the assessioners'. The assessioners who were instructed to lease the lands 'for the term of life, lives or years to such as would give most', decided after an appraisal of the land-market in Cornwall to grant leases of only seven years' duration; with these short leases providing the opportunity to reassess the value of the holdings at frequent intervals in what was obviously a period of increasing pressure on the land.

As all conventionary leases were due to expire at the same time in 1333 it would appear that an assession similar to that of 1333 had been held a certain number of years before, but although the paucity of manorial documents for this period makes any precise statements hazardous, the weight of evidence suggests that 1333 assession was in fact the first of its kind, at least for fifty years. The ministers' account of 1332 bears no traces at all of an assession system and follows almost exactly the form of accounting that had been in use since 1287/8, and which was to be transformed after 1333.[2] In addition many of the assessionable manors had been leased during Queen Isabella's tenure of the Earldom (1317–30), and the leases on some of them had not expired until 1331. Furthermore, none of the surveys made between 1327 and 1332 give any indication that a regular system of assessions was then in force.[3] The concerted termination of all conventionary leases at Michaelmas 1333 seems to have been deliberately manipulated by the administration of John of Eltham as part of a policy to secure greater revenues from

[1] D.C.O. 471.
[2] Compare the account of 1331/2 (P.R.O. E.372/158, m. 46) with that of 1335/6 made after the introduction of the assession system (P.R.O. SC.6.1094/13).
[3] P.R.O. E.142/41.

the manors and to achieve the benefits in efficiency which were enjoyed when all tenancies were leased at the same time and for the same term.

The introduction of regular assessions brought with it changes in the status of many tenants, namely a large increase in the numbers of conventionaries, and the creation of a new category called unfree conventionary tenure. A comparison of the numbers of *nativi* and *conventionarii* on the assessionable manors in 1300 or 1327–32 with the numbers of *nativi de stipite*, and *nativi* and *liberi conventionarii* after the assession of 1333, as given in Table 2 below, reveals that the *nativi* or *villani* had become either *nativi conventionarii* or *nativi de stipite*, and the *conventionarii* had become

TABLE 2   *The numbers and status of customary tenants in the early fourteenth century*

	1300[a]		1327–32[b]		1333–40[c]		
	Conventionarii	Villani	Conventionarii	Nativi	Liberi Conventionarii	Nativi Conventionarii	Nativi de Stipite
Rillaton	7	6	—	—	3	10	5
Climsland	23	81	25	69	28	49	18
Calstock	14	53	—	—	29	49	8
Trematon	29	21	38	25	37	16	6
Liskeard	41	26	46	36	49	34	4
Helstone-in-Triggshire and Penmayne	33	78	—	—	37	72	11
Tintagel	14	28	25	30	26	30	0
Talskiddy	2	1	4	3	3	3	0
Restormel	2	12	0	15	0	8	8
Penlyne	22	2	—	—	20	1	1
Penkneth	9	6	—	—	7	3	7
Tewington	43	11	52	12	52	6	5
Tybesta	28	21	37	16	36	14	4
Tywarnhaile	12	15	—	—	11	15	2
Moresk	20	19	—	—	24	20	2
Helston-in-Kirrier	76	11	102	6	102	5	2

Sources: [a] P.R.O. E.152/8; C.133, file 95. [b] P.R.O. SC.11. Roll 153.
[c] D.C.O. 471; P.R.O. E.120/1.

The Obligations and the Legal Status of Tenants

liberi conventionarii. In certain of the surveys made between 1330 and 1332 the division of the *nativi* can be seen taking place: for example on the survey of Tywarnhaile manor the unfree tenants were first listed *en bloc*, and then against the names of many of them *de stip'* or *conv'* was written in a different hand.

From the many disputes concerning the status of Duchy tenants coming before the council of the Black Prince it is evident that it was not always a straightforward process to determine whether a person was free or unfree. Sometimes the Duchy accused tenants of servile origins, whilst at other times an enquiry was set up as the result of a personal initiative or grudge. But regardless of the origin of the dispute, a speedy and apparently scrupulously fair inquisition was set in motion by the higher administration of the Prince, and these inquisitions often found in favour of the tenant.[1] A particularly interesting dispute, which in this instance went in the Duchy's favour, arose concerning Roger Scoria of Climsland manor in 1356. At the assession held in this year at Climsland Roger was forced to take a holding *de stipite* under strong protest, as he claimed he was a free man and a cleric. The Duchy officials on the other hand asserted he was unfree and next in line to inherit the holding. Against Roger Scoria's name on the assession roll it is explicitly stated that 'Roger has said that he was compelled to take the land against his will', and that he claimed such compulsion was contrary to the ancient customs of Cornwall and thus also contrary to the common law of England.[2] It is also stated on the roll that Roger had given notice of appeal to the lord's court. His appeal came up before the Prince's council on 13 February 1357 and a sub-committee of lawyers was formed from within the council to decide 'whether or not it was proper to allow the custom whereby Roger claimed to be free'.[3] Evidently the council did not decide in Roger's favour, but he was still determined to gain his freedom and later in the same year he was granted 'licence to enter Holy Church and receive all Holy Orders, both minor and major',[4] and in 1363 he finally obtained his freedom on payment of a fine of £4.[5]

The conventionary system of tenure, as it was reconstituted in

[1] See, for example, *B.P.R.* II, 139-40.
[2] D.C.O. 472a, Climsland.
[3] *B.P.R.* II, 108.
[4] *B.P.R.* II, 118.
[5] *Ibid.* p. 201.

1333, did not persist unchanged for much longer than a century; its efficient administration depended upon constant vigilance and surveillance and this was not always forthcoming. No reassessment of the rents of conventionary lands was made on those manors which passed out of the direct control of the Duchy in the later middle ages. Even when manors remained in Duchy hands the efficient administration of the system was not guaranteed, and for a period under Richard II at the close of the fourteenth century assessions were frequently delayed and even when held served merely to confirm the annual rents and assession fines already in force. In the fourth and fifth decades of the fifteenth century, fourteen- and twenty-one-year leases were widely adopted; furthermore the cost of these leases became inflexible: upon those Duchy manors notably in the east of Cornwall, where demand for land was maintained in the fifteenth century assession fines were frozen, in sharp contrast to the preceding hundred years which had seen them increase almost continuously, and upon those Duchy manors in central and western Cornwall the assession fines in force in the early fifteenth century were also taken as the maximum, but reductions were allowed in response to a prolonged slump in demand for land.[1] By the early sixteenth century the seven-yearly assessional term had once more become standard practice, but despite a resurgence in demand for land assession fines remained fixed;[2] and tenants by the early seventeenth century had assumed an hereditary title to the lands they held, which the Duchy, with some legal justification, contested.[3]

In contrast to the relaxation of the aspects of conventionary tenure described above, manorial discipline and a number of servile exactions were strictly maintained on Duchy manors throughout the later middle ages.[4] In particular *merchet*, *chevage*, and death duties continued to be exacted with only rare exceptions, although

---

[1] These matters are discussed in greater detail in later chapters.

[2] P.R.O. E.306/2/14 ff.; D.C.O. 482 ff.

[3] Richard Carew supported the tenants with some vigour (*Survey of Cornwall*, pp. 36–7); but John Norden, who was also the Duchy Surveyor, stated quite firmly that conventionaries held *ad voluntatem domini* and that their tenure was 'at every taking finable at the Lordes pleasure, and heriotable' (*Description of Cornwall*, p. 25).

[4] Extreme conservatism in manorial administration also existed in Devon (Finberg, *Tavistock Abbey*, pp. 258–9).

leyrite was abandoned. Very few manumissions can be traced in the fifteenth century and, although a number were granted in the sixteenth century, unfree status continued into the reign of James I.[1] Even by 1640 many of the lesser conditions of conventionary tenure were the same as they had been over three hundred years before.[2]

[1] For sixteenth-century manumissions see A. L. Rowse, 'The Duchy of Cornwall', *Gentleman's Magazine* (January 1937), p. 44. For tenure in villeinage in 1628 see *Calendar of State Papers, Domestic 1628–9*, p. 7.

[2] M. Coate, 'The Duchy of Cornwall', pp. 144–6.

4

THE ASSESSIONABLE MANORS FROM THE LATE THIRTEENTH CENTURY TO THE EVE OF THE BLACK DEATH: 1287–1347

It is in the closing decades of the thirteenth century that the first continuous threads of the history of the seventeen Cornish manors, later to be known as the assessionable manors, can be picked up; a time when they formed part of the extensive estates of Edmund, Earl of Cornwall. Exactly two centuries span the period from Domesday to the earliest surviving manorial document, and the fortunes of the manors during this time must remain unknown to us. Furthermore, the documentation when it starts in 1287/8[1] is comparatively sparse and uninformative over the next fifty years, yet it is sufficient to provide an indispensable introduction to the ensuing era in the history of the manors, lasting from 1337 to the downfall of the Yorkists in 1485, which is by contrast admirably documented.[2]

There is barely a trace of demesne cultivation to be found on any of the assessionable manors in our period and, with the exception of a number of deer-parks, all lands lay in the hands of tenants. Some small-scale arable farming on demesnes is in evidence on the earliest manorial account (1287/8) on the manors of Helstone-in-Triggshire and Calstock, but the next available account some nine years later shows it had been abandoned.[3] The final ill-fated attempt at demesne cultivation, this time using the Old Deer Park of Helstone-in-Triggshire, was made in 1336 whilst the manors were in the hands of Edward III in the year before Prince Edward was made Duke of

---

[1] P.R.O. SC.6.816/9. This is a much defaced account with one edge completely rotted away. It can be tentatively dated, however, from the name of the accountant, Roger de Ingepenne who was steward and sheriff of the Cornish estates of the Earldom from 1285–88 (P.R.O. *Lists and Indexes*, IX, 21); see also Midgley, *Ministers' Accounts*, I, xxv, xxxviii.

[2] For a chronological list of the medieval manorial account rolls of the Duchy see below, pp. 298–9.

[3] P.R.O. E.119/1.

Cornwall.[1] High winds and incessant rain almost completely ruined the harvest and led to the immediate relinquishing of the project, and the lack of any further experiments during the middle ages. Thus we are deprived of the fascinating and valuable details of the running of Cornish farms, of the distribution of rural resources, of the yields and prices of agrarian produce, and we are left with what appears at first sight to be mundane and unpromising material. But it is hoped that the history of the seventeen Cornish demesne manors of the Duchy in the later middle ages can be much more than a dull catalogue of rents.

The 30 years from 1287 to the accession of Queen Isabella to the estates of the Earldom in 1317 appear from the accounts to have been a period of inertia and possibly of economic stagnation. Scarcely any fluctuations occurred in 'Rents of Assize'.[2] Such inflexibility was not wholly the result of customary limitations, for some 50 per cent of customary tenants and some 40 per cent of total customary rents were conventionary, and the basis of this tenure should have been a constant reassessment of value. Yet we find the leases of conventionaries in this period were invariably renewed upon exactly the terms that had prevailed before, nor does there appear to have been any significant change in the small fines levied upon the granting of new leases.[3] Certain allowances to the 'Rents of Assize' of five manors were granted in the form of 'decayed rents', however, and in 1295/6 £12 7s. 7¼d. was allowed against a total manorial charge of approximately £380,[4] whilst in 1297/8 £11 13s. 5½d. was allowed, which included a new decay of £2 7s. 4½d. for the waste of Godolghan on Tintagel manor which could not be leased *propter exilium tenentium hoc anno*.[5] In successive accounts the causes of these 'decays of rent' are attributed to the default or lack of tenants, with the exception of Tywarnhaile manor,

---

[1] P.R.O. SC.6.1094/14.

[2] Small increases were, however, effected on certain manors between 1287/8 and 1296/7, and the account of the latter year (P.R.O. E.119/1) gives details of unsuccessful attempts to raise the 'Rents of Assize' of Liskeard and Trematon manors. Such examples are exceptional, however, and there were to be no further attempts to alter these rents before 1317.

[3] See, for example, the fines paid *pro respectu habendo* and *pro terra tenenda per convencionem* under the headings '*Fines, Perquisita et Relevia*' (P.R.O. SC.6.811/2–811/4).

[4] P.R.O. E.119/1, m. 23 d.   [5] P.R.O. SC.6.811/1, m. 2 d.

situated on the Atlantic coast, where the wasting of lands by sand was given as the explanation[1]—although this decay too can probably be attributed to a fall in demand for land as in times of population pressure such a misfortune would not have led to so lengthy a retreat from cultivation.[2] As would be expected, it is a feature of 'decays of rent' in this period that the land which suffered diminished rents or for which no tenants at all could be found was land of poor quality—mostly waste and moorland.

The same static qualities found in 'Rents of Assize' are also observable in the rents and farms of almost all manorial properties. Farms of land not included in 'Rents of Assize' remained stationary, and the farms of fisheries and ferries remained unchanged for many years. Furthermore, on only three manors was there any variation in the farms of manorial corn or fulling mills.

This overall lack of movement in rents and farms in the generation from 1288 to 1317 appears, however, to mask rather than demonstrate the underlying economic and social trends of the period. Some knowledge of these underlying trends can be gleaned from sources of revenue which responded more closely to economic fluctuations, and a slightly more dynamic picture emerges. On some of the Cornish manors variable revenues were obtained from the annual sales of pasture, the cultivation of areas of waste land for short periods, and assarting, and these form the substance of Table 3.

Perhaps the best indication of movements in demand for land can be obtained from the granting of licences permitting the cultivation of areas of waste land for short periods; land which had either previously been put to no agricultural use whatsoever or served only as rough pasture.[3] Each licence stipulated the rent to be charged, the length of time the land would remain under cultivation, and invariably contained a clause which ruled that a reduced rent, or even no rent at all, was payable if the land failed to yield a crop.[4] Rents for *baticium* were high and usually ranged from 1s. to 1s. 8d. per acre on manors in central and eastern Cornwall down to 6d. on

[1] For example, P.R.O. SC.6.811/2.

[2] For 'decays of rent' caused by sand at other periods see below, p. 151.

[3] Such land brought in from the waste was termed *baticium*. The cultivation of this land is also discussed above, p. 14.

[4] See for example P.R.O. SC.6.811/8, 811/9, Moresk, Tybesta, Tywarnhaile.

TABLE 3   *Revenues from lands not included in 'Rents of Assize', 1297–1317*

	Rillaton	Climsland	Calstock	Penlyne	Liskeard	Tybesta	Tewington	Tintagel	Tywarnhaile	Moresk	Helston-in-Kirrier	Total
	£ s. d.	£ s. d.	£ s. d.	s. d.	£ s. d.	£ s. d.	£ s. d.	£ s. d.	£ s. d.	£ s. d.	£ s. d.	£ s. d.
1297	nil	nil	nil	nil	2 14 6½	2 3	2 13 5	nil	8 9	6 14 0	nil	12 12 11½
1298	nil	nil	nil	nil	2 14 6½	6	2 0 11	nil	6 3	6 4 9	1 0	11 7 11½
1301	nil	2 3	nil	nil	nil	8	1 4	nil	7 3	2 12 6	nil	3 4 0
1302	nil	nil	nil	nil	nil	nil	nil	nil	10 0	2 10 6	nil	3 0 6
1303	nil	3 0	nil	nil	nil	7 0	nil	nil	1 4 9	2 10 10	nil	3 18 1
1304	2 0	1 0	nil	nil	nil	6 8	6 4	nil	1 5 6	2 12 1½	nil	4 13 7½
1305	nil	6	nil	nil	nil	8 6	nil	nil	1 14 3	2 19 6	9 6	5 2 3
1306	1 6 0	nil	7 6	nil	nil	1 13 6	nil	nil	2 8 10½	2 16 2	1 3 0	9 15 5½
1315	1 5 0	1½	3 2 6	1	nil	nil	nil	nil	1 0 9	3 6 5½	7½	9 16 6½
1316	1 7 0	nil	1 5 0	6 4	8 9 0	1 2 6	nil	1 9 6	3 5 6	4 17 4	2 11	24 13 9½
1317	1 7 0	9 6	1 0 0	6 1	5 17 3	12 6	nil	nil	19 0	4 11 11	2 11	18 14 4½

This table contains the revenues charged against each reeve's account for annual sales of pasture, the cultivation of areas of waste land, and assarts; i.e. those revenues from the land capable of fluctuation in this period.

The information presented should be used with discretion as at best it can only give a vague and partial picture of the short-term fluctuations in demand for pasture and arable. Notwithstanding, the overall cycle remains clear.

D

Helston-in-Kirrier in the far west; the period of cultivation varied from as little as two years to as long as five years. Unfortunately, owing to the contracted nature of the entries in the accounts it is not possible to throw any light on the frequency with which any particular area of waste was used as arable. The cultivation of waste and moorland was an extremely costly and troublesome business and this helps to explain why it was never of more than marginal importance on the assessionable manors. The revenues obtained by the Earldom from the sale of licences do form, however, a distinct cycle in the period from 1287/8 to 1316/17, falling from a peak at the close of the thirteenth century and recovering strongly by the second decade of the fourteenth.

Whereas the vast bulk of all pasture on the assessionable manors at this time was leased for long periods, at Climsland the pastures of the deer-park of Carrybullock, and at Helston-in-Kirrier the pastures of the great moor of Gondywrath, were sold year by year at variable rents and in fluctuating amounts; and both pastures produced revenues which show a falling trend from 1296/7 lasting to the end of the first decade of the fourteenth century, followed by a marked recovery. The first assarts recorded in this period were made on the westerly manors of Tybesta and Tywarnhaile in 1303/4 and 1304/5 respectively.[1] In the account of 1305/6 first mention is made of substantial assarts in the moor of Gondywrath, again in the west of the county, for which annual rents of 20s. 6d. were paid.[2] By 1314/15 further small extensions to the area of cultivable land at Moresk and Penlyne had also been made.[3]

The cycle described above, and evident in Table 3, is paralleled in the receipts from sales of turbary at Helstone-in-Triggshire and Helston-in-Kirrier which increased significantly in the second decade of the fourteenth century,[4] as did the farm of the large fish weir at Calstock.[5]

With the accession of Queen Isabella to the estates of the Earldom in 1317 it is no longer necessary to search the accounts for possible indirect indications of underlying economic and social conditions,

[1] P.R.O. SC.6.811/5, 811/6.   [2] P.R.O. SC.6.811/7
[3] P.R.O. SC.6.811/12.   [4] Below, p. 189.
[5] The farm was raised from £8 to £10 in 1316/17 (P.R.O. SC.6.811/5, 811/6).

for evidence of a progressively increasing demand for land becomes at once abundant, which contrasts sharply with the apparent stagnation of the preceding 30 years. It is probable that the Cornish economy did not suffer a prolonged setback from the effects of the series of famines which devastated much of England and Europe from 1315 to 1319;[1] indeed Cornwall was frequently called upon to supply grain and victuals to other parts of England in these critical years.[2]

The administration of Isabella adopted a more flexible and businesslike approach to the running of the manors than had been practised while they were in the hands of Edward II and Gaveston, and by 1324 a number of the rents of conventionary tenures had been raised, many substantial assarts had been made, and on some manors considerably increased revenues were derived from lands which had been converted from pasture into arable.[3] Typical of such increases was the £4 received from divers lands at Calstock which had previously rendered £3, the 8s. received from the waste of Tolfronde newly assarted at Tybesta, and the 8s. received from the wastes of Helsbury and Hamknolle at Helstone-in-Triggshire *ultra 3s 6d quos inde reddebant pro pastura et nunc dimittunt ad colendum*. Furthermore the 'decay' of £2 7s. 4d. of the rent of Godolghan waste at Tintagel fell to 5s. 4d. as £2 2s. 0d. was received from tenants. The farms of a number of manorial mills were also increased substantially between 1317 and 1324.

Furthermore, five manors were put out to farm, and the amounts of the farm were in each case greater than the highest recorded profits that the manors had ever produced for the Earldom.[4] The western manors of Helston-in-Kirrier, Moresk and Tywarnhaile,

---

[1] One of the most comprehensive studies of these famines is: H. S. Lucas, 'The Great European Famine of 1315–1316 and 1317', *Speculum*, v (1930).

[2] See for example the safe conducts granted to merchants enabling them to take foodstuffs from Cornwall to London and other parts of the realm: *C.C.R. 1313–1318*, p. 461; *C.P.R. 1313–1317*, pp. 447, 458, 465, 625.

[3] P.R.O. E.370/5/19. The conversion of pasture to arable can be interpreted as evidence of population pressure. See M. M. Postan, 'Village Livestock in the Thirteenth Century', *Ec. H.R.*, 2nd ser., xv (1962).

[4] P.R.O. E.370/5/19. No trace can be found of any earlier farms of manors in the period from 1287/8, although Edward II granted the manor of Moresk to Adam de Carleton in 1309 (P.R.O. SC.6.811/10); this manor was back in royal hands by 1313/14 (P.R.O. SC.6.811/12).

were leased to William Melbourne, the rector of Lanihorne, and a number of other leading Cornish figures of which William Pasford was one.[1] The farm of Moresk and Tywarnhaile manors was assessed at £70 annually; they had been worth some £60 annually to the Earldom from 1315 to 1317. It was agreed that £80 annually should be paid for the farm of Helston-in-Kirrier manor, which was some £15 more than it had realised as profits in 1317. The manor and borough of Liskeard were farmed to John de Valletort for a seven-year term at Easter 1321, the farm of the manor being £38 annually, which compared favourably with the average of £30 profits that it had produced from 1315 to 1317.[2] Trematon manor with all appurtenances, including the borough of Saltash and the ferry of Lenne, was leased from 1320 for seven years to Robert Bandyn for an annual farm of £86.

Increasing demand for land provided ample scope for enhancing manorial revenues and to this end, each manor was surveyed between 1326 and 1331.[3] The tenants, the rents they paid, and their holdings are all listed individually in these surveys, in addition to a complete valuation of manorial properties. Despite considerable variations in the methods used by the surveyors, difficulties in exact dating, and the vague and often ambiguous manner in which information is presented, it is possible to discern further and more widespread increments to rents and farms, and on those manors that were surveyed last of all conventionary rents were raised substantially.[4] For example, of rents totalling £57 19s. od. on Helston-in-Kirrier, £18 17s. 9d. was 'new increment'.

Edward III's grant of the estates of the Earldom of Cornwall to John of Eltham in 1333, after Isabella had fallen out of favour, put another new administrative hierarchy into power and precipitated a

[1] For a survey of some of the business activities of William Pasford see below, pp. 238–9.
[2] The Valletorts were a leading Cornish family who had previously held the Honour of Trematon; it was purchased from them by Richard, Earl of Cornwall, in 1270 (Midgley, *Ministers' Accounts*, I, xxiii; N. Denholm-Young, *Richard of Cornwall* (Oxford, 1947), pp. 164, 169). The Valletorts continued to lay claim to the Honour, however, until it was formally surrendered in 1338 by Henry le Pomeray in exchange for a pardon (*C.C.R., 1337–1339*, p. 387; *C.P.R., 1338–1340*, p. 16).
[3] P.R.O. E.142/41.
[4] The manors of Helston-in-Kirrier, Moresk and Tywarnhaile could not be surveyed until their lease to William Melbourne had expired.

further critical appraisal of the administration of the Cornish manors, with the result that many villeins were transformed into conventionaries and the rents of conventionary tenures made subject to frequent regular reassessments.[1] In 1333 a special commission led by Sir Richard de Chabernon reported that it would be to the benefit of the Earl if the conventionary lands of the assessionable manors were demised on leases lasting from seven years to seven years.[2] A short lease was thought to be most advisable in a period when the value of land was rising steadily. Reference is made in the report of the commission to exacting the 'true value' of the conventionary lands, and this was accomplished in 1333 by an increase of rents and by the imposition of a fine, called an assession fine. Adjustments to the level of these assession fines soon became the means of varying the 'prices' of the tenures when necessary at each subsequent assession, with the actual rent invariably remaining fixed.[3] The new assession fines varied considerably from holding to holding, but were far higher than the nominal fines that had been payable previously when conventionary leases had been renewed from time to time.

The conversion of many unfree tenures, which had been held on fixed rents, into conventionary tenures held on freely adjustable rents, and the placing of the conventionary tenures themselves on an economic basis resulted in substantial increases to the total revenues derived from the lands and other properties of the seventeen assessionable manors after 1333. The increases were of such magnitude as to suggest that the piecemeal increments made in the time of Queen Isabella from 1317 to 1331 had not been sufficient to keep pace with rising values. The annual rents of conventionary lands were subjected to considerable increments in the spring of 1333, but at this time the most important method of bringing the 'price' of these lands into line with their true market value was the imposition of assession fines. In Table 4 an attempt has been made to trace the steep rise in total charges, made up of both annual rents and assession

---

[1] See also pp. 74–7 above.
[2] Preamble to the assession roll of 1333, D.C.O. 471.
[3] The assession fine itself became almost equivalent to an annual rent when from the assession of 1347 each fine was made payable over the first six years of the seven years of the assessional period.

fines, on the conventionary and villein lands between 1297 and 1340. An exact computation is impossible, as the entry fines in the period before the assession system was introduced cannot be isolated with complete accuracy from the various sources of revenues comprising judicial profits. Nevertheless, the increases in revenues from conventionary lands were of such spectacular proportions that it is worth while attempting some tabulation of them, although of necessity it must be to a significant extent based upon estimates. A study of the profits of the courts of assessionable manors before 1333 reveals that generally considerably less than one third of the total judicial profits was derived each year from fines imposed upon entry into conventionary lands and renewals of conventionary leases, so that any inaccuracies in the first three columns of Table 4, which contain average annual rents plus one third of the profits of court, verge on the side of under-estimation rather than over-estimation. It can be discerned in Table 4 that the increases effected by 1323/4 were in many instances quite substantial, but on every manor they were completely overshadowed by those increases made in the ensuing decade which succeeded in raising the charges upon the conventionary and villein lands of the Cornish manors of the Earldom by proportions ranging upwards from 30 to 40 per cent on Tewington and Moresk manors to as much as 100 per cent or even more on the manors of Liskeard and Trematon. Unfortunately it is impossible to relate these overall increases to the individual holdings on each of the manors, although this can be achieved from 1333 with the aid of assession rolls.[1] The farms of all manorial mills not held in freehold were also raised substantially, as can be seen in Table 5.

John of Eltham held the estates of the Earldom of Cornwall for barely five years, nevertheless during this brief tenure the awareness of his administration of the abundant opportunities to extract greater profits from the assessionable manors resulted in a number of fundamental reforms; the most important of which was undoubtedly the transformation of conventionary tenure from a virtually inflexible form of landholding into one acutely sensitive to changes in demand for land. On assuming control in 1337 the officials of young

[1] Examples are given in Appendix B.

Prince Edward adopted the same general policies of management as had been formulated under the late Earl, and sought to consolidate

TABLE 4 *The approximate aggregate annual rents of conventionary and villein lands, 1297–1340*

	1297–1308			1315–1317			1324			1333–1340		
	£	s.	d.	£	s.	d.	£	s.	d.	£	s.	d.
Rillaton	2	18	7	4	2	11	3	0	9	4	4	3
Climsland	15	18	11	16	2	9	17	8	0	26	4	8
Calstock	14	0	6	15	18	0	18	12	8	28	0	5
Trematon	16	14	7	16	14	7	Farmed			31	19	0
Liskeard	15	8	2	19	17	5	Farmed			41	12	9
Restormel	5	0	3	5	0	3	5	8	6	5	13	8
Penlyne	4	17	5	5	0	3	5	8	7	7	8	3
Tewington	24	19	5	24	8	3	25	5	8	31	0	2
Tybesta	21	15	4	21	6	6	27	14	2	34	7	0
Talskiddy	3	0	0	3	0	0	3	0	0	3	12	0[a]
Tywarnhaile	11	19	2	12	18	10	Farmed			18	0	8
Moresk	25	7	10	26	5	5	Farmed			35	16	7
Helston-in-Kirrier	35	14	11	36	13	11	Farmed			67	1	6
Tintagel	20	9	11	22	18	9	22	12	3	34	7	5
Helstone-in-Triggshire and Penmayne	36	11	10	36	11	10	36	3	9	49	2	10

[a] No assession fines charged on this manor in 1333.

This table contains, as accurately as can be estimated, the total charges upon conventionary and villein lands, including both annual rents and assession fines. For the period 1297–1324 one third of the average profits of the manorial courts have been added to the annual rents to allow for revenues derived from payments that were replaced by assession fines after 1333. In the fourth column, one seventh of the assession fine imposed in 1333 has been added to the annual rent, thus averaging the fine over the seven years of the conventionary lease. The totals are the amounts the reeve was charged to deliver, 'allowances' and 'decays' have been deducted. The totals are not the amounts actually delivered by the reeve to the receiver, which cannot be discovered. Rents paid by free tenants for lands held in freehold have not been included as they were fixed by custom throughout the period, except for occasional fluctuations of minor importance. To have included these rents would have restricted the ability of the table to reflect underlying economic movements with accuracy.

and extend the new conventionary system which had already received the formal approval of Edward III.[1] Less than two months after the creation of the Duchy of Cornwall instructions were

[1] *C.F.R. 1337–1347*, p. 4.

issued for an exhaustive survey to be made of all possessions of the Duke of Cornwall, in order to provide the essential up-to-date information upon which to base the government of the estates. The result was the momentous Caption of Seisin.[1]

TABLE 5 *Farms of manorial mills, 1317–33*

	Rillaton	Penlyne	Tintagel	Calstock	Tybesta	Helston-in-Kirrier	Tywarnhaile
	£ s. d.	£ s. d.	£ s. d.	£ s. d.	£ s. d.	£ s. d.	£ s. d.
1317	1 0 0	1 3 6	4 13 4	2 9 0	3 6 8	5 6 8	18 0
1324	1 0 0	1 6 6	4 13 4	3 15 8	5 0 0	—	—
1326–31	1 6 8	1 6 6	4 13 4	—	5 0 0	6 13 4	—
1333[a]	1 13 4	2 8 0	5 6 8	4 15 8	5 0 0	9 6 8	1 6 8

[a] These farms do not include assession fines and therefore tend to understate the charge a little.

Rillaton—one corn mill
Penlyne—one corn mill, one small fulling mill
Tintagel—three corn mills
Calstock—one corn mill, one fulling mill
Tybesta—two corn mills, one fulling mill
Helston-in-Kirrier—two corn mills
Tywarnhaile—half of one corn mill (other half held in freehold)

The capital cost involved in keeping the mills in good repair throughout the period covered by this table was borne wholly by the farmer. No record of expenditure on repairs is available.

It is evident from 1338/9, the date of the first ministers' account of the Duchy of Cornwall, that a reappraisal of many sources of revenue had taken place.[2] Customary rents in kind, long since commuted into money payments, had been revalued. For example, a pound of pepper for which a shilling had been accepted since 1287/8 was valued at 14d. in 1338/9, and after the assession of 1347 2s. was demanded.[3] At Liskeard the ancient custom of carrying wine was

[1] P.R.O. E.120/1. A transcript of this key document is at present being prepared for publication in the *Transactions of the Devon and Cornwall Record Association* by P. L. Hull.
[2] P.R.O. SC.6.816/11.
[3] P.R.O. SC.6.816/9 and D.C.O. 4 ff.

commuted for 2s. 2d. in 1338/9 instead of the 2s. that had previously been paid, and monetary payments in lieu of rents in kind that had lapsed on Moresk manor were again exacted. Although these small increments to the customary rents added very little to the total profits of manors they were indicative of the spirit of efficiency with which the new administration approached the running of the estates.

On a much wider scale, it was part of Duchy policy to make fuller use of the pasture facilities afforded by the four Cornish manorial deer-parks than had been accomplished in earlier years; and in the Caption of Seisin the estimated value of potential sales of pasture in the parks, over and above that needed for the sustenance of the deer, was listed. Although the welfare of the deer continued to be the primary consideration, the annual revenues obtained from the pasture of the deer-parks in the first years of the Duchy were more than double those achieved twenty years earlier, whilst the deer-park of Helsbury and Lanteglos, part of the manor of Helstone-in-Triggshire, that had rarely been worth anything at all as pasture between 1297 and 1317, realised more than £4 annually in the thirteen-forties.

Increases in revenues comparable to those derived from the leases of conventionary lands and mills in the 1330s were often also obtained from the leases and sale of other manorial properties, such as fisheries, ferries, and turbaries. Perhaps the most spectacular rise was in the profits from the sale of turbary on the manor of Helston-in-Kirrier, which increased from an annual average of £6 in the first decade of the fourteenth century to some £16 in the following decade, whilst in 1338/9 no less than £35 was obtained. The receipts from the other large turbary situated on Helstone-in-Triggshire manor showed a similar rising trend over the same period, although the increases were of more modest proportions.

The net result of the substantial growth in conventionary rents and in many other sources of manorial revenue since the second decade of the fourteenth century was an increase of approximately 70 per cent in the profitability of the seventeen assessionable manors. From an annual average of approximately £375 between 1297 and 1306, the aggregate amount that the manorial reeves were charged to deliver to the receiver rose to almost £550 in 1338/9, which in turn becomes almost £650 if one seventh of the assession fines payable for the seven-year leases granted in 1333 is included.[1]

Increased efficiency in the administration of the manors no doubt played an important part in securing greater profits. But a background of considerable population pressure is indisputable, although the lack of any statistical information concerning population movements in early fourteenth-century Cornwall means that no quantitative appreciation of trends can be made.[2] Much work remains to be done on the economy of medieval Cornwall and at present it is not possible to state with certainty whether the rising revenues from the assessionable manors at this time were typical of the county as a whole; but recent archaeological investigations lend support to a thesis of population pressure leading to the colonisation of wild and intractable lands.[3] Cornwall thus does not appear to have been subjected to those conditions found in many regions of England at this time, where over-population appears to have resulted in rising death-rates and a consequent slackening of pressure on the land.[4]

The third and fourth decades of the fourteenth century constituted a boom period throughout the Cornish economy, with a remarkable growth in tin-mining activity occurring simultaneously with the most substantial and rapid increases to rents and farms on Duchy manors. Tin production, which after considerable increases in the first decades of the fourteenth century had attained almost one

---

[1] The assession fines fixed at the assession of 1333 were in fact made payable over the first three years of the assessional term (i.e. 1333/4 to 1335/6).

[2] Records of institutions to the Cornish benefices of the Diocese of Exeter are available and have been tabulated in Appendix E (below, pp. 292–6); but they are of real value only for periods of sharply falling population.

[3] Although work on documentary sources has hardly begun, archaeological evidence does exist which suggests that Cornwall experienced considerable population pressure in the fourteenth century before the Black Death. See, for example: Balchin, *Cornwall*, pp. 40–3; W. G. Hoskins, *Making of the English Landscape* (1955), p. 81; *Med. Arch.* VII (1963), 272–94.

[4] The thesis that settlement and population in England began to contract many years before the Black Death has largely been formulated by Professor M. M. Postan (for a summary of his position see *Cambridge Economic History of Europe*, I (2nd edn, ed. M. M. Postan, Cambridge (1966), 556–70)). Miss Harvey has challenged the validity of this view (*T.R.H.S.*, 5th ser., XVI (1965), 23–42), although she is forced to conclude that the first half of the fourteenth century saw little expansion. A recent article by A. H. R. Baker (*Ec. H.R.*, 2nd ser., XIX (1966), 518–32) lends support to the contraction thesis.

million lbs annually by 1323/4, suddenly embarked upon a burst of exceptional expansion and by 1331/2 had attained the unprecedented level of 1,643,000 lbs.[1]

The upward reappraisal of rent levels in the spring of 1333 had by 1340 proved a resounding success: almost without exception manors were able to sustain the greatly increased values that had been put upon their conventionary lands and properties with scarcely any arrears or vacancies. And although at first Duchy officials did meet some resistance from recalcitrant local ministers who refused to account in full, this was soon settled.[2]

Helston-in-Kirrier manor was the exception, and its reeve appears to have encountered difficulties in collecting money soon after the assession of 1333. This manor had grown in area with remarkable speed between 1300 and 1333, incorporating vast tracts of moorland into its rent roll;[3] and the value of the manor was also enhanced by the sharply rising rents of its more anciently settled land. As a result of these twin movements receipts from customary lands had increased from an annual average of £36–7 in the first two decades of the fourteenth century,[4] to more than £67 in 1333.[5] The particular stimulus for this increase seems to have been the exceptional growth of mining activity both within the manor and in close proximity to it; for not only did the production of tin rise steeply in each of the four main Cornish stannaries in the late thirteen-twenties, but it also appears that Penwith-and-Kirrier ousted Blackmore from its position as the foremost mining district.[6] Having a rapidly expanding mining community in close proximity must have greatly enhanced demand for both land and foodstuffs. Many miners pastured a few animals and some even cultivated a small piece of arable, but it is

---

[1] For a graph of tin presented for coinage see Appendix C.
[2] Below, pp. 196–7.
[3] The Inquisition *Post Mortem* made in 1300 (P.R.O. E.152/8) gives the area of the customary lands of Helston-in-Kirrier as no more than 40 Cornish acres (perhaps 2,000–3,000 statute acres); in the Caption of Seisin of 1337 (P.R.O. E.120/1) the customary lands measured 5,000 statute acres.
[4] P.R.O. SC.6.811/1–16.
[5] D.C.O. 471.
[6] In 1317 both Penwith-and-Kirrier and Blackmore stannaries had the same number of miners paying '*tribulage*', but by 1324 Penwith-and-Kirrier had twice as many as Blackmore (compare P.R.O. SC.6.811/15 and 811/16 with P.R.O. E.370/5/19; see also Lewis, *Stannaries*, Appendix O, p. 267).

probable that mining communities relied upon the food market for the greater part of their needs.[1] The joint demand for food and land had its effect upon rents, and Helston-in-Kirrier was also ideally situated for assarting and colonisation, lying as it did amongst wide expanses of uninhabited moorland. The turning-point of both the rising demand for the lands of Helston-in-Kirrier and the production of tin occurred towards the end of the thirteen-thirties. At this time, tin production began to decline quite appreciably, until from 1339 to 1342 it averaged little more than a million lbs each year, a drop of almost 40 per cent in ten years. The first extant ministers' account after the assession of 1333 is that of 1338/9, nevertheless it gives details of the insolvency of Helston-in-Kirrier reeves since the foundation of the Duchy in 1337;[2] £14 9s. 1½d. was outstanding from the account of 1336/7 and £25 4s. 1¼d. from that of 1337/8, and it was found necessary to commit both reeves to Launceston gaol.[3] But the insolvency was not cured and Gervase Trevithek, reeve in 1338/9, left office owing £25 4s. 2d. In retrospect the Duchy made some allowances against outstanding debts for 'lands in the hands of the lord because of the poverty of their tenants', and 14s. 4d. was also deducted from the farm of the mill of Melyngoys 'as many of the tenants who had owed suit had relinquished their holdings'.[4]

Conventionary leases on all assessionable manors were due to expire at Michaelmas 1340, so in March and April 1340 a body of commissioners visited each manor in turn to prepare new leases for the ensuing seven years.[5] This assession provided the Duchy administration with its first opportunity to alter the annual rents and assession fines imposed during the time of John of Eltham, but in fact very few readjustments were carried out. Of course a complete reappraisal of the price of land on Helston-in-Kirrier manor was essential, but elsewhere rents remained very much as they were,

---

[1] Stannary court rolls, *passim*.
[2] P.R.O. SC.6.816/11. There is an account of part of the year 1335/6, compiled whilst the manors were in the hands of Edward III after the death of John of Eltham (P.R.O. SC.6.1094/13).
[3] P.R.O. SC.6.816/11, receivers' account.
[4] P.R.O. SC.6.816/12.
[5] A record of the leases made in 1340 of Climsland, Rillaton and part of Calstock manors is contained in P.R.O. SC.11, Roll 153.

although occasionally small increments were added to the assession fines of holdings which were taken by new tenants. At Helston, although total assession fines payable by the tenants of the manor fell from £84 15s. 8d. to £67 18s. 5d., substantial amounts of land were left unleased; land that was only profitable to farm in times of exceptional demand.

The rapid upward movement in the price of land on the Cornish manors had thus been halted by 1340, and the thirteen-forties saw the maintenance of high though not increasing revenues for the Duchy. A further detailed survey of the resources of Duchy manors in Cornwall was undertaken in March 1345 by a commission headed by William de Cusancia and Hugo de Berwyk, only eight years after the making of the Caption of Seisin.[1] The necessity of yet another survey is not readily apparent, but it did examine the free tenancies in some detail, as no record of them was kept in the assession rolls. As a result a number of small increments were added to the 'Rents of Assize'. In addition the new survey contained revised estimates of the value of many manorial properties, such as the pasture in the deer-parks and the turbaries, and subsequent to the survey reeves had to compare the receipts they had obtained with the yield estimated by the surveyors, and explain any deficiencies.

The general stability of conventionary rents on all Duchy manors, with the exception of Helston-in-Kirrier, was again confirmed by the assession of 1347 when the vast bulk of leases were once more enacted on the same terms as had been agreed in 1333.[2] There were some scattered increases in the levels of assession fines usually, however, only upon holdings which changed hands at the assession. Very few holdings were left unleased. An audit compiled in 1347 shows that, with the notable exception of Helston-in-Kirrier, arrears of no more than a few shillings had been incurred by any reeve.[3]

On the far western manor of Helston-in-Kirrier, particularly susceptible to fluctuations in mining activity, the land market continued to become progressively more depressed in the thirteen-

[1] Fragments of this survey survive in the Duchy of Cornwall Office, the Cornwall County Record Office, Cambridge University Library, and the Public Record Office.
[2] D.C.O. 472.   [3] P.R.O. SC.6.812/3; see also Chapter 8, Figs 3–13.

forties. The modest reductions in annual rents and assession fines accomplished at the assession of 1340 achieved little. An enquiry was held at Helston in July 1342 by the auditors of the ministers' accounts sent down from London; they examined the validity of a multitude of claims for allowances against the manorial charge and sought to lease lands that persisted *in manu domini*, but with little success.[1] The next extant account, 1344/5, tells us that the auditors had once again been sent to Helston to set up a court of enquiry, and widespread reductions in rents were granted by them including accepting only £1 16s. 0d. for 12½ holdings that had earlier been leased for £6 1s. 4d. annually. Twelve holdings that had been leased at the assession of 1340 for £5 18s. 4d. were confirmed to be worth only £2 4s. 9d. as pasture.[2] Although this enquiry uncovered certain malpractices on the part of previous manorial officials, it is quite plain that the root of the troubles that Helston-in-Kirrier was experiencing at this time lay in a substantial fall in the demand for land and in a widespread inability on the part of the tenants to pay the rents and assession fines they had contracted to pay in the assession of 1340, rather than in dishonesty. In a detailed summary of outstanding arrears compiled by the auditors in 1345 we learn that the reeves of the manor in 1337, 1338, 1341, 1342, and 1343, along with the authorised collectors of conventionary fines from 1341 to 1344 were all in gaol at Launceston for their indebtedness. The pathetic attempts of some of these bankrupts to pay off their debts had failed to arouse compassion,[3] and the administration of the Duchy steadfastly refused to relent. Many of these unfortunates, more the victims of economic circumstances and harsh treatment than their own inefficiency or dishonesty, were imprisoned until they died of plague in the Black Death.[4] Michael Mynithi, who was reeve of Helston manor for two years from 1340 to 1342, fared better, however, for after being imprisoned for a number of years he escaped and fled to Devon.[5]

But no further arrests of the manorial officials of Helston were

[1] D.C.O. 1. [2] D.C.O. 2.
[3] See, for example, the small amounts paid off by John Nanslo and John Basset in 1340 and 1342 (P.R.O. SC.6.816/12; D.C.O. 1).
[4] P.R.O. SC.6.812/7. [5] *Ibid*

made after 1344 and the administration of the Duke appears to have resigned itself to the inevitability of progressively mounting arrears, at least until the next assession could establish lower rent levels. The attitude of the administration was fully justified, for in the ensuing years up to the assession of 1347 an average of only a little over half of the declining annual charge of this manor reached the Duchy receiver each year.[1] The first-hand experience gained by the auditors on their visits must have impressed them with the need for expertise in the management of this particular manor; it had become painfully obvious that a reeve could not cope, and a professional bailiff was appointed to run the manor, with an annual fee of 60s. 8d.[2]

Further signs of enlightenment are evident in the policy adopted by the Duchy at the assession held at Helston in 1347. In order to encourage the leasing of lands not in demand, the Duchy agreed to slashing reductions in annual rents and assession fines, and even upon holdings that were being leased again by sitting tenants fines were often reduced. The success of these measures is attested by the fact that, despite a halving of the total assession fines payable by conventionary tenants, aggregate rent receipts actually rose and much less land was left vacant. A typical example of the scale of the reductions on this manor was the leasing of a messuage and 46 acres in the vill of Caroscorn that had lain vacant since 1340, for 10s. per annum—it had commanded an annual rent of 23s. and an assession fine of 20s. at the assession of 1333. The values of more expensive lands, and therefore presumably more fertile lands, were maintained far better than the values of waste and moorlands, which in the majority of cases declined catastrophically if they could be leased at all. In relatively fertile hamlets, such as Hellistoth, Lisgree, and Pencois, rents fell by approximately only 15 per cent from 1333 to 1347, suggesting once again that the lack of demand for the vast tracts of poor quality land, after the short-lived phenomenal burst of activity in western tin mines in the early thirteen-thirties had subsided, was the primary cause of the dramatic decline in rent receipts from conventionary lands and the chronic insolvency which Helston-in-Kirrier manor experienced after 1333.

[1] Appendix A, Fig. 13.   [2] D.C.O. 3.

Few English estates can have had more surveys made of their tenants than the assessionable manors in the generation before the Black Death; and certainly no series comparable to that of these Cornish manors survives. The first surveys were drawn up between 1326 and 1331 while the estates of the Earldom of Cornwall were in the hands of Queen Isabella and then Edward III. The rolls of the first regular assession followed in 1333, and the information contained in them is complemented by the very detailed Caption of Seisin made a few months after the foundation of the Duchy of Cornwall in 1337. The next survey was that of the assession of 1340, following seven years after the inauguration of the system in 1333, and in 1345 a further comprehensive extent similar in scope to the Caption of Seisin was made. Finally in 1347 the last assession before the Black Death was enacted. These six surveys, containing lists of the names of all the conventionary and villein tenants of the Duchy manors together with the size and location of their holdings, the rents and assession fines due from them, and often also the names of the previous holders, enable an unusually comprehensive picture of tenants and their holdings to be constructed.[1]

One of the most striking features of the land market in the decade before the Black Death was the frequency with which conventionary holdings changed hands. Although the precise numbers of tenants surrendering their leases cannot be determined until after 1337, it is quite plain from the earliest of the surveys that the proportion was substantial and it tended to increase before the outbreak of plague in 1349. Less than half the conventionary holdings of western and central Duchy manors are recorded as being in the hands of the same tenant in the Caption of Seisin of 1337 and in the assession roll of 1347. Indeed on the manor of Helston-in-Kirrier in the far west of Cornwall only 18 out of a sample of 83 holdings were held in 1347 by the tenants who had held them ten years earlier, and furthermore it is evident that many of the holdings had changed hands more than once in this decade. On the assessionable manors in the east and north-east of Cornwall, however, the proportion of holdings which changed hands was lower, averaging some 30–40 per cent.

[1] See also Chapter 2 above.

The increase in life tenancies in the thirteen-forties did something to encourage longer tenancies, but life tenancies were never more than a very small proportion of all tenancies, and they were for the most part granted only to Duchy officials or to Duchy tenants who were capable of leasing substantial quantities of land.[1]

A change of tenant could occur for a multitude of reasons. Apart from death the personal preferences of tenants for one holding rather than another played a significant part. For example, we learn that in 1345 on Tintagel manor both John Chapman and John Morris had given up the holdings they had leased in 1340 in order to lease others of apparently similar size and quality,[2] and at the assession of 1347 on Climsland manor Richard Pouvre surrendered a holding consisting of a messuage and 16 acres in Donnhouse in order to lease a messuage and 32 acres in Oldelynes.[3] Very few holdings appear to have remained in the hands of a single family for long periods, and the inheritance of holdings was surprisingly rare. The majority of incoming tenants were persons leasing land from the Duchy for the first time, although with new tenants it is often impossible to tell whether they had previously been resident on the manor or had recently migrated there in order to obtain land. The Midwinter and Underwood families appear to have migrated to Climsland in 1340 with the express purpose of securing land, and beside the names of each member of these families who leased land in the assession of 1340 it is stated: *ad hoc electus per homagium*.[4] The Midwinters leased a total of four holdings containing some 92½ acres of land and 4 acres of waste. At the next assession two of these holdings were surrendered and Drogo Iota, who had lost his holding to Roger Midwinter in 1340, was able to regain it.

Another interesting feature of conventionary landholding demonstrated in the surveys of the thirteen-forties was the division of holdings and aggregations of holdings between a number of tenants. The most striking example of this phenomenon occurred on the small manor of Penkneth when, at the assession of 1347, three out of the five free conventionary tenants on the manor lost part of their holdings to new tenants, but continued to hold with depleted

---

[1] Above, pp. 70–1.
[2] Extent of William de Cusancia, D.C.O. Library.
[3] D.C.O. 472.
[4] P.R.O. SC.11. Roll 153, Climsland.

lands.[1] At the same time on Tewington manor a vacated holding was divided into two and leased to two new tenants, and two other holdings were also split up. At Trematon Nicholas Poda gave up $3\frac{1}{2}$ acres of his 7-acre holding for Robert Eliot to lease. Many examples also exist at this time of tenants failing to add to their existing holdings even when rights of inheritance offered opportunities.[2] John Biagga, of Helston-in-Triggshire manor, paid a heriot of 5d. but gave up his own holding before taking possession of his father's. While at Tybesta on the death of Henry de Nanstallan his son Christopher leased only 9 acres of his father's 18-acre holding. At Climsland such behaviour was repeated many times.

On the Cornish manors of the Duchy before the Black Death there were remarkably few traces of a peasant aristocracy, despite the free market in land.[3] Those tenants who did lease large amounts of land were almost exclusively officials or favourites of the Duchy, or industrial and commercial entrepreneurs.[4] On each assessionable manor virtually every conventionary holding was in the hands of a different tenant, and holdings when vacated were far more likely to have been taken by tenants who had not previously held land from the Duchy than by established tenants increasing the size of their holdings. The predominant tendency in the fourth and fifth decades of the fourteenth century was towards the creation of even smaller holdings.

The division of the conventionary lands amongst increasing numbers of tenants has an obvious explanation in the mounting pressure on the land caused by population growth, and undoubtedly such pressure was a major factor. But the division of holdings was at its most prevalent in the 1347 assession, when to all intents and purposes the price of the conventionary land had remained stable for fourteen years. Further, this phenomenon was not confined to manors that were maintaining their levels of revenue production. At Helston-in-Kirrier in 1347, for example, a holding of 140 acres was split into three parts for new tenants to lease, and a 120-acre holding and a 100-acre holding were each split in half. One possible

---

[1] D.C.O. 472.
[2] I.e., the right to succeed to a holding within the life of the conventionary lease.
[3] See Table 17 below, p. 226.　　　　　　　　　　　　[4] Below, pp. 235–52.

explanation of this trend is that the pressure upon conventionary lands had become so great and rents so high that there was a growing inability upon the part of many tenants to pay the rents that were currently prevailing in the land market. Such a state of affairs would force many tenants to take less land, whilst ensuring that the surplus put onto the market had a very good chance of being leased. Among the many indications of land hunger at this time the most direct is the statement made by the reeve of Tybesta that 'no chevage has been received from all others who have gone from Cornwall to England and are beggars there'.[1]

In the half-century from the first available manorial documents to the eve of the Black Death the fortunes of the assessionable manors had experienced a full cycle. The peak of the late thirteenth century had been succeeded by stagnation and a slight depression, which in turn had been succeeded by the remarkable boom of the thirteen-thirties. The Duchy inherited the Cornish estates at a most favourable time, with manorial values some 70 per cent higher than they had been in the first decade of the century, and arrears, with one exception, negligible. The overall picture was most satisfactory from the Duchy's point of view, but the level of rents and the occupation of lands depended primarily upon the level of population and the level of employment in the tin mines, and both of these variables were shortly to plunge dramatically and throw the rural economy into a state of flux.

[1] P.R.O. SC.6.816/11.

5

THE BLACK DEATH AND
AFTERMATH: 1348-1356

The Black Death struck Cornwall without warning in the early spring of 1349; the relative isolation and the scattered nature of settlement failed to secure any significant measure of immunity, and plague ravaged the length and breadth of the county.[1] As we have seen, the preceding decades had contained few indications of declining population or falling demand for land on Duchy manors; so that, with the exception of Helston-in-Kirrier, the Black Death struck at buoyant agrarian economies, and not at ones already slipping into depression.

The effects of plague upon the rural economy are explicit in each manorial account and it is possible to examine them in great detail, but assessing the scale of the mortalities is a far more difficult task. The only source from which one can attempt to compile a continuous statistical inference of death-rate is the institutions of priests to Cornish benefices of the diocese of Exeter, and institutions are a far from perfect source. Fortunately, however, the registers of the Bishops of Exeter enable almost unbroken year-by-year totals of institutions to be constructed from 1272.[2]

The numbers of institutions in the generation before 1348/9 follow no consistent trend, and the early thirteen-forties gave no indication whatsoever of the abundance of institutions that was to follow. There was an average of 4.2 institutions annually in the decade before 1349, but in the twelve months commencing March 1349 no less than 85 institutions were effected, more than twenty times the number in an average year. Table 6 below which gives the

---

[1] Thorold Rogers in 1866 conjectured that Cornwall enjoyed comparative immunity from the Black Death (*History of Agriculture and Prices in England*, 1 (Oxford, 1866), 601-2; but it has long since been realised that the extreme south-west of England suffered grievously from plague (F. A. Gasquet, *The Great Pestilence* (1893), pp. 87-91; *Reg. Grandisson*, III (1899), lxv-lxx).

[2] A graph of institutions from 1272 to 1455 is contained in Appendix E, together with a critical appraisal of their value in demographic studies.

monthly totals of institutions presents evidence which correlates with Duchy sources in placing the most intense visitation of the plague between Easter and Michaelmas 1349.

TABLE 6 *Monthly totals of institutions of priests to Cornish benefices, 1348–50*

	April	May	June	July	Aug.	Sept.	Oct.	Nov.	Dec.	Jan.	Feb.	March
1348/9	0	0	0	1	1	4	0	1	0	3	3	5
1349/50	13	12	14	13	6	9	5	4	1	2	1	0
1350	2	3	0	2								

From the manorial accounts of the Duchy we learn that John de Rill, reeve of Rillaton manor, died on 12 March 1349; William Carnek, bailiff of Helston-in-Kirrier manor, died the day before Easter (Saturday, 11 April); and Lucas Cerle had to be relieved of his duties as reeve of Liskeard late in March 'because of his extreme feebleness'. And, most conclusively, we are told that plague struck the manor of Rillaton, and by inference all Duchy manors, just before Easter 1349.[1]

The ferocity and ubiquity of pestilence in Cornwall, evident in the virtual collapse of tin-mining,[2] is also attested by the profits of the courts of Duchy manors in all parts of the county, which in 1348/9, swelled by revenues from death-duties, were from two to four times as great as those of an average year.[3] But such evidence as this can give only vague indications of the incidence of plague, for receipts from death duties depended upon the wealth and relative numbers of the free, free conventionary, and unfree tenants who perished,[4] and furthermore the surfeit of goods forfeited to lands in 1349 led to a dramatic fall in prices. We are told, for example, that the reeve of Calstock could only obtain 18d. for each ox he sold in November

[1] D.C.O. 4.
[2] Tin presented for coinage in the year ending Michaelmas 1351 totalled only 237,408 lbs, barely one-fifth of the amount presented each year from 1340/2 (below, Appendix C).
[3] D.C.O. 4.
[4] The estate of each category of tenant owed different death duties; see above, p. 63.

1349,[1] which was barely a quarter of the price ruling in preceding years.[2]

An unbroken series of ministers' accounts stretching from the outbreak of plague (1348/9) to the following assession (1355/6) enables a detailed year-by-year picture of the immediate consequences of the loss of life upon Duchy manors to be reconstructed. One immediate consequence of the pestilence was that conventionary and villein tenants throughout the Duchy manors in Cornwall refused to pay the instalments of assession fines and tallage that were due at Easter and Michaelmas 1349. The account of 1348/9 states that 'it was not possible to exact payment of the fines and tallage as the greater part of the tenants had died in the plague, whilst surviving tenants who appeared at court were so impoverished that they would relinquish their holdings if the fines and tallages were not remitted'.[3]

It appears that the decision to concur with the tenants' demands was first taken at local level by the receiver and steward of the Cornish estates, who wisely saw this measure as a far better alternative to facing a wholesale abandonment of lands. Their decision was soon ratified by the full council of the Prince, and the fines and tallage imposed upon conventionary and villein tenants at the assession of 1347 were completely written off after only two out of the 12 instalments had been paid.[4]

To facilitate the study of the years immediately following the Black Death, the Duchy manors may be divided into four groups, according to the extent to which they were disrupted and the speed and completeness of their recovery; such a division happily corresponds closely to the geographical locations of the manors.[5] Manors in the extreme south-east of Cornwall, namely Climsland, Rillaton, Calstock, and Trematon, were the least disrupted by plague;[6]

[1] D.C.O. 5.
[2] The experience of Cornish reeves was apparently typical of many other parts of England: *Chronicon Henrici Knighton*, ed. J. R. Lumby (Rolls Series, 1889–95), II, 62; Sir Roger Twysden, *Historiae Anglicanae Scriptores* X (London, 1652), col. 2699.
[3] D.C.O. 4, Rillaton.
[4] The first two instalments were presumably paid as usual at Easter and Michaelmas 1347/8, although the ministers' account for this year had not survived.
[5] See map p. XIV.
[6] Table 7, pp. 106–7, below.

but evidently not because of exceptionally light mortalities in this region; on the contrary, if one may judge from the number of heriot animals left unsold in November, an exceptionally high proportion of tenants must have died.¹ The year 1349/50, the first accounting year after the Black Death, was the least productive of rents for the Duchy and revenues from the manorial courts sank once more to normal levels. In this year on manors in all parts of the county the largest numbers of holdings and the greatest acreages of pasture lay untenanted and unproductive, although on the aforementioned south-eastern manors such vacant lands invariably accounted for only small proportions of total farmlands, even so soon after the pestilence. At Climsland only 8 out of approximately 100 conventionary and villein holdings and the pasture of Hengesdown were *in manu domini*, and almost a third of previous rents was received from herbage payments upon them. At Calstock the farm of the manor house and the ancient demesne was reduced from £4 to £2 14s. od. per annum, but only four holdings and some waste land worth little more than 20s. annually in 1347 were vacant, whilst at Trematon conditions were just a little worse, with nine holdings, worth some 10 per cent of the total rent roll of the manor *in manu domini*.²

The succeeding years brought further rapid progress towards complete recovery on these south-eastern manors; it is apparent that the initial shock of the dramatic fall in population only temporarily impeded demand for land. At Rillaton by Michaelmas 1350, and at Trematon by Michaelmas 1351, all holdings were being leased at their former annual rents on contracts lasting until the following assession, although of course no assession fines were payable. At Climsland from 1352/3 only a single holding was not leased on a permanent basis, and at Calstock only three holdings were technically *in manu domini*, although each of these realised substantial rents on yearly leases. Thus within months of the devastating mortalities of the Black Death all holdings of *terra* were fully occupied and only a

¹ At Michaelmas 1349 the reeve of Climsland had 47 animals from 40 heriots unsold, and the reeve of Calstock had 44 animals from 53 heriots (*sic*). In 1347 the manors had respectively, 95 and 86 holdings liable to render animals on their tenants' death.
² Similar analysis of the position of Rillaton manor in this year is impossible as the end of the membrane containing the account of this manor is badly rotted.

small amount of waste was vacant.[1] The remission of assession fines meant that revenues obtained by the Duchy from the lands of these manors were a third lower than those agreed in 1347.

TABLE 7   *Vacancies and decays of rent, 1350–6*

(a) *Climsland*

Approximate number of conventionary and villein holdings: 100
Annual rents: £16 1s. 11d.   Assession fines and tallage: £73
Approximate expected annual yield based on the 1347 assession:[a] £26 9s. 11d.

	Holdings in lord's hands	'Decayed rents'			Allowances granted by Duchy			Rent yield of customary lands		
		£	s.	d.	£	s.	d.	£	s.	d.
1349–50	8		1 4	7	10	8	0	14	17	4
1350–1	7		1 0	8	10	8	0	15	1	3
1351–2	3		15	10	10	8	0	15	6	2
1352–3	1		13	4	10	8	0	15	8	8
1353–4	1		13	4	10	8	0	15	8	8
1354–5	1		13	4	10	8	0	15	8	8
1355–6	1		13	4	10	8	0	15	8	8

[a] i.e. annual rents plus one seventh of total assession fines and tallage. The same calculation has been made for Calstock, Rillaton and Trematon; and Tintagel, Helstone-in-Triggshire, Liskeard, Penlyne, Tewington and Tybesta (Tables 8 and 9, below).

(b) *Calstock*

Approximate number of conventionary and villein holdings: 80
Annual rents: £18 0s. 0d.   Assession fines and tallage: £60
Approximate expected annual yield based on the 1347 assession: £26 10s. 0d.

	Holdings in lord's hands	'Decayed rents'			Allowances granted by Duchy			Rent yield of customary lands		
		£	s.	d.	£	s.	d.	£	s.	d.
1349–50	—	—			8	11	4	—		
1350–1	3		2 18	1	8	11	4	15	0	7
1351–2	3		1 16	1	8	11	4	16	2	7
1352–3	3		1 3	11	8	11	4	16	14	9
1353–4	3		1 3	11	8	11	4	16	14	9
1354–5	4		1 2	11	8	11	4	16	15	9
1355–6	3		1 3	11	8	11	4	16	14	9

[1] At Calstock 90 acres of waste produced only a few shillings from herbage. At Climsland Hengesdown pastures were worth only 8s. compared with the 16s. 8d. agreed at the assession of 1347.

The Black Death and Aftermath: 1348–56

(c) Rillaton

Approximate number of conventionary and villein holdings: 14
Annual rents: £5 2s. 9d.   Assession fines and tallage: £9 5s. 2d.
Approximate expected annual yield based on 1347 assession: £6 9s. 2d.

	Holdings in lord's hands	'Decayed rents'	Allowances granted by Duchy			Rent yield of customary lands		
			£	s.	d.	£	s.	d.
1349–50	—	—	1	5	11	—		
1350–1	nil	nil	1	5	11	5	2	9
1351–2	nil	nil	1	5	11	5	2	9
1352–3	nil	nil	1	5	11	5	2	9
1353–4	nil	nil	1	5	11	5	2	9
1354–5	nil	nil	1	5	11	5	2	9
1355–6	nil	nil	1	5	11	5	2	9

(d) Trematon

Approximate number of conventionary and villein holdings: 60
Annual rents: £20 7s. 8d.   Assession fines and tallage: £82 4s. 8d.
Approximate expected annual yield based on 1347 assession: £32 2s. 7d.

	Holdings in lord's hands	'Decayed rents'			Allowances granted by Duchy			Rent yield of customary lands		
		£	s.	d.	£	s.	d.	£	s.	d.
1349–50	9	2	6	0	11	15	0	18	1	8
1350–1	6	1	19	2	11	15	0	18	8	6
1351–2	nil		2	6	11	15	0	20	5	2
1352–3	nil	nil			11	15	0	20	7	8
1353–4	nil	nil			11	15	0	20	7	8
1354–5	nil	nil			11	15	0	20	7	8
1355–6	nil	nil			11	15	0	20	7	8

The Black Death threatened to have more serious and more lasting consequences on the manors of Helstone-in-Triggshire and Tintagel in the north-east of Cornwall, and on Tybesta and Tewington in central Cornwall. For whereas less than one in ten conventionary and villein holdings on the south-eastern manors had been listed as vacant in the account of 1349/50, on the north-eastern and central manors the proportion was twice as high. One of the factors behind this contrast may well have been the differences in the ratio of assession fines to rents between the manors in these groups.[1] On the manors of Calstock, Climsland, Trematon and Rillaton the total tallage and assession fines imposed on conventionary and villein lands in 1347 were approximately as great as four years' annual rents, whilst the assession fines and tallage on the lands of Helstone-in-Triggshire, Tintagel and Tybesta manors were barely double the annual rents, and on Tewington manor they were little more than a single year's rents. Consequently the Duchy's decision to remit assession fines and tallage led to a considerably greater reduction in the price of the customary lands of manors in south-east Cornwall; for whereas the aggregate annual charges upon the customary lands of these manors fell by more than a third, those upon the lands of Helstone-in-Triggshire, Tintagel, Tybesta, and Tewington manors fell by as little as one fifth or even less.

At a meeting of the Prince's council on 29 May 1350 it was decided to sanction further allowances to the rents of north-eastern and central manors in order to combat the widespread vacancies.[2] Against the accounts of 1349/50 the whole of the Michaelmas term's rents of the conventionary and villein tenants of Helstone-in-Triggshire manor were remitted, and 30s. 2d. allowed against those of Tybesta manor, in order to alleviate poverty and encourage tenants to remain on the land.[3] In the following year a quarter of each tenant's yearly rent was remitted upon Helstone-in-Triggshire, Tintagel, and Tybesta manors, although on Tewington only half of the rents due to be paid at the Michaelmas term was remitted, a sum equal to one sixth of the annual rent.[4] And from 1351/2 until the assession of 1356, conventionary and villein tenants on all manors in this region paid only three quarters of their former annual rents, and no assession fines.[5]

These new measures were successful in securing the continued occupation of lands that were already tenanted, and the taking up of leases to all but insignificant amounts of those lands that had remained without tenants since the pestilence. By Michaelmas 1351

---

[1] Full details of the ratio of assession fines to rents of each holding are contained in the roll of the 1347 assession: D.C.O. 472.
[2] For examples see P.R.O. SC.6.817/1, Tewington. [3] D.C.O. 5.
[4] P.R.O. SC.6.817/1. [5] P.R.O. SC.6.817/2; D.C.O. 5 ff.

there was only a single vacant holding on these four manors compared with the 51 which had been vacant in 1349/50, and henceforth the 'decays of rents' on Tintagel, Tybesta and Tewington were to consist solely of the statutory allowances to rents and assession fines sanctioned by the Duchy administration.

Nevertheless, despite the decline in vacant holdings, the revenues obtained by the Duchy from the conventionary and villein lands of manors in central and north-east Cornwall did not rise, for on each manor the 25 per cent reduction in the rents represented a greater sum than the loss of revenues from the holdings that had been vacant. But the wisdom of the policies of the Duchy should not be judged on this evidence alone, for no further holdings were surrendered, and it was the immediate threat of a large-scale movement to throw holdings into the lord's hands that had been one of the major factors prompting the Duchy to take the action they did.[1] The loss of revenue from vacant holdings was a serious problem, but even more serious was the rapid deterioration of both land and buildings during prolonged vacancies and the considerable capital expenditure needed to render them suitable for farming again.[2]

TABLE 8   *Vacancies and decays of rent, 1350–6*

(a) *Tintagel*

Approximate number of conventionary and villein holdings: 50
Annual rents: £23   Assession fines and tallage: £42
Approximate expected annual yield based on the 1347 assession: £29

	Holdings in lord's hands	'Decayed rents'			Allowances granted by Duchy			Rent yield of customary lands		
		£	s.	d.	£	s.	d.	£	s.	d.
1349–50	10	4	15	7	6	0	1	18	4	4
1350–1	nil		6	8	10	18	2	17	15	2
1351–2	nil		nil		12	2	1	16	18	11
1352–3	nil		nil		12	5	3	16	15	9
1353–4	nil		nil		12	5	3	16	15	9
1354–5	nil		nil		12	5	3	16	15	9
1355–6	nil		nil		12	5	3	16	15	9

[1] Most allowances are accompanied by an explanation which invariably refers to the poverty of the tenants and the need to assist them to remain on their holdings.
[2] Greater allowances of annual rents and assession fines had to be granted to tenants who leased holdings which had been vacant for a number of years.

(b) Helstone-in-Triggshire

Approximate number of conventionary and villein holdings: 100
Annual rents: £37 10s. od. Assession fines and tallage: £66
Approximate expected annual yield based on the 1347 assession: £45

	Holdings in lord's hands	'Decayed rents'			Allowances granted by Duchy			Rent yield of customary lands		
		£	s.	d.	£	s.	d.	£	s.	d.
1349–50	17	5	11	5	16	4	1	23	4	6
1350–1	13	5	16	1	16	8	4	23	15	7
1351–2	1		—		17	8	11		—	
1352–3	1	18	8		16	15	10	27	5	6
1353–4	1	18	8		16	15	10	27	5	6
1354–5	1	18	8		16	15	10	27	5	6
1355–6	1	18	8		16	15	10	27	5	6

(c) Tewington

Approximate number of conventionary and villein holdings: 65
Annual rents: approx. £23 10s. od. Assession fines and tallage: £32
Approximate expected annual yield based on 1347 assession: £28

	Holdings in lord's hands	'Decayed rents'			Allowances granted by Duchy			Rent yield of customary lands		
		£	s.	d.	£	s.	d.	£	s.	d.
1349–50	16	5	19	9	4	10	10	17	10	5
1350–1	16	6	7	10	8	7	10	13	4	4
1351–2	nil	1	1	4	10	15	10	16	1	10
1352–3	nil	13	4		10	14	7	16	12	1
1353–4	nil	13	4		10	14	7	16	12	1
1354–5	nil	13	4		10	14	7	16	12	1
1355–6	nil	13	4		10	14	7	16	12	1

(d) Tybesta

Approximate number of conventionary and villein holdings: 55
Annual rents: £23 10s. od. Assession fines and tallage: £55
Approximate expected annual yield based on 1347 assession: £31 6s. od.

	Holdings in lord's hands	'Decayed rents'			Allowances granted by Duchy			Rent yield of customary lands		
		£	s.	d.	£	s.	d.	£	s.	d.
1349–50	8	4	1	6	9	7	8	17	11	8
1350–1	7	4	4	6	12	17	5	14	5	1
1351–2	nil	3	0		13	4	5	17	18	7
1352–3	nil	1	0		13	3	5	18	2	7
1353–4	nil	1	0		13	3	5	18	2	7
1354–5	nil	1	0		13	3	5	18	2	7
1355–6	nil	1	0		13	3	5	18	2	7

The Black Death and Aftermath: 1348–56

In the west of the county both Moresk and Tywarnhaile manors appear to have suffered particularly severe set-backs after the plague struck them in 1349, and by April 1350 Moresk had 23 holdings *in manu domini* out of a total of no more than 50 holdings on the manor.[1] The Duchy, however, absolved itself from responsibility and in April 1350 Moresk and Tywarnhaile, together with the small north-eastern manor of Penmayne, were granted to Walter de Wodeland,[2] to enjoy for the life of himself and his heirs during the Prince's own life, in lieu of an annuity of 100 marks.[3] The grant was limited to the life of the Prince, presumably so as not to break the terms of the Great Charter of the Duchy.[4] Considering that the average annual profits the Duchy had obtained from these three manors in the decade before the Black Death had been little more than 100 marks, Walter does not seem to have received a generous exchange. When these manors returned to the Duchy on the death of Walter in 1370, however, they were worth about £70 annually.[5]

In view of the chronic problems of Helston-in-Kirrier, the most westerly of the assessionable manors, in the decade before 1349 it was to be expected that this manor would have been subjected to considerable disruption by the Black Death,[6] but the catastrophic decline in the demand for land, no doubt intensified by the slump in mining which followed the mortality, would have confounded even the most pessimistic of prognostications. In the year of the plague £46 9s. 4½d. was allowed against a total manorial charge of £109 14s. 9½d. for vacant holdings, for reductions in the farms of the manorial mills, and for tenants defaulting in their rent payments.[7] In the following year (1349/50) we are told that 66 holdings, out of a total of approximately 100 on the manor, were in the hands of the lord, and rents totalling £28 2s. 7d. were lost from this source alone, with a further £7 16s. 0½d. conceded to certain poor tenants by the

---

[1] D.C.O. 5.
[2] Walter de Wodeland was a trusted member of the household of Prince Edward; he was often sold marriages and wardships which had accrued to the Duchy (*B.P.R.* II, 2, 27, 47, 186). He also appears as a witness to a number of council proceedings (*ibid.* pp. 64, 71), and he held a number of other manors in Cornwall (*ibid.* p. 87).
[3] D.C.O. 5. Moresk; Cornwall C.R.O. MTD 31/1, m. BBB; *B.P.R.* II, 50.
[4] Above, p. 6.
[5] P.R.O. SC.6.816/1, 816/2.
[6] Above, pp. 93–7.   [7] D.C.O. 4.

auditors.[1] Thus, over half of the total charge upon customary lands was lost in this year. At Michaelmas 1350 well over half of the total area of the manor, probably amounting to almost 3,000 acres, was lying idle and of no value at all to the Duchy,[2] and persistent arrears were a cause of great concern.[3]

As Helston-in-Kirrier was so badly afflicted the administration of the Duchy decided to reduce all the landed annual rents of the manor by a third, with the exception of the freeholdings, and furthermore the auditors were given discretionary powers to allow additional relief to be given to individual tenants when it was needed.[4] The Duchy steward of the Cornish estates visited Helston-in-Kirrier before the start of the new accounting year in Michaelmas 1352 in an attempt to apply the Duchy policy of concessions with more success than it had hitherto achieved, and by leasing some of the plethora of vacant holdings to secure a more acceptable level of revenue.[5] Armed with far greater powers than the bailiff ever aspired to possess and no doubt some excellent salesmanship, the steward succeeded in leasing many of the vacant holdings at half their former annual rents, and some at even two thirds rents; furthermore in a general rationalisation, much vacant land that had little chance of being leased by itself was put into the 'manorial chase', thus boosting the value of this perquisite.[6] In the following year the acreage lying in the lord's hands fell even further,[7] and subsequent years continued to show modest increases in the area of land under cultivation and in rent receipts.[8]

It was decided that the general condonation of assessment fines and tallage on the small manors of Penlyne, Penkneth, and Restormel clustered around the borough of Lostwithiel, and the extensive manor of Liskeard, some 12 miles to the east of the same borough, was sufficient and that no further reductions should be made. The

---

[1] D.C.O. 5.   [2] P.R.O. SC.6.817/1.
[3] The auditors in 1350 were instructed to 'find the cause of the arrears of £62 9s. od.' (above, p. 47).
[4] P.R.O. SC.6.817/1.   [5] P.R.O. SC.6.817/3.
[6] The manorial chase was a collection of rough pasture lands leased to a single tenant, who may well have sub-let to other tenants. With the additional lands put into the chase by the steward, the farm of the chase and toll-tin rights rose from 7s. in 1351/2 to 40s. in 1352/3.
[7] P.R.O. SC.6.817/4.   [8] See Appendix A, Fig. 13.

initial impact of the Black Death had caused considerable areas of these manors to be left vacant, and the account of 1349/50 lists more than a third of the customary lands of Restormel manor and more than a quarter of those of Penlyne and Liskeard as being in the lord's hands.[1] Both Restormel and Penkneth progressed rapidly in subsequent years towards a full occupation of all holdings, but a very substantial proportion of vacancies persisted on both Liskeard and Penlyne manors.[2] The conventionary and villein lands of Liskeard, like those of the other eastern Cornish manors discussed earlier, had a high ratio of total assession fines and tallage to annual rents, and in the assession of 1347 conventionary and villein rents had totalled a little over £26 and assession fines and tallage more than £106.[3] The condonation of the assession fines in 1349 thus had the overall effect of reducing substantially the price of the customary lands; nevertheless 10 holdings, some 12 per cent of the total, remained *in manu domini* from the time of the pestilence until the assession of 1356, producing only a small portion of their former rents from the annual sale of herbage rights upon them.[4] The

TABLE 9   *Vacancies and decays of rent, 1350–6*

(a) *Liskeard*
Approximate number of conventionary and villein holdings: 80
Annual rents: £26   Assession fines and tallage: £105
Approximate expected annual yield based on 1347 assession: £41

	Holdings in lord's hands	'Decayed rents'			Allowances granted by Duchy			Rent yield of customary lands		
		£	s.	d.	£	s.	d.	£	s.	d.
1349–50	19	8	0	4	15	0	0	17	19	8
1350–1	16	8	0	7	15	0	0	17	19	5
1351–2	12	5	18	6	15	0	0	20	1	6
1352–3	12	5	18	8	15	0	0	20	1	4
1353–4	10	4	16	8	15	0	0	21	3	4
1354–5	10	5	5	3	15	0	0	20	14	9
1355–6	10	4	12	6	15	0	0	21	7	6

[1] D.C.O. 5.   [2] Table 9.   [3] D.C.O. 472.
[4] See, for example, the account of 1356, the last year before the new assession took effect: transcript of account of 29/30 Edward III, D.C.O. Library.

(b) *Penlyne*

Approximate number of conventionary and villein holdings: 22

Annual rents: £6 3s. 7d.   Assession fines and tallage: £30 4s. 10d.

Approximate expected annual yield based on 1347 assession: £6 12s. 10d.

	Holdings in lord's hands	'Decayed rents'			Allowances granted by Duchy		Rent yield of customary lands		
		£	s.	d.	s.	d.	£	s.	d.
1349–50	5	—			9	3	—		
1350–1	8	1	1	7	13	7	4	17	11
1351–2	6		14	2	9	3	5	9	5
1352–3	6		13	2	9	3	5	10	5
1353–4	6		13	2	9	3	5	10	5
1354–5	6		13	2	9	3	5	10	5
1355–6	6		13	2	9	3	5	10	5

slackness of the demand for these holdings was to some extent the result of peculiar local conditions of which some explanation can be given.

The remission of assession fines and tallage on Liskeard, as on all manors, did not produce an exactly proportionate reduction in the prices of all holdings, for some had greater assession fines relative to rents than did others. The absence of assession fines could lead to a complete reversal of previous valuations, as can be seen from the following examples taken from Trematon manor.[1]

A messuage and 14 acres in Wadsworth — annual rent 4s. — assession fine 30s. annual charge 8s. 3d.[2]

A messuage and 15 acres in Worflenton — annual rent 5s. — assession fine 15s. annual charge 7s. 2d.

A messuage and 16 acres in Stoke — annual rent 5s. — assession fine 18s. 4d. annual charge 7s. 7d.

A messuage and 15 acres in Boraton — annual rent 5s. — assession fine 30s. annual charge 9s. 3d.

Thus, whilst in 1347 the holding in Wadsworth was considered to be worth more than those in Worflenton or Stoke, after the remission of assession fines it was charged with less rent than either

[1] D.C.O. 472. Further examples can be found in Appendix B.

[2] Annual charge = annual rent plus ⅐ of assession fine.

of them. The most expensive of the four holdings in 1347, the messuage and 15 acres in Boraton, was charged with the same rent as the holdings in Worflenton and Stoke from 1349 to 1356. For the most part it was the lands which had the highest ratio of assessment fines to rents that were the most in demand, and consequently most expensive. The average holding on Liskeard manor after the assession of 1347 had an assession fine approximately four to five times as great as the annual rent upon it. On each of the eight holdings listed in the following table which remained *in manu domini* until the assession of 1356, the ratio of assession fines to rents was substantially below average. Consequently the remission of assession fines reduced the annual charge of these holdings by proportionately lesser amounts than those of most other holdings on the manor.

TABLE 10 *Conventionary lands* in manu domini *on Liskeard manor 1349–56*[a]

Holding	Assession fine			Annual rent			Annual charge pre-1349		
	£	s.	d.	£	s.	d.	£	s.	d.
A messuage and 33 acres in Doubleboys	1	3	4		8	0		11	4
A messuage 32 acres Doubleboys	1	3	4		8	0		11	4
A messuage 42 acres in Doubleboys	1	10	0		10	0		14	3
1 messuage 42 acres Doubleboys	1	6	8		10	0		13	10
1 messuage 42 acres Doubleboys	1	5	0		10	0		13	7
1 messuage 40 acres Looden		8	0		8	5		9	7
1 messuage 30 acres Cremabit		16	8		10	6		12	11
1 messuage 13 acres Penquyt	1	3	0	1	0	0	1	3	3

[a] This table is based upon the 1347 assession roll (D.C.O. 47) and subsequent ministers' accounts.

Doubleboys contained some difficult farming country to the west of Liskeard, and was probably most useful as pasture.[1] The five holdings in Doubleboys were to spend long periods in the lord's hands in the ensuing years of the middle ages, despite a general rise

[1] We know it was used as pasture in 1435 (P.R.O. SC.2.159/6, court held at Liskeard, 18 February).

E

in the demand for land on Liskeard.[1] The lands of Looden were waste, whilst the holding in Penquyt was grossly overvalued at an annual rent of 20s., as the corn mill that belonged to the holding had fallen into complete decay, and in the assession of 1356 the rent of this holding was reduced to 4s.[2]

The land that was difficult or impossible to lease after the pestilence, was almost without exception the land that had previously been leased for below-average rents which was in turn invariably waste and poorest quality *terra*. There was an abundance of pasture after the pestilence: fewer people were seeking land, and good quality herbage and pasture was usually obtainable at cheap rates on the holdings of *terra* that were left unleased. Furthermore farmers may well have been forced to leave untilled a greater proportion of their own holdings than they had been accustomed to, owing to the shortage and increased cost of labour, and would thus have needed to rent less. The abundance of grazing land was reflected in the low level of profits from the sales of agistment in Duchy deer-parks in the decade after the plague.[3]

The policies initiated by the Duchy in 1349 to deal with the unprecedented crises caused by the Great Plague were remarkable both in their wisdom and their foresight. Dramatic falls in revenues from the manors were not met by reactionary measures seeking to enforce contracts made in times far more favourable to landlords, nor by vain attempts to recreate by legislation the conditions that had prevailed before the Black Death; instead the Duchy introduced a plan of action which showed a comprehensive understanding of the economic and social factors involved in the problems it faced. Not only was it fully realised that the value of land had fallen sharply, but also the initiative was taken by the Duchy to reduce rents in an attempt to bring them into line with the new levels of demand and help to ensure that vacant lands were leased, thereby avoiding the loss of revenues, the wastage and depreciation of resources, and the

[1] Below, Appendix B, Table 23.
[2] Two copies of the proceedings of the 1351 assession exist: D.C.O. 472 and P.R.O. E.306/2/1.
[3] Below, pp. 182–3.

misery caused to small landholders when the price of land was left at unrealistically high levels for long after population had fallen. Furthermore, when it was appreciated that the remission of assession fines alone was going to prove insufficient to effect a complete refilling of the vacant holdings on all manors, it was decided, just twelve months after the first serious outbreak of plague, to reduce annual rents in proportion to the requirements of individual manors.

The central administration saw the necessity of acting swiftly and of being kept fully informed of the conditions prevailing on the local estates. The auditors were sent down to Cornwall in February 1350 to conduct an exhaustive enquiry into the conditions of the estates and to take appropriate action,[1] and on 11 December 1351 many local officials, including the steward, the receiver and the auditors of the Cornish estates, were summoned to appear before the council at London to report on the state of their bailiwicks.[2] Furthermore in the Trinity term of 1354 the steward was called upon to report to the Royal Exchequer and account for the 'decays' in the revenues from his county.[3] The local officials of the Duchy must have been extremely busy in the hectic years after the plague; lands had to be leased, decreases in rents and farms assessed and ratified, and a multitude of claims for allowances investigated. But despite all the pressures of the vast numbers of additional tasks thrown upon it in these years the administration never allowed disruption to degenerate into chaos.

The falls in the rent levels of conventionary and villein lands were paralleled by trends in receipts from most other manorial properties. Sales of turbary and receipts from toll-tin slumped dramatically and revenues from sales of herbage and pasture in deer-parks dropped significantly. Immediately the pestilence struck the Cornish manors allowances and reductions were made to the farms of manorial mills held by lease and not freehold.[4] Farmers could not be expected to pay the full farms when the ranks of the tenants owing suit had been so seriously depleted, and furthermore the remission of assession

---

[1] County Museum, Truro: transcript of Mt Edgecumbe White Book, pp. 15–17.
[2] *B.P.R.* III, 54.   [3] P.R.O. E.368/126.   [4] D.C.O. 4 ff.; P.R.O. SC.6.817/1 ff.

fines made very little difference to the annual farm as the fines were invariably small. Some mills persisted in the lord's hands after the pestilence and could not be leased,[1] others were leased only when their farms had been slashed by half[2] or even more,[3] and in certain cases the Duchy undertook for the first time to meet repair costs.[4] The failure of the majority of farms in the decade after the Black Death to regain anything approaching their former levels, even when situated upon manors whose lands were soon fully reoccupied, suggests there may well have been some relaxation in the enforcement of suit, although owing to the lack of court-rolls at this time any explanation must remain largely a matter of speculation.

As might be expected in these troubled times, the state of repair of manorial mills declined rapidly, and the frequent changes in lessees may often have resulted in a mill being relinquished in a state of advanced disrepair, thus perpetuating and encouraging the tendency towards lower farms. Heavy and constant capital expenditure was needed to keep mills in a good state of repair, and in a short space of time a neglected mill might become completely unworkable. At Restormel after the manorial corn mill had remained vacant for at least three years it was rebuilt by the Duchy at a cost of 55s. 5d.,[5] the two corn mills at Camelford and Kenstock were completely reconstructed in 1356 at a cost to the Duchy of £10 6s. 1d.,[6] and 21s. 5d. had to be spent on repairs to the mill of Polscoth at Penlyne before it was leased to John de Purlee.[7] But the Duchy did not always consider it judicious to reconstruct mills, and after an estimate on the cost of rebuilding the ruined mill of Penquyt on Liskeard manor had been submitted to the Prince's council it was decided that it would be unwise to proceed.[8]

The total profits yielded by the assessionable manors in 1348/9 were barely 25 per cent lower than those of an average year of the early thirteen-forties, being cushioned by inordinately high receipts

---

[1] For example, the mills of Restormel and Penlyne. In addition the corn mills of the borough of Lostwithiel were left *in manu domini*.
[2] *Ibid.* Calstock, Trematon, Tewington. [3] *Ibid.* Helston-in-Kirrier
[4] *Ibid.* Calstock, Helstone-in-Triggshire. [5] P.R.O. SC.6.817/3.
[6] Transcript of account of 29–30 Edward III, D.C.O. Library.
[7] P.R.O. SC.6.812/7; *B.P.R.* II, 100.
[8] *B.P.R.* II, 74; this mill was never rebuilt in the later middle ages.

from the manorial courts. But the following year saw a further sharp fall and in 1350/1 the deepest point in the depression was reached when profits slumped to £375, some 40 per cent lower than those of 1347. Subsequent years brought a progressive recovery with £75 added to the profits by 1354/5. Insolvency did not persist for long, and after initial disruption to the system of revenue collection from 1348 to 1350, when substantial portions of the manorial charges did not reach the receiver,[1] finances were once again restored to an even keel. By 1350/1 very few traces of indebtedness were in evidence, and the series of receivers' accounts which run from 1351 to 1357 show that reeves were settling their annual accounts almost in full and that large-scale arrears were almost non-existent. Serious indebtedness on the assessionable manors, like the severe contraction of the area of land under cultivation, was of very short duration, and once again the efficiency of the Duchy administration had played a major part in this achievement.

Favoured by cheap rents the ranks of the tenantry had remarkably few gaps within a year or two of the Black Death. This swift reoccupation of what must have been a multitude of holdings made vacant by plague could be accounted for in three ways: first and probably most of all, by the existence of a substantial body of landless persons living on the manors before 1348/9; secondly, by a migration of persons seeking land from other areas and other occupations; and finally, by surviving tenants taking more land. As we have seen, much evidence points towards Cornwall having experienced considerable population pressure in the 1330s and 1340s. The rapid rise in rents and the splitting of holdings suggests the presence of a large body of landless on Duchy manors at this time, as indeed do the lists of contributors to the royal subsidy of 1327 which include the names of many persons who lived on the assessionable manors but apparently did not hold land there.[2] As the majority of tenants who leased land in 1356 had unfamiliar names, and only 10–25 per cent of holdings remained in the same

---

[1] The amounts paid over by the reeves in these years are contained at the foot of each manor's account.
[2] Compare P.R.O. E.179/87/7 and 87/37 with P.R.O. E.142/41; see also below, p. 219.

hands as 1347, the implication is that vacant holdings were filled more by persons who do not seem to have leased land from the Duchy before than by tenants enlarging their farms or by inheritance.[1]

A high degree of mobility in Cornwall at this time seems likely. The scale of migration from industrial occupations into agriculture should not be underestimated, indeed the failure of tin production in the thirteen-fifties to attain more than 40 per cent of the levels achieved in the thirteen-forties in the face of an almost 100 per cent occupation of the land may well reflect the results of a large-scale migration from mining into farming; with landholding or even farm labouring appealing far more than the arduous and dangerous life of the miner.[2] The mortalities of 1349 may well have stretched the resources of many of conventionary and villein tenants to the full. A great deal of attention is devoted in Duchy records after the plague to the impoverished condition of the bulk of tenants, and both the remission of assession fines and reduction of rents were apparently based upon the need to give financial assistance to tenants who were so poor that they might otherwise have been forced to flee from their holdings. The duties exacted by the Duchy on the deaths of tenants must have placed a crushing burden upon many families. The death of a free conventionary tenant required the payment of his best beast as heriot, and possibly also his second best beast as mortuary to the Church; in addition his successor was required to pay a small sum of money for acknowledgement. Unfree tenants owed the whole of their goods and possessions to the Duchy on death, and even if in practice only two thirds were forfeited, and these normally resold to his family at prices well below their true value, the effect upon his household could well have been ruinous. Furthermore even those families which escaped the

---

[1] See Table 17, pp. 226–8, below.

[2] Throughout the medieval and early modern periods, tin-mining appears to have been able to attract labour easily only in times of large surplus population. Wages paid by the Crown, both in the late thirteenth century and in the late fifteenth century, for work in Devon silver mines were almost identical to those paid by the Duchy for work of an inestimably more congenial nature on buildings or in parks: Salzman, 'Mines and Stannaries', pp. 71–3; Lewis, *Stannaries*, pp. 194–7. See also Lewis, *op cit.* pp. 216–17 for an account of the appalling working conditions in the stannaries in the late sixteenth century.

plague, protected perhaps by the scattered nature of the settlement on the assessionable manors, may well have had their farming routine severely impeded.

Some analysis of the whole course of the Cornish rural economy in the later fourteenth century is contained in the following chapter;[1] nevertheless it is apposite at this point to make some preliminary attempt to explain the attractions of tenant farming in the thirteen-fifties, for the tenurial structure of the assessionable manors left little scope for the Duchy to compel persons to take land against their will. Cornish farmers in the years immediately following the Black Death faced a number of serious problems, of which the shortage and high cost of labour was perhaps the most important.[2] The farmers of all except the smallest holdings, if they practised arable husbandry, would have had to employ some labour at the busiest times of the farming year, but the average holding at this time was not large enough to have required much regular hired labour.[3] To compensate for labour problems, the thirteen-fifties may well have been a decade of high agricultural prices,[4] and with rents at levels almost a third lower than they had been before 1348/9, one must doubt whether tenant farming was much less attractive as long as farmers had been left with sufficient capital to practise it efficiently.

[1] Below, pp. 139–47.
[2] According to Duchy records the cost of unskilled labour rose from 1½d. to 2d. in the 1350s, and the actual rise may well have been greater (Appendix D below). The stannaries experienced a desperate shortage of labour and the Justices of Labourers visited Cornwall at least twice in the late 1350s.
[3] Below, pp. 226–9.
[4] See for example M. M. Postan, 'Some Economic Evidence of Declining Population in the Later Middle Ages', *Ec. H.R.*, 2nd ser., II (1950), 226; E. H. Phelps Brown and S. V. Hopkins, 'Seven Centuries of the Price of Consumables compared with Builders' Wage-Rates', *Economica*, new. ser., XXIII (1956). For the demand for foodstuffs in late fourteenth-century Cornwall, see below, pp. 146–7.

6

THE LATER FOURTEENTH
CENTURY: 1356–1399

A cataclysmic picture of the effects of the Black Death upon the rural economy of England is no longer acceptable, yet the speed and completeness of the recovery of many Cornish manors from the mortality was perhaps unusual; by the mid-thirteen-fifties few traces of the ravages of plague were in evidence.[1] With the exception of Helston-in-Kirrier, the only far western manor whose fortunes we can trace at this time,[2] scarcely a handful of holdings were vacant, and furthermore by 1356 it appears that the remission of assession fines and tallage and the reductions in rents granted by the Duchy in 1349/50 had become progressively over-generous. The conventionary leases enacted in 1347 should have expired at Michaelmas 1354, but they were allowed to persist until it was finally decided that an assession should be held in the spring of 1356, with new leases taking effect the following Michaelmas.[3] At the assession on manors throughout Cornwall the rents of conventionary lands rose substantially and frequently regained pre-plague levels.

It is apparent that the remission of assession fines and tallage had given the tenants of Rillaton, Climsland, Calstock, and Trematon manors in south-east Cornwall a number of years of privileged tenure at rents appreciably less than they would have been willing to pay in more competitive circumstances, for almost without exception the conventionary and villein lands of these manors were taken at the assession of 1356 on the same terms as had prevailed nine years earlier in 1347. What is more, on a few holdings assession

---

[1] See the graphs of manorial profits (Chapter 8, pp. 201–17, below) and of aggregate rents (Appendix A, pp. 262–6, below); see also Appendix B (pp. 278–87, below) for the rents of individual conventionary holdings.
[2] The two other western manors of the Duchy, Moresk and Tywarnhaile, had been granted to Walter de Wodeland (above, p. 111).
[3] *B.P.R.* II, 91. For the enrolments of this assession see D.C.O. 472; P.R.O. E. 306/2/1.

fines were raised to new peaks, as for example the three holdings leased by William Fraunceys at Rillaton, for which he paid a fine of 20s., double that imposed in 1347. Almost all the available land on these south-eastern manors was leased in 1356, although a few of the less attractive holdings and areas of waste at Climsland and Calstock required reductions in their rents before they were taken. By Michaelmas 1356 only a single holding at Climsland and four holdings at Calstock remained vacant, and even these subsequently realised some revenues from herbage payments.[1] Demand was very slack, however, for 180 acres of waste at Calstock, and only 4s. 10d. was received from payment for herbage, although it had been worth more than 20s. annually in 1347/8.

The lands which proved difficult to lease at the assession of 1356 in south-east Cornwall comprised only a tiny proportion of the total, and they did little to retard the general advance of Duchy rent receipts, which in the years when the instalments of assession fines were paid were as high, or even higher, than they had been after the assession of 1347 before the population of the county had been decimated by plague.

A similar spectacular recovery in the value of conventionary leases was negotiated in the spring of 1356 on Duchy manors in central Cornwall, including Tybesta, Tewington, and the smaller manors of Restormel, Penlyne, and Penkneth. At Tewington and Restormel all available lands were leased with the same annual rents and assession fines as had prevailed in 1347, whilst at Penlyne and Penkneth the greater part of the conventionary lands were taken with only an occasional lowering of fines. At Tybesta the assession resulted in about two thirds of the conventionary holdings being taken on the same terms as in 1347, whilst the remainder were leased with reduced assession fines. When a reduction was negotiated it was for the most part of less than 20 per cent, although on poorer lands and waste lands especially those that had remained

---

[1] Land which was not leased at assessions, usually held in the spring before the Michaelmas at which leases were to take effect, was kept open to offers. Frequently such land was leased at former annual rents and assession fines between the assession and the start of the new term; but often it was leased on a year to year basis for a rent only—no assession fines being payable. Alternatively the reeve might only be able to raise a portion of its former rent from herbage payments.

in manu domini since the Black Death, fines had often to be completely wiped out before land could be leased.

On these manors in central Cornwall, as on those in the south-east, only negligible amounts of land were left untaken at the assession; namely three holdings and six acres of waste at Tybesta and three holdings at Penlyne, and by Michaelmas 1356, the start of the seven-year term, two of Tybesta's vacant holdings had been leased for the full term at their former rents, and two of the vacant holdings of Penlyne were realising their former annual rents on a year to year basis, although no assession fines were being paid. As the majority of the conventionary lands in this group of manors were leased on the same terms as had been agreed in 1347 and no lands were altogether valueless, the aggregate totals of annual rents and assession fines based on the assession of 1356 were only marginally below those based on the assession held nine years earlier.

At the assession of 1356 held at Tintagel in north-east Cornwall all conventionary and villein land was leased at full rents, which compared favourably with the assession of 1347 when six holdings and the pastures of Godolghan had been left vacant. In contrast on the neighbouring manor of Helstone-in-Triggshire and on Liskeard manor, which lay to the south of Bodmin moor, many assession fines were lowered. The majority of holdings at Helstone were demised by the Duchy assessioners with fines some 20 per cent below those of 1347, and a few could command no assession fines at all; nevertheless all available land was leased. On Duchy manors throughout the county the value of waste invariably fell more sharply than that of *terra*, and Helstone-in-Triggshire was no exception; here, for example, Nicholas Kernek leased four separate areas of waste amounting to 138 acres upon which no assession fine at all was levied 'because it is waste and unfit, and because it was in the lord's hands at the time of the pestilence'.[1] At Liskeard 27 out of the 84 conventionary holdings leased in 1356 commanded lower assession fines than they had in 1347, with once again the most drastic reductions reserved for lands which had remained vacant or on temporary leases since 1348/9. Furthermore four holdings were not leased and, together with some small areas of vacant waste

[1] D.C.O. 472.

land, they produced only a small portion of their former rents from sales of herbage.

The reductions in assession fines and the small areas of land not leased on a permanent basis were sufficient to keep the aggregate rent receipts from Helstone-in-Triggshire and Liskeard somewhat below the levels of 1347/8; but as can be seen from the graphs in Appendix B the assession of 1356 marked a massive recovery from the depths to which receipts had plunged immediately after the plague.

Helston-in-Kirrier manor, after the granting of Moresk and Tywarnhaile to Walter de Wodeland in 1350, was the only representative of the western regions of Cornwall under the direct administration of the Duchy. To a manor faltering before 1349 the Black Death had inflicted the most grievous wounds, but some measure of recovery was in evidence before the spring of 1356. Although the valuations agreed between tenants and the officials of the assession were almost without exception substantially below those that had been agreed for the same lands in 1347, they were nevertheless generally well in advance of the land values which had prevailed in the seven years after the Black Death, when one third of the annual rents and the whole of the assession fines had been remitted. It was exceptional at Helston-in-Kirrier in 1356 if a holding was burdened with an assession fine, but a small number of holdings of good quality land did command fines, some of which were even as high as they had been in 1347. A further indication of the deeply depressed conditions prevailing on this manor was the quantity of land left in the lord's hands after the assession, which was so great that it was divided by the assessioners into two categories: the first comprising lands which had been leased at the assession of Edmund of Kendale in 1347 and left vacant at the present assession, and the second comprising lands leased at the assession of Jacob of Woodstock in 1340 and not since. Together these two categories accounted for almost 2,000 acres, or some 40 per cent of the total area of the manor in conventionary and villein tenure. An analysis based upon area alone can, however, be misleading for the value of the vacant land amounted to considerably less than 40 per cent of the total rent roll of the manor, as the land *in manu domini* was invariably of the poorer sort which when leased had commanded lower rents than the land which continued to be occupied. Some of this vacant land realised a little from herbage payments in the years after the assession, but much remained completely valueless, except for the small increment it may have added to the farm of the manorial chase with which it was often grouped. Nevertheless, overall the assession of 1356 at Helston-in-Kirrier was a qualified success for the Duchy administration, and from an average of £35 per annum between 1353 and 1356 the charge upon conventionary lands rose to an average of £55 annually between 1359 and 1362, although of course it was still much below the peak based upon the assession of 1333.

The assession of 1356 thus demonstrated clearly the strength of the recovery of demand for land throughout Cornwall within seven years of the Black Death. A large number of holdings were leased at the rents which had obtained before the plague, and many more at rents only slightly lower; furthermore, with the solitary exception of Helston-in-Kirrier, none of the assessionable manors had more than a handful of vacant holdings, and scarcely any land was completely valueless to the Duchy. The rents of some assessionable lands may, however, have been set too high in 1356, for soon after the assession had been completed the conventionary tenants of Climsland, Calstock, Rillaton, Trematon, and Helston-in-Kirrier petitioned the Prince and his council complaining that 'the auditors, steward, and receiver [i.e. the officials of the assession] had compelled them to take their lands at higher rents and farms than they had been wont to pay, on pain of being utterly removed from the lands and their houses'.[1] What this petition really tells us of demand conditions in these years is rather obscure. The tenants had agreed to take the lands on the terms put forward by the assessioners in 1356 as they were afraid of being dispossessed, but 'because of the many disasters and losses they had suffered in a short time to their crops and animals' they claimed yet again that 'they must needs leave the prince's lands and become beggars unless the prince will be pleased to mitigate their fines'. Although the evidence of subsequent assessions does not suggest that conventionary tenants were being asked

[1] *B.P.R.* II, 117.

to pay too much for their lands in 1356, during the Black Prince's tenure of the Duchy of Cornwall such petitions and pleas for aid from his 'poor tenants' usually met with a favourable reception. Accordingly it was decided that an enquiry should be held into circumstances surrounding the 1356 assession on the south-eastern manors and upon Helston-in-Kirrier; furthermore, with the intention of creating conditions 'wherein the said tenants could hold and enjoy the lands they had taken without being ruined', the receiver was instructed to allow 'delay and respite' of payments of assession fines. It is probable that the Prince received further petitions of a similar nature from the tenants of other assessionable manors for 'in consideration of the hard times there have been of late in Cornwall' he subsequently pardoned all his conventionary and villein tenants the instalments of their assession fines and tallage for the whole of the year ending Michaelmas 1357.[1] It was not the Prince's intention, however, that the holders of life tenancies should also have their fines pardoned, for life tenancies were rightly considered to be preferable to the seven-year contract of the conventionary tenant, if the enhanced payments due in the first three years of tenure could be met.[2]

It would be unjust to see mere self-interest behind the many acts of kindness and mercy rendered on behalf of the Black Prince to his 'poor tenants'. One has only to skim the pages of his council registers to discover that his estates were often governed with a degree of benevolence that far exceeded the feudal obligations of a lord to his tenants, and with a spirit of charity pitifully wanting in the administration of many ecclesiastical estates at this time.[3]

---

[1] *B.P.R.* II, 133. This order promulgated by the council refers only to conventionary tenants, but in fact villeins were also excused from paying their instalments of tallage (P.R.O. SC.6.817/5; D.C.O. 11).

[2] Fines three times as great as the assession fines for a seven-year lease were sometimes made payable over the first three years of a life tenancy.

[3] See, for example, in the early months of the first year of his Cornish register (*B.P.R.* II)—*p. 8*: The receiver is ordered to 'deal equitably and rightly' with 'the prince's tenants' in a matter concerning disputed payments. *p. 9*: The Prince takes the side of his tenants to protect them from 'many oppressions and extortions' committed against them in the name of the Archdeacon of Cornwall. *p. 18*: A directive that the 'poor persons' who have 'concealed tin beyond the time when it ought to have been coined', but 'who would be injured too much by the forfeiture thereof' should instead make 'such suitable fines as they can bear'. *p. 22*: the Prince orders that a petitioner, Reynold

The magnanimity with which the Prince conducted his affairs is all the more laudable in view of the desperate impecunity that dogged him for most of his life.[1]

After the initial remission of assession fines and tallage for Michaelmas 1356/7 the full amounts were paid for all conventionary and villein lands until 1361/2, and despite the continued depressed state of the farms of manorial mills receipts from Duchy manors in all parts of Cornwall except the west were within reach of their pre-plague levels and in a number of instances were significantly higher; and what is more there was no appreciable accumulation of arrears. Even the profits of Helston-in-Kirrier manor in the far west had made a substantial recovery aided by a tremendous growth in the value of the manorial turbary, and even if the total charge of this manor was less than it had been in the decade before the plague a far greater proportion of it was reaching the hands of the Duchy receiver each year.

Once again, however, when agrarian conditions in Cornwall were buoyant, the county was struck by a further succession of disasters. First, a devastating storm swept the land, probably towards the close of 1361. With admirable concern for the well-being of their tenants the council of the Black Prince ordered the steward and the receiver of the Cornish estates 'to go in person from manor to manor and from place to place, investigate the estate of each of the Prince's tenants and respite a portion of rent where necessary'. The Black Prince himself considered the welfare of his tenants of such importance that he personally gave the steward more detailed instructions before the council meeting.[2] Secondly, as is apparent from the numbers of institutions of priests to Cornish benefices, a second outbreak of plague raged in Cornwall in both 1360/1 and 1361/2. A comparison of the numbers of institutions in the two years

---

Trenansaustel, 'receives without delay what rights and reason demand' and 'marvels greatly that Reynold and other such poor folk are importuning him and his council so much, bringing their suit to him from such distant parts and upon such petty matters'.
[1] The Prince always regarded his revenues as insufficient to maintain his estate and to carry on the wars against the King's enemies (T. F. Tout, *Chapters in the Administrative History of Medieval England*, 6 vols (Manchester, 1920–33), V, 292–3).
[2] *B.P.R.* II, 188–9.

1348/50 with those of 1360/2 would suggest that the second pestilence was fully two thirds as virulent as the Black Death; although
this is perhaps too precise a conclusion to be drawn from such
evidence.[1] Unfortunately the ministers' account for 1360/1 is
missing, but that for 1361/2 contains many evidences of the pestilence, and a separate membrane was attached to the record of each
manor confirming the moneys received from the sale of *bona
nativorum*.[2] As in 1348/50 no assessionable manor was completely
isolated from the plague, but if one may judge from the revenues
derived from death duties in 1361/2 the south-eastern manors appear
to have been particularly severely hit, and from Climsland, Castock,
and Trematon a total of £10 18s. od. was received from the sale of
bona nativorum compared with £15 9s. od. in 1348/9. In order to
bring a measure of relief to their tenants the Duchy forgave them
the final instalments of assession fines and tallage which were due to
be met at Easter and Michaelmas 1363.[3]

This second severe outbreak of plague appears to have had
extremely limited effects on the agrarian economy of Cornwall, even
though it came little more than a decade after the Black Death.
At the assession of 1364 the remarkable buoyancy of demand for
land almost everywhere in the county, with the exception of the far
west, was once again demonstrated; many assession fines were
raised, few were lowered, and only small amounts of poor quality
land were left untaken.[4] At Helston-in-Kirrier alone was the plague
the cause of an agrarian crisis, and only in this manor was a fresh
crop of holdings thrown into the lord's hands. But once again tin-
mining suffered to a greater extent than agriculture and very low
levels of output persisted for much of the decade.[5]

Throughout the second half of the fourteenth century demand for
land on the Cornish manors of the Duchy was maintained, despite
the number of severe drawbacks to farming that were present in
these times; whilst on some manors, particularly those in the south-
east of the county, the value of land rose to unprecedented levels.

Rillaton and Climsland, of all Duchy manors, demonstrate most

[1] 98 institutions were recorded in 1349 and 1350, and 63 in 1361 and 1362.
[2] P.R.O. SC.6.817/8.   [3] D.C.O. 15, Rillaton.
[4] D.C.O. 473.   [5] *See* Appendix C.

convincingly an increasing demand for land in the generation after the Black Death.[1] In the assession of 1356 the total fines and tallage imposed on the conventionary and villein lands of Climsland manor amounted to £63 7s. 5d.,[2] not far below the £72 15s. 10d. of 1347.[3] Even at the assession of 1364, immediately after the second outbreak of plague, the total of fines and tallage rose to £74 4s. 5d.,[4] seven years later it rose still higher to £86 17s. 4d.,[5] and the sum agreed between the tenants of Climsland and the assessors of Princess Joan, widow of the Black Prince, at the assession of 1378 amounted to £93 12s. 5d.[6] At Rillaton aggregate assession fines and tallage rose from £8 7s. 0½d. in 1356 to £11 10s. 9d. by 1371. As a result of these increases the aggregate rents upon conventionary and villein lands rose in this period by 20 per cent at Climsland and more than 30 per cent at Rillaton. Unfortunately for our analysis the manors of Calstock and Trematon were granted in 1369 to Nigel Loheryng, the favoured yeoman of Prince Edward, together with a number of other Duchy properties in Cornwall,[7] and all available record of them is then lost to us. Nevertheless, before this grant was made, almost without exception the rents of individual holdings on these manors were as high or even higher than they had ever been before, and the aggregate annual rent receipts virtually the same as 1347.[8]

The effect of the steadily increasing assession fines upon the annual payments due from holdings on the assessionable manors in south-east Cornwall can be seen from the typical example (p. 131) from Climsland manor.[9]

The total charge on the conventionary and villein lands of Tintagel and Helstone-in-Triggshire manors in the north-east of Cornwall, together with that of Liskeard manor to the south of Bodmin moor, grew steadily after 1356 until at the death of the

---

[1] Annual rents invariably remained stable whilst changes in demand were reflected in fluctuations in assession fines (above, pp. 53–4).
[2] D.C.O. 472a; P.R.O. E.306/2/1.
[3] D.C.O. 472.   [4] D.C.O. 473.
[5] D.C.O. 475.   [6] P.R.O. E.306/2/3.
[7] P.R.O. SC.6.818/1, 818/2, letter of the Prince dated 1 December 1369.
[8] It is legitimate to use the term 'rent receipts', as arrears never reached more than negligible proportions in the later fourteenth and the fifteenth centuries.
[9] Many further examples from a wide range of manors are contained in Appendix B.

A messuage and 28 acres in Kenston, annual rent 4s. 8d.

	Assession fine	Annual charge
	£ s. d.	s. d.
1347–8	1 0 0	7 6
1348–57	nil[a]	4 8
1357–64[a]	1 0 0	7 6
1364–71	1 2 0	7 10
1371–8	1 4 0	8 1
1378–85	1 5 0	8 3

[a] Assession fine remitted by order of the Duchy from 1348–57 and 1362/3.

Black Prince in 1376 they were almost as high as in the thirteen-forties. But on these manors the determination of the total charge was a less straightforward process than on the south-eastern manors where steadily rising assession fines between 1356 and 1378 were accompanied by an almost complete leasing of available lands, for on Tintagel, Helstone-in-Triggshire and Liskeard manors the effects of increased assession fines on the majority of holdings that were leased were sometimes negated by an expansion in the acreage left untaken at an assession, which could subsequently be rented only on temporary leases without assession fines. For example, on both Tintagel and Liskeard at the assession of 1364 fines were raised on many holdings, but other holdings were left untaken and subsequently leased without assession fines, with the result that there was only a small increase in the aggregate charges. In the second half of the fourteenth century there were clear signs of a divergence of the trends in the valuations put upon lands of differing qualities on these manors and this was to be a leading feature of the demand for land throughout Cornwall after the Black Death.[1]

As the graphs of Appendix B show, the net result of the assessions of 1356, 1364, 1371 and 1378 held on Tintagel, Helstone-in-Triggshire and Liskeard manors was that the aggregate profitability of the conventionary and villein lands slowly but surely regained the same level as that achieved in 1347. By 1378 the rents of the majority

[1] Below, pp. 271–2.

of individual holdings were higher than 1347, but the falling values of a small proportion of lands meant that, in aggregate, total rent receipts were approximately the same as they had been immediately before the Black Death.

In central Cornwall by 1356 aggregate rent receipts from the conventionary and villein lands of Tewington, Tybesta, Penlyne, Penkneth, and Restormel manors had attained approximately the same levels as those of the decade before the Black Death,[1] and the succeeding assessions of 1364, 1371, and 1378 brought little change either to these totals or to the rents of the individual holdings which made up these manors. In every assession after 1347 both the annual rents and the assession fines of the holdings of Tewington manor remained stationary. During the same period at Tybesta, modest increases to the fines of a number of holdings in 1364 and 1371 raised the aggregate total of fines paid by the tenants from just under £38 in 1356 to over £47 in 1378, but the effect on the total charge of the lands of this manor was only slight. Few holdings were ever left untaken on any of the manors in central Cornwall at the assessions held after the Black Death, and those that were realised their former annual rents when leased on year-to-year contracts, although they were not burdened with assession fines.

In contrast the aggregate revenues the Duchy received from the lands of the western manors of Helston-in-Kirrier, Tywarnhaile, and Moresk in the later fourteenth century never matched those attained in the years after the assession of John of Eltham in 1333. At Helston the assession of 1364 marked a deterioration in the demand for land from the position reached before the second plague of 1360/2. The economy of this manor was so delicately balanced that this pestilence severely affected the leasing of land, and the account of 1363/4 shows that twelve holdings with rents totalling £6 7s. 2d. had been abandoned as a result of the mortalities.[2] In the assession of 1364 a few of the holdings at Helston that had been left vacant since the assession of 1356 were leased once again, but far greater numbers of other holdings were thrown into the lord's hands. This assession was marked by falling fines and, where no fines existed on a holding,

[1] Appendix A, Figs 6 and 7.   [2] P.R.O. SC.6.817/9–10.

by falling annual rents. But once again the value of areas of good quality land was maintained or even enhanced.[1] Even the opportunity to lease on favourable terms and at much reduced rents failed to arrest the rapid increase in the acreage of unwanted lands, and in the assessional term after 1364 almost half of the manor was once again left vacant, with some 1,700 acres rendered completely valueless to the Duchy. But as previously, the relative value of each acre of land that was leased was on average far greater than the value of each acre of unwanted land when it had last been taken; the aggregate annual rents and fines of the lands leased in 1364 amounted to almost £46 compared with only a little over £12 that the remaining vacant half of the manor had realised when it had last been leased. The subsequent assessions of 1371 and 1378 registered an improvement, and the total revenues from the conventionary lands of this manor totalled between £50 and £55, or approximately the same as from 1358 to 1362; and the average sum delivered each year by the bailiff to the receiver was not far short of that which was actually received by the Duchy in the decade before the Black Death.[2]

On the death of Walter de Wodeland early in 1370 the assessionable manors of Tywarnhaile and Moresk in the west of Cornwall and the tiny manor of Penmayne in the north-east returned to the control of the Duchy.[3] An account of the profits of these manors for the last three terms of the year of Walter's death is contained in the ministers' account of 1369/70,[4] demonstrating the speed with which the administrative machinery of the Duchy was set in motion; and in the following year full details of these manors are included.[5] Unfortunately as 1370/1 was the final year of the assessional period no fines were paid by the conventionary tenants and it is not possible therefore to arrive at an estimate of the total value of the lands of these manors immediately before 1371. Nevertheless, the charges upon the lands of both manors based upon the assession of 1371 were not far below those based upon that of 1347, although

[1] See the examples of Carily, Roslyn and Tresperson hamlets in Appendix B.
[2] For the heavy arrears in the 1340s see Chapter 8, Fig. 13.
[3] These manors had been granted to Walter in 1350.
[4] P.R.O. SC.6.818/1, 818/2.
[5] P.R.O. SC.6.818/3.

at Moresk a number of assession fines were reduced and lands that had formerly been worth £5 17s. 1d. were left unleased.[1]

The growth in the aggregate revenues from the conventionary and villein lands of all assessionable manors after the immediate effects of the Black Death had been overcome was assisted in a small way by the conversion of many villein tenures (i.e. those held by *nativi de stipite*) into conventionary tenures, and by progressive increments to the tallage paid by those who remained villeins. Before the plague of 1349 the disparity between the amounts paid by conventionary tenants and the amounts paid by hereditary villein tenants for holdings of identical size and quality was most marked, for the thirteen-thirties had seen sharp increases in the assession fines of conventionary tenants whereas the tallage of the *nativi de stipite*, restrained by manorial custom, was only subjected to modest increases. An example of the resultant divergence in rents can be given from Climsland manor in 1347, using two holdings in the hamlet of Ovese, one of which consisted of a messuage and 16 acres and was held in free conventionary tenure for an annual rent of 2s. 8d. and an assession fine of 15s., which together resulted in an annual charge on the holding of 4s. 10d.; and the other consisting of a messuage and 24 acres which was held *de stipite* for an annual rent of 2s. 4d. and tallage of 5s., amounting to an annual charge of less than 3s. 1d.[2] The great mortality of 1349 caused the numbers of *nativi de stipite* to fall sharply as whole lines of succession were wiped out. The transfer of a holding previously in the hands of a *nativus de stipite* into conventionary tenure usually resulted in a sharp rise in its value to the Duchy.[3] But the lack of heirs was not the only reason for the diminishing numbers of *nativi*, for on occasion the Duchy upgraded the *nativi* either into unfree conventionaries or even into free conventionaries, invariably accompanying this upgrading with suitable increases in assession fines. The tallage upon those holdings that remained in the hands of *nativi de*

[1] D.C.O. 475, P.R.O. E.306/2/2.

[2] D.C.O. 472.

[3] An example of such a rise in value is the messuage and 27½ acres at Rillaton which realised 2s. 10d. annual rent and 2s. tallage in 1347 (D.C.O. 472). In 1356 it was leased in free conventionary tenure for the same annual rent but an assession fine of 18s. (D.C.O. 472a; P.R.O. E.306/2/1).

stipite was increased by small amounts at every opportunity in the later fourteenth century, irrespective of whether the assession fines of similar conventionary holdings were being raised or lowered, and as a result of these continuous increments the charges upon villein holdings were brought more into line with those of comparable conventionary lands. By 1392 the tallage on the messuage and 24 acres in Ovese mentioned earlier was fixed at 16s. 8d., whilst the assession fine on the 16-acre holding in conventionary tenure had only increased to 17s.[1]

The farms of manorial mills on Duchy manors in all parts of Cornwall failed to recover fully to the levels attained before the Black Death, despite the almost complete occupation of lands at rents at least as high as they had been before 1348/9. This suggests that enforcement of suit to the mills may have been relaxed, but many other factors could also influence the value of mills to potential farmers and any firm conclusion as to the causes of these depressed farms is impossible.[2] A good example of the scale of the decline in such farms in the course of the second half of the fourteenth century is furnished by the two corn mills of Camelford and Kenstock on Helstone-in-Triggshire manor; in 1345 they were leased in conventionary tenure for an annual rent of £13 6s. 8d.,[3] but by the late fourteenth century they were worth only £9 6s. 8d. to the Duchy.[4]

In contrast to the farms of mills many other sources of manorial revenue after the Black Death followed the same general course as the rents of conventionary and villein lands. By the death of the Black Prince in 1376, receipts from the sales of pasture rights in the deer-parks of the Duchy had regained or even exceeded the levels attained in the thirteen-forties.[5] No doubt the demand for pasture in the parks rose as the number of vacant holdings declined and so diminished the supply of cheap alternative grazing facilities available on a short-term or temporary basis. But fluctuations in supply, of which we must remain ignorant, depending upon such factors as

[1] P.R.O. E.306/2/5.
[2] For a fuller discussion see below, pp. 175–7.
[3] Extent of William de Cusancia, D.C.O. Library.
[4] P.R.O. E.306/2/3.

[5] Below, pp. 182–3.

the numbers of deer and the amount of grazing reserved for them, may also have played a significant part.

The profits of most manorial courts, which usually accounted for between 10 and 20 per cent of total manorial profits, were considerably higher by the end of the third quarter of the fourteenth century than they had been between 1339 and 1347.[1] Only the profits of Helston-in-Kirrier court, with far fewer tenants owing suit, showed a decrease over this period, whilst the average annual profits of the courts of Rillaton, Climsland, Liskeard and Tybesta almost doubled between the foundation of the Duchy in 1337 and the death of the first Duke some forty years later. There are remarkably few traces of a relaxation in manorial discipline after the Black Death, and the full quota of thirteen annual courts was maintained almost without exception. The rise in the profits of the courts attests both the resilience of manorial institutions in Cornwall and the ability of the Duchy to enforce their observance, and contrasts most strongly with the general loosening of discipline found elsewhere in England at this time.

Increasing rent receipts from the mass of the conventionary and villein lands and rising revenues from manorial courts combined to push the profits of almost all the Duchy's Cornish manors to new heights in the thirteen-seventies. The graphs in Chapter 8 are a revelation, as they show that in this decade the profitability of manors in east, north and central Cornwall was, almost without exception, greater than ever before.[2] Plague, increased wages, and the constant threat of invasion[3] had not managed to reduce demand for land in Cornwall at this time. Not only were the manorial charges higher, but also the receivers' accounts show they were being delivered promptly and invariably in full. Even on the western manors of Moresk and Tywarnhaile total charges were only marginally below what they had been in the thirteen-forties.

On the death of Edward the Black Prince in 1376 the estates of the Duchy of Cornwall reverted to Edward III.[4] Hugh de Segrave was

[1] Below, p. 195.
[2] Using the Adjusted Profits schedule, which averages seven-yearly assession fines and tallage over seven years.
[3] Below, pp. 144–5.
[4] Edward III as ruling monarch was the next in line of succession according to the terms of the charter of creation (above, pp. 6–7).

accordingly appointed steward of all the Cornish lands[1] and an assessment of their average annual value based upon the accounts of 1373, 1374, and 1375 was made by the executors.[2] The King then proceeded to divide the Duchy estates in Cornwall between his grandson Richard, and Joan the widow of the Black Prince. By doing this he flagrantly broke many of the clauses of the Duchy charter that he had himself so carefully caused to be drawn up, and in particular that which stated that the Duchy must reside in the first-born son of the ruling monarch, or in default of such a son, in the hands of the monarch himself. Princess Joan received as her dower a portion calculated to be worth one third of the total value of the estates, which included most of the assessionable manors, namely: Rillaton, Tewington, Helston-in-Kirrier, Moresk, Tywarnhaile, Penmayne, Penlyne, Tintagel, Tybesta and Talskiddy.[3] In addition Nigel Loheryng granted to her one third of the Duchy estates he held, which included the manors of Calstock and Trematon.[4] The remaining two thirds by value of the Cornish estates of the Duchy were granted to Richard, and included the manors of Climsland, Liskeard, Helstone-in-Triggshire, Penkneth, and Restormel;[5] but in 1378 Richard, then king, ceded the last-named manor to Princess Joan, apparently in exchange for Rillaton and Penlyne.[6]

Throughout his reign Richard II showed little desire to retain possession of any of the assessionable manors, although he saw to it that he retained most deer-parks and castles. In 1377 he ceded Helstone-in-Triggshire to Sir Richard Abberbury for life,[7] and in 1382 the manors of Climsland and Liskeard were given to his wife Anne on her coronation for life.[8] On the death of Princess Joan in

[1] *C.P.R. 1374–1377*, p. 293.
[2] P.R.O. C.47/9/57.
[3] *C.P.R. 1374–1377*, pp. 374–7; *C.C.R. 1374–1377*, pp. 407–8.
[4] *C.C.R. 1385–1389*, p. 389. The assession roll of 1378 contains details of the tenants of one third part of the manors of Calstock and Trematon, by value, and the farms of one third part of the mills of the manors and other perquisites (P.R.O. E.306/2/3).
[5] *C.C.R. 1374–1377*, p. 421, *C.P.R. 1374–1377*, p. 389.
[6] *C.P.R. 1377–1381*, p. 156; P.R.O. SC.6.818/8.
[7] P.R.O. SC.6.818/6; D.C.O. 21. Sir Richard Abberbury was one of the three *magistri* of the young Richard; he had been a knight in the service of the Black Prince (May McKisack, *The Fourteenth Century* (Oxford, 1959, p. 424)).
[8] *C.C.R. 1389–1392*, p. 273.

1385[1] the assessionable manors that had been in her possession were used to support other members of the royal family and retainers,[2] a policy which Richard resolutely followed throughout his reign.[3] Richard himself kept possession of only a few of the smallest manors, in particular Rillaton, Restormel, Penmayne, Penkneth, and Penlyne; although for a number of years the only manor he retained was Penkneth.[4]

Consequently our knowledge of Duchy manors in the last quarter of the fourteenth century is extremely sparse. The only manors for which accounts have survived were, with a few exceptions, those which remained in royal hands, and these manors were very small and in no way typical of the Cornish manors of the Duchy as a whole.[5] Thus it would be presumptuous to draw conclusions concerning the state of the agrarian economy of the county from the evidence of these manors alone. Whilst in Richard's hands this group of small manors was not managed with any conspicuous efficiency, and the holding of assessions was frequently delayed for many years after the legal expiry of leases,[6] and when held they served merely to confirm the levels of annual rents and assession fines already in force.[7] Nevertheless, from the receivers' accounts it is possible to discover that the profits of these manors were paid regularly and without significant arrears.[8]

As for all the other assessionable manors in the last quarter of the fourteenth century a comparison of conditions in the early years of

---

[1] P.R.O. C.136/41.
[2] See, for example, *C.P.R. 1385–1389*, p. 17; *ibid. 1391–1396*, p. 102; *ibid. 1396–1399*, p. 48. John of Cornwall on his death in 1397 held the Duchy manors of Calstock, Trematon, Restormel, Moresk, Penkneth, Penlyne, Tewington, and Tintagel (P.R.O. C.139/114).
[3] Apparently the dispersion of the assessionable manors was carried even further; see *C.R.P. 1385–1389*, p. 48, in which Princess Joan granted the manor of Tywarnhaile to William de Clifford for the term of her life.
[4] See, for example, P.R.O. SC.6.818/11, 818/12.
[5] There are one or two accounts of the ministers of Princess Joan and Queen Anne.
[6] See, for example, P.R.O. SC.6.819/7 for 20–21 Richard II, in which the conventionary rents and fines of the tenants of Penmayne are still being based upon the assession held in the ninth year of the reign.
[7] See Appendix A, Fig. 2b for Rillaton manor.
[8] See Chapter 8, Fig. 4. In 1394 (D.C.O. 31), however, the reeves of the manors and boroughs in royal hands were imprisoned for their arrears, at the most only £2 2s. od., but released subsequently on payment. The reason for such drastic action is not readily apparent.

The Later Fourteenth Century: 1356–99

Henry IV's reign, when records begin again, with the early years of Richard II's reign when records cease, must suffice; such a comparison suggests that the period was one of stability with no evidence at all of either declining demand for land or falling manorial profits.

There was no immediate spectacular increase in the average size of holding leased from the Duchy in Cornwall after the Black Death, but definite and progressive increases in the numbers of tenants leasing more than a single holding can be discerned, especially during the reign of Richard II.[1] Even at the close of the fourteenth century, however, by far the greatest proportion of conventionary tenants were still leasing single holdings, very few tenants held lands worth more than 20s. annually,[2] and the conventionary lands continued to be divided almost without exception into small- (under 20 acres) and medium- (20–40 acres) sized holdings. The shortage and high cost of labour may well have proved a crucial factor in limiting the size of tenant farms,[3] although it is not to be assumed that persons leasing lands from the Duchy invariably farmed all that they leased, for a great deal of sub-letting, especially of the larger holdings can be traced.[4] The lack of large numbers of extensive farms does not preclude farming for the market, however, and the farmers of small- and medium-sized holdings apparently sold produce regularly.[5]

Although it was an era of high and even rising land prices, the second half of the fourteenth century was not a period of pressure on land for subsistence; it was the attraction of farming for the market which appears to have supported land values in Cornwall. It is this distinction that helps to explain the apparently contradictory trends

[1] Table 17, pp. 226–8 below.
[2] The value of holdings in terms of annual rents has been taken as the yardstick in determining the scale of leasing by conventionary tenants. Vast differences in the rent per acre, in particular between good quality land and waste, means that any assessment in terms of acreage would be misleading.
[3] The enforcement of the Statutes of Labourers by landlords could also work against the interests of large-scale tenant farmers. See, for example, Elizabeth Levett, 'A note on the Statute of Labourers', *Ec. H.R.* iv, 1932.
[4] See below, pp. 232–5.
[5] Large numbers of conventionary and villein tenants holding 15 acres or more (see P.R.O. E. 306/2/1; D.C.O. 472a) can be found amongst the persons indicted before the justices at Michaelmas 1359 for using false weights and measures (P.R.O. J.I.125/1).

in the prices of certain lands after the Black Death, when increases in rents on most holdings were accompanied by stagnant or falling rents on some, and a significant number of other holdings persistently remained vacant. In times of rapidly expanding population marginal lands, lands of indifferent quality might be brought into cultivation in a desperate quest to secure subsistence or increase the supply of foodstuffs to the market. High prices for agrarian produce, cheap labour, and for innumerable small subsistence farmers the struggle to avert starvation, led to the cultivation of even the most intractable of soils and to the payment of substantial rents for them. In times of relatively low population, however, such infertile lands were bound to suffer in comparison with better quality soils. After the Black Death the dominant factor determining the value of a particular holding in Cornwall was likely to have been the amount of profit it would yield to the farmer when its produce was sold, and in such an analysis of profitability the better soils were rendered more attractive even at enhanced rents. Poorer soils needed extensive preparation before they could be sown or used as satisfactory pasture and, at a time when the cost of a day's unskilled labour was almost equivalent to the rent of an acre of land for a whole year, it can be appreciated that the process of preparation could be very expensive indeed.[1] In contrast, more fertile soils would yield better returns in terms of animal products or grain with the expenditure of considerably less labour. Such considerations help to explain the vast acreages left vacant at Helston-in-Kirrier after the mid-fourteenth century, and also the persistently low rental of waste and moorland on Duchy manors all over Cornwall; for such land was probably suitable for use only as rough pasture in these more spacious times, whilst the rents for holdings on good soils with access to expanding markets rose spectacularly.[2]

Conditions on the assessionable manors at the end of Edward III's reign with few vacant holdings, the rents of most lands as high or even higher than ever before, and scarcely a trace of arrears was most satisfactory for the Duchy. A number of other examples of

---

[1] See p. 13 above, for fifteenth- and sixteenth-century estimates of the cost of preparing pasture for use as arable.

[2] For the whole question of differential rent movements on the assessionable manors, and the factors behind them, see below, pp. 271–7.

comparatively high landlords' incomes can be found at this time elsewhere in England.[1] The pressure on land in the first half of the fourteenth century had become so great in many parts of England that landlords often found it relatively easy to fill vacant holdings after 1348/9, especially on fertile land.[2] High selling prices for their produce[3] may have cushioned many demesne cultivators against the effects of increased costs of production,[4] and doubly so if they were able to draw upon copious supplies of cheap compulsory labour. Furthermore, the discipline of the manorial court could do much to compel tenants to remain on their holdings and pay rents rendered immobile by the custom of the manor.[5] Such advantages did not accrue to the Duke of Cornwall, for on his Cornish estates,

[1] For examples of high landlords' incomes that have been published see: G. A. Holmes, *The Estates of the Higher Nobility in Fourteenth Century England* (Cambridge, 1957), pp. 114–15; A. E. Levett, 'The Black Death on the Estates of the See of Winchester', *Oxford Studies in Social and Legal History*, v (Oxford, 1916), 123. For a substantial recovery by the 1370s see J. A. Raftis, *The Estates of Ramsey Abbey—A Study in Economic Growth and Organisation* (Toronto, 1957), p. 265.

[2] For detailed descriptions of the ease with which vacant holdings were refilled after the Great Plague see: Levett, *op. cit.* pp. 84–6; Raftis, *op. cit.* pp. 252–3; F. M. Page, *The Estates of Crowland Abbey* (Cambridge, 1934), pp. 122–4. The fertility of the soil was an important factor and on manors less favourably situated serious vacancies could persist; see for example the neglected studies of Miss Shillington, *V.C.H. Hampshire*, v, 420–1; and Adolphus Ballard, 'The Manors of Witney, Brightwell, and Downton' in *Oxford Studies in Social and Legal History*, v, pp. 197–9. Furthermore, it would be wrong to assume that holdings were always re-let on the terms which had been prevailing before the plague. See for example, the reservations expressed by Raftis (*op. cit.* p. 253) and the calculations of Professor Postan ('Some Economic Evidence of Declining Population in the Later Middle Ages', p. 242, n. 1), which estimate the fall in the value to the lord of re-lets on Taunton manor to have been as great as 75 per cent and on Forncett approximately 60 per cent.

[3] The prices of most foodstuffs kept high until the 1370s. Most price series are still based upon Thorold Rogers' researches; for a systematic treatment of his figures see G. F. Steffen, *Geschichte der Englischen Lohnarbeiter*, vol. 1 (Stuttgart, 1901). For wheat prices (derived from the Bishop of Winchester's estates) see Postan, 'Some Economic Evidence', p. 226; and W. H. Beveridge, 'The Yield and Price of Corn in the Middle Ages', *Economic History*, May 1927. Movements in the price of Phelps Brown's 'composite unit of consumables' are also of value ('Seven Centuries of the Prices of Consumables, compared with Builders' Wage-Rates', *Economica*, new ser., XXIII, 1956).

[4] For wages, see E. H. Phelps Brown and S. V. Hopkins, 'Seven Centuries of Building Wages', *Economica*, new ser., XXII (1955); and Postan, *op. cit.* pp. 226, 233–5. For the cost of raw materials likely to have been used in farming, see Thorold Rogers, *History of Agriculture and Prices in England*, II (Oxford, 1866); E. Perroy, 'Les Crises du XIVe Siècle', *Annales*, IV (1949), 176.

[5] For a reassessment of the extent and effectiveness of attempts by lords to repress their customary tenants in the later fourteenth century, see R. H. Hilton, *The Decline of Serfdom in Medieval England* (Studies in Economic History, 1969), p. 36 ff.

as we have seen, the prevailing system of tenure left demand for land almost completely at the play of free market forces. There is a striking lack of information concerning freely negotiable rents and farms in England, and it is in these free leases that the demand for land and its productivity, and the profitability of tenant farming is most likely to be clearly reflected.

A major turning point in the fortunes of most English landlords occurred in the last quarter of the fourteenth century. Against a background of successive plagues and peasant discontent, manorial discipline weakened. Further sharp rises in wage-rates in the last two decades of the century were accompanied, for the first time since the Black Death, by a disastrous fall in grain prices, and the basis of demesne farming, and perhaps of much large-scale farming for the market, was at last undermined.[1] Landlords abandoned farming, rents tumbled, arrears multiplied, and vacancies proliferated.[2] It was in this period that the assessionable manors can be seen most clearly to have experienced fortunes quite contrary to those of estates which have been studied in many other parts of England. For these Cornish manors, the last quarter of the fourteenth century appears to have been a time of consolidation and high landlord's incomes, whilst the first quarter of the fifteenth century must be viewed as a period of unprecedented, and as yet unparalleled, prosperity for many of the manors of the Duchy, with a further resurgence of demand for land on the others.[3] For an explanation of these exceptional trends the particular conditions influencing the agrarian economy of Cornwall need to be examined in some detail; a task made especially difficult by the complete absence of statistical information concerning the yield and price of agrarian produce. The effects of plague in Cornwall in the second half of the fourteenth century can be traced clearly in wage-rates and the shortage of labour,[4] and in the vicissitudes of tin-mining.[5] The drop in the

---

[1] For evidence see p. 141, n. 3 and 4.
[2] For detailed accounts of the difficulties of landlords in the last quarter of the fourteenth century see: Raftis, *The Estates of Ramsey Abbey*, p. 265; Page, *The Estates of Crowland Abbey*, pp. 152–3; Holmes, *The Estates of Higher Nobility*, pp. 115–20.
[3] See Chapter 7 below.
[4] The daily wage-rates of unskilled and semi-skilled labourers hired by the Duchy in Cornwall doubled between 1349 and 1389. See Appendix D, pp. 290–1.
[5] Sharp set-backs in tin production followed the plagues of 1348/9 and 1361/2. Possibly further outbreaks of plague also occurred in the 1370s.

production of tin after 1348/9 was catastrophic.¹ Although the Black Death did not 'almost ruin the stannaries',² the process of recovery after 1348/9 was a tortuous one, fraught with many relapses. It was not until the thirteen-eighties that production once again reached the levels of the thirteen-forties, despite the fact that the price of tin in Cornwall in the second half of the century was more than double that of the first half,³ and only in the first decade of the fifteenth century were the peaks of production achieved in the thirteen-thirties equalled. Tin-mining suffered relatively more from the consequences of the fall in population experienced by Cornwall than did agriculture, and farming in the thirteen-seventies may well have provided the livelihood of a far greater proportion of the decimated population than it had in the decade before the plague struck the country.⁴ The stannaries suffered from an acute shortage of labour in the later fourteenth century and the court rolls are full of suits invoking the Statutes of Labourers, and of reference to workmen being seduced away from the employers to whom they were contracted.⁵

The hiring of labour to repair the castles, buildings and parks of the Duchy in the later middle ages provides an excellent source of wage statistics. In the thirteen-fifties, the daily wage of an unskilled labourer rose from 1½d. to 2d., and that of a semi-skilled labourer from 3d. to 3½d.⁶ But even higher wages may well have been paid by local Duchy officials and successfully disguised on the ministers'

¹ The amount of tin presented for coinage fell from an average of almost 1,200,000 lbs annually between 1340 and 1342, to less than 240,000 lbs in 1350/1.
² Assertion made by Lewis, *Stannaries*, p. 40.
³ The price of each pound of tin purchased by the Duchy for building works in Cornwall cost ¾d. or 1d. in the late thirteenth and early fourteenth centuries. Immediately after the Black Death the price rose to 3d., but by the late fourteenth century had settled at 2½d. per pound (P.R.O. E.101/461/11 ff; receivers' accounts, *passim*).
⁴ See also above, p. 120.
⁵ The earliest of the court rolls after the Black Death, that for Blackmore stannary from Michaelmas 29 Edward III (P.R.O. SC.2.156/26), contains many references to *serviens* breaking their contracts or being 'stolen', as indeed does a contemporaneous court roll of the stannary of Penwith and Kirrier (SC.2.161/81). Such cases remained a feature of court proceedings throughout the fourteenth century; see for example the rolls of the court of Foweymore stannary, 1–3 Henry IV (P.R.O. SC.2.159/1). The Black Prince's council in 1359 rightly attributed the low level of production of the stannaries partly 'to the lack of workers since the pestilence' (*B.P.R.* II, 158).
⁶ See Appendix D below for a graph of wage rates in the later middle ages.

accounts at our disposal.[1] Only once was an amended wage enrolled on an account, and this was in 1348/9 when the reeve of Liskeard tried unsuccessfully to claim 3d. instead of 2d. per day for a man employed in the deer-park, and 1½d. per perch instead of 1¼d. for repairs to the park hedges.[2] The shortage of labour in Cornwall and the high price it commanded brought a number of visits from the Justices of Labourers in the later thirteen-fifties.[3] In the thirteen-eighties a further sharp rise in Cornish wage-rates took place. According to Duchy sources the daily wage of an unskilled labourer rose from 2d. to 3d. and of a semi-skilled from 3½d. to 4d. A further factor forcing up the cost of farming was the sharp increase in the price of many raw materials, such as iron, lead, nails and lime, which followed the Great Plague. In the second half of the fourteenth century the Duchy had often to pay twice as much for the building materials it purchased in Cornwall as it had before 1348/9.[4]

But the prosperity of the assessionable manors in the second half of the fourteenth century must also be considered in the light of a number of factors, other than purely economic ones, which adversely affected farming. One such factor was the vulnerability of the Cornish coast, of particular significance in the later middle ages because of prolonged hostilities with both France and Spain; and many assessionable manors were situated by the sea.[5] The victory of the English navy at Sluys in 1340 did serve for a time to protect Cornwall from the threat of invasion, a taste of which had already been experienced when the vill of Sutton, adjacent to Plymouth,

---

[1] An easy means of effecting higher wages was to claim for more days of labour than were actually worked; for other methods see Thorold Rogers, *Six Centuries of Work and Wages* (1894), pp. 229–30.

[2] D.C.O. 4, Liskeard.

[3] Some of the proceedings of the Justices are contained in P.R.O. J.I.1/125, unfortunately this roll is not detailed enough to enable any conclusions to be made as to the scale of abuses against the Statutes. The revenues from the proceedings, which included prosecutions against breaches of the current legislation on weights and measures, amounted to £144 15s. 5d. (D.C.O. 13, Sheriff's account). Edward III granted this sum to the Black Prince to assist him in the expense of preparing for war (*B.P.R.* IV, 41). See also: B. H. Putnam, *The Place in Legal History of Sir William Shareshull* (Cambridge, 1950), pp. 71 ff.

[4] P.R.O. E.101/461/11 ff.; receivers' accounts, *passim*.

[5] E.g. Tintagel, Penmayne, Tywarnhaile, Moresk, Tewington and Trematon.

was sacked in 1339;[1] but this relative security did not last for long and the thirteen-fifties were punctuated by frequent urgent messages from the council of the Duchy calling for the Cornish castles to be repaired and manned.[2] Finally in 1372 at La Rochelle the English supremacy at sea was lost and Cornwall was laid open to attack. Fowey was attacked and burnt by Spaniards in 1378.[3] In order to combat the dangers of imminent invasion, 'knights and esquires' were forced to remain in Cornwall, and those tenants of the Duchy holding by military service were compelled to find 'men-at-arms, hobelers, archers, victuals, and other services', including the repair of the castles.[4] Richard II also directed that large-scale repairs should be carried out on Tintagel and Trematon castles, and garrisons were also established in them.[5] The people of Cornwall were far from unaware of the dangers they faced, and frequent petitions were addressed to the King and Parliament requesting protection for the coasts.[6]

Another adverse factor was the continuous drain on the manpower of Cornwall through the loss of Cornishmen to fight overseas. This must have exacerbated the effects of the plague, and contemporary records contain many references to recruiting campaigns. In 1363 the Black Prince himself visited Cornwall with the express purpose of raising men for his forthcoming Spanish ventures.[7] In 1381 the steward of the Cornish lands of Princess Joan was paid an additional £13 6s. 8d. for raising recruits for campaigns against France and Spain.[8] The frequency with which the absence of plaintiff, defendant or witness at proceedings of the stannary courts is excused 'because in the service of the king' attests the success of Cornish recruiting.

It is not possible, without a much fuller investigation of all Cornish

---

[1] P.R.O. SC.6.816/11, Trematon. See also: *C.P.R. 1338–1340*, p. 279.
[2] *B.P.R.* II, 9, 60, 128, 136, 149, 166, 168. The high rate of expenditure on castle repairs is contained in contemporary receivers' accounts.
[3] *V.C.H. Cornwall*, I, 48.
[4] *C.P.R. 1377–1381*, pp. 271, 455; *ibid. 1388–1392*, p. 95.
[5] See, for example, heavy repair costs in 1385 and 1386, and also the details of the garrisons: P.R.O. SC.6.813/7, 813/8.
[6] See, for example, *Rot. Parl.* II, 307, 311; III, pp. 5, 42, 162; P.R.O. E.197, file 102, no. 5068; *ibid.* file 104, no. 5162; *ibid.* file 333, no. E.1063.
L. E. Elliot-Binns, *Medieval Cornwall* (1955), p. 93.　　　　[8] P.R.O. SC.6.813/1.

sources, to do more than hazard a few suggestions as to the context in which the Duchy manors existed in the later middle ages. Nevertheless some aspects of the late medieval Cornish economy need explanation. Despite the influence of all the adverse factors outlined above, tenant farming appears to have remained an attractive proposition in the later fourteenth century, and rents on all except the western manors of the Duchy were maintained at or above their pre-Black Death levels. A considerable migration from tin-mining seems to have supplemented the previously landless agrarian classes and bolstered demand for land immediately after 1348/9, for, as we have seen, mining was a hard and dangerous occupation with little evidence to suggest that labourers in Cornish mines were compensated by high wages.

There was a substantial market for foodstuffs in medieval Cornwall created by the large proportion of the population which engaged in occupations other than agriculture, and the need to revictual ships.[1] Furthermore, great demands were also placed upon the land by the vast, albeit intermittent, purchases of victuals in the county to furnish the war effort, no doubt facilitated by the ease of communications with Gascony and the close ties of the Black Prince with Cornwall.[2]

The Duchy haveners' accounts supply a further indication which, although unsatisfactory in many ways, serves to emphasise the demand for grain in Cornwall in the second half of the fourteenth century. These accounts, listing the value of imports of grain into Cornwall by aliens paying 'maltot' must considerably understate the true value of Cornish imports. 'Maltot' was an *ad valorem* duty which was apt to be grossly undervalued; furthermore the efficiency with which the havener performed his duties appears to have varied considerably from year to year, and the vast numbers of ports and havens along the Cornish coastline and their inaccessibility must have rendered his task most arduous, even with the assistance of a number of deputies.

Although no statistics of agrarian prices in late medieval Cornwall

[1] For a fuller discussion, see Chapter 1, pp. 32–6.
[2] See, for example, *B.P.R.* II, 69, 77, *B.P.R.* IV, 18; *C.P.R. 1350–54*, p. 358.

TABLE 11   *The value of grain imported into Cornwall by aliens (as recorded in the Duchy haveners' accounts)*

1356	£104	1360	£23
1357	£190	1364	more than £100
1358	£5	1366	£16
1359	£10	1370	more than £200

have so far come to light, evidence of grain prices from Devon lends support to the thesis of maintained or even increasing demand for foodstuffs in the half-century after the Black Death. Records of the grain sales of certain Tavistock Abbey manors, although too slight to bear the weight of firm conclusions, suggest that prices rose after the mid-fourteenth century;[1] furthermore the admirable series of Exeter wheat prices, continuous from the second decade of the fourteenth century, show that if the decade of the great famines (1310 to 1319) is excluded, decennial average prices in the second half of the century were consistently higher than those in the first half.[2]

The thirteen-eighties which brought a further rise in Cornish wage-rates, putting unskilled rates twice as high as they had been before the Black Death, did not herald declining rents. The resilience of the land market must have been in part due to the considerable prosperity enjoyed by tin-mining. The output of tin between 1380 and 1420 at times rose to greater levels than those of the thirteen-forties and almost equalled the highest production figures ever recorded,[3] thus generating a massive demand for foodstuffs which in turn pushed up the demand for land. Indeed, if the assessionable manors had been managed with more efficiency in the last quarter of the fourteenth century there might well have been further sharp increases in conventionary rents, but as it was these increases were delayed until the accession of Henry IV.

[1] Finberg, *Tavistock Abbey*, pp. 116–28.
[2] W. H. Beveridge, 'A Statistical Crime of the Seventeenth Century', *J.E.B.H.* (August 1929).
[3] Appendix C.

7

THE FIFTEENTH CENTURY

Tales of falling land rents, of retreating cultivation, of dilapidated holdings, and often also of chronic insolvency, pervade the rural history of the fifteenth century. From regions as far apart as Cumberland, Northumberland[1] and Durham[2] in the north, to Sussex[3] and Hampshire[4] in the south, from Wales[5] through the Midlands[6] to East Anglia, Lincolnshire and Essex,[7] and from Somerset[8] and Wiltshire[9] to Kent[10] can be drawn a picture of the effects upon agrarian society of a severely contracted demand for land.

Modern scholarship, circumscribed instead of guided by hypotheses of the inevitable effects on demand for land of a drastic fall in population in a peasant agrarian society,[11] and lacking an adequate

[1] J. M. W. Bean, *The Estates of the Percy Family, 1416–1537* (Oxford, 1958), pp. 22–9, 29–35.
[2] E. M. Halcrow, 'The Decline of Demesne Farming on the Estates of Durham Cathedral Priory', *Ec. H.R.*, 2nd ser., VII (1955).
[3] Bean, *op. cit.* pp. 17–21.
[4] *V.C.H. Hampshire*, V (1912), 421–3.
[5] T. B. Pugh, *The Marcher Lordships of South Wales, 1415–1536* (Cardiff, 1963), pp. 274–80; W. Rees, *South Wales and the March 1284–1415* (Oxford, 1924), pp. 149–53.
[6] R. H. Hilton, 'A Study of the Pre-History of English Enclosure in the Fifteenth Century', *Studi in Onore di Armando Sapori*, I (Milan, 1957), 680–1; R. H. Hilton, *The Economic Development of some Leicestershire Estates in the fourteenth and fifteenth centuries* (Oxford, 1947), pp. 79–88; W. G. Hoskins, *The Midland Peasant* (1957), pp. 83–6.
[7] Raftis, *Ramsey Abbey*, pp. 265, 292–3; F. G. Davenport, *The Economic Development of a Norfolk Manor, 1086–1565* (Cambridge, 1906), pp. 56–9; H. E. Hallam, 'The Agrarian Economy of South Lincolnshire in the 15th Century', *Nottingham Medieval Studies*, XI (1967); R. H. Britnell, 'Production for the Market on a small 14th Century Estate', *Ec. H.R.*, 2nd ser., XIX (1966), 386–7.
[8] Postan, 'Economic Evidence', pp. 237, 239.
[9] Postan, *art. cit.* p. 237; *V.C.H. Wiltshire*, IV, 40–1; R. C. Payne, 'The Agricultural Estates in Wiltshire of the Duchy of Lancaster in the 13th, 14th and 15th Centuries', London Ph.D. thesis (1939).
[10] The Kent land-market may well have not suffered to the same extent as most other parts of England. But for a mid-fifteenth-century depression see F. R. H. Du Boulay, *The Lordship of Canterbury* (1966), pp. 225–6.
[11] Many of the most crucial of these hypotheses have been formulated by Professor M. M. Postan; for example: 'in a society so predominantly agricultural and an agricultural system so predominantly "peasant" as those of medieval England, changes in

range of regional studies, has allowed for no significant exceptions to the universal depression of the land-market. But evidence from Cornwall, and possibly also from larger areas of south-west England,[1] suggest that it is wrong to assume that the fall in population, which occurred during the fourteenth century *per se* produced a slump in demand for land in all parts of the country: even in so unsophisticated a pre-industrial economy as medieval England. The economy of Cornwall, although firmly based upon agriculture, had many other branches of primary importance including mining, fishing, and shipping, as well as quarrying, and shipbuilding which assumed some importance in the course of the fifteenth century, and textile production which flourished in west Devon.

The rapid and complete resurgence of the annual rents and assession fines of the bulk of the conventionary lands of the Duchy in Cornwall to the levels attained in the decade before the Black Death, as shown in previous chapters, has given a significant indication that demand for land in Cornwall could run contrary to that in other parts of England. By the opening years of Richard II's reign, with the exception of the westerly manors, rent receipts were as high or even higher than ever before, and with the resumption of the records from the opening years of Henry IV's reign the first quarter of the fifteenth century is revealed as a period of exceptional growth in Cornish land values.

Henry of Lancaster created his eldest son Duke of Cornwall on assuming the throne in 1399, after the overthrow of Richard II. Attempts to regroup the scattered manorial estates of the Duchy were not completely successful despite the determination of Parliament, and only nine of the seventeen assessionable manors were granted to the new Duke whilst the remaining eight were allowed to rest in the hands of the Huntingdons who were important royal

---

population must *ex hypothesi* have a direct effect on demand for land' ('Economic Evidence', p. 236). Professor Postan has frequently drawn attention to the limitations of his hypotheses, calling them 'mere outlines' which need to be filled with 'local detail and accident' ('Histoire Economique Moyen Ages', *IXe Congrès International de Sciences Historiques*, I, Rapports (Paris, 1950)); nevertheless, discussion has persistently centred on the reconstruction of a deceptively uniform picture of the English rural economy.

[1] See, for example, Finberg, *Tavistock Abbey*, pp. 255–6; Finberg and Hoskins, *Devonshire Studies*, pp. 233–49.

retainers. Fortunately for the purposes of our study, however, the nine manors placed under direct control of the Duchy were widely dispersed throughout the county, and their records form virtually a continuous series for the whole of the fifteenth century, thus enabling a fairly comprehensive picture of regional developments to be drawn. Of the manors still in Duchy hands, Rillaton, Climsland, and Liskeard lay in the south-eastern parts of the county, the extensive manor of Helstone-in-Triggshire and the small manor of Penmayne lay in the north-east, Tybesta manor and 97 acres at Talskiddy in central Cornwall, and Tywarnhaile and Helston-in-Kirrier in the western regions.

An assession was held on each of these nine manors in 1399 just before Prince Henry was made Duke, but on the whole it merely reaffirmed leases on the same terms as had prevailed over the preceding seven years, and on many manors since the early years of Richard II's reign.[1] On assessionable manors in the east of Cornwall, both to the north and the south and at Tybesta close by Truro, no adjustments were made in 1399 to the rents of holdings, and without exception the aggregate charges on conventionary and villein lands in these regions remained very much at the levels that had existed at the time of the last available account in the thirteen-seventies.[2]

In the far west the recovery in rent levels had been appreciably slower and far from complete, and by the close of the fourteenth century the conventionary and villein lands of Helston-in-Kirrier and Tywarnhaile were still worth considerably less than they had been in 1347, no doubt affected to a greater extent than eastern manors by the tortuous course of tin production.[3] For the land-market of Helston-in-Kirrier the last twenty years of the fourteenth century brought few changes; but Tywarnhaile manor proved to be the exception for it had apparently been in the grip of a depression since the thirteen-eighties, which had resulted in a fall in the charge

---

[1] The roll of the 1399 assession is missing, but the terms of the leases made at this assession can be deduced from the rolls of the succeeding assession of 1406 (P.R.O. E.306/2/7, 2/8). The aggregates of conventionary and villein assession fines and annual rents are obtainable from contemporary ministers' accounts (P.R.O. SC.6.819/10 ff.; D.C.O. 35 f.).

[2] Appendix A.

[3] See Appendix C for a graph of amounts of tin presented for coinage.

on the conventionary and villein lands of approximately 25 per cent. The ministers' account of 1399–1400 gives some indication of the difficulties this manor was experiencing,[1] for in this year Tywarnhaile was visited by a group of officials who reassessed the value of many holdings *propter paupertatem tenentium*, and allowed 55s. 4d. for lands *in manu domini* by default of tenants and because of the serious damage inflicted by sand blown from the sea onto neighbouring holdings.

A number of sectors of the economy of south-west England experienced a boom in the closing decades of the fourteenth century and the first quarter of the fifteenth. From the late thirteen-eighties until the early fourteen-twenties the output of tin was maintained at peaks comparable with those of the previous highest recorded levels achieved in the fourth and fifth decades of the fourteenth century. Furthermore, textile manufacturing in the south-west entered, in the early fifteenth century, upon a phase of very rapid expansion in which west Devon and the eastern extremities of Cornwall played a significant part.[2]

Once again growth in the non-agrarian sectors of the economy coincided with a sharp increase in demand for land throughout Cornwall. It was on south-eastern manors that the most spectacular advances in the value of land were registered. At the Climsland assession of 1406 the assession fines of the majority of holdings that were leased had increments of between 30 and 40 per cent placed upon them,[3] followed by a further average increment of some 10 per cent in 1413.[4] The subsequent assessions of 1420[5] and 1427[6] brought further increases, but usually of more modest proportions involving only a few pence per holding. The rate of increase of assession fines on the small manor of Rillaton was even more spectacular; for between 1406 and 1427 the total for the manor rose from £11 16s. 4d. to £21 8s. 5d., an increase of almost 90 per cent. At Liskeard the rate of growth of both assession fines and total revenues from the land was slower and less continuous than on the

[1] P.R.O. SC.6.819/10. [2] Discussed in greater detail below, pp. 169–71.
[3] P.R.O. E.306/2/7, 2/8.
[4] Increases registered at this assession can be determined from the roll of the succeeding assession.
[5] P.R.O. E.306/2/10. [6] D.C.O. 476.

more easterly manors of Climsland and Rillaton, and the assession of 1427 actually resulted in a fall in both; notwithstanding, aggregate assession fines rose by 40 per cent in this period.

It should be noted that in the face of the sharp increases in the rents of the vast majority of holdings, on both Climsland and Liskeard some lands fell in value. At Climsland in 1406 more than 150 acres of *terra* were left untaken at the assession, to be leased subsequently on temporary contracts without assession fines, and the area of such lands had grown to almost 300 acres by 1420 and 1427. At Liskeard the 1427 assession resulted in a significant acreage of land being left unleased.[1] But such lands were rarely more than 10 per cent of the total area of customary lands and did little to retard the appreciation in the aggregate rentals of Rillaton, Climsland and Liskeard, which from 1406 to 1427 rose by more than 30, 20 and 15 per cent respectively.[2]

The effects these increases had upon the rents of the individual conventionary holdings of this group of south-eastern manors can be seen from the following examples, each of which has been selected as typical of the general movement of land values. Many further examples are contained in Appendix B below.

TABLE 12 *Movements in the rents of individual conventionary holdings, 1347–1427*

	(a) Liskeard					
	A messuage and 40 acres in Trevekker, annual rent 5s. 6d.		A messuage and 25 acres in Trewythe-lan, annual rent 7s. 3d.		A messuage and 26 acres in Sturte, annual rent 8s.	
Date of assession	Fine	Charge	Fine	Charge	Fine	Charge
	s. d.	s. d.	s. d.	s. d.	s. d.	s. d.
1347	32 0	10 1	30 0	11 6	30 0	12 3
1371	33 4	10 3	40 0	13 0	30 0	12 3
1399	35 0	10 6	40 0	13 0	33 4	12 9
1406	40 0	11 3	50 0	14 5	40 0	13 9
1413	40 0	11 3	50 0	14 5	40 0	13 9
1420	53 4	13 1	60 0	15 10	48 8	14 11
1427	56 8	13 7	62 0	16 1	50 4	15 2

[1] The disparate trends in the rents of individual holdings are discussed below, pp. 271–7.　　　　　　　　　[2] Appendix A, Figs 1, 2b, 3.

(b) Climsland

Date of assessment	A messuage and 23 acres in Fontendrine, annual rent 3s. 10d.		A messuage and 32 acres in Mirfield, annual rent 4s.		A messuage and 32 acres in Putte, annual rent 4s.	
	Fine	Charge	Fine	Charge	Fine	Charge
	s. d.	s. d.	s. d.	s. d.	s. d.	s. d.
1347	20 0	6 8	20 0	6 10	18 0	6 7
1371	21 0	6 10	20 0	6 10	21 0	7 0
1399	21 0	6 10	23 0	7 3	23 0	7 3
1406	26 8	7 8	24 0	7 5	26 0	7 9
1413	28 8	7 11	31 0	8 5	29 0	8 2
1420	30 0	8 1	32 0	8 7	30 0	8 3
1427	32 0	8 5	34 0	8 10	31 8	8 7

Fine = Assessment fine payable over the seven-year assessionable term.
Charge = Annual rent plus one seventh of the assessment fine.

The rental of conventionary and villein land at Helstone-in-Triggshire and Penmayne in the north-east of Cornwall also appreciated substantially in the first quarter of the fifteenth century; although greater diversity in the quality of land there meant even less uniformity in the rent movements of individual holdings than there was on south-eastern manors. This lack of uniformity was demonstrated in the assessment of 1406 at Helstone-in-Triggshire when, although the assessment fines of a large number of holdings were raised by an average of almost a third, those of the remainder were either increased by a few pence only or left untouched. All available holdings were leased at this assessment and only a small acreage of waste was left untaken; as a result the average annual receipts from customary lands increased from just under £46 to almost £48. An increasing demand for land was also in evidence on Penmayne manor when in 1406 the total assessment fines payable by the conventionary and villein tenants was increased from £3 12s. 6d. to £4 4s. od.

The following assessment brought little change to the revenues from the lands of these two north-eastern manors, but in that of 1420 most of the conventionary tenants of Helstone-in-Triggshire manor were burdened with a novel and unique imposition termed *donum*.

This 'gift' was paid by almost all conventionary tenants at the rate of one half or one third of their assession fines, the assession fines themselves being still payable. It was explicitly guaranteed on the assession roll that this 'gift' would not be used as a precedent to burden the tenants with similar demands at future assessions. Those conventionary tenants that made no *ex gratia* payment had the fines on their holdings increased, although not by comparable amounts. As a result of this payment, which for indeterminate reasons was restricted to the manor of Helstone-in-Triggshire, £29 4s. 8d. was collected in addition to assession fines totalling £69 15s. 4d., which was the highest recorded total of assession fines to date. The donation to the king appears to have been, to all intents and purposes, compulsory, and equivalent to an increase in assession fines of more than 40 per cent, yet this was accomplished with only a single eight-acre holding left in the hands of the lord after the assession. The strength of the demand for the lands of this manor is even more remarkable when we learn that the farm of the manorial corn mills was reduced at this assession from £9 16s. od. to £9 4s. 8d., *causa minime pestilenciam*.

The terms of the grant of *donum* by the tenants of Helstone-in-Triggshire manor may well have implied that those tenants who paid it should not have their assession fines increased in the future. Indeed the subsequent assession brought no changes to the fines of tenants whose holdings had borne the imposition seven years before, whilst the fines of some of the small number of holdings which had not were increased. On the other hand, although it had been explicitly stated in 1420 that the *donum* should not be taken as a precedent, 40s. was taken from the tenants of Helstone-in-Triggshire manor in 1427 'for the holding of their lands until the next assession', in addition to the normal assession fines which served exactly the same purpose. The assession of 1427 demonstrated an unexpected fall in demand for land on this manor, for even if the £29 4s. 8d. of *donum* is not added to the annual rents and fines of the 1420 assession the rent receipts in the seven years after 1427 were considerably lower. In contrast both assession fines and aggregate rent receipts from Penmayne manor increased slightly after the assession of 1427.

The Fifteenth Century

As we have seen, the westerly manors of the Duchy of Cornwall provided somewhat of a contrast with those in the east. Nevertheless although the customary lands of Tybesta, Tywarnhaile and Helston-in-Kirrier were worth less than they had been before the Black Death, and rent receipts from Tybesta and Tywarnhaile had fallen since 1380, these manors also experienced a resurgence in demand for land in the opening decades of the fifteenth century. Most of the lands leased in the assession of 1406 on Helston-in-Kirrier manor were charged with fines considerably in excess of any period since the plague of 1348/9, and upon many holdings not burdened with fines annual rents were increased. Another indication of the rising demand for land on this manor was the sharply enhanced farm of the manorial chase. The effect of these adjustments upon the Duchy's rent receipts was restricted, however, by the persistence of a considerable body of unleased land comprising approximately 2,000 acres. But as a certain amount of this land was taken on year-to-year contracts for quite high rents, receipts from Helston-in-Kirrier were at their highest recorded level since the Black Death in the seven years following the assession. At Tybesta in 1406 fines on the majority of holdings were increased by a few pence each, which resulted in a small overall growth in the charge on customary lands. At Tywarnhaile, however, the total assession fines payable by the tenants of the manor fell sharply from £15 to £7, but this fall was probably the consequence of a rationalisation of land values rather than a response to further falls in demand for land, for all vacant holdings were taken up at the assession and a modest increase in aggregate rent receipts resulted.

Whilst the aggregate revenues from the conventionary lands of Duchy manors in the east of Cornwall continued to increase, those of the westerly manors had generally reached their peak for the fifteenth century by 1410. Unfortunately all record of the manor of Helston-in-Kirrier is lost to us from 1415, when it was re-granted to the Sarnsfelds after an appeal to Henry V.[1] From the assession of 1413 rent receipts from Tybesta and Tywarnhaile manors began to fall, albeit hesitantly and almost imperceptibly at first. Increments added to the assession fines of many holdings on Tybesta in 1420

[1] C.C.R. 1413–1419, p. 247.

were offset by a marked growth in the numbers of holdings left in the lord's hands and subsequently leased on yearly contracts without fines. The assession of 1420 at Tywarnhaile demonstrated the effects of a severe slump in the demand for land, much more clearly; hardly a single holding was charged with an assession fine, and the total paid fell from more than £6 to 13s. 4½d., and furthermore a substantial area of land left untaken. And although progressively successful attempts were made to lease these vacant lands in the years after the assession and each year marked a further recovery of receipts, the levels attained before 1420 were not equalled.[1]

It is from the fifteen-twenties that the divergence between the value of the lands of the western and of the eastern assessionable manors becomes most pronounced—a decade in which wage-rates rose for the third time since the Black Death[2] and the stannaries entered upon fifty years of continuously declining output. Between the assessions of 1420 and 1434 the total assession fines payable by the conventionary tenants of Tybesta fell from £41 to £26 and many holdings were left *in manu domini*, whilst demand for land at Tywarnhaile continued to languish.

The efficiency with which the assession system was managed deteriorated in the reign of Henry VI. Although manorial profits continued to be calculated without significant arrears, the rents of conventionary lands were allowed to stagnate and the standard lease became twenty-one years in length instead of seven years. No assession fines on the holdings of any manors were increased after 1427, and the fines fixed in this year at Climsland, Rillaton, Liskeard, and Helstone-in-Triggshire were to persist unchanged throughout the fifteenth century,[3] whilst at Tybesta and Tywarnhaile, faced with a falling demand for land, the assession fines and annual rents of the 1406 assession were taken as the ceiling and allowances against these granted as they were needed in ensuing assessions.

---

[1] For example, D.C.O. 44, when Richard Sody went from Tywarnhaile to the annual auditors' court at Lostwithiel to lease land.

[2] In the 1420s the daily wage of an unskilled labourer employed by the Duchy rose from 3d. to 4d., and that of a semi-skilled man from 4d. to 5d. or 6d., see below, Appendix D.

[3] The sole exceptions were the increments of a few pence each added to the fines of a number of holdings on Liskeard manor in 1441.

The Fifteenth Century

A new element was introduced into the assession system when in 1434 the conventionary tenants of Helstone-in-Triggshire and Rillaton manors were given the opportunity of renewing their leases for the usual seven-year term or entering into a twenty-one year contract.[1] These experimental long-term leases were possibly introduced to assist Henry VI financially as well as to ease the burdens upon the administration, for the assession fines, although three times as great as those for the normal seven-year term, were made payable over the usual six-year period. It appears that more than half the tenants of Rillaton opted for the twenty-one-year contract, most probably encouraged by the expectation that the value of land on their manor would continue to rise, but on Helstone-in-Triggshire by far the greater part of the tenants, perhaps some 85 per cent of the total, elected to take the shorter lease, no doubt influenced for their part by the fact that assession fines on their manor had not risen since 1413 and the terms of the *donum* of 1420 probably inhibited any further increases.

At the succeeding assession of 1441 it was decided to extend, wherever possible, the granting of longer leases and further encouragement was given to tenants who would take twenty-one-year leases by making the fines for them payable in eighteen instalments over the whole term, thus putting them on a comparable basis with the fines for seven-year leases.[2] Once again, however, all the conventionary tenants of Climsland and Liskeard manors took their lands for only seven years, and at Rillaton the leases made in 1434 for seven years were again renewed for the same term. More success was achieved, however, at Helstone-in-Triggshire, for those lands that had not been leased for twenty-one years in 1434 were taken for fourteen years, thus contriving all conventionary leases to expire in 1455. On the westerly manors of Tybesta and Tywarnhaile, afflicted by a continuing decline in demand for land, longer leases still proved unpopular and less than a third of the conventionary lands of Tywarnhaile were taken on the longer lease, whilst at Tybesta four fifths continued to be leased for seven years.

Finally, in the following assession of 1448 long leases met with

D.C.O. 48.   [2] D.C.O. 478.

more widespread success, and all conventionary lands of Climsland and Liskeard were taken on twenty-one-year contracts, and even at Tybesta the twenty-one-year term predominated.[1] Whatever advantages they brought to the Duchy administration, long-term leases robbed the conventionary system of tenure of much of its flexibility and efficiency, making it more difficult to adjust rents to relatively short-term fluctuations in demand.

Although after 1427 no adjustments of any importance were made to the assession fines of any holdings except those of the western manors, the 1441 assession saw the conventionary tenants of all manors burdened with payments termed *recognitio*; such payments had been exacted at the preceding assession from the tenants of Climsland and Helstone-in-Triggshire alone. The sums payable varied considerably from manor to manor and also from holding to holding within each manor, apparently in accordance with the value of the land. At Climsland 95 conventionary tenants paid £6 *recognitio*, at Liskeard 75 tenants paid only 40s. 8d., whilst at Tybesta and Tywarnhaile only 4s. 6d. and 13s. 4d. respectively was demanded.

Despite further increases in wage-rates and falling tin-production, which by the late fourteen-thirties was averaging little more than half the amounts produced in the first decade of the fifteenth century,[2] there was still no slump in demand for land upon the south-eastern manors of the Duchy for which we have records, and the assessions of 1441 and 1448, with the lengthening of leases to twenty-one years, served merely to stabilize rent levels, although in 1441 small increments of a few pence each had been added to the assession fines of those holdings which were leased for seven years only, possibly to act as a disincentive. In the course of the first thirty years of the fifteenth century both the rents of individual conventionary holdings and the aggregate rent levels of the manors in this region had been increased steadily,[3] and by the accession of Edward IV in 1460 rent receipts from the customary lands of Rillaton were 40 per cent higher than they had been in 1400 and

---

[1] P.R.O. E.306/2/11. [2] Below, Appendix C.
[3] For movements in aggregate rent levels see Appendix A, for the rent movements of individual holdings see Appendix B. 'Rents' and 'rent-levels' refer of course to the total charges upon the lands, made up of both annual rents and assession fines.

fully 75 per cent higher than 1347, whilst those from Climsland were 30 per cent higher and more than 50 per cent higher respectively. At Liskeard although the upward trend in rents had been neither so spectacular nor so continuous, and on occasion had even been reversed, by 1460 Duchy rent receipts from this manor were approximately 15 per cent higher than they had been in 1400 and 1347, although at their peak between 1434 and 1448 they had been as much as 20 per cent higher.

The payment of *donum* by the tenants of Helstone-in-Triggshire at the assession of 1427 complicates the analysis of demand for land on this manor, but each succeeding assession brought lower rent receipts until by 1456 they were no higher than in the thirteen-forties. The customary lands of the small manor of Penmayne also situated in the north-east of Cornwall were worth a little more at the accession of Edward IV than they had been before the plague of 1348/9.

By 1460 the decline in demand for land in the more westerly parts of Cornwall had forced rent receipts from Tybesta and Tywarnhaile manors well below their pre-Black Death levels. Falling assession fines and a growing number of vacant holdings resulted in a further decline of more than 10 per cent in the values of customary lands of both manors to the Duchy between 1400 and 1460.

In 1453 the infant Prince Edward, first-born son of Henry VI, was granted the estates of the Duchy of Cornwall. For the benefit of the new Duke the eight assessionable manors alienated with one exception since the reign of Richard II, namely Calstock, Trematon, Restormel, Moresk, Tintagel, Penmayne, Tewington, and Helston-in-Kirrier were restored to the Duchy.[1] Thus once again the full complement of seventeen assessionable manors lay in the hands of the Duchy, where they were to reside for the rest of our period. We must remain ignorant of the detailed vicissitudes of economic fortune experienced by these eight manors in the period for which we have no record of them. Nevertheless it will be worth while to attempt a comparison of the value of their conventionary lands in

[1] D.C.O. 57.

1459 with that of the time of our last record of them, in the context of the wider knowledge we have of other assessionable manors within their respective regions.

The continuous records of the south-eastern manors of Calstock and Trematon which become available from 1459 were the first since the manors were granted to Nigel Loherying in 1369.[1] Unlike the neighbouring manors of Rillaton, Climsland, and Liskeard, assession fines had not been increased at all in the intervening years; in fact each conventionary holding on Calstock and Trematon appears to have been burdened with exactly the same annual rent and assession fine as it had at the assession of 1356 more than a century earlier.[2] Thus one of the most important principles of the assession system had been ignored by the succession of feoffees of these manors.

An assession was held on Calstock and Trematon manors by Duchy officials in 1458 when the conventionary lands were demised for twenty-one years.[3] The assessioners must have appreciated that the lands of these manors were grossly undervalued when compared with those of other Duchy manors in the region, but inflexible assession fines had long since been the custom on all Duchy manors. Nevertheless, some attempt was made to redress the discrepancy by imposing substantial payments for *recognitio* on the conventionary tenants of these manors which amounted to more than 11 per cent of the total assession fines on Calstock and almost 20 per cent on Trematon; a much heavier burden than was imposed on the tenants of Climsland and Liskeard manors whose *recognitio* amounted to less than 5 per cent and barely 2 per cent respectively of the sums payable in assession fines.

Although we are denied the most obvious indicator of demand for land—fluctuations in the value of conventionary lands—there are incontrovertible signs of a 'prosperity' on both Trematon and Calstock manors in the later fifteenth century, which was comparable with that experienced by other south-eastern manors. No lands were left *in manu domini* on either manor, and allowances of rents and

---

[1] Above, pp. 129–30. [2] Compare D.C.O. 472a with D.C.O. 482.
[3] The 1458 assession roll is missing but see the ministers' account of 1458–9; D.C.O. 52.

assession fines to facilitate repairs to buildings and enclosures frequently found on assessionable manors in other regions of Cornwall,[1] are completely absent from the ministers' accounts of Trematon and Calstock, as they are also from those of Rillaton and Climsland. In addition, in 1463 Roger Bond was granted a licence to construct two mills on Glamaryn water at Calstock manor and to maintain them at his own expense. One mill was a 'blowyngmille' and the other a corn mill.[2] The construction of a 'blowyngmille' for the smelting of tin, is most significant as it coincides with the collection of substantial sums for toll-tin on Duchy manors in south-east Cornwall. No record of any previous receipts from the sale of tin received as toll had been recorded on Calstock and Climsland manors since the late thirteenth century, and on Rillaton since the Black Death; it is possible that eastern Cornwall was now sharing in the increased production of tin achieved by Devon in the early years of Edward IV's reign.[3]

But the continued buoyancy of the land-market of south-east Cornwall in Edward IV's reign was not shared by Duchy manors in other parts of the county, on the contrary, the manors in central and western Cornwall were in the grip of a severe depression. A major factor in this depression must have been the slump in the activity of the western stannaries which forced production to a level as low as that of the later thirteen-fifties just after the Black Death, which was barely 40 per cent of the average amount mined annually in the first decade of the fifteenth century.

Records of Tintagel manor, neighbour to Helstone-in-Triggshire in the north-east, paint a picture of slack demand for land in the mid-fifteenth century, and rent receipts were much lower than they had been when records had ceased in 1382. The conventionary lands of both Tintagel and Helstone-in-Triggshire, whose rent receipts had been falling since 1427, were leased for only seven-year terms from 1460. In 1465 the conventionaries of Tintagel contracted to pay assession fines amounting to less than £16, compared with fines of more than £40 agreed at the assessions of 1347

---

[1] See below, pp. 163-5.   [2] D.C.O. 64.
[3] The output of Devon tin mines appears to have risen appreciably from 1460 (Lewis, *Stannaries*, Appendix J, p. 253).

and 1378.[1] Consequently the rents of the lands of this manor were approximately 20 per cent lower than those based on the mid-fourteenth-century assessions, although in Edward IV's reign the quantities of land left *in manu domini* were not substantial. Rent receipts from Helstone-in-Triggshire in the fourteen-sixties were the lowest since those based on the assessions of 1356 and 1364. Individual assession fines were not reduced on Helstone but left at their 1420 levels; the drop in receipts was caused by greater amounts of land being left vacant at the assession and subsequently leased on a year-to-year basis without fines, and from allowances given to tenants for the repairing of holdings. But a measure of recovery was evident on both these manors in the fourteen-seventies. The two small manors of Penmayne and Talskiddy managed to resist the fall in demand for land to greater effect, and receipts from their lands in the latter part of the fifteenth century were maintained at levels almost as high as those of the thirteen-forties.

The cluster of small manors around the borough of Lostwithiel, comprising Restormel, Penlyne, and Penkneth, fared much better on the whole than assessionable manors farther west and although their conventionary lands were no longer subject to any assession fines,[2] rent receipts had fallen little since records of them were last available in Richard II's reign. The manor of Tewington, on the other hand, displayed all the symptoms of a severely depressed land-market in 1460, the date of the first fifteenth-century account of this manor. On Tewington, situated close to the stannary of Blackmore, few holdings were burdened with assession fines.[3] Indeed, the whole manor was assessed to pay fines of only £4 13s. od. in 1465, and £2 19s. od. in 1472, compared with fines of £26 6s. 8d. agreed in 1378.[4] Other signs of depression are easily discernible: some annual rents had been reduced, an aid was hired each year to assist the reeve in the running of the manor and in particular in the collection of money,[5] and frequently substantial sums were granted to tenants to assist them in constructing new buildings, repairing

[1] D.C.O. 472; P.R.O. E.306/2/3.   [2] See, for example, P.R.O. SC.6.822/1.
[3] P.R.O. E.306/2/12.   [4] P.R.O. E.306/2/3.
[5] D.C.O. 57 ff. Jacob Chidley was consistently rewarded for assisting the reeve of Tewington. In 1461 he received 6s. 8d. in fees and half the value of a boat which was wrecked on the shores of the manor and worth 10s.

old, or maintaining the enclosures around their holdings. It was in the period between the assessions of 1465 and 1479 that the aggregate rent receipts from the lands of this manor sank to levels fully one third below those of the thirteen-forties and thirteen-seventies.

Rent receipts from neighbouring Tybesta manor, as we have seen, had been declining steadily since 1427, but during the reign of Edward IV this trend was arrested and even reversed. The overall effect of the decline had been far less spectacular than on Tewington where highly-priced lands had tended to become relatively more overvalued in the second half of the fifteenth century, and by the end of our period in 1485 the rent receipts from the conventionary lands of Tybesta were little more than 15 per cent below what they had been a century earlier.

The land-market in the far west of Cornwall was even more depressed. By the late fourteen-sixties the conventionary lands of Tywarnhaile were worth little more than half as much in aggregate as they had been in 1347 and after the assession of 1378, though a slight measure of recovery followed soon afterwards. Records of Moresk and Helston-in-Kirrier manors, returned to the Duchy by 1459, tell a similar story. At the assession of 1465 fines were almost non-existent at Moresk, amounting to less than £4 for the whole manor, and aggregate rent receipts were barely half those produced in the decade before the Black Death. At Helston-in-Kirrier almost half the lands of the manor lay uncultivated and nearly 1,000 acres had lain vacant for so long that it was described as *jacent in foresta*.[1] No assession fines at all were payable on any of the conventionary lands of the manor and rent receipts were more than a third less than they had been in the first quarter of the century.[2]

A symptom of the torpid land-market which prevailed on all but the south-eastern manors by the second half of the fifteenth century, was the policy followed by the Duchy of granting cash discounts to tenants to facilitate the repair of the buildings and enclosures of

---

[1] Under a separate heading on the assession roll such lands are described as *vastabant per plures annos elapsos et jacent in foresta* (P.R.O. E.306/2/12).

[2] A comparison with the 1340s is difficult as the manorial charge was then seriously in arrears and so gives a false picture of the value of the manor to the Duchy (see above, pp. 93–7).

their holdings. Some exceptional early examples of such arrangements can be found on the Assession Roll of 1406; Nicholas
Reynold took an 80-acre holding on Liskeard manor paying only
the annual rent of 17s. for it; the assession fine which had previously
been 30s. was remitted on condition that Nicholas, in addition to
the cattle shed (*boverium*) he had already built, undertook to construct a new house (*aula*) and a new barn (*grangia*). It was specified
by the assessors that if the buildings were not erected within two
years Nicholas would be evicted.[1] In the assession of 1420 held at
Helstone-in-Triggshire, John Brewer was excused making *donum*
to Henry V for two holdings because he agreed to construct at his
own expense 'houses, barns, and sheep-folds' as well as other
buildings. Although the conventionary system with its relatively
short leases must have encouraged the running down of capital
stock the Duchy had rarely found it necessary to make cash grants
towards reconstruction in times of buoyant demand for land.[2]
The terms of the normal conventionary lease did serve to protect
the Duchy from the abuse of holdings by tenants and the clause
demanding that holdings should be returned in the same state as
they were originally leased was stressed in the second half of the
fifteenth century on the assession rolls. With the continued slackening of demand for land in many parts of Cornwall in the later
fifteenth century the system of allowances for repairs and improvements grew even more widespread, and in Edward IV's reign they
can be found on almost every account. It became standard practice
for the assessors to authorise allowances for repairs and improvements at the assession, with the agreed sums being disbursed in
instalments in ensuing years. For example, in 1455/6, the first year of
a new assessional term, a total of £4 19s. 6d. was allowed to the
conventionary tenants of Tybesta manor:[3] 42s. for repairs to a
holding in the lord's hands, three separate sums of 13s. 4d. for the

---

[1] P.R.O. E.306/2/7, 2/8.
[2] It is significant that no such allowances were given to the tenants of any of the south-
eastern manors during the fifteenth century. There were, however, some dilapidated
holdings on these manors as inquisitions carried out through the manorial courts
testify: P.R.O. SC.2/158/12, court held at Calstock, 4 February, 11 Edward IV;
P.R.O. SC.2/159/32, court held at Stoke Climsland, 17 December, 6 Edward IV.
[3] P.R.O. SC.6.821/9.

repair of enclosures of three holdings, and 7s. 6d. to a tenant whose farm buildings and other goods had been destroyed by fire. The Duchy not only made cash grants to restore holdings to a reasonable state of repair, improvements were also encouraged and it was often willing to meet part of the cost of new enclosures.[1]

Movements in the rent of land tell much of economic fluctuations on manors whose lands were all in the hands of tenants; and on the assessionable manors in the later fifteenth century land rents, including 'Rents of Assize', comprised at least 75 per cent of total manorial revenues. Yet rents alone are only part of the story, and trends in a number of other branches of revenue are available for study.

It has been noted in earlier chapters that farms of manorial corn mills failed to recover to the same extent as landed rents after the Black Death.[2] By the late fifteenth century many mills were being leased for farms less than half of what they had commanded in the thirteen-forties, even upon manors whose rents were comparable with pre-Black Death levels. This state of affairs persisted despite the fact that the Duchy generally assumed responsibility for repairs to mills in the late fifteenth century. Yet there continued to be a demand for mills, and new ones were built in Edward IV's reign at Calstock[3] and Penkneth, and expensive reconstructions were carried out on the mills of Tintagel.[4]

The revenues which the Duchy obtained from some manorial properties depended upon the extent to which it was considered suitable to exploit them. Two such sources of revenue were the deer-parks[5] and the manorial woodlands.[6] By the fifteenth century the annual expenditure on repairs to the enclosures of the deer-parks fully absorbed the revenues obtained from the sales of agistment, and intermittent large-scale projects such as the rebuilding

---

[1] For example, in 1463 5s. was granted towards the cost of enclosing a piece of waste on Helstone-in-Triggshire manor (P.R.O. SC.6.822/1).
[2] See, for example, pp. 118, 135 above.
[3] D.C.O. 64.
[4] P.R.O. SC.6.821/11, Penkneth and Tintagel.
[5] See also below pp. 179–84.
[6] See also below pp. 184–6.

of lodges[1] or the construction of feeding-troughs,[2] resulted in a considerable loss to the Duchy. Some of the Cornish manors were quite well wooded in the middle ages. The policy of the Duchy towards woodlands had always been one of conservation at the expense of easy profits, although it is not possible to discover whether the woodlands were cleared whilst manors were out of Duchy hands.[3] From the middle years of Edward IV's reign, however, attempts were made to realise some of the capital lying dormant in woodlands, and in the nine years from 1473 to 1481, for example, £5 12s. 8d. was gained from the sale of wood at Restormel.[4]

In contrast the size of revenues from other sources depended upon factors usually outside the control of the Duchy. Two such sources of revenue were turbaries[5] and the sale of tin, which was rendered as toll to the Duchy as a proportion of the amount dug within the bounds of the assessionable manors.[6] The sums derived from the sale of toll-tin varied according to the general level of mining activity, the price of tin, and the location of mines. The renewed mining activity evident in the latter part of Edward IV's reign led to a marked rise in toll-tin receipts on a number of manors. In contrast the later fifteenth century saw a complete collapse in the revenues derived from the sale of turbary on Helston-in-Kirrier and Helstone-in-Triggshire manors, the sites of the two largest Duchy turbaries. By 1459 a mere 5s. annually was obtained from the turbary on Helston-in-Kirrier compared with £20–30 realised in the thirteen-fifties. Whilst at Helstone-in-Triggshire all revenues from turbary ceased after 1468. Demand for turves was still very high but apparently supplies were exhausted.[7]

[1] The lodge of Helsbury and Langteglos park, attached to the manor of Helstone-in-Triggshire, was rebuilt just before 1448 at a cost of at least £68 10s. 0½d.; 12 acres of underwood were also used in the operations.
[2] See, for example, P.R.O. SC.6.812/7, Restormel.
[3] It is apparent that the manors were not always well cared for; see, for example, *C.P.R. 1429–1436*, p. 133.
[4] D.C.O. f.: P.R.O. SC.6.822/2 ff.
[5] See also below, pp. 186–9.   [6] See also below, pp. 188–91.
[7] It was stated in 1466 that all the turbary in Cornwall had been used and that its scarcity was holding back the production of tin (*C.P.R. 1461–1467*, p. 482). Turves were apparently used for the first smelting of the ore, which was usually performed near its place of extraction.

The Fifteenth Century

The Cornish manors of the Duchy were governed with conservatism in the later middle ages and the fifteenth century brought no collapse of manorial discipline. The full complement of thirteen courts continued to be held each year, almost without exception and, although receipts from the courts were invariably lower in the fifteenth century than they had been in the fourteenth, there were no signs of any severe decline in judicial profits.[1] There is in fact very little evidence of growing inefficiency in the Duchy administration during the fifteenth century despite the prolonged dynastic struggles of the age which involved the Duchy both through its intimate connection with the Crown and through serious local disturbances.[2] The seventeen assessionable manors were worth approximately 15 per cent less to the Duchy in each year of Edward IV's reign than they had been over a century earlier, before the Black Death.[3] The money due from the manorial reeves continued to be collected without the accumulation of serious arrears, even from those manors whose lands had ceased to be in great demand. On the Cornish manors of the Duchy, in contrast to conditions prevailing on many other estates in the later middle ages, rents could fall without the amassing of arrears; and the frequent reassessments of the value of land through the assession system, coupled with generous allowances, must have played a significant part in achieving this commendable solvency.[4]

It would be injudicious to offer a detailed explanation of the sharply contrasting rent trends displayed by Duchy manors in eastern and western Cornwall in the later middle ages, especially when hampered by the complete absence of statistical information concerning the yield and price of agrarian produce; nevertheless some explanation is called for and it seems obvious that we must look to the influence upon demand for land of the non-agrarian sectors of the

---

[1] Below, pp. 193–6.
[2] For civil disorder in Cornwall see: C. L. Kingsford, *Prejudice and Promise in Fifteenth Century England* (Oxford, 1925), pp. 54–7, Chapter IV *passim*.
[3] See below, pp. 199–201.
[4] Arrears found elsewhere in England were sometimes the result of failure to adjust rents to new levels of demand, and the use of out-of-date rentals. This state of affairs was largely avoided on the assessionable manors by the assession system.

regional economy as well as to population movements. It must always be borne in mind that the economic structure of Cornwall contrasted sharply with that of many regions of England, in that the dominance of agriculture was constantly being challenged by tin-mining and seafaring.[1] Consequently there was always a considerable market for agrarian produce created by those sectors of the population not practising farming at all, or not managing to supply all their requirements.

Mining was undoubtedly the most important of all the various non-agrarian activities which influenced demand for land, and fortunately our knowledge of tin-mining is extremely full. One must not, however, discount a sympathetic connection between the output of tin and the size of the Cornish population at various times in the later middle ages. When the level of tin production was high and many employed in mining, demand for foodstuffs within the county must have risen and in turn pushed up the level of demand for land. We can see in the records of Duchy manors that in times of intense mining activity, as in the thirteen-thirties and forties, the demands of miners for food and land, both pasture and arable, exerted a tremendous influence on adjacent farming areas, forcing up rents and encouraging colonisation.[2] The small square fields typical of mining regions and visible from aerial photographs and 6-inch Ordnance Survey maps[3] can also be traced in the assession rolls of the 'mining manors' of Tywarnhaile and Tewington. On these manors small holdings predominated, and in the decades before the Black Death plots of 5 or even $2\frac{1}{2}$ acres can be found divided between two or three tenants.[4] At the same time at Helston-in-Kirrier, where fertile land was scarce, vast areas of poor quality moorland were brought into use, but it was land which could profitably support cultivation only when employment in mining was extremely high; and with the drastic slump in production and

---

[1] For a fuller discussion of the importance of the various forms of economic activity in medieval Cornwall see above, pp. 29–36.
[2] For seventeenth- and eighteenth-century examples of the stimulus given to agriculture by large mining populations in Derbyshire and Cornwall respectively see: Joan Thirsk, 'Industries in the Countryside', *Essays in the Economic and Social History of Tudor and Stuart England*, ed. F. J. Fisher (Cambridge, 1961), p. 73; J. Rowe, *Cornwall in the Age of the Industrial Revolution* (Liverpool, 1953), p. 231.
[3] Balchin, *Cornwall*, pp. 50, 101.   [4] For example, D.C.O. 472.

employment after 1349 almost 2,000 acres were to remain almost permanently vacant.

A comparison of rent trends on the westerly manors of Helston-in-Kirrier, Tywarnhaile, and Tybesta with trends in the production of tin reveals an intimate correlation between the two throughout the fourteenth and fifteenth centuries;[1] for these manors were all relatively isolated from alternative markets. The recovery of tin production by 1400 to levels comparable with those of the thirteen-thirties was a remarkable feat, for it was almost certainly achieved with a greatly diminished population. The period of high tin output, lasting from about 1385 to 1420, marks the period of greatest demand for the lands of these manors after the Black Death; but total rent receipts as high as those of the decade before the plague were achieved from Tybesta alone, as the smaller population at the close of the fourteenth century meant a substantially reduced demand for land for purely subsistence farming. The years after the second decade of the fifteenth century brought a continuous decline in the output of tin, which was paralleled by falling rents, both reaching their lowest point in the fourteen-sixties; but both in the decades thereafter showing some tendency to rise.

But the progressively rising rents of the majority of holdings on the south-eastern manors from 1356 to 1434, and the maintenance of these high levels in the succeeding half-century when the principle of frequent reassessment was abandoned cannot be explained solely in terms of fluctuations in the level of population and the output of tin. Migration, both from mining into farming and from the poor lands of the west to the more fertile lands of the east, in the wake of the Black Death, undoubtedly played a part, but it too by no means offers a complete explanation and we must look for other influences.

Amongst such influences must have been the rapid growth of textile manufacture in the south-west. Whilst much cloth came from east Devon and even from Somerset, west Devon and the Cornish border was an important production area.[2] In the first half of the

---

[1] Compare the graph of the amounts of tin presented for coinage (Appendix C below) with the graphs of the aggregate rents of customary lands on these three manors (Appendix A, Figs 6, 8b, 9 below).

[2] H. P. R. Finberg and W. G. Hoskins, *Devonshire Studies* (1952), pp. 241–5; Finberg, *Tavistock Abbey*, pp. 150–5.

fifteenth century exports of cloth from Plymouth and the Cornish ports increased almost ten-fold, until an annual average of over 1,000 cloths were despatched overseas in the fourteen-forties, whilst exports from Exeter and the ports of east Devon rose by an almost equivalent proportion and culminated in a peak of well over 2,000 cloths annually.[1] Furthermore it is apparent from the Particulars of Customs (P.R.O. E.122), which distinguish Plymouth's exports from those of Cornish ports, that Cornwall played a more significant part in this trade than she has been given credit for. As can be seen from the following table, exports of cloth from Cornish ports accounted for almost 40 per cent of the combined exports from Plymouth and Cornwall between 1418 and 1438, although the proportion appears to have declined in ensuing years.[2]

TABLE 13   *The equivalent of cloths of assize exported, 1418–38*

	Plymouth	Fowey and Cornish ports
1418	159	69
1420[a]	204	130
1426	112	114
1427	195	64
1430	186	169
1438[a]	652	163

[a] Account covers part of the year only.

The emergence of a flourishing textile industry in the Devon and Cornwall border regions, as well as farther afield in east Devon, meant a substantial and growing market for the agricultural produce of east Cornwall; a market which provided a stimulus to both arable and pastoral husbandry—to the production of both foodstuffs and wool. The fifteenth- and sixteenth-century customs accounts of many Devon ports reveal the necessity of large-scale

[1] For statistics see E. M. Carus-Wilson and O. Coleman, *England's Export Trade, 1275–1547* (Oxford, 1962).
[2] P.R.O. E.122/113/19 ff.

The Fifteenth Century

imports of foodstuffs to feed industrial and commercial populations,[1] and the manorial records of the Duchy of Cornwall[2] and Tavistock Abbey[3] reveal also the stimulus given to sheep-rearing. Evidence of the increase of cloth manufacture in Cornwall itself can be drawn from the manorial records of Climsland. In the course of the later fourteenth and the fifteenth centuries additional fulling mills were constructed on the manor,[4] and many tenants described as 'tuckers'[5] and 'weavers'[6] leased land and buildings from the Duchy. Also of interest as indicating the large and increasing measure of economic activity on the manor are the annual *censar'* payments made by persons resident on the manor but not holding land. In 1401, 21 such persons paid *censar'*, and in 1405 no less than 40 persons.[7] And, of course, manorial records provide only a poor guide to industrial growth at this time.[8]

But textile manufacture does not provide a complete answer to the buoyant rents of eastern Cornwall. In general west country ports appear to have weathered the economic storms of the fifteenth century better than most, and the pull of these towns for supplies of foodstuffs both for resident populations and for the victualling of ships, must have proved a powerful stimulus to farming for the market. But even in the mid-fifteenth century, when cloth exports were depressed and tin production at its lowest level, there were

---

[1] For the fifteenth century see: for Plymouth, P.R.O. E.122/114 ff.; for Exeter, Touchard, 'Les Douanes municipales d'Exeter'; for Dartmouth, Laura M. Nicholls, 'The Trading Communities of Totnes and Dartmouth in the late 15th century and the early 16th century' (unpublished Exeter M.A. thesis, 1960). For the sixteenth century, see N. S. B. Gras, *The Evolution of the English Corn Market* (Harvard Economic Studies, XIII, 1915), Appendix D.

[2] Eastern Cornwall was particularly suited for sheep-rearing, and scattered court rolls reveal that a number of tenants of Liskeard manor in the fifteenth century kept large flocks of sheep: we learn, for example, that in 1412 Adam Drinker trespassed with 140 sheep (P.R.O. SC.2.160/27), that in 1445 William Blog had 40 sheep (SC.2.160/29), and that in 1451 John Russell trespassed with a flock of 60 sheep, and Robert Helyer seized 60 sheep belonging to John Hoyk (SC.2.160/30).

[3] Finberg, *Tavistock Abbey*, p. 150.

[4] In 1364 Roger Bestus built a fulling mill at his own expense (D.C.O. 473) and in 1403 Thomas Hellier, by constructing another, also at his own expense, brought the total on the manor to three (P.R.O. E.306/2/7, 2/8).

[5] See, for example, D.C.O. 478.

[6] P.R.O. SC.2.159/32, court held at Stoke, 17 December, 6 Edward IV.

[7] P.R.O. SC.6.819/10; 819/15.

[8] See for example E. M. Carus-Wilson, 'Evidences of Industrial Growth on Some Fifteenth Century Manors', *Ec. H.R.*, 2nd ser., XII, 1959.

no signs of falling demand for land on any of the south-eastern manors.

Yet again the explanation may lie in the growth of another market within easy reach. This may well have been provided by the Devon stannaries, the output of which doubled between 1450 and 1470 to fluctuate around a level approaching 25 per cent of the output of the Cornish mines, compared with less than 10 per cent in the early fifteenth century.[1] The three stannaries of Devon were centred on the towns of Chagford, Ashburton, and Tavistock, each of which lay no more than a day's journey by cart from the Duchy manors of south-east Cornwall.[2]

Cornish tax records can help to place our study of the assessionable manors in a wider context, despite the limitations placed upon their utility by the exemption of tin-miners from taxation.[3] A comparison of the tax assessment of 1334 with that of either 1514/15[4] or 1523/4[5] appears the most satisfactory, although of course no direct comparisons of absolute wealth are possible as the basis of the assessments had been altered. What can be obtained, however, is an approximate survey of changes in the relative wealth of Cornwall to other counties, and of the various regions of Cornwall to each other. A comparison of the assessment of 1334 with that of 1515 or 1524 suggests a most rapid accumulation of wealth within Cornwall in the intervening two hundred years, a rate of accumulation which was surpassed by only Devon and Middlesex.[6]

Within Cornwall the comparison reveals a considerable degree of variation.[7] It is significant that the Hundreds of East and West, which together comprised the south-east portion of the county and contained the Duchy manors of Climsland, Calstock, Rillaton,

[1] Lewis, *Stannaries*, Appendix J.
[2] A cart fully loaded could cover approximately 30 to 35 miles in a day (*Cambridge Economic History of Europe*, II (ed. M. Postan and E. E. Rich, Cambridge, 1952), 144.
[3] For a discussion of this exemption see above, p. 9.
[4] The assessments of this date have been preferred by R. S. Schofield in a recent attempt to trace changes in the relative distribution of wealth in England between the fourteenth and seventeenth centuries, *Ec. H.R.*, 2nd ser., XVIII (1965).
[5] The 1523/4 assessments have been widely used. See for example Carus-Wilson, 'Fifteenth Century Manors', pp. 191–2; A. R. Bridbury, *Economic Growth: England in the Later Middle Ages* (1962), pp. 77–82, 111.
[6] Schofield, *art. cit.*, Table 2, p. 504.
[7] For 1334 see P.R.O. E.179/87/9; for 1523–4 see P.R.O. E.359/41.

The Fifteenth Century

Trematon and Liskeard, paid between $4\frac{1}{2}$ and 5 times as much in 1524 as in 1334, while the county as a whole paid less than $2\frac{1}{2}$ times as much. In conclusion it must be borne in mind, however, that the sixteenth-century assessments were made when the Cornish economy had apparently effected a recovery from the relative slump of Edward IV's reign, when the output of Cornish tin once again approached the peaks of previous centuries,[1] and when the export trade of the south-west was enjoying an unprecedented boom.[2]

[1] Lewis, *The Stannaries*, Appendix J, p. 253. The output of tin doubled between the mid-fourteen-sixties and the second decade of the sixteenth century.

[2] G. Schanz, *Englische Handelspolitik gegen Ende des Mittelalters* (Leipzig, 1881), II, ff. 39, 109; Carus-Wilson and Coleman, *England's Export Trade*, pp. 144–5, 154–5; Finberg and Hoskins, *Devonshire Studies*, p. 244; Rowse, *Tudor Cornwall*, pp. 70–1; E. M. Carus-Wilson, *The Expansion of Exeter at the Close of the Middle Ages* (Exeter, 1963), p. 29 ff.

8

SEIGNEURIAL REVENUES AND THE EXPLOITATION OF MANORIAL ASSETS

From the closing decades of the thirteenth century rents and judicial profits provided almost the whole of the revenues from the seventeen assessionable manors, although on certain manors valuable natural assets such as turbaries or fisheries supplied additional income. The annual rents and assession fines imposed on conventionary lands were by far the most important single source of revenue, and at the creation of the Duchy in 1337 they amounted to well over half the total profits of many manors. Furthermore, by the close of the middle ages the extinction of *nativi de stipite* tenancies, large increases in conventionary rents on eastern manors, and the eventual decline of the profits of courts and farms of mills, had created for the conventionary lands a position of even greater importance. The proportionate contribution of the 'Rents of Assize', which comprised the rents of free tenancies and certain customary payments, varied immensely from manor to manor being only partly dependent on the amount of land in the hands of free tenants, but on all manors it remained less than 25 per cent of the value of conventionary leases. In preceding chapters much has been said of the vicissitudes in the value of the conventionary lands to the Duchy, in this chapter a little will be said of the other sources of seigneurial revenue and of their importance to the manorial economies.

MANORIAL MILLS

All but the smallest of the assessionable manors had corn mills, some having as many as three, and Climsland, Calstock, Tybesta, Penlyne, and Moresk also possessed seigneurial fulling mills.[1] Without exception it was the policy of successive administrations to

[1] For the prevalence of fulling mills in medieval Cornwall see: E. M. Carus-Wilson, 'An Industrial Revolution of the Thirteenth Century', *Ec. H.R.*, XI (1941), 49–50; Henderson, *Essays in Cornish History*, pp. 204–10.

farm the mills whenever possible. The farm of Climsland mill was fixed as it was held in freehold, whilst the mills of a number of other manors were held by boroughs as part of the terms of the borough chaters.[1] Those mills that were not held on fixed farms were demised by the Duchy using a modified form of conventionary tenure, the terms of the *conventio* being much more flexible than those made for lands; for example, many of the usual conditions of conventionary tenure were waived, millers were rarely liable to serve as reeve or tithingman and heriots were usually either excused completely or commuted to a small money payment,[2] in addition mills were not always leased for terms of the same length as conventionary lands.[3]

Fluctuations in the farms of manorial corn mills have been used as indicators of the economic prosperity of agriculture and, in conjunction with other evidence, as a means of measuring demand for land, but it is apparent that the use of the farms in this way is fraught with many inherent pitfalls, for they were determined by a multitude of divers factors, of which the prosperity of agriculture was only one. The amount of rent a miller was prepared to pay for a mill depended broadly upon his estimated excess of receipts over necessary expenditure, i.e., profit. The most fundamental determinants of the receipts of a miller were the quantity and quality of grain brought to the mill, the level of the toll or charge for grinding, and prevailing grain prices. Superficial impressions of the quantity of grain brought to a mill can often be deduced from the size of the manor and the numbers of tenants who owed suit. But even an assessment of limited accuracy cannot be made without an analysis of the acreage of arable, yields per acre, and the efficiency of enforcement of suit to the mill: and such analysis is invariably impossible even to attempt.

The factors which influenced the receipts of millers, outlined above, are only one side of the problem, and the siting of a mill[4]

[1] See above, p. 59.
[2] See for example the lease made at Tintagel in 1371 (P.R.O. E.306/2/2).
[3] See for example a lease of four years at Calstock in 1356 (D.C.O. 472a); one of 12 years at Helstone-in-Triggshire in 1342 (D.C.O. 1).
[4] The efficiency of a mill depended largely upon its watercourse, and some mills were useless in dry seasons, or at best could be used only intermittently.

and its maintenance were also of paramount importance. The up-keep of mills was an expensive process, which from Duchy evidence could cost almost 20 per cent of the annual farm.[1] Consequently, if the miller were required by the terms of his lease to bear the whole cost of upkeep he would be prepared to pay a lower farm than if he were assisted by the lord. The actual costs of maintaining a mill in good repair depended in turn upon the cost of labour and upon the prices of raw materials.

All these factors and many more which influenced the farms of mills could and did vary greatly in the course of the later middle ages, and many of them combined to force down the farms of mills after the Black Death regardless of the 'prosperity' of agriculture. The general tendency in many parts of England was towards the relaxation of customary manorial dues and services which resulted in a less strict enforcement of suit to mill; furthermore, the mono-poly enjoyed by many seigneurial mills was being undermined as new mills were constructed. In later fourteenth- and fifteenth-century England much land lay in the lord's hands, and there was some movement towards pastoral husbandry at the expense of arable, thus further reducing the amount of grain brought to manorial mills. In addition the price of grain remained low in many regions throughout the fifteenth century, whilst on the expenditure side wages and the cost of raw materials rose sharply. It was thus almost impossible for the farms of mills to be maintained in these circum-stances.

The dangers of using the farms of mills as a substitute for land rents or even as a supplementary source of information on the agrarian economy are strikingly emphasised by the evidence of Duchy manors. After the Black Death trends in the farms of mills show little if any correlation with trends in the rent of conventionary land, and even upon those manors where in the early fifteenth century rents rose far above their pre-1349 levels the farms of mills sometimes attained barely half their former totals.

[1] See, for example, the graph (Fig. 1, p. 178) of the expenditure by the Duchy on the upkeep of the mills of Helstone-in-Triggshire manor. An even greater proportion of the farm of the mill held by the borough of Lostwithiel was expended by the Duchy upon its upkeep in the fifteenth century.

Seigneurial Revenues and Manorial Assets

The Black Death was the turning point of the upward rise of the farms of mills leased in conventionary tenure which had been taking place since the thirteen-twenties.[1] Deaths of tenants and vacant holdings caused a drastic fall in the value of the mills immediately after the plague, and the Duchy was forced to reduce farms and even to repair mills with its own capital. Without exception the freely negotiable farms of both corn and fulling mills failed to regain their pre-plague levels in the later fourteenth century, although no great difficulty was experienced in leasing them at reduced rents. By the later fifteenth century the farms of many mills had declined even further and in addition the Duchy sometimes undertook to meet repair costs. It can be seen from the graph (p. 178) of Camelford and Kenstock mills that by Edward IV's reign the mills were virtually valueless, although in 1345 they had been worth £13 6s. 8d. annually.

For certain manors, in particular Helston-in-Kirrier whose mills declined in value from £9 6s. 8d. in 1347[2] to 28s. in 1465,[3] the fall in the value of mills to the Duchy may well have been the result of diminished corn production, but for the manors of eastern Cornwall this explanation is inadequate. Some of the resons can no doubt be found in a probable relaxation of enforcement of suit, and to confirm the continued and possibly even increasing demand for milling facilities in central and eastern Cornwall in the later fifteenth century, a number of new mills were constructed by entrepreneurs on Penkneth, Calstock, and Tintagel manors.[4]

The farms of fulling mills in central and western Cornwall declined in the same manner as those of corn mills. For example, the farm of the *fullereticum* of Moresk manor fell from 7s. in the early fourteenth century[5] to only 2s. in the late fifteenth.[6] But in the east of the county the expansion of textile production led to a proliferation of mills, although manorial documents can only provide a partial picture of the scale of industrial developments.[7]

[1] Above, pp. 90, 117–18.
[2] D.C.O. 472.
[3] P.R.O. E.306/2/12.
[4] Above, pp. 160, 165.
[5] P.R.O. E.120/1.
[6] P.R.O. SC.6.822/1.
[7] Above, pp. 169–71.

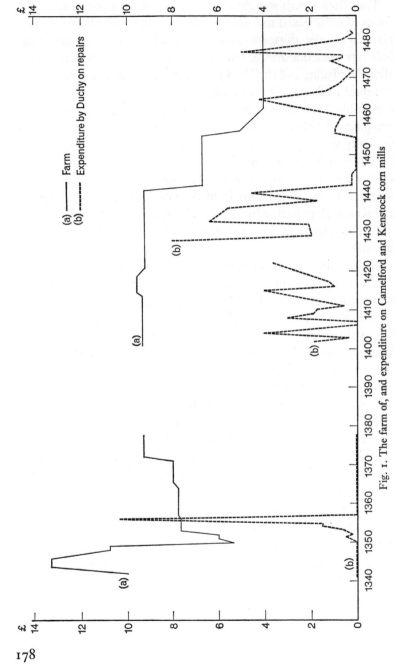

Fig. 1. The farm of, and expenditure on Camelford and Kenstock corn mills

Seigneurial Revenues and Manorial Assets

DEER-PARKS

There were seven Duchy deer-parks in Cornwall in the middle ages and they are described in some detail in the Caption of Seisin of 1337.[1] The smallest parks were attached to the castles of Launceston and Trematon and contained only 15 and 42 deer respectively. Much larger was the park of Carrybullock, appended to Climsland manor, which was three leagues in circumference and held 150 deer. To the north of Carrybullock lay the park of Helsbury and Lanteglos, in Helstone-in-Triggshire manor, which had 180 deer, and to the east lay Liskeard park with 200 deer. The largest of the Duchy parks was Restormel with 300 deer, which lay adjacent to the castle and manor of Restormel where the Dukes, and the Earls before them, usually resided on the rare occasions when they visited Cornwall.[2] All these parks had been in existence in the time of Earl Edmund, together with the park of Penlyne which was deparked before the Duchy was created,[3] but their area had not always remained constant.[4]

The maintenance of the parks was a costly item of expenditure for the Duchy. Each of the large parks had a full-time parker to administer it at an annual salary ranging from 45s. 6d. to £4 11s. 0d., according to his responsibilities.[5] Continuous repairs had to be made to the hedges, walls, and ditches surrounding the parks, as well as occasional large-scale expenditure on hunting lodges. In

[1] P.R.O. E.120/1. See also Henderson, *Essays in Cornish History*, pp. 157–62.
[2] Edmund made his home at Restormel in the later years of his life (Henderson, *op. cit.* p. 51). The Black Prince always stayed at Restormel when he visited Cornwall; see, for example, *B.P.R.* II, 113, 198, 202, 204.
[3] The Penlyne park was enlarged in 1296/7 causing a 'decay' of 6s. 4½d. in the 'Rents of Assize' of the manor (P.R.O. E.119/1). By 1337, however, there were no deer at Penlyne and the park was worth 15s. as pasture (P.R.O. E.120/1).
[4] For example, Restormel park was enlarged in 1297/8 by 3½ Cornish furlongs at the expense of 32s. 6d. in rents (P.R.O. SC.6.811/1), and again in 1345 (D.C.O. 2). Helsbury and Lanteglos park was made larger before 1337 (see the Caption of Seisin in which it is shown that certain tenants had been given lands in exchange for those which were included in the park).
[5] The stipends of parkers, as of all Duchy officials, remained remarkably constant in the later middle ages, and in Edward IV's reign inquiries were initiated to determine the stipends and fees paid to officials in Edward III's reign a century earlier (P.R.O. C.47/52/2, pieces 55 and 56). At various times in the fourteenth and fifteenth centuries there were 'surveyors of game' and masters of venison in Cornwall; see, for example, *B.P.R.* II, 8, 14, 15; *C.P.R. 1429–1436*, p. 428.

G

addition it was sometimes necessary to provide feeding-troughs for the deer[1] and extra fodder for their winter feed.[2] Although the amount of money spent each year on the parks fluctuated in the course of the fourteenth and fifteenth centuries the approximate annual running costs of the major parks was as follows: Restormel from £7 to £8, Climsland £6, Liskeard £5 to £6, and Helstone-in-Triggshire £4. But these totals do not include certain large-scale repairs which were paid from the receivers' funds and not the reeves', and might cost anything from £20 to £70.[3]

The Earldom derived very little income from the deer-parks. Some parks had been used for arable demesne in 1288,[4] but this scheme was abandoned soon afterwards and sales of pasture and agistment brought in scant profit, as can be seen from Table 14.[5] Under the Earls agistment and pasture rights were usually leased for long periods at low rents, but with the assumption of the estates by Queen Isabella some attempt was made to exact greater revenues; it was not until the creation of the Duchy, however, that sums approaching the full potential profitability of the parks were realised. But even under the Duchy the foremost consideration was always the welfare of the deer, which appears to have taken precedence at all times over the making of profits. Many examples of the preoccupation of the Duchy with the welfare of the deer can be given, especially during the tenure of the Black Prince. In 1342 the parkers of Liskeard and Restormel were instructed to restrict the numbers of animals pasturing in the parks because of the large number of deer there,[6] and whenever the Black Prince planned to visit Cornwall his arrival was preceded by and his stay accompanied by, complete prohibitions on the sale of agistment in the parks, so that the deer population might increase;[7] this explains the total absence of sales of agistment in many parks in the years 1354/7 and 1362/3.

[1] For example, P.R.O. SC.6.812/7, which contains details of feeding-troughs built in Restormel park at a cost of £17 3s. 3d.
[2] For example, P.R.O. SC.6.817/8, Restormel; *B.P.R.* II, 76.
[3] For example see: D.C.O. 8, for the complete re-hedging of Liskeard park at a cost of £20; P.R.O. SC.6.821/7, for details of expenses of at least £68 10s. 0½d. incurred in the making of a new lodge in the park of Helsbury and Lanteglos.
[4] P.R.O. SC.6.816/9. The tenants of those manors with parks were sometimes liable for ploughing services (above, p. 65).
[5] Below, pp. 182–3.   [6] D.C.O. 1.   [7] For example, *B.P.R.* II, 71.

Agistment in the parks was sold at prices which varied according to both the capacity of the animal to consume and the season. The prices, which varied little in the later middle ages, ranged from as little as 3d. for the summer agistment of a calf up to 5d. or 6d. for a cow or an ox, and 10d. for a horse. The cost of winter agistment was approximately half that of summer.

As the revenues from the sales of agistment depended upon both supply and demand factors their interpretation is a most complex exercise. But in general the trends are plain and Table 14 (p. 182) shows that the levels of revenues achieved in the thirteen-forties were usually maintained until the middle of the fifteenth century, with the exception of the immediate post-Black Death period. In the fourteen-forties the Duchy embarked upon a policy of farming the agistment and pannage rights of the parks *en bloc* to a single person or to a partnership, usually composed of Duchy officials. In 1449 the sole rights to the agistment of animals and the pannage of pigs in Liskeard park were farmed to Thomas Bodulgate, the Duchy havener and keeper of Restormel park, and John Trevilian, the steward of the Devon lands of the Duchy, for an annual rent of 20s.[1] The farm of the agistment and pannage was to stay at this level for the rest of the fifteenth century except for a short-lived contract made with Thomas Clemence, Controller of Duchy Works, in which Thomas agreed to maintain the enclosures of the park at his own expense in return for the pasture and pannage rights. That this arrangement apparently only lasted for a single year is not surprising as the repair costs in previous years had often amounted to more than twice the 20s. of the prevailing farm.[2] The pasture and pannage rights in Helsbury and Lanteglos park were leased in 1449 to John Arundell for life for £1 6s. 8d. per annum,[3] just after the lodge had been reconstructed at a cost of almost £70. This lease ran until 1459 when a new lease was made upon more competitive terms, which raised the farm to 40s. annually, the level at which it was to remain for the rest of the century.[4] At Climsland a

---

[1] D.C.O. 53. These two also farmed the manors of Restormel, Penlyne, Penkneth, Moresk, Tintagel and Tewington, together with the Duchy boroughs of Lostwithiel and Camelford (D.C.O. 205).
[2] D.C.O. 60.   [3] D.C.O. 53.   [4] D.C.O. 57.

TABLE 14 *Receipts from the sales of pasture in parks*

	Restormel	Helstone-in-Triggshire	Liskeard	Climsland
	s. d.	s. d.	s. d.	s. d.
1297	7 8	nil	13 4	14 4
1298	7 8	nil	13 4	14 10
1301	7 8	nil	13 4	12 9
1302	7 8	nil	13 4	7 3
1303	7 8	nil	13 4	7 4
1304	7 8	30 8	13 4	8 0
1305	7 8	nil	13 4	7 6
1306	7 8	nil	13 4	
1307	7 8	nil	13 4	
1315	7 8	nil	13 4	8 0
1316	7 8	13 4	27 4	13 4
1317	7 8	3 0	26 0	13 7
1339	14 11	113 0	26 7	35 6
1340	11 4	83 4	14 0	
1342	19 9	97 4	23 11	40 0
1345	10 1	88 4	23 2	35 4
1347	19 7	85 0	nil	35 8
1349	19 5	29 8	nil	18 2
1350	16 10		9 0	21 9
1351	23 0	18 9	10 7	15 5
1352	22 0	39 6	10 3	22 0

	Restormel	Helstone-in-Triggshire	Liskeard	Climsland
	s. d.	s. d.	s. d.	s. d.
1374	59 2	87 9	25 8	40 0
1375	49 0	92 6	28 2	34 6
1377		42 0	17 0	21 1
1378			18 2	28 3
1379			16 8	
1388	60 6			
1391	54 4			
1392	37 2			
1394	49 4			
1401		128 8	47 8	15 11
1402		63 7	38 4	15 6
1403		105 6	40 6	17 10
1404		91 7	46 6	17 10
1405		94 11	46 4	
1406		101 0		19 0
1407		85 8	52 8	20 6
1408		87 11	48 4	20 6
1409		49 4	46 0	25 0
1410		62 4	45 10	24 0
1411		78 8	49 0	26 8
1412		95 11	32 8	29 8

Park pasture receipts

Year				
1353	21 7	46 6	22 0	11 7
1354	nil	36 1	21 4	29 3
1355	nil	nil	nil	nil
1356	nil	nil	nil	nil
1357	nil	4 0	26 7	8½
1358	3 8	61 0	12 7	22 6
1359	20 7	62 0	11 0	27 1
1360	17 1	62 6	9 9	36 9
1362	nil	nil	19 5	26 2
1363	nil	nil	25 0	27 6
1364	12 3	34 0	16 3	31 0
1366	35 0	56 10	32 1	34 7
1369	35 8	48 5	18 5	27 7
1370	30 0	53 4	19 8	26 6
1371	30 0	nil	26 8	
1372	36 0	84 0	26 8	30 4
1373	45 8	77 0	26 10	26 2

Year			
1415	58 0	21 8	26 6
1416	57 5	26 0	25 8
1417	81 4	30 1	21 2
1418	49 1	28 0	24 6
1422	48 5	23 4	22 3
1423	39 9	24 10	21 9
1426	53 4	22 6	17 5
1427	40 4	22 10	20 1
1428	44 7	24 8	21 1
1429	66 4	28 2	23 6
1432	82 7	27 8	21 8
1434	73 4	25 8	16 6
1436	82 10	30 10	8 2
1438	83 8	18 8	24 7
1440	86 10	22 2	23 3
1442	65 7	20 6	22 9
1445	50 5	12 4	27 10

The pasture in Helstone-in-Triggshire park was farmed for 20s. annually from 1449 to 1457, and for 40s. annually from 1459 to 1485.

The pasture at Liskeard park was farmed for 20s. annually from 1449 to 1485.

The pasture in Climsland park was farmed for 26s. 8d. annually from 1449 to 1458; in 1459 it realised 21s. 3d, in 1460—23s. 3d., in 1462—20s., 1463—20s. 3d. From 1467 to 1485 a lease was granted in return for the upkeep of the park by the lessee.

No records of Restormel manor exist from 1394 to 1459, as it was not in Duchy hands. Records available after 1459 show that no revenues were obtained by the Duchy from sales of pasture as the park was invariably in the hands of favoured retainers who paid no farm.

The nil receipts recorded from 1354 to 1357 and 1362 to 1363 resulted from visits of the Black Prince to Cornwall, and the desire to build up stocks of deer.

lease of the agistment in the park of only seven years was given to John Nailer, the parker of Carrybullock park, also in 1449 at an annual rent of 26s. 8d.[1] When this lease expired it was not renewed, and once again agistment was sold annually, although it realised on average little more than 20s. until a new contract was entered into by Alfred Cornborough in 1462. Under the terms of this contract Alfred, the Custodian of Duchy Fees in Cornwall, agreed to maintain the enclosures of the park at his own expense and was granted underwood to this end by the Duchy.[2] In the ten years preceding this contract the Duchy had spent a little over 20s. annually on the maintenance of enclosures.

Scant use was ever made by Dukes of Cornwall of the facilities afforded by the parks. The Black Prince visited Cornwall three times and certainly hunted whilst he was there, but subsequent medieval Dukes apparently did not visit Cornwall at all.[3] Deer were occasionally given as gifts,[4] but on the whole the parks appear to have been enjoyed more by trespassers than by the Dukes.[5] A continual and substantial net deficit of expenditure over receipts was encountered by the Duchy throughout the fourteenth and fifteenth centuries, and the parks constituted an expensive and rather unnecessary luxury. The de-parking by Henry VIII was a sensible economy.

WOODLANDS

Although a much greater area of Cornwall was more thickly wooded in the middle ages than it is today,[6] timber and wood were still in very short supply and as such were treated as valuable commodities. Certain of the south-eastern manors of the Duchy appear to have contained the most extensive wooded areas on the manorial estates

[1] D.C.O. 53.
[2] D.C.O. 60. The terms of Alfred's lease also stated that he should '*faciet totam terram in parco predicto, ubi bosc' et petre non impedunt fossat', adhustam ac zabulat' voc Bete arat' et seminat'* '(D.C.O. 480).
[3] There are no traces of any further visits in the documentation of the estates. See also Rowse, 'The Duchy of Cornwall', p. 51.
[4] See for example, *B.P.R.* II, 206, 209.
[5] There were innumerable commissions formed throughout the fourteenth and fifteenth centuries to combat trespassers hunting in Duchy parks; for one example see: *C.P.R. 1340–1343*, pp. 582–3.
[6] See Henderson, *Essays in Cornish History*, pp. 135–51.

in the fourteenth and fifteenth centuries; in particular Liskeard, Calstock, Restormel, Penlyne, Rillaton and Climsland, with their woods lying for the most part in the fertile valleys of the Tamar and Fowey.[1] Although no surveys of the woodlands are extant it is probable that Liskeard had the largest area of woodland of all. It lay in six separate regions, namely Doublebois, Clyner, Conyngswood, Heghwood, Knylly and Oldepark, each of which was committed to the care of a woodward who was elected annually by the homage.[2] At Calstock there were three separate woods called Hirgard, Northwood and Crinscombe.

The Duchy looked upon woods almost exclusively as a source of building material to be conserved and protected, and not as a source of revenue, although some income was received from the sale of dead and fallen trees which were especially numerous after high winds. In addition the woodlands provided small and occasional revenues from the sale of woodland pasture and pannage, from furze and ferns, wild honey and bird traps.[3]

In times of desperate impecunity, however, the Duchy had sometimes to resort to the sale of timber to raise capital, as for example in 1359 when the Black Prince was making expensive preparations for war in the face of severely reduced revenues from his estates. On 11 August of this year the council of the Prince issued the following directive to the receiver of Cornwall: 'inasmuch as the prince is in great need of money at present, to sell part of the underwood called "herigard" within the prince's manor of Calstock, and part of the underwood called "Dublebois" within the prince's manor of Liskird, and part of the other underwoods in the parts of Cornwall which are outside the prince's parks, as the steward shall advise, and to enclose the woods so cut down with a hedge so that beasts may not enter and do damage to the new growth'.[4] The ministers' account of 1359/60 gives details of consequent sales of wood at

---

[1] In the Domesday survey Helston-in-Kirrier, Moresk, and Tybesta manors are listed as having considerable acreages of woodland, but the demands of mining may well have led to early destruction of woodlands (Henderson, *op. cit.* pp. 135, 151).

[2] See for example, P.R.O. SC.2.160/26, courts held at Liskeard, 2 Henry IV.

[3] The bird-traps or snares were designated *volatoriis* in the thirteenth and fourteenth centuries and *cockrodes* in the fifteenth; they commanded a rental of 6d. each on Climsland at the creation of the Duchy, but only 3d. each by the late fifteenth century.

[4] *B.P.R.* II, 155.

Liskeard totalling £27 16s. 5d. It was sold by the acre at prices ranging from 5s. to 21s.[1]

The Duchy made heavy demands upon the woodlands for timber used in the construction and maintenance of capital equipment. Castles, manor-houses, and hunting-lodges had to be repaired, parks had to be re-fenced and feeding-troughs built for the deer, and the tenants of lands and mills were usually granted sufficient large timber for essential renovations. Occasionally also gifts of trees and wood were made to religious houses,[2] or to favoured retainers and officials.[3]

The tenants of villein and conventionary holdings had no rights to the trees and brushwood growing on the lands they leased. But it is evident from manorial court rolls that many tenants did cut down trees and steal wood from the Duchy, sometimes on a grand scale.[4] Despite the Duchy's policy of conservation a gradual contraction in the area of woodland must have occurred in the course of the later middle ages, and woodlands may well have been severely damaged when manors passed out of Duchy hands.[5] There are no traces of any systematic planting of new trees by the Duchy.

TURBARIES

Turves were a most valuable commodity in medieval Cornwall, a county with an enormous demand for fuel, but only limited supplies. Much of the demand for fuel came from mining and stress was laid in tinners' charters upon the right to dig turves,[6] which were used in the first smelting of the ore.[7] A number of assessionable manors

---

[1] D.C.O. 13.

[2] For example, *B.P.R.* II, 65, 87, 181.

[3] *Ibid.* 82, 142, 180.

[4] It appears the fines imposed on tenants stealing wood or trees served more as a price for the amount stolen than as a deterrent, see below, pp. 223–4.

[5] It is apparent that manors which were granted out by the Crown or the Dukes of Cornwall were not always conscientiously managed. See, for example, *C.P.R. 1429–1436*, p. 133.

[6] See, for example, the charters of 1201 and 1305 (transcribed in Lewis, *Stannaries*, Appendices B and D, pp. 238, 239–41).

[7] Tin ore was smelted twice, once by the miners themselves and once by a professional smelter (Lewis, *op. cit.* pp. 16–17).

obtained revenues from turbaries, though many sources of supply were exhausted early in the fourteenth century. The two most valuable Duchy turbaries in Cornwall lay in the manors of Helston-in-Kirrier and Helstone-in-Triggshire, and the revenues derived from them have been tabulated below (Table 15).

Most striking is the tremendous increase in the sales of turbary on Helston-in-Kirrier manor over the first forty years of the fourteenth century, which correlates closely with rising tin production. Perhaps some of the figures given in the table below even understate the actual growth in receipts, for it is evident that sales were declining before 1339. The Inquisition *Post Mortem* made on the death of Earl Edmund in 1300 valued the turbary of Helston-in-Kirrier at 40s. per annum, substantially less than the £4 12s. 11d. and £7 17s. 1d. actually realised in 1298 and 1301 respectively.[1] The extent of the manor made in 1331[2] and the Caption of Seisin of 1337[3] valued the turbary at £40, thus it appears that the £35 of 1339 was probably consistently and significantly surpassed in the early thirteen-thirties, if one accepts that the extents of 1331 and 1337 are understatements also.

Receipts from the turbaries of both Helston-in-Kirrier and Helstone-in-Triggshire began to decline before the Great Plague of 1348/9, and fell dramatically in the years immediately after. But at Helston-in-Kirrier there was a swift recovery, and by 1359 the total receipts from the turbary were greater than for any year of which we have record before the plague. In this recovery the resilience of demand for turves may well have played only a minor part. In 1353 the council of the Black Prince sitting in London advised that the wasteful practices of allowing all persons to dig the turbary of Helston-in-Kirrier at will without 'livery of the ministers of the Prince', and 'the pricing of the turves so dug afterwards' was leading to great losses, and it was decided that 'the turbary shall henceforth be sold either by the day or by plots'.[4] But increased efficiency in management was only one of the factors making for increased receipts, for the account of 1359/60 makes a distinction between £5 19s. 5d. received from the sales of turbary proper and £16 4s.

[1] P.R.O. E.152/8.   [2] P.R.O. E.142/41.
[3] P.R.O. E.120/1.   [4] *B.P.R.* II, 52.

5½d. from *turba carbonum* (probably peat-charcoal).[1] The Duchy apparently took a toll of 12d. per load of peat-charcoal which was estimated to be half its value.[2] By the next available account, that of 1361/2, however, the seam appears to have been exhausted and henceforth the substantially lower receipts came exclusively from turves.[3]

The fifteenth century was to bring the complete exhaustion of all turbaries on the assessionable manors. The farm of the turbary on Helstone-in-Triggshire manor, which had been fixed at 40s. in 1366,[4] declined continually from the first decade of the fifteenth century until it was no more than 6s. 8d. in 1442, and by 1468 no revenues at all were obtained. The turbary of Helston-in-Kirrier was worth only 40s. by 1405, and slowly but consistently it fell to £1 14s. 6d. by 1415 when the manor was re-granted to the Sarnsfelds. When records of this manor are next available in 1459 the turbary was worth only 5s. 8d. and like that of Helstone-in-Triggshire it was soon to be completely exhausted.

The shortage of turbary throughout the county was acute in the later fifteenth century, and with the rising output of tin in both Devon and Cornwall from the late fourteen-sixties the situation became critical. In 1466 it was granted that 'stannarymen and their servants may dig turves in Dartmoor [another part of the southwestern estates of the Duchy of Cornwall], and take them back to Cornwall to melt their tin with, with pasture for their beasts, as the lands, moors, wastes, and groves in their own county have been so devastated of turf they cannot get enough to melt their tin and they have left unworked many mines to the diminution of coinage to 300 marks and more yearly'.[5]

TOLL-TIN

Every Cornish landowner had the right to exact as toll a certain

---

[1] D.C.O. 13. For peat-charcoal in south-west England see D. H. Woolner, 'Peat-Charcoal', *Devon and Cornwall Notes and Queries*, vol. VIII, part 5 (Oct. 1965).
[2] D.C.O. 15, Helston-in-Kirrier.
[3] P.R.O. SC.6.817/8.
[4] It was farmed to John Gyneys, who also leased the two manorial corn mills for £8 (D.C.O. 17, 18).
[5] *C.P.R. 1461–1467*, p. 482.

TABLE 15   Receipts from turbaries

	Helston-in-Kirrier			Helstone-in-Triggshire				Helston-in-Kirrier			Helstone-in-Triggshire		
	£	s.	d.	£	s.	d.		£	s.	d.	£	s.	d.
1297	4	12	4	1	5	5	1369	9	3	0	2	0	0
1298	4	12	11	1	4	6	1370	15	5	6	2	0	0
1301	7	17	1	1	0	7	1371	8	1	3	2	0	0
1302	6	17	5	1	0	8	1372	5	1	2	2	0	0
1303	7	1	5	1	0	6	1373	14	0	4	2	0	0
1304	6	13	11	1	0	7	1374	10	0	0	2	0	0
1305	6	6	0	1	0	5	1375						
1306	6	17	5	1	0	8	1377						
1307	6	15	2	1	1	10	1378	8	7	4			
1315	9	4	1	1	9	0	1379						
1316	16	4	6	1	12	1	1380	6	0	1			
1317	16	10	0	1	12	0	1382	3	18	2			
1324				1	13	6							
1339	35	0	3	1	18	10	1401				2	0	0
1340	31	5	6	1	19	2	1402				2	0	3
1342	23	1	4	1	16	5	1403				1	12	5
1345				1	17	8	1404				1	8	0
1347	23	10	0	1	6	11	1405	2	0	0	1	4	0
1349	6	18	7		6	1	1407	2	2	5	1	0	0
1350	8	9	8				1408	2	1	2	1	3	4
1351	5	8	2		13	4	1409	1	16	0	1	3	4
1352	6	17	8		9	6	1410	1	19	2	1	3	4
1353	16	12	1		9	10	1411	1	19	6	1	3	4
1354	16	11	8		9	4	1415	1	12	10	1	6	8
1355	21	8	2		9	5	1417	1	14	6	1	6	8
1356	25	13	11				1422–33				1	6	8
1357	30	2	6		12	0	1434–41					10	4
1358	31	18	8		11	9	1442–55					6	8
1359	36	18	4		11	6	1459		5	8	nil		
1360	22	3	10				1460		5	4	nil		
1362	6	12	8		12	3	1462		5	4	nil		
1363	3	17	4		15	5	1463		3	2	nil		
1364	10	16	11	1	14	5	1467–85		nil		nil		
1366	12	1	6	2	0	0							

proportion of all tin dug up within the bounds of his land. The
ratio of the toll levied by the Duchy in the later middle ages

unfortunately cannot be determined, but it is evident from other contemporary sources that it could be as little as one fifteenth of the tin dug or as much as one third.[1] In 1361 John de Treeures petitioned the council of the Prince stating he and his ancestors before him had received from tinners in his waste moor one third part of the tin they dug as toll, but lately fully sixty tinners had entered his demesne, 'which bears wheat, barley, oats, hay and peas, and is as good and fair as any soil in Cornwall', and were ruining the land. John claimed that 'the toll on the demesne should be increased beyond that on the moor, inasmuch as the land in the one case is worth more than in the other'.[2] On the assessionable manors toll was collected in kind by the reeve or his assistant and appraised at the last manorial court held before Michaelmas. It was the value put upon the tin at this court that the reeve was charged to deliver to the Duchy receiver, and not the sum he actually sold it for. As an alternative arrangement the rights of the Duchy to exact toll were sometimes farmed.

Although toll-tin was obtained from almost all assessionable manors in the course of the later middle ages, thus attesting the ubiquity of tin veins within the county,[3] the amounts obtained varied according to the proximity of manors to the main centres of mining activity and the amount of waste and moorland contained within their boundaries.[4] Whilst on most manors receipts tended to be small and intermittent, usually amounting to less than 10s. per annum and often to only a few pence, receipts from the western manors of Tywarnhaile and Helston-in-Kirrier, and from Tewington, lying on the southern tip of Blackmore stannary, were frequently substantial, and often higher in the fifteenth century than they had been in the fourteenth. At Tywarnhaile in the first half of the fifteenth century receipts had averaged approximately 20s. annually, or some 5 per cent of total manorial profits; whilst at Helston-in-Kirrier before the manor passed out of Duchy hands in 1415, they were even

---

[1] Lewis (*Stannaries*, p. 160) states that toll generally consisted of the fifteenth disk.
[2] *B.P.R.* II, 180.
[3] The only exceptions were Tintagel and Trematon. Unfortunately few continuous records of toll-tin receipts are available as they were often aggregated under 'Profits of Court' on the ministers' accounts.
[4] Tin was far more likely to lie amongst waste and moorland than good quality land.

higher at £4, almost 6 per cent of total profits. The fourteen-seventies brought renewed mining activity and at Tywarnhaile revenues from toll-tin jumped sharply to an average of more than £8 each year, whilst being maintained at £4 at Helston-in-Kirrier.

FISHERIES

The Duchy had freshwater fisheries in six of the seventeen assessionable manors. The most valuable of all belonged to the manor of Calstock and was located on the Tamar, extending from the rock called Tokelyng Torre upstream as far as Halton Pool.[1] A great weir called *Le Hacche* or *La Pool* spanned the Tamar and served to catch large quantities of salmon, trout, lampreys, and other fish. The upkeep of the weir was provided for by the labour services of certain of the free, conventionary, and villein tenants of Calstock, which amounted in all to more than 150 days' work. But the services were only rarely used, as the fishing rights and weir were usually farmed by the Duchy, with the farmer being responsible for maintenance, and consequently they were commuted for 1d. each. The farm of the fishing rights and weir realised £8 10s. 0d. and later £10 annually in the first half of the fourteenth century. After the Black Death had caused a fall in the farm the 'abbot and convent of Tavistock' secured a lease in perpetuity at the old farm of £10, and William Tavistock, the sitting tenant, was evicted after receiving 60s. in compensation from the abbot.[2]

Another important fishery lay in the Fowey river and extended 'from the port of St Saviour (Polruan) to the bridge of Reprenne (Respryn near Lanhydrock) as far as two oxen yoked together can go'.[3] In the first half of the fourteenth century this fishery was leased for 50s. annually, before passing into the hands of the burgesses of Lostwithiel who farmed it together with two corn mills for £13 6s. 8d. With the Black Death the fishery lapsed into the hands of the Duchy who sold fishing rights each year to whoever would take them,[4] but on average less than 20s. was realised annually and the weir appears to have fallen into complete disrepair. In 1365/6 a new

---

[1] See also Finberg, *Tavistock Abbey*, pp. 161–3.   [2] *B.P.R.* II, 70–1.
[3] P.R.O. E.152/8; P.R.O. C.133, file 95.   [4] *B.P.R.* II, 25.

lease was made with the burgesses of Lostwithiel for £4 annually, but also included were the profits of the maritime court of Lostwithiel and the farm of the local port dues called 'killage' which together were probably worth £2 annually.[1] When the borough returned to Duchy hands at the close of Henry VI's reign the fishery itself was worth only 6s. 8d.[2]

Two Duchy fisheries were held in freehold for fixed farms throughout the later middle ages: Liskeard fishery on the East Looe was held for 13s. 4d., and a small fishery at Tybesta for only 6d. Another tiny fishery at Penlyne was mentioned in 1301, and again in 1303 when it was farmed for 9d., but no subsequent trace of it can be found.[3] A fishery on the Lynher belonging to the manor of Trematon was worth 5s. to the Duchy when taken by the burgesses of Saltash. A few pence each year had been received on this manor from a toll on oysters caught in the Tamar estuary early in the fourteenth century, but there was no trace of this payment after the creation of the Duchy. The remaining fishery lay in the manor of Tewington and was leased for 4s. before 1337. In 1364 it was leased, together with the farm of the *traventria*, apparently a toll on alien fishermen, for 16s.[4]

Revenues were also obtained on Tintagel and Trematon manors from fines imposed on the inhabitants of those manors who beached their fishing boats on the lord's land. Exacted at the rate of 12d. per annum for each boat, they averaged somewhat less than 15s. each year at Tintagel and less than 5s. at Trematon.

FERRIES

Two of the three Duchy ferries in Cornwall crossed the Tamar. The most important was appended to Trematon manor and connected Saltash with Devon, landing at Little Ash where 35 acres of land belonging to the Duchy were divided into two holdings. The ferry was farmed for £8 10s. 0d. from 1301 until the burgesses of Saltash leased it for £10 during Queen Isabella's tenure of the estates. The Earldom and later the Duchy assumed responsibility for providing

[1] D.C.O. 17, 18.
[3] P.R.O. SC.6.811/2, 811/4.
[2] See, for example, D.C.O. 57.
[4] D.C.O. 473.

boats, and in 1298 a new one was supplied at a cost of 49s. 4d.,[1] and in 1351 another was provided for 66s. 8d.[2] In 1356, however, the Black Prince granted the ferry to William Lenche, his 'porter', for good service in England and Gascony, particularly at the battle of Poitiers where he lost an eye 'to the great emblemishing of his person'.[3] William continued to hold the ferry until the Honour of Trematon was granted to Nigel Loheryng, but nevertheless it appears that he granted the ferry on lease to the burgesses of Saltash as the Prince had done before him,[4] and the burgesses subsequently retained possession of the ferry throughout the fifteenth century.

The other Duchy ferries were of less importance.[5] One belonged to Calstock manor and was held in freehold for 2s. 6d., the other crossed the estuary of the Camel between the manor of Penmayne and the port of Padstow, and was called Black Rock Passage. In the early fourteenth century all the tenants of Penmayne rented it for 13s.

MANORIAL COURTS

Profits from manorial courts remained an important source of revenue for the Duchy throughout the later middle ages. On most manors during this period 13 courts were held each year, which included two views of frankpledge. The courts, especially in the fifteenth century, appeared to be geared more to the raising of money than to the enforcement of manorial discipline, for there were at that time no labour services and very little compulsory holding of land. The revenues from the courts can be divided into four main categories: fines for breaches or relaxation of seigneurial authority, death duties, the incidents of villeinage, and the small fines imposed for the normal run of rural misdemeanours.

At the first court held after Michaelmas, which was invariably the most profitable for the Duchy, the officials of the manor would be

---

[1] P.R.O. SC.6.811/1.   [2] P.R.O. SC.6.817/1.   [3] B.P.R. II, 98–9.
[4] The ferry was leased to the burgesses in 1357 (*B.P.R.* II, 122) and it seems likely that William left in force the lease made between the Duchy and the burgesses in 1356 (D.C.O. 472a, Trematon).
[5] For a general discussion of these ferries see Henderson, *Essays in Cornish History*, pp. 163–7.

elected and fines would be exacted from those who declined to serve. Other tenants would seek relaxation of suit to the court for the coming year, and occasionally exemption from suit of mill. The unfree who wished to live beyond the bounds of their native manor would make fine for licence to do so.

Death duties could take three different forms according to the status of tenants. Free tenants were liable to a relief of 12s. 6d. for each Cornish acre of land held, free conventionary tenants for a heriot of the best beast they possessed for each holding that they leased; and the unfree conventionaries and villeins were liable to forfeit all their goods and chattels to the lord. In addition the incoming tenant would be liable to pay a recognizance. A similar recognizance was also payable when holdings changed hands within the term of the conventionary leases.

The unfree were of course liable to more exactions than the free, and in particular paid fines for permission to marry, for fornication, and for licence to dwell outside their native manor. Fines for permission to marry could vary from as little as 12d. to as much as 6s. 8d. depending upon the circumstances. On the other hand fines for fornication were fixed at 5s. 1d., not only on the assessionable manors but also apparently on many other Cornish manors as well as some Devon manors.[1]

Table 16 shows the trends of the profits of the courts of those assessionable manors for which records are abundant in the fourteenth and fifteenth centuries. The creation of the Duchy brought a tightening of manorial discipline and considerably enhanced revenues from the manorial courts, despite the introduction of the assession system under which assession fines were accounted for separately as opposed to being grouped with the profits of court as they had been under the Earls. The second half of the fourteenth century saw a substantial rise in revenues which was mainly attributable to increased death duties occasioned by the series of plagues which struck Cornwall. The fifteenth century brought no collapse in manorial discipline and the full complement of 13 courts annually continued to be held on all but the smallest manors.

---

[1] On estates of Tavistock Abbey fines for *leywrite* were levied at 5s. 0½d. (Finberg, *Tavistock Abbey*, p. 78).

Although no trace of any fines for *leywrite* can be found on fifteenth-century court rolls, fines for licence to marry continued to be rigorously imposed upon the unfree. These fines usually amounted to 5s. each on Liskeard manor, although 20d. was a common exaction on Climsland and Calstock in Edward IV's reign. The efficiency of manorial courts in exacting these fines is demonstrated by the case of John Scoria of Calstock. It was presented at the court of 20 January 1470 that John Scoria, *nativus domini*, who was at that time paying 12d. annually for permission to live outside the manor at Plympton, had married without first obtaining permission. On 3 April in the same year it was duly recorded that John had made a payment of 20d. for the licence in dispute.[1]

The right of the Duke to seize all the goods and chattels of his unfree tenants on death had been challenged in 1382, but without success. Throughout the fifteenth century bond tenants continued to be subjected to this imposition, although it became standard practice to allow 'the expenses incurred in the death of the tenant' to be deducted along with one third of the value of his estate.

The decline in the levels of profits of court in the fifteenth

TABLE 16   *Profits of the manorial courts*[a]

	Helstone-in-Triggshire			Rillaton			Climsland			Liskeard			Tybesta			Tywarn-haile			Helston-in-Kirrier		
	£	s.	d.	£	s.	d.	£	s.	d.	£	s.	d.	£	s.	d.	£	s.	d.	£	s.	d.
1297–07	7	10	0	1	0	0	7	10	0	3	10	0	3	0	0	2	10	0	4	10	0
1315–17	—			1	10	0	6	10	0	4	10	0	4	0	0	2	10	0	5	10	0
1339–47	9	10	0	2	0	0	6	0	0	5	0	0	4	0	0	3	10	0	8	0	0
1351–64	9	0	0	3	0	0	9	0	0	8	10	0	7	10	0	—			8	10	0
1365–77	10	0	0	3	10	0	10	10	0	9	10	0	8	0	0	3	10	0[b]	6	0	0
1400–20	5	10	0	2	10	0	7	10	0	5	0	0	3	0	0	1	10	0	3	0	0[c]
1421–60	4	10	0	2	0	0	4	10	0	4	10	0	3	0	0	1	10	0	—		
1461–85	4	0	0	2	10	0	4	10	0	4	10	0	2	10	0	1	10	0	3	10	0

[a] All figures to nearest 10s.
[b] Based upon accounts from 1372 to 1382.
[c] Based upon accounts from 1406 to 1415.

[1] P.R.O. SC.2.158/12.

century was apparently due to the combined influence of many factors, amongst which the slow fall in the numbers of the unfree may have played a major part. But as a manorial institution the court remained virtually unaltered throughout the later middle ages, and unfree status was to continue on the assessionable manors, in name at least, until the reign of James I.[1]

MANORIAL PROFITS AND THEIR COLLECTION

The profits of the assessionable manors were second in importance to the stannaries as a source of Duchy revenue from Cornwall. Before the Black Death when all the manors were in Duchy hands they provided approximately 15–18 per cent of Cornish revenues, and probably almost 25 per cent in Edward IV's reign when receipts from most other sources had slumped.

Whilst the assessionable manors formed part of the Earldom of Cornwall from 1297 to 1306, profits averaged £380 annually and fluctuated very little from year to year. Despite the scarcity of evidence concerning the collection of manorial revenues at this time there is no reason to believe there was any serious indebtedness.[2] The steady rise in profits, apparent from the assumption of the estates by Queen Isabella in 1317, was transformed into a veritable flood tide by the increased efficiency of the administrations of John of Eltham and the Black Prince, which took full advantage of increasing demand for land. In response the value of the assessionable manors leapt to an annual average of almost £600 in the thirteen-forties, over 50 per cent more than they had been worth in the first decade of the century.

The administration of the Duchy at first encountered considerable difficulty in securing payments from local ministers. The receivers' accounts of 1338/9 and 1339/40 tell a story of some disorder and of a chronic inability on the part of the receiver to collect money due to him from manorial reeves.[3] It appears that substantial sums were

---

[1] *Calendar of State Papers Domestic, 1628–9*, p. 7.
[2] For example, by the time the account of 29 Edward I (P.R.O. SC.6.811/2) had been enrolled on the Pipe Roll (P.R.O. E.372/146), Thomas de la Hyde, the receiver, had accounted for all but £11 7s. od. of his total charge from Cornwall of £1,733 17s. 8d.
[3] P.R.O. SC.6.816/11 and 12, receivers' accounts.

left owing for a number of years after the creation of the Duchy in 1337—a state of affairs which prevailed throughout the estates in Cornwall and in other parts of the country,[1] and which seems to have been due to recalcitrance on the part of local officials rather than underlying economic troubles, of which there is little sign apart from Helston-in-Kirrier manor.[2] For a number of years before 1342 reeves in arrears had been arrested and delivered into the hands of the keeper of Launceston gaol, who was also the Duchy receiver. Most reeves were, however, released immediately upon finding sufficient security for their debts, again with the exception of the reeves of Helston-in-Kirrier manor whose debts had reached such spectacular proportions they were kept in prison. But it was in 1342 that the Duchy first took sterner and, as it proved, more successful measures to cure the insolvency. A special meeting of the Prince's council was held in Cornwall, including amongst its members royal justices, and soon afterwards parties of horsemen and footsoldiers were despatched from Restormel castle to the manors of Helston-in-Kirrier, Moresk, Liskeard, Tintagel and Helstone-in-Triggshire to distrain for outstanding debts.[3] From this year until the outbreak of the Black Death in the spring of 1349 there was no further insolvency on the assessionable manors.

This short period of indebtedness was to be one of the rare periods when the Duchy experienced any difficulty at all in the collection of revenues throughout the fourteenth and fifteenth centuries. No doubt a major part in this achievement was played by the generous allowances made to tenants in need and the frequency with which rent levels were reassessed through the conventionary system. Even the Black Death had only a short-lived effect on the solvency of the manors, and from 1350/1 profits, although sharply diminished, were being paid almost in full.[4]

After the assession of 1356, in the years when enstalments of assession fines were paid, total profits from the Duchy manors were

---

[1] The accounts of the bailiffs of the hundreds and stannaries were also seriously in arrears. There was considerable opposition and some refusal throughout the Prince's estates to account at his exchequer which was set-up in 1345 (T. F. Tout, *Chapters in the Administrative History of Medieval England* (6 vols, Manchester, 1920–33), v, 324).
[2] For the peculiar conditions affecting this manor see above, pp. 93–7.
[3] D.C.O. 1, receivers' account.   [4] See, for example, P.R.O. SC.6.817/1 ff., 812/6 f.

less than 10 per cent lower than they had been before the plague, if the value of the three manors ceded to Walter de Wodeland in 1350 is taken into account.[1] This healthy state of affairs continued until the closing years of the life of the Black Prince when the manorial estates began to be broken up. In 1369 Nigel Loheryng was granted Calstock and Trematon manors for life, and on the death of the Prince in 1376 the remaining Duchy manors were divided between his son and his widow. Subsequent grants during the reign of Richard II led to an almost complete dispersion of the assessionable manors, with Richard for most years receiving less than £30 annually from the manors in his hands.

Henry IV was only partly successful in his attempt to regroup the Duchy estates in the hands of his son who was created Duke of Cornwall in 1399, and until 1456 more than half the assessionable manors were to remain outside the direct control of the Duchy. Trematon, Calstock, Restormel, Penlyne, Penkneth, Tewington, Moresk, and Tintagel manors as well as certain other Duchy properties in Cornwall were allowed to remain in the possession of Elizabeth, Countess of Huntingdon, and her husband John, for life, with the proviso that if Elizabeth died before John he should pay 100 marks for retaining the estates.[2] Helston-in-Kirrier manor, which had been restored to the Duchy in 1406 was re-granted to the Sarnsfelds in 1415 on appeal.[3] And when the manors in the hands of the Huntingdons finally reverted to the Duchy in 1443 they were immediately farmed or invested in retainers, none remaining in Duchy possession.[4]

In 1456 Edward of Westminster, first-born son of Henry VI,

---

[1] These three manors were valued at 100 marks by the Duchy (above, p. 111).

[2] *Rot. Parl.* III, 531–2; P.R.O. SC.6.813/22.

[3] *C.C.R. 1413–1419*, p. 247.

[4] In 1443 Restormel, Penlyne, Penkneth, Moresk, Tintagel and Tewington together with two Duchy boroughs were farmed to Thomas Bodulgate and John Trevilian for seven years (*C.F.R. 1431–1445*, p. 187), this was later changed to a life tenancy at £80 per annum (*C.P.R. 1446–1452*, p. 80). In 1451 they were farmed to John Trevilian and Henry, Duke of Exeter, for £91 10s. od. annually (D.C.O. 206). John, Duke of Exeter, was granted the Calstock and Trematon manors in 1444 (*C.P.R. 1441–1446*, p. 267). Helston-in-Kirrier manor and borough were granted to John Arundell and John Trevilian in 1444 (*C.P.R. 1441–1446*, p. 322). In 1455 they were in the hands of John Nanfan who held them on a twenty-year lease for £50 per annum (D.C.O. 206).

became Duke of Cornwall, and all seventeen assessionable manors were granted to him; they were to remain in Duchy hands throughout the rest of our period. From 1459 to 1484 the annual profits of the manors averaged just under £500, or almost 20 per cent lower than they had been when all seventeen manors were last in Duchy hands in the thirteen-forties; but if the severe insolvency of Helston-in-Kirrier manor in the earlier period is taken into account, then actual receipts were perhaps only 15 per cent lower. We have seen how the value of mills, turbaries, agistment, manorial courts and many other sources of manorial revenue declined in the course of the later middle ages on manors in all parts of Cornwall, but despite these trends profits from some south-eastern manors in the later fifteenth century were considerably higher than they had ever been before. These manors were exceptions, however, and all others were worth considerably less than they had been before the Black Death, or in the case of Helstone-in-Triggshire manor than it had been in the first half of the fifteenth century.

GRAPHS OF MANORIAL PROFITS

The following graphs are an attempt to render the mass of information concerning the profitability and solvency of the assessionable manors contained in the ministers' and receivers' accounts into a convenient and easily assimilable form. No graphs have been constructed of the profitability of the small manors of Talskiddy, Penmayne, Penlyne, Restormel, and Penkneth; and owing to the complexity of the accounting procedure used for Trematon manor, which involved receipts from a large number of knights' fees and the ports of Plymouth and Saltash, it has not proved possible to compile accurate statistics of the profitability of this manor.

Profits

This schedule portrays the amounts manorial reeves were required to pay to the receiver in any given year; it does not include arrears. Receipts and expenses totally unconnected with the manors, which on rare occasions found their way on to the accounts, have been excluded.

Adjusted profits

This schedule has been created by manipulating the data in the ministers' accounts to suit the needs of the historian, and it is an attempt to put the manorial profits into a form which obviates unreal fluctuations and facilitates accurate comparisons over the whole course of the fourteenth and fifteenth centuries. To this end, expenses such as those paid for repairs to castles and deer-parks, which fluctuated considerably from year to year, and those paid as salaries to constables, chaplains, and parkers, which were sometimes debited to reeves' accounts and sometimes the receivers', have not been deducted from manorial profits; similarly, receipts such as those from the farms of the bailiwicks of hundreds and stannaries have not been credited. Furthermore, the amounts due from assession fines and tallage on conventionary and villein lands, which were payable in instalments over the first six years of the seven-year assessional term, have been averaged over each year of the term, thus avoiding the technical fall in the values of manors every seventh year.

Details of all the adjustments that have been made are noted on the graphs below. On manors where there were no extraordinary expenses or receipts the *Profits* and *Adjusted Profits* schedules will be identical for the periods when no assession fines were levied, i.e., 1297–1324 and 1349–57.

Receipts

These are the amounts paid to the receiver in the year indicated, and have been extracted from the receivers' accounts. They can include payments of the charge of the current year as well as payments of arrears, if any, of previous years. Receivers' accounts were compiled after manorial accounts had been audited.

1296/7 = accounting year Michaelmas 1296 to Michaelmas 1297.

To facilitate the accurate scanning of both line and bar schedules it has been necessary to split the vertical axes of most figures.

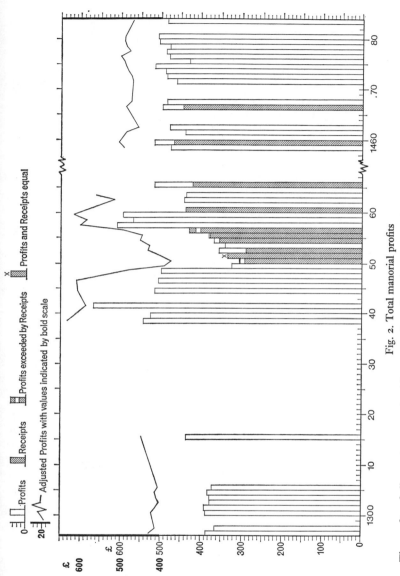

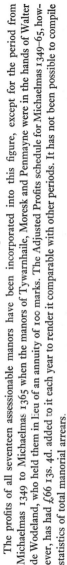

Fig. 2. Total manorial profits

The profits of all seventeen assessionable manors have been incorporated into this figure, except for the period from Michaelmas 1349 to Michaelmas 1365 when the manors of Tywarnhaile, Moresk and Penmayne were in the hands of Walter de Wodeland, who held them in lieu of an annuity of 100 marks. The Adjusted Profits schedule for Michaelmas 1349–65, however, has had £66 13s. 4d. added to it each year to render it comparable with other periods. It has not been possible to compile statistics of total manorial arrears.

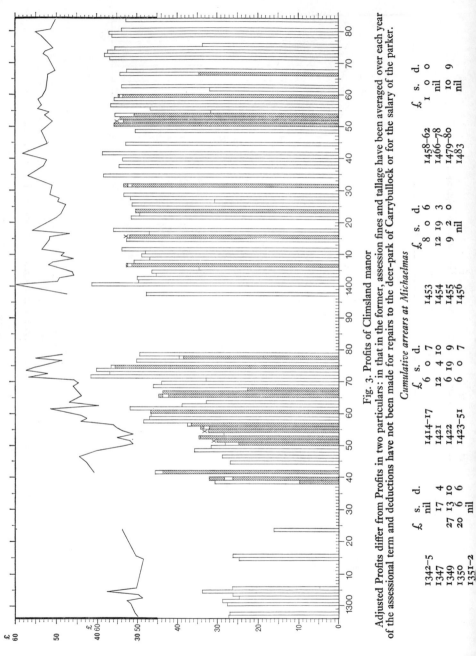

Fig. 3. Profits of Climsland manor

Adjusted Profits differ from Profits in two particulars: in that in the former, assession fines and tallage have been averaged over each year of the assessional term and deductions have not been made for repairs to the deer-park of Carrybullock or for the salary of the parker.

Cumulative arrears at Michaelmas

	£	s.	d.			£	s.	d.
1342–5			nil		1414–17	6	0	7
1347		17	4		1421	12	4	10
1349	27	13	10		1422	6	19	9
1350	20	6	6		1423–51	6	0	7
1351–2			nil					

	£	s.	d.			£	s.	d.
1453	8	0	6		1458–62	1	0	0
1454	12	19	3		1466–78			nil
1455	9	2	0		1479–80		10	9
1456			nil		1483			nil

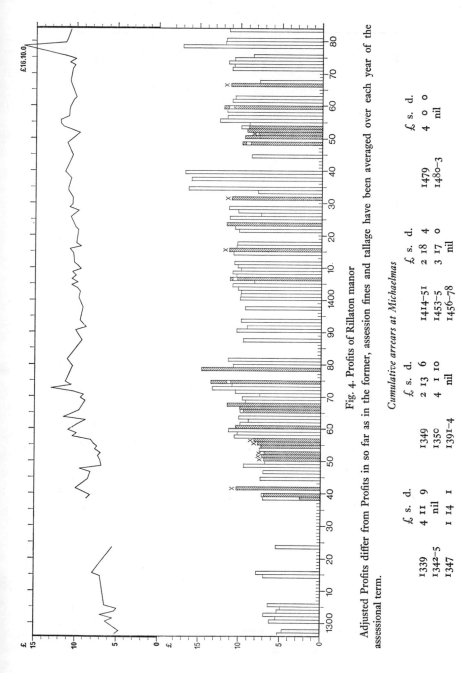

Fig. 4. Profits of Rillaton manor

Adjusted Profits differ from Profits in so far as in the former, assession fines and tallage have been averaged over each year of the assessional term.

Cumulative arrears at Michaelmas

	£	s.	d.		£	s.	d.		£	s.	d.
1339	4	11	9	1349	2	13	6	1414–51	2	18	4
1342–5		nil		1350	4	1	10	1453–5	3	17	0
1347	1	14	1	1391–4		nil		1456–78		nil	

	£	s.	d.
1479	4	0	0
1480–3		nil	

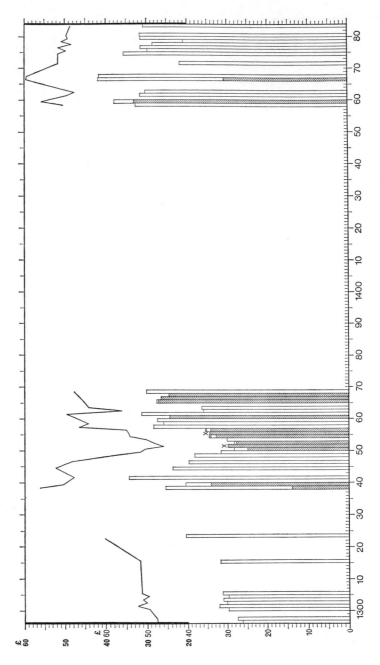

Fig. 5. Profits of Calstock manor

In addition to the usual adjustments made to revenues from assession fines and tallage, Adjusted Profits differ from Profits in that money expended on the cost of repairing the fish weir of Calstock have not been deducted.

Profits and Adjusted Profits for 1466/7 and 1467/8 include a fine of £10 13s. 8d. imposed on the Abbot of Tavistock for a breach of the terms of the contract upon which he leased the 'great fish weir' from the Duchy.

Cumulative arrears at Michaelmas

	£	s.	d.		£	s.	d.		£	s.	d.
1345	15	16	10	1458–61		nil		1478		8	4
1347		19	1	1462–6		10	5	1479		12	4
1349	25	12	2	1467	11	4	0	1480	1	10	8
1350	19	11	4	1471		nil		1483		nil	
1351	2	6	4	1474	7	0	0				
1352	3	4	5	1475–7		nil					

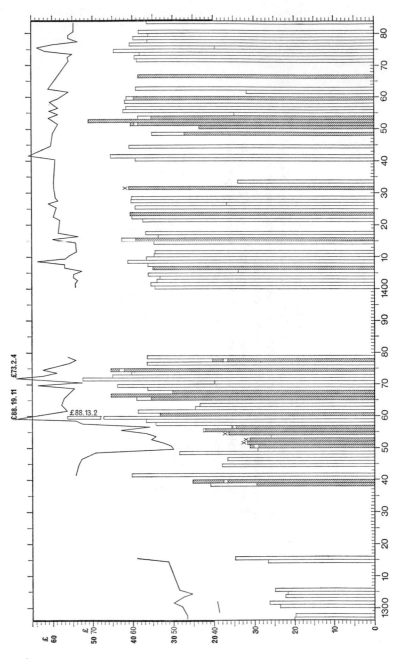

Fig. 6. Profits of Liskeard manor

In addition to the usual adjustments made to revenues from assession fines and tallage, Adjusted Profits differ from Profits in that expenditure on the park and manor house, and the salary of the parker have not been deducted.

The Profits and Adjusted Profits for 1359/60 were swelled by receipts from the sale of wood totalling £27 16s. 5d.

Cumulative arrears at Michaelmas

	£	s.	d.		£	s.	d.		£	s.	d.		£	s.	d.
1342	1	11	3	1414	18	8	2	1456		nil		1472	4	2	0
1347	1	16	4	1415–44	8	10	0	1458	14	3	7	1473	11	1	6
1349	47	15	2	1448	11	3	9	1459	23	10	9	1474	23	15	6
1350	33	13	6	1451	30	13	5	1461	11	6	5	1475	13	1	6
1351	12	3	4	1453	22	2	8	1462	12	8	8	1476	11	10	0
1352	13	19	10	1454	26	4	9	1466	20	15	10	1477–83	12	3	4
1353	10	4	11	1455	40	3	4	1471	3	4	6				

The arrears from 1466–83 consisted almost exclusively of unpaid amercements levied in the manorial court.

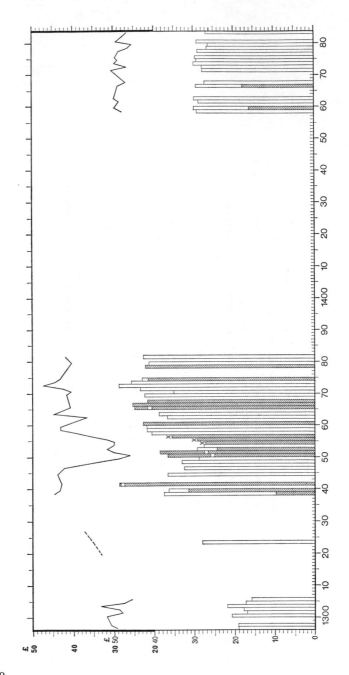

Fig. 7. Profits of Tintagel manor

In addition to the usual adjustments made to revenues from assession fines and tallage, Adjusted Profits differ from Profits in that expenditure on Tintagel castle and the salaries of the constable and chaplain employed there has not been deducted.

Cumulative arrears at Michaelmas

	£	s.	d.		£	s.	d.		£	s.	d.
1342	7	7	7	1458	2	13	5	1467	86	8	2
1345	20	10	7	1459	1	2	0	1471–3		nil	
1347		4	0	1461	19	16	6	1474–80	12	6	2
1349	26	16	7	1462	32	6	3	1483		nil	
1350	39	4	7	1466	76	2	2				

The arrears contracted between 1461 and 1467 consist exclusively of the annual stipend of £13 13s. 9d. paid by the reeve to Thomas Clemence, constable of Tintagel castle and controller of Duchy building works in Cornwall, but which had not, as yet, been allowed by the receiver.

The arrears of £12 6s. 2d. outstanding from 1474–80 consisted of repairs to Tintagel castle, executed on the orders of John Robyn, yeoman of the King, but not allowed by the receiver.

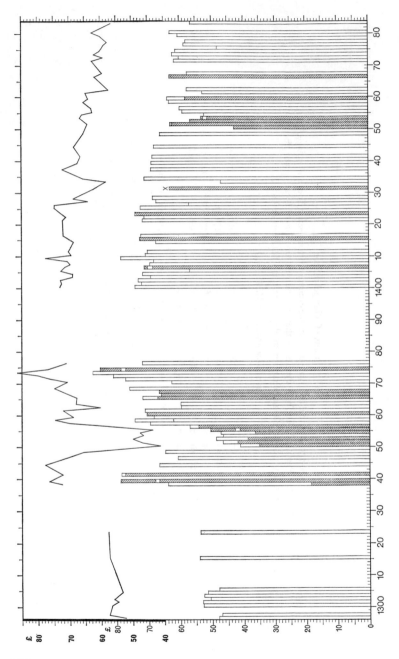

Fig. 8. Profits of Helstone-in-Triggshire manor

From 1297 until 1351 the profits of the small manor of Penmayne and the borough of Camelford were included on Helstone-in-Triggshire's accounts; these profits have been separated as accurately as possible from those of Helstone-in-Triggshire manor, but no totals of arrears can be given until after 1351.

Adjusted Profits differ from Profits in that revenues from assession fines and tallage have been averaged over each year of the assessionable term and expenditure on the park of Helsbury and Lanteglos has not been deducted.

Cumulative arrears at Michaelmas

	£ s. d.		£ s. d.		£ s. d.
1414	15 0 0	1431–44	8 1 2	1461	3 6 8
1416	12 3 8	1448	55 0 0	1462	5 0 0
1421	12 18 8	1451	92 8 7	1466	2 6 8
1422	20 5 5	1453	96 10 9	1467	1 6 8
1425	8 6 2	1454	94 19 8	1471	nil
1426	11 9 8	1455	88 2 10	1477	2 10 0
1427	13 17 6	1456–8	nil	1478–80	10 0 0
1428	14 15 4	1459	1 15 0	1483	nil

The arrears contracted between 1448 and 1455 consist almost exclusively of expenditure incurred in the rebuilding of a hunting lodge in the manorial deer-park which was for a time not allowed by the receiver.

H

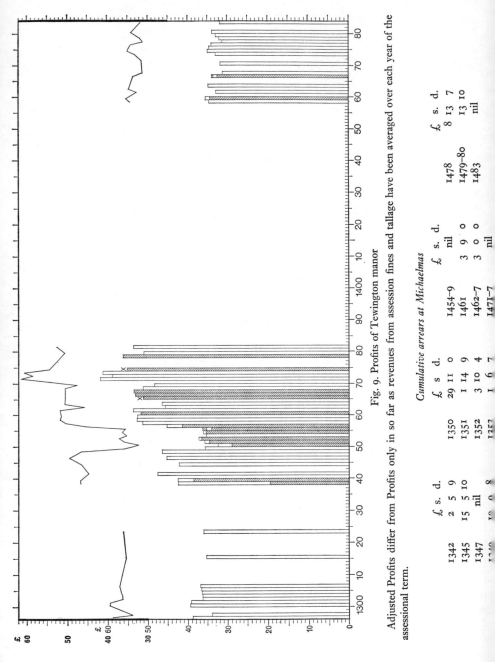

Fig. 9. Profits of Tewington manor

Adjusted Profits differ from Profits only in so far as revenues from assession fines and tallage have been averaged over each year of the assessional term.

Cumulative arrears at Michaelmas

	£	s.	d.
1342	2	5	9
1345	15	5	10
1347			nil
134?	10	0	8

	£	s	d.
1350	29	11	0
1351	1	14	9
1352	3	10	4
135?	1	6	7

	£	s.	d.
1454-9			nil
1461	3	9	0
1462-7	3	0	0
1471-7			nil

	£	s.	d.
1478	8	13	7
1479-80		13	10
1483			nil

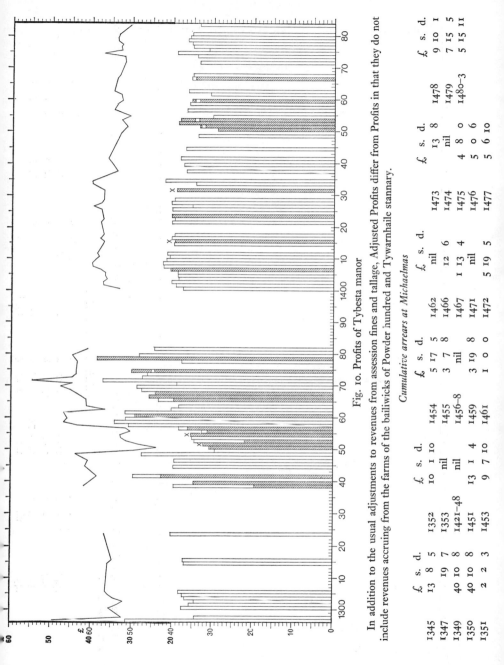

Fig. 10. Profits of Tybesta manor

In addition to the usual adjustments to revenues from assession fines and tallage, Adjusted Profits differ from Profits in that they do not include revenues accruing from the farms of the bailiwicks of Powder hundred and Tywarnhaile stannary.

Cumulative arrears at Michaelmas

Year	£	s.	d.		Year	£	s.	d.
1345	13	8	5		1352	10	1	10
1347		19	7		1353		nil	
1349	40	10	8		1421–48		nil	
1350	40	10	8		1451	13	1	4
1351	2	2	3		1453	9	7	10

Year	£	s.	d.		Year	£	s.	d.
1454	5	17	5		1462		nil	
1455	3	7	8		1466		12	6
1456–8		nil			1467	1	13	4
1459	3	19	8		1471		nil	
1461	1	0	0		1472	5	19	5

Year	£	s.	d.		Year	£	s.	d.
1473		13	8		1478	9	10	1
1474		nil			1479	7	15	5
1475	4	8	0		1480–3	5	15	11
1476	5	0	6					
1477	5	6	10					

213

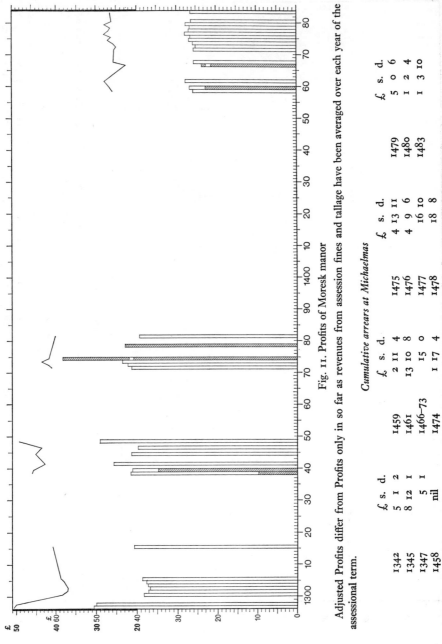

Fig. 11. Profits of Moresk manor

Adjusted Profits differ from Profits only in so far as revenues from assession fines and tallage have been averaged over each year of the assessional term.

Cumulative arrears at Michaelmas

	£	s.	d.		£	s.	d.		£	s.	d.		£	s.	d.
1342	5	1	2	1459	2	11	4	1475	4	13	11	1479	5	0	6
1345	8	12	1	1461	13	10	8	1476	4	9	6	1480	1	2	4
1347		5	1	1466–73		15	0	1477		16	10	1483	1	3	10
1458		nil		1474	1	17	4	1478		18	8				

214

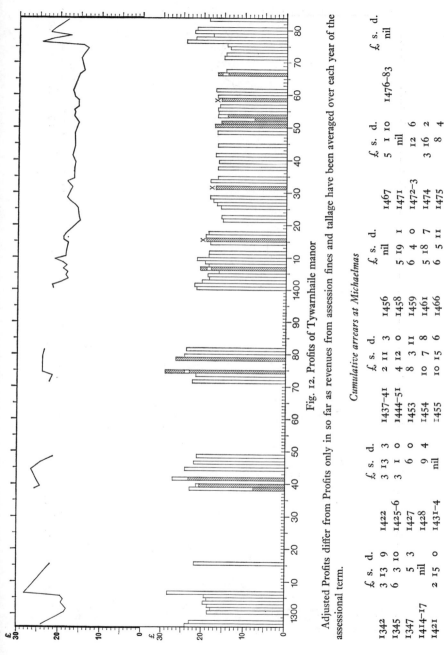

Fig. 12. Profits of Tywarnhaile manor

Adjusted Profits differ from Profits only in so far as revenues from assession fines and tallage have been averaged over each year of the assessional term.

Cumulative arrears at Michaelmas

	£	s.	d.		£	s.	d.		£	s.	d.		£	s.	d.		£	s.	d.		£	s.	d.
1342	3	13	9	1422	3	13	3	1437–41	2	11	3	1456		nil		1467	5	1	10	1476–83		nil	
1345	6	3	10	1425–6	3	1	0	1444–51	4	12	0	1458	5	19	1	1471		nil					
1347		5	3	1427		6	0	1453	8	3	11	1459	6	4	0	1472–3		12	6				
1414–17		nil		1428		9	4	1454	10	7	8	1461	5	18	7	1474	3	16	2				
1421	2	15	0	1431–4		nil		1455	10	15	6	1466	6	5	11	1475		8	4				

215

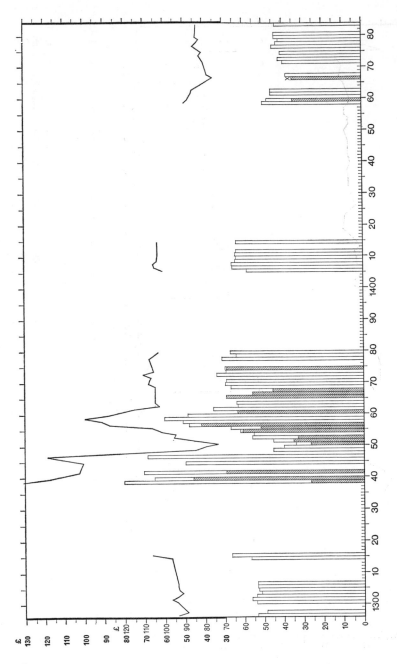

Fig. 13. Profits of Helston-in-Kirrier manor

Adjusted Profits differ from Profits only in so far as revenues from assession fines and tallage have been averaged over each year of the assessional term.

The serious indebtedness of the manorial officials in the 1340s should be noted (above, pp. 93–7), as both Profits and Adjusted Profits for these years tend to exaggerate the value of this manor to the Duchy.

Cumulative arrears at Michaelmas

	£	s.	d.			£	s.	d.
1339	30	10	1		1466–7	11	0	0
1340	110	0	0	(estimated)	1471	2	6	5
1345	128	14	1		1473		12	6
1458	1	10	0		1474–83		nil	
1459	1	0	0					
1461	12	0	1					
1462	15	16	8					

9

SOME ASPECTS OF RURAL
SOCIETY

Impressive advances have been made in recent years towards the writing of a meaningful social history of medieval England, but it is apparent that the social histories of many regions will remain largely unwritten since illuminating documents in sufficient quantities are not available. We are perhaps able to learn more about the inhabitants of the Cornish manors of the Duchy of Cornwall than we can about the inhabitants of the majority of estates in remote parts of medieval Britain, the lack of a good series of manorial court rolls of Duchy manors being more than compensated by the existence of unusually fertile alternative sources, namely assession rolls, council registers, and petitions. Much of interest can also be gleaned from extra-manorial sources, of which the most useful are tax and judicial records.

The tenants of the assessionable manors in the later middle ages fall into two main groups: free and customary. It is of the customary tenants that our knowledge is most full, for almost continuous records of their names and landholdings are contained in the assession rolls of the fourteenth and fifteenth centuries. The free tenants, who for the most part held large amounts of land for nominal rents and services, are listed in detail at only two points in time: in the decades preceding the Black Death,[1] and in the reign of Edward IV.[2] Conventionary lands, as we have seen, formed the bulk of all the lands of the assessionable manors and were leased at regular intervals in an almost free market, thus they could be taken by any who could satisfy and were willing to accept the conditions of tenure.[3] Consequently conventionary tenants were a heterogeneous

---

[1] The first detailed surveys of the free tenants were those made between 1326 and 1332 (P.R.O. E.142/41). These were followed in 1337 by the Caption of Seisin (P.R.O. E.120/1), and in 1345 by the survey of William de Cusancia, fragments of which survive in the Duchy of Cornwall Office, the Cornwall County Record Office, Cambridge University Library and the Public Record Office.   [2] D.C.O. 480.
[3] For a discussion of the conditions of conventionary tenure see Chapter 3, above.

body, which at various times in the later middle ages included Duchy officials, burgesses, merchants, tin-mining entrepreneurs, and clerics, as well as peasant farmers.

MOBILITY AND EMPLOYMENT

The lists of persons holding land from the Duchy contained in assession rolls provide only a partial survey of the inhabitants of Duchy manors, for many residents did not hold land directly from the Duchy, being sub-tenants of free tenants or of customary tenants amongst whom sub-letting was common. Many were also agricultural labourers, craftsmen, miners, fishermen, etc., and one must also take account of the existence of a substantial body of under-employed, unemployed, and unemployable, who remain almost completely hidden from sight in the middle ages but who are all too evident in the succeeding centuries of Tudor and Stuart England.

A comparison of tenants listed in the manorial surveys drawn up by the administration of the Earldom of Cornwall between 1326 and 1332 with persons paying the royal subsidy of 1327, reveals a multitude of persons listed as dwelling on the assessionable manors who do not appear to have held land from the Earldom of Cornwall.[1] Similarly a substantial proportion of landholders did not pay the subsidy, presumably because they had less than the minimum level of wealth, or gained exemption through having connections with tin-mining, or because they did not live on their holding. For example, despite only 95 persons being listed as tenants of Helston-in-Kirrier manor in 1331, more than 125 persons, many of whom were not tenants, are recorded as dwelling within the boundaries of the same manor in the subsidy lists made four years earlier. In the fifteenth century, in the east of Cornwall in particular, it became standard practice for persons living on Duchy manors without leasing land to pay a tax of a penny per year, *censaria pro libertatem eiusdem manerii habendo*, and substantial numbers are recorded paying this tax.[2]

[1] For the subsidy of 1327 see P.R.O. E.179/87/7, 87/37. For the manorial surveys see P.R.O. E.142/41. A comparison is facilitated by names in the subsidy returns occasionally being grouped under manors instead of parishes, e.g. Helston-in-Kirrier and Calstock.   [2] See, for example, P.R.O. SC.6.819/10 and 819/15.

Rural Society

The overall impression created by Cornish sources is that society was fluid, with persons frequently moving from occupation to occupation and from region to region. The violent fluctuations which occurred in the output of tin over relatively short periods show just how reliant this sector of the economy must have been on a migrant labour force. An indication of the scale of mobility in agrarian society, particularly in evidence in the first half of the fourteenth century, was the frequency with which conventionary holdings changed hands, and the fact that in the majority of cases the incoming tenant cannot be traced as having leased land from the Duchy before. From the earliest rentals of 1326 to 1333 a remarkable turnover in conventionary tenants is evident on all manors, and barely half the tenants listed as holding land in 1337 remained in possession at the assession of 1347. The pestilence of 1348/9, combined with the tendency to change, resulted in only 10–25 per cent of holdings being leased in 1356 by those who had leased them at the preceding assession nine years earlier. But as conditions became increasingly more settled in the later fourteenth century so progressively greater proportions of the tenantry re-leased their holdings at successive assessions, until no less than 85 per cent of the conventionary tenants of the eastern manors of Climsland and Liskeard leased the same holdings in 1371 as they had in 1364. Conditions appear to have remained relatively more settled throughout most of the fifteenth century, especially upon those manors whose lands were in great demand. For example, at the 1427 assession some 60–70 per cent of the conventionaries of Helstone-in-Triggshire and Liskeard renewed their leases for a further seven-year term, whilst an even greater proportion did so at Climsland. The favouring of longer tenancies was assisted by the introduction of fourteen- and twenty-one-year leases, which predominated for a while after 1441.

The evidence of the average length of tenancies provided by the assession rolls is, however, only partial and in many instances can be misleading. From manorial court rolls it is apparent that many tenancies did not even last the seven years of the original agreement, and a number of holdings may well have changed hands more than once during this term. As long as the sitting tenant could find another who was willing and able to take his holding on the same terms as he himself had leased it, the Duchy generally offered no objections to a transfer. The court rolls of Duchy manors contain many examples of holdings changing hands with the consent of the court and on payment of a small fine for *recognitio*, usually 6d. or 8d. For example, in the 12 months from Michaelmas 1431/2 there were five recorded instances of holdings, or fractions of holdings, being transferred on Liskeard manor; and three further holdings changed hands in the following year.[1] In no case did the change result from the death of a tenant. Thus the short seven-year lease sometimes proved to be of even shorter duration.

Chevage payments also provide a useful guide to the scale of migrations at some periods, although at others they cannot be isolated from the total profits of courts. The receipts from chevage in the early fourteenth century, from 1297 to the creation of the Duchy in 1337, show that substantial numbers of persons were paying for licence to dwell beyond the bounds of their native manors.[2] On certain manors, such as Moresk and Helston-in-Kirrier in the west of Cornwall, chevage payers at this time often constituted more than half as many persons as the numbers of tenants, whilst for the assessionable manors as a whole they averaged more than a quarter the numbers of tenants. The first account of the manors under Duchy administration, that of 1338/9, registers a considerable fall in receipts from chevage, especially upon the western and central manors.[3] The Black Death a decade later caused a further contraction, compatible with the fall in population, although a number of persons can be traced migrating in search of land. In the fifteenth century it becomes more difficult, and frequently impossible, to discover the total numbers of chevage payers, and yet on rare occasions not only the number but the location of migrant bond tenants is given; and in each case a marked urban bias is shown. For example, in 1438 we are told that all eight *nativi* paying chevage to Climsland court were resident in the borough of Lostwithiel, and of six *nativi* paying chevage to the court of the manor of Helstone-in-Triggshire five were resident in towns—one in Plymouth, one in

[1] P.R.O. SC.2.160/28.   [2] See P.R.O. SC.6.811/1 ff.
[3] P.R.O. SC.6.816/11, this may have been the result of administrative adjustments.

Rural Society

Lostwithiel, one in Saltash, one in St Ives, and one in the port of St Kewe close to Padstow.[1] Two years later at least six bond tenants of Helstone manor were paying chevage to live in the borough of Saltash.[2]

The level of income and the standard of living a tenant enjoyed were determined by factors other than the amount of land he leased, the rent he paid, and the profitability of farming; in particular, alternative sources of income and food-supply played a significant part.[3] The average arable farmer's year gave long periods of under-employment, whilst much of the routine tending of animals in pastoral farming could be performed by women and children. Thus even those families with fairly substantial holdings could engage in occupations other than agriculture, while for those with very small holdings some other means of livelihood was essential. We know how in Fenland communities the abundance of alternative sources of employment and food-supply enabled families to survive on in-credibly small holdings.[4] Small holdings were also common in Cornwall, many were less than 10 acres in extent, and on certain manors, such as Tewington and Tywarnhaile, holdings of 5 acres or less predominated,[5] so that here too other sources of income and food-supply were essential for survival.

Mining was perhaps the most important source of occasional employment and supplementary income. Tin seams were well scattered throughout the county, as is evidenced by toll-tin receipts which were obtained from almost all the assessionable manors at some time or other in the later middle ages. Some tenants worked tin on their own behalf or in partnerships on tin seams within their native manors,[6] but many more must have found occasional employ-ment as wage-labourers in a capitalist industry invariably short of

[1] D.C.O. 48.
[2] D.C.O. 49.
[3] The extent to which a peasant exploited the opportunities for alternative employment and income depended upon his leisure preference which has been shown to be very strong in underdeveloped countries once the basic necessities of life have been satisfied.
[4] H. E. Hallam, *Settlement and Society* (Cambridge, 1965).
[5] Above, pp. 25, 27.
[6] See, for example: P.R.O. SC.6.811/4, Tywarnhaile; P.R.O. SC.2.158/12, court held at Calstock, 18 October, 10 Edward IV; P.R.O. E.197, file 344, no. E.1266.

Rural Society

labour. Each of the assessionable manors lay within easy distance of a tin-mining region, whether it was one of the four main stannaries located in Cornwall or one of the stannaries of Devon near to the boundary with Cornwall. Royal lead and silver mines on the Cornwall and Devon borders also employed large numbers of miners, at various times in the later middle ages, many of them on temporary contracts.[1]

The sea provided both food and employment for the population of medieval Cornwall. The manors of Tintagel, Penmayne, Tewington, Moresk, and Tywarnhaile were all ideally situated for sea-fishing, and their inhabitants must have reaped much benefit from it. Some tenants owned their own boats and fished for themselves and for sale; the capital outlay on a boat and net was small.[2] Others may well have worked for professional fishermen and capitalist fleet owners farther out to sea.[3] Considerable numbers must also have found employment cleaning, preserving and packing Cornish fish for redistribution throughout England and for export. Cornwall was also rich in fresh-water fisheries, notably those situated in the Tamar and Fowey rivers.[4] The tenants of Climsland and Calstock manors bordering on the Tamar profited greatly from the abundance of salmon, trout, lampreys, and other fish to be found there, and the Abbot of Tavistock sub-let many small pools below the great weir of Calstock.[5]

Certain other local resources provided employment opportunities for tenants, such as the turbaries of Helston-in-Kirrier and Helstone-in-Triggshire manors[6] and the lime-pits of Liskeard.[7] Woods, although scarce in Cornwall, did provide a source of employment and income for some tenants, and manorial court rolls are littered with references to tenants cutting down trees for timber,[8] collecting

---

[1] Salzman, 'Mines and Stannaries', pp. 71–5; Lewis, *Stannaries*, pp. 77, 192–7.
[2] Fines of 1s. per annum were imposed on those tenants who beached a fishing boat on Duchy land. See also P.R.O. SC.2.161/18, court held at Moresk, *die Merc. ante fest. St. Luce Evang.*, 22 Richard II.
[3] For an example of a capitalist fishing enterprise, see *B.P.R.* II, 93.
[4] Above, pp. 191–2.   [5] Finberg, *Tavistock Abbey*, pp. 163–5.
[6] Above, pp. 186–9.
[7] P.R.O. SC.2.160/28, court held at Liskeard, 21 May, 10 Henry VI.
[8] See, for example: P.R.O. SC.2.161/18, court held at Moresk, *die Merc. ante fest. St. Luce Evang.*, 22 Richard II; P.R.O. SC.2.160/29, court held at Liskeard, 17 August, 24 Henry VI.

fuel and acorns,[1] and making charcoal[2] without leave of the lord, sometimes on a commercial basis. Often it seems as if the fines imposed on offenders served more as a charge for the wood taken than as a deterrent.

Part-time and occasional employment was available to many tenants within their native manors. The tenants of those manors with deer-parks, namely Helstone-in-Triggshire, Climsland, Liskeard and Restormel, were obliged to assist in the repair of the park enclosures for which they received payment at the rate of 1¼d. or 1½d. per perch; and occasionally hunting lodges and feeding-troughs needed to be repaired. A considerable and regular demand for labour was created by Duchy building projects,[3] and it was Duchy policy to use its own tenants as far as possible for building and transporting operations. Those tenants living near castles or manor houses benefited most, such as the tenants of Tintagel, Trematon, Liskeard, and the Lostwithiel group of manors, but for some projects tenants were drawn from far afield.[4] Occasionally it is possible to discover Duchy tenants plying a craft such as that of tiler, thatcher, or carpenter.[5] Additional demands for hired labour must also have come from those tenants who farmed large amounts of land, and some tenants can be seen acting as stock-keepers for neighbouring churches and institutions.[6]

In the fifteenth century the textile industry must have provided occasional and part-time employment for many persons in the east of Cornwall.[7] From the first decades of the century there were four fulling mills within the manor of Climsland, and possibly many more in the immediate vicinity. And, of course, textile production on a large scale was thriving only a few miles away in the Tavistock

[1] For example, P.R.O. SC.2.160/25, court held at Liskeard, *die Sabb. prox. post fest. St. Luce Evang.*, 30 Edward III.
[2] For example, P.R.O. SC.2.158/12, court held at Calstock, 21 May, 11 Edward IV.
[3] For a brief survey of the maintenance of Duchy buildings in Cornwall, see *The History of the King's Works* (ed. H. M. Colvin, 1963–) I, 470–3.
[4] See, for example, P.R.O. E.101/461/13, 461/20.
[5] *Ibid.*; the names of persons employed by the Duchy are listed and can be compared with those on contemporary assession rolls: P.R.O. E.306/2/7, 2/8.
[6] P.R.O. SC.2.160/31, court held at Liskeard 30 September, 34 Henry VI. See also the accounts of the stock-keepers of Trematon St Mary: P.R.O. SC.6.823/24–6.
[7] Above, pp. 169–71.

region of Devon. 'Touker' was a common surname on Climsland manor, and in the fifteenth century a number of persons leasing land from the Duchy on this manor were designated 'tuker' by profession. In addition, the wives and children of many tenants must have spun wool in their own homes,[1] and a number of tenants were also tailors and weavers.[2] Another industry which sprang to prominence in the fifteenth century was stone quarrying on Tintagel and Tewington manors. Slates and stones dug in the north-east of Cornwall were renowned throughout the south-west and also exported.[3] In the later fifteenth century, sixteen separate leases in two quarries were granted by the Duchy, and often taken by tenants who also leased land on the manor.[4]

CONVENTIONARY LANDHOLDINGS, 1333–1504

The assession system as practised on the Cornish manors of the Duchy presents us with a unique opportunity for the study of landholding in the fourteenth and fifteenth centuries, for the assession rolls provide an almost continuous record of the names of tenants, and the size, location, and rent of their holdings. Nevertheless, there are pitfalls in the interpretation of the rolls, and as we have seen, a tenant could hold land on a sub-lease or on non-Duchy manors, and no trace of this would remain.

The wide divergencies in the quality of land and the size of holdings from manor to manor, and even within the same manor, create difficulties in the tabulation of trends in the size or value of landholdings accumulated by tenants. Extreme variations in rents per acre occasioned by extreme variations in fertility and suitability for farming render any comparison of tenancies by acreage almost valueless. For example, on Helston-in-Kirrier manor many hold-

---

[1] We know that Cornwall acted as a supplier of yarn to the big cloth centres of Devon in the sixteenth and seventeenth centuries: W. G. Hoskins, *Industry, Trade and People in Exeter, 1688–1800* (Manchester, 1935), p. 29; J. C. A. Whetter, 'The Economic History of Cornwall in the 17th Century' (London Ph.D. thesis, 1965), p. 13.

[2] See, for example, John Rothe, weaver and collector of fines (P.R.O. SC.2.159/32, court held at Stoke, 17 December, 6 Edward IV). See also the lands leased by John Byle, tailor, and John Byle, weaver, in 1504 (D.C.O. 483, Climsland).

[3] Above, p. 35.

[4] See, for example, the assession roll of 5 Edward IV: P.R.O. E.306/2/12.

Rural Society

ings of over 100 acres were regularly leased for rents of less than 10s., whilst on Tywarnhaile and Tewington some lands were rented for more than a shilling per acre. Consequently an analysis based upon the rental of the holdings of conventionaries and *nativi de stipite* has been adopted for the most part in Table 17.[1] This method also has its deficiencies, however, for rents fluctuated in the course of the fourteenth and fifteenth centuries. Column (1) of the Table contains the numbers of tenants leasing more than a single holding of land.[2] Although the size and value of the holdings varied immensely such

TABLE 17   *The distribution of holdings, 1337–1504*

Column (1) Number of tenants leasing more than a single holding.
Column (2) Number of tenants leasing land of 20s. and up to 29s. 11d. rent.
Column (3) Number of tenants leasing land of more than 30s. rent.
Column (4) Approximate number of holdings leased at the assession.
Column (5) Approximate rental of all holdings leased.

Areas of waste land have not been included as holdings in columns (1) and (4), but rents of waste land have been taken into account when compiling columns (2), (3), and (5).

Sources: The Caption of Seisin of 1337 and subsequent assession rolls.

Climsland

	(1)	(2)	(3)	(4)	(5)
					£ s. d.
1337	0	0	0	102	—
1347	0	0	0	100	26 10 0
1356	6	0	0	97	23 10 0
1364	5	0	0	101	26 10 0
1371	10	0	0	99	28 10 0
1392	14	1	0	96	28 0 0
1406	15	0	0	100	31 0 0
1427	13	1	0	94	33 10 0
1441	12	0	0	97	36 0 0
1448	12	1	0	102	37 10 0
1469	17	0	0	101	38 0 0
1504	17	0	0	102	38 0 0

[1] Rentals calculated by averaging assession fines over each year of the lease and adding it to the annual rent.
[2] The *terra* of the assessionable manors was divided into holdings which were maintained intact on most manors for the whole of the later middle ages (above, pp. 10–11).

Rural Society

Liskeard

	(1)	(2)	(3)	(4)	(5) £ s. d.		
1337	2	2	0	85	—		
1347	3	2	1	80	41	0	0
1364	4	4	0	72	33	10	0
1371	7	4	0	72	35	10	0
1392	12	3	1	80	40	10	0
1406	12	3	0	79	41	0	0
1420	8	3	0	75	42	10	0
1427	11	5	2	78	42	10	0
1448	10	3	2	78	44	0	0
1469	14	3	4	74	—		
1504	14	3	2	80	49	0	0

Helstone-in-Triggshire

	(1)	(2)	(3)	(4)	(5) £ s. d.		
1337	3	0	0	96	—		
1347	4	0	1	95	—		
1356	7	0	2	93	43	0	0
1364	8	0	1	96	44	0	0
1371	8	1	1	90	46	0	0
1406	5	1	1	89	46	10	0
1427	8	5	1	85	45	10	0
1441	15	5	2	84	45	10	0
1462	20	5	2	84	43	10	0
1469	21	6	2	85	46	0	0
1504	22	15	3	93	50	0	0

Tybesta

	(1)	(2)	(3)	(4)	(5) £ s. d.		
1337	2	3	0	55	—		
1347	6	4	1	58	31	0	0
1356	3	3	1	54	26	0	0
1364	15	5	5	53	28	0	0
1371	10	3	1	58	28	10	0
1378	12	7	1	59	29	10	0
1406	10	6	1	53	27	0	0
1420	11	10	0	45	24	10	0
1427	12	5	5	—	—		

1462	14	5	5	49	26 10 0
1469	16	8	4	48	24 0 0
1504	17	6	4	51	27 10 0

| | | | *Tywarnhaile* | | |
	(1)	(2)	(3)	(4)	(5)
					£ s. d.
1337	8	3	0	43	—
1347	7	3	0	43	15 0 0
1371	9	1	0	39	12 10 0
1406	4	0	0	40	12 10 0
1427	9	0	0	35	10 10 0
1441	11	0	1	40	11 0 0
1462	8	2	0	32	10 0 0
1469	6	1	1	25	7 10 0
1504	9	1	1	37	12 10 0

an analysis does provide at least a good general guide to tenant landholding. Columns (2) and (3) contain the numbers of tenants holding lands with annual rentals of from 20s. to 29s. 11d., and 30s. and more respectively; thus they may include tenants leasing only a single holding if its rent was 20s. or more, but such holdings were extremely rare.

The formulation of general trends in the size of tenancies from the evidence of the assession rolls of individual manors is fraught with complications. As has been explained in previous chapters, trends in the demand for land and the price of land could exhibit contrasting characteristics from manor to manor, being dependent upon differing factors. Trends in demand for land on the eastern and on the western manors of the Duchy ran contrary to each other for long periods. Nevertheless, on all manors for which tables have been constructed, with the possible exception of the westerly manor of Tywarnhaile,[1] a certain approximate uniformity is undeniable.

In the decades before the Black Death there were remarkably few traces of a peasant aristocracy; as the tables show, it was excep-

[1] Tywarnhaile was composed of holdings of extremely small dimensions. It was also peculiarly susceptible to fluctuations in mining activity and the encroachment of sand, which led to many vacant holdings in the late fourteenth and fifteenth centuries.

tional for a conventionary or villein tenant to be in possession of more than a single holding of land. This was a time of population pressure, holdings were changing hands frequently, and the general trend was towards the creation of even smaller units of land through the division of holdings between tenants and the breaking down of such groupings of holdings that did exist. Vacated holdings were far more likely to be leased by tenants who had not held land from the Duchy before than by established tenants increasing the size of their holdings.[1] In the period 1330–47 only nine conventionary tenants can be traced who leased lands with an annual rented value in excess of 40s., and none of these were peasant farmers; rather they were merchants, mining entrepreneurs, or Duchy officials, to whom the leasing of land was only a small part of their economic activities.[2]

The Black Death brought no general long-term slump in demand for land on the assessionable manors. At the first assession held after the plague a growth in the numbers of tenants leasing more than a single holding is evident on most manors.[3] But growth was not spectacular, and the vacancies caused by the unprecedented mortality were in general not filled by existing tenants expanding the size of their holdings but rather by migrants and those who had previously been landless. The closing decades of the fourteenth century brought a progressive increase in the numbers of fairly substantial holdings, although only a few really large tenancies were created, and even these were often held by tenants who had extensive business interests besides farming.

During the first twenty-five years of the fifteenth century, a time of expansion in Cornwall, the trend towards multiple holdings was arrested and frequently reversed. But with the slackening of demand for land in ensuing decades, an increasing number of substantial tenancies were created, until by the reign of Edward IV on some manors it was often the tenant leasing a single holding who was in the minority. Perhaps the most spectacular example of this process occurred on Helstone-in-Triggshire manor, where in 1427 only eight tenants held more than one holding and only six held lands

---

[1] Above, pp. 99–101.
[2] These nine tenancies are examined in detail below, pp. 235–41.
[3] The assession of 1356: D.C.O. 472a.

worth more than 20s. each year; by 1504 after eighty years of virtually stationary rents no less than twenty-two tenants held more than a single holding and eighteen rented lands worth more than 20s. each year. Upon those manors not listed in the tables a similar trend in landholding is evident. At Helston-in-Kirrier by the end of the fifteenth century, for example, the manor was almost exclusively in the hands of tenants leasing complete hamlets, whereas in the early fourteenth century these hamlets had been divided between as many as five tenants, or even more.[1] Throughout the fifteenth century on all assessionable manors holdings were being retained by their tenants for longer periods, sometimes becoming family holdings and, in contrast to the early fourteenth century, groups of holdings were often built up by a tenant over a number of assessions. The age of the yeoman peasant had dawned.

Fifteenth-century assession rolls provide many examples of tenants adding to their holdings in succeeding assessions, but once a group of holdings reached a certain size and value it frequently remained constant and often in the hands of the same family. For example, on Helstone-in-Triggshire manor at the assession of 1441 the two largest landholdings, both realising more than 40s. rent annually, were held by John Kittowe and Thomas Willott,[2] and in the assessions of 1462[3] and 1469[4] these groups of holdings remained unaltered and in the hands of Radulph Kittowe and John Willott respectively.

Throughout the fourteenth century and the first half of the fifteenth the most valuable groups of holdings were almost exclusively composed of lands of the best quality, although on occasion a single tenant did lease vast tracts of waste and pasture. Usually a tenant sought to lease a number of holdings within the same hamlet, so that he held a compact unit such as Warinus Trewithian's 7 messuages and 126 acres in Forda,[5] Henry Gartha's 6 messuages and

---

[1] A comparison between the Caption of Seisin of 1337, for example, and any assession roll of the later fifteenth century reveals the revolution in landholding that had taken place on this manor.
[2] D.C.O. 478.
[3] D.C.O. 479.
[4] D.C.O. 480.
[5] Assession of 1347: D.C.O. 472, Helstone-in-Triggshire. Most of Warinus' holdings were taken by John Colyn in the succeeding assession: D.C.O. 472a.

193 acres in the fertile hamlet of Trevelmond,[1] John Carnarthur's 6 messuages and more than 150 acres in Trevillick and Trewinnow,[2] or John Trewyk's 110 acres in Hellistoth.[3]

Thus it can be seen that the structure of conventionary land-holding was transformed in the course of the fourteenth and fifteenth centuries. If a free market in land is considered a precondition of the emergence of a 'yeoman peasantry' then the assessionable manors ought to have provided an almost ideal breeding ground,[4] and yet even here the progress towards larger landholdings was not continuous and for many manors the first quarter of the fifteenth century had seen a reversal of the trend. Progress was also slow, and the Black Death and subsequent outbreaks of plague do not appear to have been directly responsible for it; they had led to relatively minor increases in the numbers of tenants leasing larger amounts of land or more valuable holdings. A decline in the price of land is not a completely satisfactory explanation either, for at the close of the fifteenth century the average conventionary holding on the eastern manors was much larger even on manors where rents were considerably higher than they had been before the Black Death. Nevertheless, there does appear to have been some correlation between the demand for land and the size of holdings formed by the conventionary tenants, for it was in periods of stagnating or falling rent levels that the numbers of tenants with larger holdings increased most rapidly—for example, in the later fourteenth and the later fifteenth centuries.

Parallel with this movement towards larger and more valuable holdings ran a trend towards the establishment of a greater number of really substantial holdings—the holdings of a 'yeoman' tenantry. Whereas in the fourteenth century the largest and the most valuable of conventionary landholdings were in the hands of tenants who were not peasant farmers, by the second half of the fifteenth century there appear to have been many more substantial holdings leased by

---

[1] Assession of 1426: D.C.O. 476, Liskeard. Most of Henry's lands were taken by William Pomeray in the assession of 1448: P.R.O. E.306/2/11.
[2] Assession of 1504: D.C.O. 483, Tybesta.
[3] Assession of 1378: P.R.O. E.306/2/3, Helstone-in-Kirrier.
[4] R. H. Hilton, *The Economic Development of Some Leicestershire Estates in the Fourteenth and Fifteenth Centuries* (Oxford, 1947), p. 95.

genuine farming tenants. But one must always remember the prevalence of sub-leasing. Large tenancies did not necessarily mean large farms. Prevalent sub-letting on the assessionable manors in the later middle ages makes it extremely dubious to assume that Duchy tenants who appeared on assession rolls always farmed all the lands they held. All demises of conventionary land within the duration of the *conventio* had to be licensed by the manorial courts,[1] and it is from the proceedings of these courts that much of the information concerning the trade in conventionary land can be found.

It is most significant that the leases of some of the most important Duchy tenants of the fourteenth and fifteenth centuries should contain specific clauses granting exemption from having to make recourse to the manorial courts before sub-letting parts of their holdings; thus suggesting that a part of the attraction of leasing substantial holdings was to sub-let them at a profit.[2] The Duchy only granted leases for complete holdings and on terms of seven, fourteen or twenty-one years, but there was in the later middle ages an ever-present demand for smaller parcels of land on shorter terms, and it is this demand that a number of tenants sought to satisfy by acting as wholesalers in land.

It was not only those tenants who leased large amounts of land who engaged in sub-letting. Many examples can be given from manorial court rolls of tenants with holdings of a wide range of sizes who engaged in the trade in land. The methods by which land could be sub-let were manifold. The most straightforward was to apply to the manorial court for a licence. A most detailed example of this process is contained in the proceedings of Calstock manorial court for 1470 when John Dimrygge and John Felype were both licensed, upon the payment of one penny each, to lease an acre of their lands to Ranulph Volo and Radolph Barlebien respectively for a five-year term, upon condition that the two acres so demised were adequately sanded during the term of the lease, 'according to the customs of the manor'.[3] There appears to have been very little

---

[1] This regulation was stressed from the earliest assession rolls, see the preamble to the proceedings of the assession of 1347: D.C.O. 472. See also pp. 57–8 above.
[2] See, for example, the terms of the leases of William Jagow: D.C.O. 476, Tybesta; Henry Gartha: D.C.O. 478, Liskeard; John Trewyk: P.R.O. E.306/2/3, Helston-in-Kirrier.   [3] P.R.O. SC.2.158/12, court held at Calstock, 18 October, 10 Edward IV.

difference in the amount charged for a licence to sub-let whether it was duly applied for or whether a fine was eventually paid for sub-letting without licence—in all cases the amount was very small. For example, on Liskeard manor Hugo Hok paid 6d. for a licence to sub-let 3 acres of his holding in Trevelwode to John Hogge,[1] whilst John Genow was fined 2d. for demising some of the land he held in Trevekka to William Share without first obtaining the leave of the court.[2]

Although much of the sub-leasing appears to have been concerned with small amounts of land, frequently only an acre or so, there was also a considerable trade in larger and more valuable areas. The Duchy declined to grant leases other than for the conventional period, nevertheless, it did allow holdings, or fractions of holdings, to change hands within the life of prevailing leases as long as the incoming tenant was acceptable, and willing to take the land for the unexpired portion of the lease on the same terms as those stipulated at the assession. By these means holdings were leased, relinquished and taken up by new tenants within the assessionable term with great frequency in the fourteenth and fifteenth centuries, and many holdings were held only for a short period by the tenants who took them at the assession. Much of this interchanging of land during the term of the original lease seems to have been a means of trading in land. Often fractions of holdings were surrendered into the lord's hands to be taken by another tenant until the ensuing assession, and one suspects that some tenants who gave up parts of their holdings may possibly have been sub-letting, supplying land in smaller portions and for shorter terms than the Duchy were prepared to demise it. An example of this type of trade in land occurs in the proceedings of Climsland court of 3 February 1466, when John Calewe gave up a quarter of his holding and Thomas Maither and William Rothe both gave up half of their holdings to other tenants,[3] whilst in the court held at Liskeard in 1451 three tenants each gave up their holdings in Northbodual and William Nichol leased them all.[4]

---

[1] P.R.O. SC.2.160/31, court held at Liskeard, 3 May, 34 Henry VI.
[2] P.R.O. SC.2.160/30, court held at Liskeard, 1 December, 30 Henry VI.
[3] P.R.O. SC.2.159/32.
[4] P.R.O. SC.2.160/30, court held at Liskeard, 1 December, 30 Henry VI.

Rural Society

From amongst the multitude of cases concerning debt which fill the court rolls,[1] it is apparent that lands were often rented out by tenants for short periods in small parcels, and that tenants leasing pasture in particular frequently sold agistment and pasture rights both to other Duchy tenants and to outsiders. In 1410 Nicholas Hethe, for example, was indicted for a debt of 14d. to Thomas Harry for rent and agistment,[2] whilst in 1401 John Moyle confiscated 2 affers of John Scurra for rent owing to him.[3] On a larger scale, in 1445 William Blog of Liskeard caused 40 sheep belonging to John Hogge to be seized for 40s. of arrears of rent for land in Doublebois which had been owing for more than six months;[4] in the 1441 assession William Blog had leased 37 acres of land at Doublebois for a rent of 7s. and an assession fine of 46s. 11d.[5] Earlier in the century lands at Doublebois were also being sub-let, this time to tin-miners in very small parcels for the pasturing of their animals, for at the court of Foweymore stannary in 1435 we find that Jacob Crok, John Plonk, and Stephen Polglas were accused of owing John Russell of Liskeard 4d. each for pasture in Doublebois, whilst John Fogelysham was accused of owing him 2d.[6]

Many of the suits for trespass appear in fact to have been claims for the payment of arrears of rent for pasture. For example, Adam Drinker of Liskeard was accused of trespassing on the pasture of Walter Halbothek with 140 sheep from 25 March until the following Michaelmas,[7] and John Russell pastured 60 sheep on Walter Gartha's land from Michaelmas to Easter.[8] Tenants who found themselves without adequate pasture naturally sought to rent from those who had pasture to spare, just as they used the deer-parks of the Duchy for grazing when necessary.

Thus it can be seen that the actual distribution of land and the size of farms could be very different from the pattern of landholding

---

[1] Unfortunately the court rolls of Liskeard manor are the only continuous records of this type available.
[2] P.R.O. SC.2.160/2, court held at Liskeard, 4 January, 2 Henry V.
[3] P.R.O. SC.160/26, court held at Liskeard, *die Lune pro ante fest. St. Math Apost.*
[4] P.R.O. SC.2.160/29, court held at Liskeard, 15 October, 24 Henry VI.
[5] D.C.O. 478.
[6] P.R.O. SC.2.159/6, stannary court held at Liskeard, 18 February, 14 Henry VI.
[7] P.R.O. SC.2.160/27, court held at Liskeard, 22 July, 2 Henry V.
[8] P.R.O. SC.2.160/30 court held at Liskeard, 4 May, 30 Henry VI.

demonstrated on the assession rolls.[1] The lessees of substantial holdings can be identified, but it must remain uncertain whether they farmed all the land themselves. Land as an investment through sub-leasing appears to have been attractive to many tenants, especially at times when the shortage and high cost of labour tended to limit the size of economic farms.

SOME OUTSTANDING CONVENTIONARY TENANTS

The profusion of documentary material concerning many of the varied spheres of activity in the economy of medieval Cornwall which survives for certain parts of the fourteenth and fifteenth centuries, makes it worth while to examine in detail some of the more outstanding conventionary tenants, and in general the relationship between landholding and industry and trade.

In the period from 1324 to 1347 only nine conventionary tenants can be traced leasing lands worth in excess of 40s. rent annually; the holdings of these tenants are given in Table 18. Fortunately these nine tenants need not remain just names, for we can learn much of the business activities of all of them and as a result show each of them to have been more of a speculator in real estate than a farmer, and also that for the majority of these tenants the holding of land was only a small part of their economic interests.[2] Land was, of course, one of the commonest forms of investment for gains made in trade or industry, at least until the eighteenth century, and many merchants and burgesses bought or leased land either as a temporary speculative measure or as a means of providing for old age and retirement.[3]

The first three tenants listed in Table 18 were Duchy officials. The most substantial holdings of conventionary lands on Duchy

[1] Sub-leasing is evident from the earliest manorial records. See, for example: account of 25–26 Edward I, P.R.O. SC.6.811/1, Tintagel; 29–30 Edward I, P.R.O. SC.6.811/3, Trematon.

[2] The quarter century before the Black Death of 1348–9 was most rich in manorial surveys, no less than six were made of each assessionable manor between 1326 and 1347. This period also has a number of lists of the burgesses of certain Cornish boroughs, a record of persons paying the subsidy of 1327, and a number of tin coinage rolls.

[3] See S. Thrupp, *The Merchant Class of Medieval London* (Chicago, 1948), p. 120 ff.

TABLE 18 *Substantial conventionary landholders, 1324–1347*

Tenant	Manor	Holding	Rent
			£ s. d.
Richard Bakhampton[a]	Calstock, Moresk, Liskeard, and Tintagel	Approx. 400 acres *terrae et vastae*	10 17 0
John de Park[b]	Liskeard	A messuage and 93 acres	2 3 7
Michael Wastel[c]	Talskiddy	6 messuages and 96 acres	4 2 7
William Pasford[d] (with Alex de Cantock)	Extensive holdings of pasture and waste on Tewington and Penlyne manors		2 1 8
Warin Trewithian[e]	Helstone-in-Triggshire	7 messuages and 126 acres	3 0 0 (approx.)
John Yurl, Chaplain[f]	Helston-in-Kirrier	4 messuages and 69 acres	3 12 0
John de St Neulina[g]	Helston-in-Kirrier	3 messuages and 47 acres and 300 acres of waste	4 6 9
Laurence Pengarth[h]	Moresk	3 messuages and 81 acres	2 2 0
William Trespreson[i]	Helston-in-Kirrier	A messuage and 56 acres	2 1 6

[a] Lands held from 1333 to the Black Death. See, for example, P.R.O. E.120/1; D.C.O. 472.
[b] 1337; P.R.O. E.120/1, Liskeard.
[c] 1347; D.C.O. 472, Talskiddy.
[d] 1324; P.R.O. E.370/5/19.
[e] 1347; D.C.O. 472, Helstone-in-Triggshire.
[f] 1333; D.C.O. 471, Helston-in-Kirrier.
[g] 1337; P.R.O. E.120/1, Helston-in-Kirrier.
[h] 1337; *ibid.* Moresk.
[i] 1337; *ibid.* Helston-in-Kirrier.

manors in the early fourteenth century, or indeed throughout the fourteenth and fifteenth centuries, were held by Richard Bakhampton. Richard had been the trusted steward of the Cornish estates of John of Eltham.[1] The rents paid by Richard for the lands he held

[1] John of Eltham was Earl of Cornwall from 1328 to 1336.

do not appear to have been substantially below the true market value, but as a special favour for the services he had rendered to John of Eltham he was allowed to hold them for life.[1] John de Park was keeper of the Prince's park at Liskeard,[2] and sometime keeper of the tinners' jail at Lostwithiel and weigher of tin.[3] Michael Wastel was the receiver of coinage dues under the sheriff and receiver of the Cornish estates of the Duchy, Sir Robert Beaupel.[4] Another prominent official in Cornwall who held extensive lands, was John Dabernoun, who amongst other offices held the stewardship and shrievality of the Cornish estates of the Duchy and was constable of a number of Duchy castles in the south-west.[5] In 1347 John was granted a life tenancy of 3 messuages and 2½ Cornish acres on Trematon manor for an annual rent of approximately 30s.[6] John of Kendale, parker and constable of Restormel, was yet another Duchy official leasing substantial amounts of land; in 1342 he was granted for life 3 messuages, 75 acres and a rood of land on the manor of Penlyne, close to Restormel.[7]

These members of the Duchy administration, men of rank and influence building up estates within the estates, were almost certainly sub-letting the lands they held and not farming them. We are told, for instance, that Richard Bakhampton demised the lands he held in Calstock to various tenants.[8] Such men looked upon the holding of land as a sound investment, and land management usually constituted only one of their economic activities. John Dabernoun speculated in land on a grand scale,[9] and on the death of Richard Bakhampton he took over his holdings in Calstock;[10] he

[1] *C.P.R. 1334–1338*, pp. 235, 236; *ibid. 1340–1343*, p. 13.
[2] See, for example, *B.P.R.* I, 114 *ter*.
[3] *Ibid.* pp. 71, 150, 151.
[4] *B.P.R.* II, 187.
[5] See index of *B.P.R.* II, for a multitude of references.
[6] D.C.O. 472, Trematon. John Dabernoun was granted these lands after the death of Henry de Erth.
[7] D.C.O. Roll I, Penlyne.
[8] *B.P.R.* II, p. 97.
[9] See, for example, *B.P.R.* I, 99, wherein it is stated that John was given possession of some lands forfeited to the Duke of Cornwall by statutes merchant, paying 20 marks yearly for them, a greater sum than the lands were worth according to an extent in the Duke's possession. He also granted a sub-manor to the Abbot of Tavistock (Finberg, *Tavistock Abbey*, p. 18).
[10] D.C.O. 5, Calstock.

also leased the Duchy rights and perquisites in the harbour of Sutton, next to Plymouth, for an annual farm of £6 13s. 4d.[1] Richard Bakhampton did not restrict himself to landholding either: he held property in the town of Callington,[2] he was involved in commercial transactions,[3] and he was also charged coinage duty on substantial amounts of tin.[4] Similarly Michael Wastel, from his considerable financial resources,[5] also speculated heavily in the tin trade[6] and had commercial connections with London.[7] Further evidence of the desire of Duchy officials to speculate in real estate is furnished by John de Moveroun, sometime receiver of the Cornish estates,[8] who in 1347 took the great fish weir of Calstock on lease from the Duchy for an annual farm of £10.[9]

The next two tenants on Table 18, William Pasford and Warin Trewithian were prominent burgesses and merchants. In 1337 William Pasford can also be traced leasing at Tewington two corn mills, the waste of Wallan, and the pasture of the wood.[10] Investigation amongst contemporary Cornish records reveals William as one of the leading merchants of the county in the later middle ages. He was a Lostwithiel burgess,[11] and together with another Lostwithiel burgess, Alex de Cantock, was assessed to pay 6s. 8d. in the subsidy of 1327—the joint highest assessments in the borough.[12] But William apparently also held property in other parishes.[13] He was also a

---

[1] *Ibid.* Trematon.
[2] *C.P.R. 1340–1343*, p. 181.
[3] *C.C.R. 1341–1343*, p. 137.
[4] 942 lbs at Truro, 9 March, 6 Edward III, P.R.O. E.101/262/22. 2,196 lbs at Lostwithiel, 26 March, 7 Edward III, P.R.O. E.101/262/26. Tin coinage dues appear frequently to have been paid by the purchaser of the tin and not the producer.
[5] He took on the responsibility of paying the arrears of Sir Robert Beaupel who had been sheriff and receiver of Cornwall, which amounted to £1,175 5s. od., and succeeded in paying off a great part (*B.P.R.* II, 27, 40, 55, 127).
[6] 1,240 lbs at Lostwithiel, 9 December, 5 Edward III, P.R.O. E.101/262/21; 5,480 lbs at Lostwithiel, 26 March, 7 Edward III, P.R.O. E.101/262/26 and Lostwithiel 28 September, 7 Edward III, P.R.O. E.101/262/29; 5,576 lbs at Lostwithiel, 27 July, 8 Edward III, P.R.O. E.101/262/30 and 263/1.
[7] *B.P.R.* I, 65.
[8] For a list of his offices see *B.P.R.* I and II, *passim*.
[9] D.C.O. 472, Calstock.
[10] P.R.O. E.120/1, Tewington.
[11] *Ibid.* m. 7., William held only 2 burgages for a rent of 7d.
[12] P.R.O. E.179/87/7, m. 14.
[13] A William Pasford was assessed at 23d. in the parish of Eglosmerther (*ibid.* m. 14).

member of the consortium which had leased the manors of Tywarnhaile, Moresk and Helston-in-Kirrier from Queen Isabella for £150 annually.[1] As a merchant his commercial activities were extensive. He is recorded as owing £300 to the Bardi of Florence in 1326,[2] and in 1331 he acknowledged debts of £300 to Robert Bilkemore giving as security his chattels in Devon as well as in Cornwall.[3] William was granted safe conducts to trade throughout the realm in 1332 and 1333,[4] and when wine was purchased in Cornwall for the Scots wars in 1322 and 1329 he supplied most of it.[5] As would be expected William's interests also included the tin trade, as did those of most leading burgesses and merchants in Cornwall. As a joint lessee with Thomas Quoynte of Lostwithiel he farmed the offices of weigher of tin and custodian of the tinners' jail, together with two houses called the 'Blouynghous and Weghynghous' in Lostwithiel, in which the tin brought for coinage was smelted and weighed,[6] as well as a number of cellars in the borough.[7] In 1332 William was charged with the coinage of nearly 14 thousandweight of tin on behalf of German de Bray,[8] and in 1334 he can be seen coining tin on his own behalf.[9] An insight into the extent of his dealings in tin is given by his debts of coinage duty which in 1334 amounted to £65.[10] As a leading member of the community William took his place in the administrative system of the south-western counties, and was appointed, amongst other offices, as one of the collectors of the subsidy on alien imported wine in 1323,[11] and controller of the King's silver mines of Devon in 1332.[12]

Warin Trewithian was one of the leading Tintagel burgesses, and

[1] P.R.O. E.370/5/19. See also above, p. 86.
[2] *C.C.R. 1323–1327*, p. 571.
[3] *C.C.R. 1330–1333*, p. 291.
[4] *C.P.R. 1330–1334*, pp. 246, 396.
[5] He supplied 20 tuns out of the 40 tuns of wine purchased in 1322, Alex de Cantock supplying 10 others (P.R.O. E.101/16/1). In 1329 he supplied the whole of a requisition of 40 tuns (P.R.O. C.145/111/1; *Cal. Inq. Misc. 1307–1349*, 1088).
[6] *C.F.R. 1327–1337*, p. 242; P.R.O. C.143, file 185, no. 6.
[7] See, for example, P.R.O. SC.6.816/11 ff.
[8] Coinages at Lostwithiel, 5–6 Edward III, P.R.O. E.101/260/20.
[9] 1,750 lbs at Truro, 16 March, 8 Edward III, P.R.O. E.101/262/30 and 263/1.
[10] Owed for the duty on 32 thousandweight. Salzman, 'Mines and Stannaries', p. 95.
[11] *C.F.R. 1319–1327*, p. 212.   [12] *C.P.R. 1330–1334*, p. 247.

in 1345 he held four burgages for a rent of 3s. 8d.[1] The first recorded instance of his investment in Duchy property occurred when a lease was taken on the corn mills of Camelford and Kenstock on Helstone-in-Triggshire manor in the early thirteen-forties.[2] By 1345 he had leased four holdings on Helstone-in-Triggshire manor,[3] and in the assession of 1347 he took a total of 7 messuages and 126 acres of good land in the hamlet of Forda, and was granted a life tenancy.[4] A glimpse of the commercial activities of Warin is given when he supplied sides of bacon to the Crown in 1348.[5] Unfortunately the absence of the coinage rolls of the thirteen-forties makes it impossible to determine if Warin also speculated in the tin trade.

Each of the four remaining persons who leased land worth more than 40s. rent annually before the Black Death were tenants of the western manors, and each can be traced as having interests in tin as well as in land. John Yourl was a cleric,[6] he also paid the coinage duty on 1472 lbs of tin in 1334;[7] William Trespreson was charged for the duty on 224 lbs in 1332,[8] and John de St Neulina for a total of 7286 lbs in 1333.[9] John de St Neulina obviously had substantial sources of income in addition to the land he leased from the Duchy, for his tin was probably worth almost £30.[10] In the subsidy of 1327 John was assessed to pay 5s., one of the highest amounts recorded in the hundred of Kirrier.[11] Laurence Pengarth, in addition to the land he leased at Moresk, had leased some 600 acres of waste comprising the manorial chase of Helston-in-Kirrier for 26s. 8d.[12] In 1337 he was leasing a blowing-house and a corn mill on Helston-in-Kirrier manor.[13] In the proceedings of the stannary court of Penwith-and-Kirrier Laurence Pengarth can be identified suing for breach of

1 Extent of William de Cusancia, D.C.O. Library.   2 D.C.O. 1.
3 Extent of William de Cusancia, D.C.O. Library.   4 D.C.O. 472.
5 P.R.O. E.101/554/1.
6 He is described in the first assession roll (D.C.O. 471) as John Yourl, Chaplain. It is stated against his name that he was not liable for the office of reeve.
7 Coinage at Lostwithiel, 12 May, 8 Edward III, P.R.O. E.101/262/30 and 263/1.
8 Truro, 9 March, 6 Edward III, P.R.O. E.101/262/22.
9 Truro, *die Merc. in fest. St. Swithin*, 6 Edward III; Truro, 11 February, 7 Edward III: P.R.O. E.101/262/22, 262/28.
10 Tin was sold retail in Cornwall for about 1d. per lb. at this time.
11 P.R.O. E.179/87/7, m. 3 d.
12 P.R.O. E.120/1, Helston-in-Kirrier.
13 *Ibid.*

contract concerning the non-delivery of tin.[1] Both Laurence Pengarth and William Trespreson acted as assessors of tax for the levy of 1327.[2]

Thus all the nine tenants who leased land from the Duchy worth more than 40s. rent annually have been traced in other spheres of economic activity, and it is apparent that to most of them, and perhaps to all, the holding of land was secondary to other business interests. The significance of these findings is all the more remarkable when one appreciates that the difficulties of discovering tenants in other spheres are considerable and success fortuitous; for even such a remarkable collection of complementary records as those studied for the generation before the Black Death can only give a partial survey of the economic activities of these nine men. In the field of mining and the tin trade, for example, coinage rolls exist only for the early thirteen-thirties and only one stannary court roll survives for the thirty years before the plague of 1348/9.

It is even more difficult to trace the activities of less important people. Nevertheless even a superficial investigation of Cornish sources in the pre-Black Death period reveals a considerable diversification of interests amongst many Duchy tenants. Invariably the tenants leasing the most valuable holdings were concerned in activities other than farming. Many of the lessees of the more substantial landholdings on the westerly manors paid tin coinage duties, in addition to those tenants already mentioned above. On the westerly manors in particular there must have been at this time a considerable demand from the populous mining communities for small units of arable and for pasture rights.[3] In response to this demand some Duchy tenants may well have acted as wholesalers in land, leasing large amounts of land on seven-year contracts and subletting in small units and for short periods to miners.[4] Tin-mining

---

[1] P.R.O. E.101/260/1, court held at Penrin, Penwith-and-Kirrier stannary, *die Ven. prox. post fest. St. Jacob.* This document is headed: *Anno regni regi Edwardi Septimo,* but from internal evidence including the name of the sheriff and steward, it should be dated 1332/3.

[2] P.R.O. E.179/87/7, m. 3.

[3] The 1330s saw the highest levels of tin production ever attained in the middle ages (see Appendix C, p. 289).

[4] From various records, e.g. stannary court rolls, it is evident that miners frequently kept animals and cultivated land.

Rural Society

entrepreneurs may have leased lands for their workmen or servants to farm in their spare time, or as means of supplying their employees with food.

Given below in Table 19 are those tenants of westerly manors who, in what must remain a superficial survey, were found to have been connected in some way with mining or the trade in tin. It must be borne in mind that the numbers of persons paying coinage or appearing in the stannary court rolls comprised only a minute proportion of the total numbers connected in some way with the tin industry and the distribution of its product. For example, the list

TABLE 19 *Conventionary tenants on western manors in 1337 with interests in the tin trade*

Name	Holding in 1337[a]	Rent	Tin coined 1331-3[b]
Leading tenants of Helston-in-Kirrier Manor			
John Lanargh	Half of 1 messuage and 90 acres plus shares in waste	Approx. 30s.	2,610 lbs[c]
John Gyneys	1 messuage and 33 acres plus 15 acres waste	38s.	448 lbs[d]
Richard de Glyn	1 messuage and 33 acres	30s.	2,600 lbs[e]
The Bloyou family	7 messuages and 96 acres	80s.	4,202 lbs[f]
Leading tenants of Tybesta Manor			
Odo de Tybeste	3 messuages and 24 acres	19s. 6d.	2,456 lbs[g]
John de Carahoda	2 messuages and 44 acres	32s. 6d.	4,522 lbs[h]
John de Pengelly	1 messuage and 31 acres plus 20 acres waste[i]	30s.	—

[a] Based upon the Caption of Seisin: P.R.O. E.120/1.

[b] I.e. in two full years.

[c] Truro, 9 March, 6 Edward III, P.R.O. E.101/262/22; Truro, 11 February, 7 Edward III, P.R.O. E.101/262/28. John is also recorded as owing substantial sums in outstanding coinage dues, see for example P.R.O. E.142/41.

[d] Truro, 9 March, 6 Edward III, P.R.O. E.101/262/22.

[e] Truro, Saturday before Michaelmas, 6 Edward III, P.R.O. E.101/262/22.

[f] Truro, *die Merc. in fest. St. Swithin,* 6 Edward III, P.R.O. E.101/262/22.

[g] Truro, Saturday before Michaelmas, 6 Edward III, P.R.O. E.101/262/22.

[h] 814 lbs at Truro, 9 March, 6 Edward III, P.R.O. E.101/262/22; 1784 lbs at Truro 16 March, 8 Edward III; 1924 lbs at Lostwithiel, 27 July, 8 Edward III, P.R.O. E.101/262/30 and 263/1.

[i] Lands leased at assession of 1333: D.C.O. 471.

of tinners owing tax in 1316 contains some 1,300 names,[1] but the coinage rolls of 1302/3[2] or 1331/2[3] contain less than one tenth of this number of names. It is thus certain that a far greater number of tenants on the western manors were in some way connected with tin than could ever be established from coinage rolls alone, even if these were complete.

A few further pieces of information can be added concerning some of the tenants listed in Table 19. John Lanargh appears to have been a person of considerable substance, for he was assessed to pay 5s. in the royal subsidy of 1327, one of the highest assessments recorded in his hundred.[4] Richard de Glyn emerges from the court rolls of the stannary of Penwith-and-Kirrier as a 'middle-man' of great importance, and his name crops up on the proceedings of most of the courts held in 1332/3.[5] On Tybesta manor Odo de Tybeste is probably the same person as was appointed to the benefice of St Gwinear in 1338, on the recommendation of the patron, Edward the Black Prince.[6] John de Pengelly, who is not recorded as having paid coinage on tin in the records at our disposal, was nevertheless a substantial mining entrepreneur. In the stannary tax of 1307 he was assessed to pay 3s. 6d. in the district of Lamenes,[7] well above the average assessment; and his name also appears on the only available court roll of his time.[8] The connection between the lessees of the largest and most valuable holdings of the western manors and tin-mining or the tin-trade is thus established without doubt.

Farther east, the existence of a number of pre-plague borough extents and rentals enables a study to be made of those who combined rural and urban landholding. Table 20, below, contains details of certain burgesses of Tintagel and Lostwithiel who have been traced leasing land in conventionary tenure on manors adjacent to their boroughs. The borough of Tintagel was relatively small, situated in the north-east of Cornwall, within the manor of the same name. It

---

[1] P.R.O. E.372/161, m. 41. See above, pp. 30–1.
[2] P.R.O. E.101/260/25.   [3] P.R.O. E.101/262/21, 262/22.
[4] P.R.O. E.179/87/7, m. 3 d.   [5] P.R.O. E.101/260/1.
[6] *Reg. Grandisson*, III, 1338.
[7] P.R.O. E.179/87/5; P.R.O. E.372/161, m. 41.
[8] P.R.O. E.101/260/1, Penwith-and-Kirrier Stannary, court held at Trewyny, *die Sabb. prox. post. fest. St. Maria Magdal.*

TABLE 20 *The rural landholdings of Lostwithiel and Tintagel burgesses in 1337*[a]

Name	Manor	Holding[b]	Borough	Burgages	Tin[c]
Gerard Curtoys	Penlyne	5 acres, 2s.	Lostwithiel	8, rent 3s. 9d.	2,164 lbs
William Gille	Penlyne	1 mess. 4½ a., 2s. 8½d.	Lostwithiel	1, rent 3s. 4d.	
Matthew Coombe	Penlyne	3 mess. 49a., 26s. 4d.	Lostwithiel	13, 5s. 7d.	3,344 lbs
Serlo Queynte[d]	Penlyne	4 a., 3s.	Lostwithiel	4, 5s. 3d.	60 lbs
Serlo Queynte and Alex Cantok[e]	Penkneth	The moor of Penkneth	Lostwithiel	8, 4s. 3d.	
John Marchaunt	Restormel	1 mess. 10a., 6s.	Lostwithiel	1, 1½d.	4,534 lbs
Randolph Jolly, clerk	Restormel	1 mess. 10a., 6s.	Lostwithiel	2, 3d.	2,880 lbs
Robert Trewithian	Tintagel	1 mess. 16a., 11s.	Tintagel	2, 3s. 4d.	
John Herry	Tintagel	1 mess. 23a., 10s.	Tintagel	1, 5s. 6d.	
Vincent Boria	Tintagel	1 mess. 8a., 6s. 8d.	Tintagel	1, 3s. 0d.	
William Moly	Tintagel	1 mess. 7a., 5s.	Tintagel	1, 3d.	
Henry Chyna	Tintagel	1 mess. 7a., 5s.	Tintagel	1, 4d.	
John Pronta	Tintagel	1 mess. 15a., 15s.	Tintagel	1, 1s. 2d.	
Walter Langa	Helstone	1 mess. 19a., 7s.	Tintagel	1, 3d.	
John Roger	Penmayne	1 mess. 8a., 3s.	Tintagel	1, 6d.	

[a] Prepared exclusively from the Caption of Seisin of 1337: P.R.O. E.120/1.
[b] Rents exclusive of assession fines.
[c] Amounts of tin upon which coinage was paid between Michaelmas 1331 and Michaelmas 1333: P.R.O. E.101/262/21 to 262/29 *passim.*
[d] Serlo Queynte was mayor of Lostwithiel.
[e] See also above, p. 236.

had less than a hundred burgages in 1337.[1] But Lostwithiel was the third wealthiest borough in the county after Truro and Bodmin,[2] and was in no sense a 'rural borough'. Lostwithiel had a gild merchant, it was an important centre of the tin-trade and the leading coinage town of Cornwall throughout the middle ages, and it was also the centre of the local Duchy administration. In 1337 there were more than 400 burgages within Lostwithiel.[3] The status of Lostwithiel burgesses leasing land from the Duchy can be determined from the burgages they held, from the quantities of tin upon which they paid coinage duty, and occasionally from their tax assessment. The holding of farmland for these men could have been little more than a side investment for idle funds.

Although no further borough rentals are available in the Caption of Seisin of 1337 a high incidence of rural landholding amongst burgesses elsewhere is apparent from other types of record. For example, of the six burgesses either taking the farm of Saltash borough or acting as pledges to the farmers, four were holding land in the adjacent manor of Trematon.[4] As would be expected, burgesses sometimes acquired land in freehold as well as in conventionary tenure, and a number of burgesses can be traced who were free tenants of the Duchy. One example of many is Stephen de Trewynt, a leading Camelford burgess,[5] who in 1331 held 3 Cornish acres[6] in free tenure on Helstone-in-Triggshire manor and also farmed the two manorial corn mills for 10 marks.[7] Robert Lowys could be quoted as another example; he held an extraordinary number of burgages in Liskeard borough,[8] paid the very high assessment of 8s. 6d. in the subsidy of 1327,[9] and also held land and water-course rights in freehold on Liskeard manor.[10]

[1] P.R.O. E.120/1.
[2] P.R.O. E.179/87/9.
[3] P.R.O. E.120/1. In 1300 there had been only 305 burgages; P.R.O. C.133, file 95; P.R.O. E.152/8.
[4] Assession Roll of 1356; D.C.O. 472a; P.R.O. F.306/2/1.
[5] P.R.O. E.142/41, rental of Camelford.
[6] Possibly almost 200 acres by standard English measurement (above, p. 18).
[7] P.R.O. E.142/41, Helstone-in-Triggshire.
[8] These are listed in P.R.O. SC.6.1290/1, piece 9. This unusual document credits Robert with more than 30 separate holdings in Liskeard borough.
[9] P.R.O. E.179/87/7, m. 16.
[10] P.R.O. E.142/41, Liskeard.

The holding of land or mills jointly by the burgesses of a whole borough was a frequent occurrence in medieval Cornwall. Often a grant of agricultural lands was included in the terms of borough charters. For example, the charter of Helston borough includes the grant of 33 acres *terre assissi* and the meadow below the town;[1] whilst the charter of another Duchy borough, Grampound, includes 57 acres of waste, a messuage and 39 acres of land, two corn mills and a fulling mill.[2] Boroughs also leased in common in conventionary tenure from the Duchy, as was discovered when the burgesses of Tintagel took the waste of Godolghan in 1337,[3] and invariably boroughs were granted the farms of the mills of adjacent Duchy manors.[4]

Although the scope for investigation in the later fourteenth century is limited by the relative paucity of documentation concerning the varied facets of economic life in Cornwall, it is still possible to uncover some details of the activities of certain of the most important and substantial tenants and, as before the plague, they are invariably revealed as speculators rather than farmers. There were in general rather fewer tenants leasing really extensive holdings in the later fourteenth century than there had been before 1349.

Some officials of the Duchy continued to be amongst the holders of the most substantial lands, but in lesser numbers than before. John de Purlee, who acted as victualler and general factotum for the Duchy in the south-west[5] and who was a speculator in tin,[6] was

---

[1] These were the famous open-fields of Helston borough. See Henderson, *Essays in Cornish History*, p. 67.
[2] Copies of these charters are enrolled in the Caption of Seisin (P.R.O. E.120/1). Launceston borough also possessed agricultural lands (O. B. and R. Peter, *Histories of Launceston and Dunheved* (Plymouth, 1885), p. 158), as did Truro (Henderson, *op. cit.* p. 2).
[3] P.R.O. E.120/1, Tintagel Manor. The mayor and burgesses of Helston also leased 300 acres of the waste of Goenwen of Helston-in-Kirrier manor for 6s. 8d. in 1465 (P.R.O. E.306/2/12).
[4] Amongst the boroughs which farmed mills from the Duchy were: Lostwithiel, Launceston, Liskeard, Helston, Grampound and Saltash.
[5] See, for example, *B.P.R.* II, 116, 141, 142, 168. John also held a messuage in Lostwithiel borough and land in a moor in the fee of Penkneth (*ibid.* p. 160).
[6] See, for example, the stannary court rolls of Blackmore, P.R.O. SC.2.156/26. His name also appears on the rolls of Penwith-and-Kirrier stannary: P.R.O. SC.2.161/81, court held at Redruth, *die Jonis prox. post. fest. St. Fides Vir. et Mar.*

granted a life tenancy to two messuages and 36 acres and the manorial corn mill of Penlyne[1]—he was the only tenant of any significance to emerge in the later fourteenth century on this manor.

On the manor of Helston-in-Kirrier, where rents were low and much land was vacant, Henry Nanfan, the manorial bailiff, leased extensive holdings for life. In 1356 he took two messuages 40 acres and a croft for 27s. annually, and the farm of the manorial chase and toll-tin rights for 60s.[2] At the same assession his brother Richard leased a total of six messuages and 83 acres of very good quality land for 73s., also on a life tenancy. Henry Nanfan had a long and successful career in the service of the Duchy. He was appointed bailiff of Helston-in-Kirrier in 1350, and through the efficient performance of his duties in a most difficult period in the history of the manor he soon became a trusted and favoured agent.[3] In 1362 he was granted the bailiwick of the hundred of Penwith for an annual farm of 16s. 8d.[4] On being relieved as the bailiff of Helston-in-Kirrier manor Henry was made Keeper of the Prince's Fees in Cornwall and Devon,[5] a most gratifying promotion; and on the death of the Black Prince in 1376 he was appointed an auditor of the accounts of the Cornish ministers of Princess Joan.[6] Richard II's administration, however, showed Henry little favour and he was imprisoned in 1377 for arrears of the farm of Penwith bailiwick, though subsequently released.[7] Henry and his brother were tin-mining entrepreneurs on a grand scale, who often undertook considerable operations in partnership with other entrepreneurs, and whose interests extended far beyond the bounds of the stannary of Penwith-and-Kirrier.[8]

---

[1] D.C.O. 472a; P.R.O. E.306/2/1.   [2] *Ibid.*

[3] For example, in 1359 he carried the receipts from Cornwall to the household of the Prince in London (P.R.O. SC.2.1290/1). As a reward for 'good service as bailiff of the manor of Helston-in-Kirrier' Henry and his brother Richard were pardoned the fines imposed on them by William de Shareshull (*B.P.R.* II, 168, 179).

[4] See, for example, *B.P.R.* II, 197.

[5] See, for example, D.C.O. 26, account of the Keeper of the Fees.

[6] In 1382 Henry Nanfan and Jacob Gerneys were appointed to audit the accounts of the Cornish ministers of Princess Joan at Lostwithiel (P.R.O. SC.6.818/9). He also presided at the assession of 1378 (D.C.O. 200).

[7] P.R.O. SC.6.812/18.

[8] See for example, P.R.O. SC.2.161/81, 161/82, Penwith and Kirrier stannary; P.R.O. SC.2.164/34, Tywarnhaile stannary; P.R.O. SC.2.156/27, Blackmore stannary. For the scale of some of his enterprises see also *B.P.R.* II, 156-8.

Clerics took a considerable interest in leasing land[1] and frequently the vicar of a local church would take a piece of land from the Duchy. Such leasing was not always on a small scale and some clerics featured amongst the most substantial of all conventionary tenants in the late fourteenth century. For example, Ranulph the vicar of Tintagel leased four messuages and 41 acres in Malstas[2] as well as a small turbary on Helstone-in-Triggshire manor.[3] One of the most valuable tenancies on Helston-in-Kirrier manor in the later middle ages was created in 1364 by John the vicar of St Wendron when he took four messuages and 122 acres of good arable for an annual rent of approximately 34s. 9d.[4]

Speculation and investment in land by burgesses was a feature of the second half of the fourteenth century as it had been of the first, and a number of the most prominent conventionary landholders in the later fourteenth century were burgesses. Richard Juyl, a leading Saltash burgess, leased the largest holding to emerge on Trematon manor during the period for which records are available in the latter part of the century.[5] At the assession of 1356 he took three messuages and 52½ acres for an annual rent of 40s. 6d.,[6] which was reduced to 37s. 3d. in 1364 (because of the scarcity of tenants) when he renewed his lease.[7] Another Saltash burgess, John Halganer, also leased lands on Trematon manor and farmed the corn mills.[8] Both Richard Juyl and John Halganer served as reeves of Trematon manor.[9] Near by at Calstock a portion of the lands previously held by Richard Bakhampton were taken by William Stacy,[10] a prominent burgess of Tavistock.[11] William was wealthy enough to lease the Duchy salmon weir of Calstock for £8 until he was dispossessed at the instigation of the Abbot of Tavistock.[12]

---

[1] For landholding by clerics in medieval Leicestershire see W. G. Hoskins, 'The Leicestershire Country Parson', *Essays in Leicestershire History* (Liverpool, 1950), p. 6.
[2] D.C.O. 472a, Tintagel.
[3] The farm of the turbary was incorrectly placed by the scribe in Helston-in-Kirrier manor on the assession roll of 1356 (D.C.O. 472a).
[4] D.C.O. 473, Helston-in-Kirrier.
[5] He was reeve of the borough in 1362/3.
[6] D.C.O. 472a.
[7] D.C.O. 473.
[8] D.C.O. 472a.
[9] Above, p. 40.
[10] *B.P.R.* II, 61.
[11] Finberg, *Tavistock Abbey*, p. 162.
[12] *B.P.R.* II, 54, 58, 71.

Other leading conventionary tenants of the later fourteenth century were engaged in the tin-mining or the tin-trade. Nicholas Kernek, who leased extensive pastures on Helstone-in-Triggshire manor for approximately 46s. per annum,[1] appears frequently on the court rolls of Blackmore stannary in cases concerning tin.[2] As would be expected, many of the larger tenancies on the western manors of the Duchy were once again in the hands of tenants with interests in tin. The most expensive landholding on Helston-in-Kirrier manor in the fourteenth century was created by John Trewyk in 1378.[3] It consisted of over 100 acres of good quality land in Hellistoth, for which he paid 42s. each year.[4] John was no ordinary tenant, however, and he acted as bailiff of Helston-in-Kirrier manor for Philip Fower who was appointed to succeed Henry Nanfan.[5] John was also bailiff of Tywarnhaile stannary in his own right and he paid an annual farm of 5s. for this office.[6] From the frequent appearances of his name in the court rolls of various stannaries he emerges as an important tin-mining entrepreneur.[7] He had a house in Truro,[8] he rented considerable amounts of land from Robert Cowythaday,[9] acted as a middle-man,[10] and was charged the coinage duty on 3½ thousandweight of tin in 1385.[11]

Thus, one by one almost all the holders of the largest and most valuable amounts of land in the late fourteenth century have been identified as Duchy officials, merchants and burgesses, middle-men or mining entrepreneurs. This almost complete domination by essentially non-peasant tenants of the leasing of the greatest landholdings throughout the fourteenth century is an interesting commentary on the economic and social conditions of the age, for

[1] D.C.O. 472a.
[2] P.R.O. SC.2.156/26. Court rolls of Blackmore stannary, 29–31 Edward III, *passim.*
[3] P.R.O. E.306/2/3.   [4] *Ibid.* Helston-in-Kirrier.
[5] He took office in 1370/1 (P.R.O. SC.6.818/3), and remained until records of the manor cease in 1382.
[6] 1371 assession at Tybesta: P.R.O. E.306/2/2; D.C.O. 475. 1378 assession at Tybesta: P.R.O. E.306/2/3.
[7] For example, P.R.O. SC.2.161/81, 161/84, 164/34, etc.
[8] P.R.O. SC.2.164/34, court held at Truro, *die Merc. in Vigil. St. Matth.*, 48 Edward III.
[9] P.R.O. SC.2.161/81, court held at Marazion, *die Merc. prox. post. fest. St. Mich.*, 37 Edward III.
[10] For example P.R.O. SC.2.161/84, Redruth, *die Lune ante fest. St. Luc.*, 13 Richard II.
[11] P.R.O. E.101/263/19, coinage held at Truro, 26 September, 9 Richard II.

these men were almost certainly engaging in sub-leasing. In a free
market for land very few substantial holdings were created by peasant
farmers.

For the first sixty years of the fifteenth century records of only nine
of the seventeen assessionable manors are available.[1] From these
records there appear to have been fewer really extensive tenancies
than there had been in the first half of the fourteenth century.
A major factor in the decline in the number of tenancies worth more
than 40s. rent annually was undoubtedly the complete absence of
Duchy officials from the ranks of the conventionary tenants. One
explanation of this reversal, for Duchy officials had figured pro-
minently amongst the lessees of the most substantial and valuable
holdings in the fourteenth century, must rest in the administrative
policies of the Crown and the Dukes which, after the death of the
Black Prince in 1376, favoured the appointment of many absentee
and 'alien' officials to posts in the Cornish hierarchy.[2] We can,
however, discern during the century a progressively growing
number of yeoman peasants, probably resident on the manors, often
building up their holdings over many years, and frequently passing
them on to members of their families when they died.

Henry Gartha, a free conventionary of Liskeard manor, was the
lessee of the most valuable holding to be formed on any of the
assessionable manors of which we have record in the fifteenth
century. In the assession held in 1420 he leased a single holding of
22 acres and paid approximately 6s. 11d. rent.[3] In the following
assession held seven years later Henry increased his landholdings
tremendously by leasing a total of eight messuages and 207 acres of
land, mostly grouped in the fertile hamlet of Trevelmond some 3
miles west of Liskeard borough, along with two holdings of waste
land;[4] for his total holdings he paid £4 1s. 9d. annually to the
Duchy.[5] But the total amount of land acquired by Henry may have
been even larger than this.[6] From contemporary manorial court

[1] Above, pp. 149–50.   [2] Above, pp. 47–8.
[3] P.R.O. E.306/2/10, Liskeard. The 6s. 11d. rent includes assession fines.
[4] One holding of waste was held in partnership with Roger Gourda.
[5] D.C.O. 476.
[6] He is recorded as taking possession of Nicholas Geoffrey's holding in Cadusket in
1445 (P.R.O. SC.2.160/29, court held at Liskeard, 28 April, 24 Henry VI).

rolls he does not appear to have played a prominent part in the affairs of the manor, and he cannot be found serving in any official capacity whatsoever. The main references to him in the court rolls are concerned with suits against other tenants for debts.[1] By 1448 Henry Gartha no longer held land on Liskeard manor and many of his holdings had passed to William Pomeray who paid a total rent of £3 3s. od. for them.[2] A little more can be discovered of the activities of William Pomeray, and from frequent references in the court rolls of the stannaries of both Foweymore and Blackmore, in which he was constantly suing for outstanding debts, close economic ties with surrounding mining communities can be established.

One of the leading fifteenth-century tenants of Tybesta manor was William Jagow, who leased a total of four messuages 82 acres of land and 2½ acres of waste in the hamlet of Gorlennick on the northern tip of the manor in the assession of 1427 for 45s. 5d.[3] In the roll of the previous assession William Jagow held only two messuages and 24 acres;[4] thus like Henry Gartha he had built up a large landholding by stages and not created it at a single assession as many of the largest and most valuable of the holdings of the fourteenth century had been created. Just as the more substantial holdings were often completed in stages, so they often remained unaltered and in the hands of the same tenants for long periods.

A most typical example of the history of a number of large and valuable groups of holdings is that of Thomas Willott, a conventionary tenant of Helstone-in-Triggshire manor. At the assession of 1427 Thomas leased three messuages and 37½ acres of 16s. 6d.;[5] fourteen years later he leased a total of five messuages and 87½ acres of land, 34 acres of waste, and an escheated burgage in Camelford, paying a total of more than 45s. annually for them.[6] In the assessions of 1462[7] and 1469[8] his son John Willott can be seen leasing the same holdings.

Although most of the extensive tenancies consisted of holdings of good quality lands a few were composed exclusively of waste and

[1] See, for example, P.R.O. SC.2.160/28, 160/29.
[2] P.R.O. E.306/2/11, Liskeard.
[3] D.C.O. 476.
[4] P.R.O. E.306/2/10.
[5] D.C.O. 476.
[6] D.C.O. 478.
[7] D.C.O. 479.
[8] D.C.O. 480.

pasture, especially on the manors of Helston-in-Kirrier, Helstone-in-Triggshire and Liskeard. For example, John Gille of Helstone-in-Triggshire speculated in pasture when he leased three holdings of poor quality land in Tregoodwell on the eastern edge of the manor close to Bodmin moor, and extensive waste pastures in nearby Corndon.[1] Although the pastures of Doublebois on Liskeard manor were never in great demand after the Black Death[2] and were frequently left unleased, on occasion a tenant would take a substantial amount of them if the terms of his lease were made acceptable.[3]

SOME OBSERVATIONS ON THE ECONOMIC STATUS OF CONVENTIONARY AND VILLEIN TENANTS

The conventionary tenants of the Duchy of Cornwall in the later middle ages were, as has already been shown, a truly remarkable grouping of heterogeneous elements, comprising amongst others, figures of considerable political significance, wealthy merchants and industrialists, and clerics, as well as more typical peasant farmers. Mention has been made of the wealth and scope of the activities of a number of outstanding tenants, so it is now intended to make a few observations on the status of more typical tenants.

It must always be borne in mind that the information we have of the wealth of the bulk of the tenants is not completely reliable. The land a conventionary or villein tenant held directly from the Duchy may well have been only a part of his total holdings; within the manor he might also have been a sub-tenant of other conventionary or villein tenants, or of the free tenants, many of whom almost certainly engaged in sub-letting on a grand scale. A number of conventionary tenants can be identified holding land outside their native manors. In addition tenants must often have had sources of

[1] John Gille apparently first leased these lands in 1406 (P.R.O. E.306/2/7, 2/8), and held them until 1434 (D.C.O. 476).
[2] Below, Appendix B.
[3] For example, in 1392 John Goly leased 5 messuages and 191 acres of Doublebois for more than 53s. (P.R.O. E.306/2/4). Thomas . . . leased 3 messuages and 126 acres of Doublebois for 30s. in 1448 (P.R.O. E.306/2/4). Thomas Clemence held extensive pastures in Doublebois and Looden worth 36s. in 1469 (D.C.O. 480). John Harry leased much of Doublebois in 1504 for 48s. 8d. (D.C.O. 483).

Rural Society

income apart from their land, which are rarely possible to discover. The incompleteness of the information generally at our disposal is stressed by a comparison of the extent and value of landholdings and wealth of their tenants as assessed for subsidy, which reveals no close correlation. The details of the comparison are given in Table 21.

TABLE 21 *Landholdings compared with subsidy assessment,*
1327–31

Tenant	Holding[a]	Rent		Tax[b]		Status
	Liskeard manor[c]					
		s.	d.	s.	d.	
Robert Tympellon	½ Cornish acre	3	0		7	*Nativus*
David Leen	¼ Cornish acre ½ ferl.	7	0		7	*Conventionarius*
William de Clyker	1 piece terre			3	1 0	*Conventionarius*
Roger Clerk	¼ Cornish acre and 1 piece	7	3		7	*Conventionarius*
Walter Bromhoyt	3 Cornish ferl.	6	8		7	*Conventionarius*
Simon Rosnornan	½ Cornish acre	3	3		9	*Nativus*
John Boduel	½ Cornish acre	3	7		9	*Nativus*
Radulph Boduel	3 Cornish ferl.	4	6		9	*Nativus*
Richard Gourda	½ Cornish acre	2	3		8	*Conventionarius*
	Helston-in-Kirrier manor[d]					
John Basset	⎫	7	0		9	*Conventionarius*
Oliver Bodily	⎪	9	0		7	*Conventionarius*
Reginald Bodily	⎪	3	0		7	*Conventionarius*
John Sken	The extent of landholdings	20	4	2	0	*Conventionarius*
Peter Primatyn	cannot be determined	6	8½		6	*Conventionarius*
John Scurra	⎪	4	0		6	*Conventionarius*
Richard Menethy	⎪	16	0		6	*Conventionarius*
Andrew Sampite	⎭	7	4		6	*Nativus*

[a] Extent of lands in Cornish acres, as contained in P.R.O. E.142/41.
[b] P.R.O. E.179/87/7, subsidy of one fifteenth levied in 1327.
[c] Rental made in 1329.
[d] Rental made in 1331.

Few tenants holding land directly from the Duchy could have been members of the lowest and poorest strata of Cornish rural society, for they leased complete holdings in a free market and paid

253

an economic rent. Each person before being granted a lease had to satisfy the authorities as to his solvency and credit-worthiness, and find two other tenants who were prepared to stand as pledges to his credit.[1] There are few records of arrears being contracted by conventionary tenants which could not be recouped by distraining on their property. The scattered items of information throwing light on the condition of the general body of conventionaries and villeins in the later fourteenth and the fifteenth centuries reinforces the impression that they were not struggling in poverty but instead maintaining a reasonable standard of living for the times. For example, tenants often had large amounts of ready cash to hand, as the payment of the heavy fines demanded in manorial courts suggests. Heriots were invariably paid promptly, and in the form of a valuable animal such as a horse, cow or ox.

The wealth of certain tenants in livestock can be assessed from the proceedings of Liskeard manorial court, and in the following examples most tenants leased only a single holding from the Duchy. In 1412 Adam Drinker trespassed with 140 head of sheep;[2] in 1445 William Blog had 40 sheep[3] and William Gonhilet had 22 assorted animals, namely oxen, cows and steers stolen;[4] and in 1451 John Russell trespassed with a flock of 60 sheep and Robert Helyer seized 60 sheep and 4 cows belonging to John Hoyk.[5]

Perhaps most informative of all are the inventories of the goods and chattels of unfree tenants, which by the custom of the assessionable manors were all ceded to the Duchy on death.[6] Unfortunately these too have a number of serious limitations, being scarce and showing a tendency towards extreme underestimation of both the quantity and value of the goods listed. Nevertheless, although the available inventories are too few to provide a satisfactory sample, it is worth while discussing a number of the more complete of them as they cast light upon farming practices as well as upon the wealth of their owners. The earliest available inventory lists the goods of a

---

[1] Above, p. 55.
[2] P.R.O. SC.2.160/27, court held at Liskeard, 22 July, 2 Henry V.
[3] P.R.O. SC.2.160/29, court held at Liskeard, 15 October, 24 Henry VI.
[4] P.R.O. SC.2.160/29, court held at Liskeard, 28 April, 24 Henry VI.
[5] P.R.O. SC.2.160/30, court held at Liskeard, 20 January, 30 Henry VI.
[6] Above, p. 63.

bond-tenant called Walter, of Liskeard manor, who died in 1358 and left corn in his barn, 2 oxen, 2 steers, 4 cows, 36 sheep, and a number of boxes, pots and pans, as well as a quantity of other goods.[1] In 1404 the goods left by another unfree tenant of this manor were recorded and they consisted of 4 oxen, a horse, a heifer, 3 cows, and an undisclosed quantity of sheep and other goods, together with 1½ acres of wheat.[2] John Johan, an unfree tenant of Liskeard manor, who died in 1417, left only 4 sheep, 3 quarters of wheat, and 3 old boxes, after a heriot had been paid.[3] At the other extreme John Randolf, also of Liskeard, who died in 1409, left 14 cattle, 60 sheep, corn unharvested to the value of 40s., and various household goods to the value of 10s.[4]

John Randolf does not appear to have been an important tenant of the Duchy for in 1406 he had leased only a single messuage and 40 acres of poorish land in Newhouse for less than 6s. per annum.[5] Another inventory concerns the possessions of Richard de Fentenwausaut, who as reeve of Helstone-in-Triggshire manor had left his account in arrears. His goods, as assessed in 1342, were considerable; they comprised 2 oxen, 2 steers, 6 young oxen, 4 heifers, 2 cows, 3 calves, 40 sheep, boars worth 10s., corn worth 3s. 9d., and other goods worth together almost 50s.[6]

Finally, the abundant possessions of Matthew de Treveggen, another bond-tenant of Helstone-in-Triggshire manor, serve to emphasise both the advancement that could be achieved by the unfree and the discrepancy which could sometimes exist between the amount of land leased from the Duchy and the wealth of a tenant. Matthew held only a single messuage from the Duchy in 1347, yet a list of his goods and chattels made in 1351 includes 40 assorted animals valued at 33s., 5 marks in cash, agricultural implements worth 6s. 8d., a woman's robe worth 5s., and a gold buckle worth 3s. 4d.[7] On his death the reeve of Helstone-in-Triggshire arrested goods of Matthew's consisting of 6 oxen, 4 cows, 2 acres of wheat, 2 acres of oats, and other possessions to the value of £10, but more

[1] P.R.O. SC.2.160/25.
[2] P.R.O. SC.6.819/15; D.C.O. 33.
[3] P.R.O. SC.2.160/27, court held at Liskeard, 22 January, 7 Henry V.
[4] D.C.O. 38 and 39.   [5] P.R.O. E.306/2/7 and 2/8.
[6] D.C.O. 1, Helstone-in-Triggshire.   [7] P.R.O. SC.6.817/1.

interesting still is the fact that Matthew had purchased a Cornish acre (perhaps 40–50 English acres) in the hamlet of St Fenten.[1] A number of other cases of bondmen achieving advancement in their economic and social status are contained in Duchy records. For example Richard Juyl, a wealthy burgess of Saltash and tenant of Trematon manor,[2] was stepson of a bond-tenant of Trematon;[3] and sons of bondmen were frequently granted leave to take Holy Orders by the Duchy.[4]

[1] *B.P.R.* II, 64–5.
[2] Above, pp. 40, 243.
[3] *B.P.R.* II, 139.
[4] See, for example, *B.P.R.* II, 118, 193; *C.P.R. 1413–1416*, p. 138.

CONCLUSION

It is perhaps useful in conclusion to draw together and summarise a few aspects of this study which could claim some significance beyond the boundaries of Cornwall. The management of lay estates has not, as yet, received much attention from medieval historians and, although this present work has not dwelt in great detail upon estate management and administrative procedures, this aspect of the history of the Cornish estates of the Duchy of Cornwall in the fourteenth and fifteenth centuries might well be recalled. One cannot fail to be impressed by the high standards of management displayed throughout most of the period under scrutiny. Despite all the potentially disruptive influences exerted on the management of royal estates, including the desperate impecunity of the later fourteenth century and the prolonged dynastic struggles of the fifteenth, the administrative machinery, at least of the Cornish estates, appeared to be so successfully institutionalised and so far-sighted in its objectives as to be able to withstand such subversive pressures. As has been demonstrated, there was some dispersion of the assessionable manors, with favourites, retainers and farmers from time to time taking over direct management of certain manors, and we have seen that the competitive nature of the assession system was eventually abandoned in the mid-fifteenth century, but at no time did manorial arrears accumulate seriously, and manorial documents exhibited no tendency to become the stereotyped falsifications often encountered elsewhere in England. Indeed in the Cornish estates at large, which ranged from boroughs to stannaries, accounts were usually rendered promptly and in full, with the only heavy arrears incurred by the Custodian of the Fees. Managerial efficiency as a factor in the determination of manorial profits needs to be emphasised; although its importance is impossible to quantify and often difficult to perceive it cannot be ignored, as the prodigious rent increases effected by new administrations on the assessionable

257

manors in the 1330s, after many decades of slack management and stable rents, eloquently testify.

Much of what is significant in this study provides a contrast with the general experience of English medieval history. In many important respects Cornwall differed markedly from most other regions; her diversified economic structure and the importance of non-customary elements in her rural social structure gave her a distinctive character. The Cornish manors of the Duchy of Cornwall lacked most of the elements seemingly crucial to manorialism or even to medievalism: the land-market was predominantly fluid and competitive, convertible husbandry was practised on enclosed holdings, and demesne cultivation and compulsory labour services were of no importance.

Clearly agricultural prosperity in Cornwall, seen in terms of the occupation of land and rent levels, was determined by a complex series of interconnected movements within the regional economy as a whole. The evidence of the assessionable manors in the 150 years after the Black Death suggests a much less direct and immediate causal link between falling population and agricultural recession than is generally encountered in medieval economies; tin-mines, fisheries, and industrial and port development all played their part in influencing demand for foodstuffs and land. We have seen how rents in south-east Cornwall soared to new peaks in the first half of the fifteenth century, boosted by a growing demand for agricultural produce from centres of industry and trade, and migration from less fertile soils; whilst in western Cornwall fluctuations in the output of tin were paralleled by fluctuations in rents. The intimate connections between agriculture, industry, and commerce are further emphasised by the manifold business interests of leading Duchy tenants.

Just as the fortunes of the seventeen Cornish manors provide contrasts with the fortunes experienced by manors in other regions of England, so within themselves were there many contrasts; each one arguing against too facile a generalisation of trends in agricultural prosperity. In the later fifteenth century, for example, we have seen that sagging rents and an abundance of vacant and dilapidated holdings on the western manors of Helston-in-Kirrier, Moresk, and Tywarnhaile contrasted sharply with buoyant rents and fully

Conclusion

occupied lands on the eastern manors of Climsland, Rillaton, Calstock, Trematon, and Liskeard. But even within these geographical groupings there were marked variations, and what is more the mass of information available in the assession rolls concerning the rents and occupation of individual pieces of land confirms that within each manor there was a profusion of contrasting and sometimes even contradictory movements. The quality of land within the same manor varied from place to place, whilst lands of equal fertility were not necessarily equally desirable, for example flat, sheltered, easily accessible holdings would generally command a higher rent than those in hilly and exposed areas. As Appendix B shows, even holdings within the same vill were not always equally desirable and rents were consequently not always identical.

In a sense therefore it is rash to generalise even about a single manor, and thus far more rash to generalise about counties or regions; but the inevitable miscellany of local experience need not argue for a narrow interpretation of evidence, or for the historian to be limited to the mere gathering and recording of information. Agrarian history involves the separation of the typical from the untypical, the normal from the exceptional, and the comparison of region with region, era with era. As we learn more and more of the varied histories of all regions so it becomes necessary to revise our models and to seek more complex and sophisticated, but no less ambitious, schemes of social and economic developments on a national and even an international scale, schemes which incorporate and allow for regional and chronological deviations, and thereby provide the essential framework for future local studies.

Appendix A
MANORIAL RENT MOVEMENTS

The graphs of this appendix represent the annual fluctuations in the aggregate monetary charges upon all conventionary and villein lands. The charges upon freehold lands have not been included, as they remained virtually static throughout the fourteenth and fifteenth centuries and would thus have restricted the ability of the graphs to mirror changes in demand for land. Rents in kind, either produce or labour, were of negligible significance on the assessionable manors.

The charges have been calculated by averaging assession fines over each year of the assessional term (seven, fourteen or twenty-one as the case may be) and adding the resultant sum to the annual rent. Payments of *recognitio*, which made their appearance in the mid-fifteenth century, have been treated in a similar manner to assession fines. Fines for life tenancies have been averaged over twenty-one years, as the Duchy usually set them at levels three times as great as those of a seven-year conventionary lease.

The intention has been to isolate the charges upon customary lands from all other sources of manorial revenue, e.g. mills, turbaries, toll-tin, etc., and this has proved possible except in the case of Tywarnhaile, the graph of which includes farms of the manorial mill. The revenues from the pastures of deer-parks have not been included as these varied according to the influence of many factors other than demand for pasture. Allowances against charges, in the form of 'decayed rents' or grants towards the maintenance of enclosures and buildings, etc., have been deducted.

Appendix A

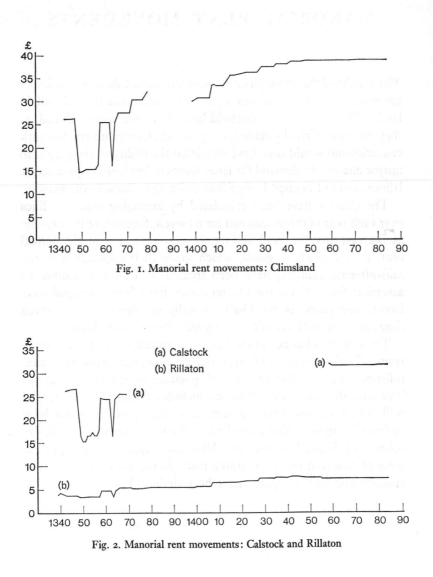

Fig. 1. Manorial rent movements: Climsland

Fig. 2. Manorial rent movements: Calstock and Rillaton

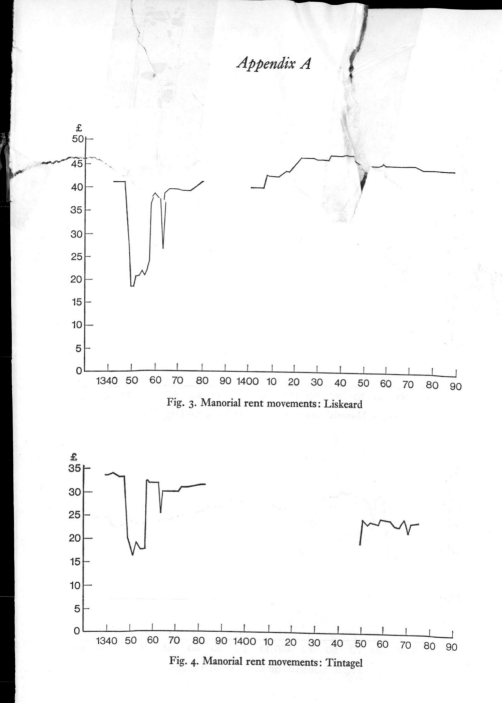

Fig. 3. Manorial rent movements: Liskeard

Fig. 4. Manorial rent movements: Tintagel

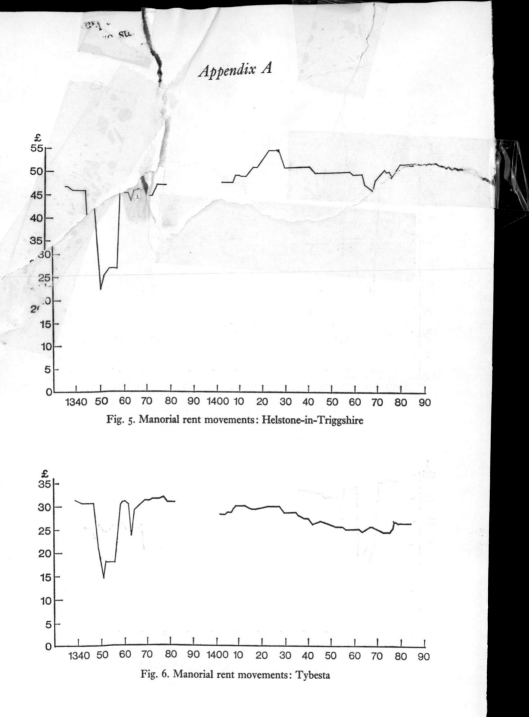

Fig. 5. Manorial rent movements: Helstone-in-Triggshire

Fig. 6. Manorial rent movements: Tybesta

264

Appendix A

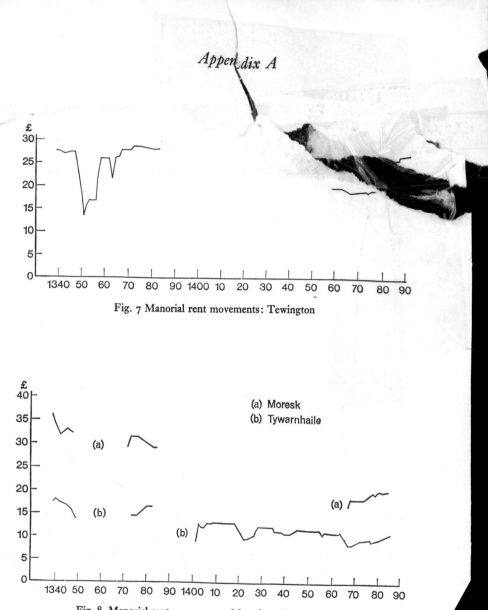

Fig. 7 Manorial rent movements: Tewington

(a) Moresk
(b) Tywarnhaile

Fig. 8. Manorial rent movements: Moresk and Tywarnhaile

265

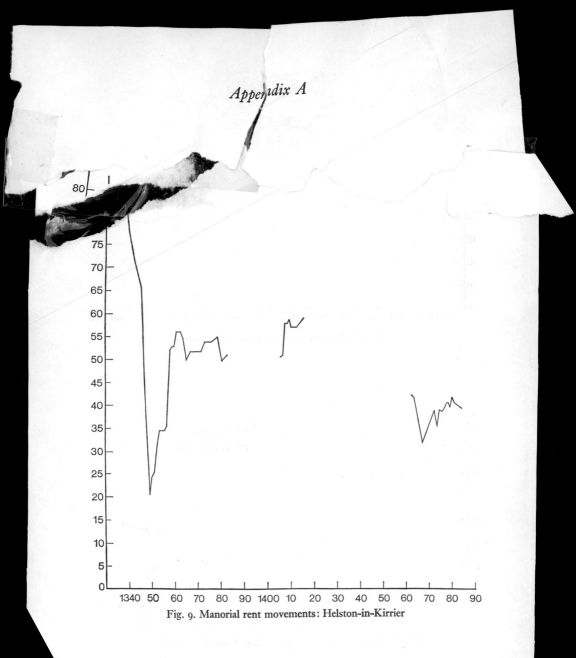

Fig. 9. Manorial rent movements: Helston-in-Kirrier

Appendix B

MOVEMENTS IN THE RENTS OF INDIVIDUAL LANDHOLDINGS:

1333–1497

Fluctuations in aggregate rent levels and landlords' incomes are an important part of any study of medieval agriculture, but the value of such composite movements has tended to become exaggerated simply because the lack of continuous evidence of the rents of particular areas of land invariably limits the scope of the historian. The excellent series of assession rolls of the manors of the Duchy of Cornwall, however, enables the rents of individual holdings and areas of land to be studied continuously throughout the fourteenth and fifteenth centuries, and as we have seen the conventionary system of tenure was such that the rent of land should have varied sympathetically with changes in demand for it. The tables contained in this appendix (below, pp. 278–87) catalogue movements in the rents of a sample of 93 conventionary holdings selected from five assessionable manors.

When broken down into their component parts the aggregate rent receipts from the assessionable manors can be seen as a fascinating miscellany of divers and often contradictory movements in the rents of the individual holdings making up each manor. For example on south-eastern manors in the 150 years after the Black Death far from uniform increases in the rents of most holdings were accompanied by stagnant or falling rents on some holdings, and a complete absence of colonisation.

Although the assession rolls are an incomparable source for rents and demand for land in Cornwall in the fourteenth and fifteenth centuries, some imperfections must be borne in mind. The ability of conventionary rents to mirror changes in demand depended upon the efficiency with which the tenurial system was administered, and upon the officials of the assessions in particular. At certain times the efficiency of the administration appears to have been in question.[1]

[1] The reign of Richard II and the second half of the fifteenth century were periods when

267

Furthermore in the early years of the assession system there seems occasionally to have been a tendency to under͟͟͟͟ certain unfree conventionary holdings relative to comparable free conventionary holdings, but this was soon corrected in successive assessio͟͟͟. 1 Another basis upon which the evidence of the assession rolls could be criticised is the fact that holdings did not necessarily remain in the same state of repair throughout our period, and as leases were short some maltreatment of holdings must have been encountered which would have been likely to influence the amount of rent a potential tenant would be willing to offer. But the reasons for wayward movements in the rents of particular holdings are often given on the assession rolls as, for example, when allowances were granted to assist in the repair of dilapidated buildings or enclosures.[2] On the other hand a particular holding might appear especially desirable, as apparently was the case with the messuage and 16 acres at Trematon which in 1371 came on to the market for the first time in forty years or more on the death of Richard Stalbat.[3] This holding seems to have been well cared for and there was a great scramble to possess it: William Moily upon securing the lease had to pay an assession fine of 22s., *incrementi quinque solidos propter brigam inter ipsa et aliis tenentibus*, at a time when few other fines were being increased. Yet, on the whole, such allowances or premiums were rare and one can presuppose a reasonably uniform state of repair amongst holdings of similar type and quality, borne out in

---

reassessments of the rents of conventionary lands in the hands of the Duchy were not undertaken (see above, pp. 137–9 and p. 156). The assession system, though often of undoubted value to the lord, could easily be abandoned; for example, the tenancies on Calstock and Trematon manors were not reassessed from the time they were granted to Nigel Loheryng in 1369 to the time they returned to the Duchy almost a century later, although the value of the tenancies on the neighbouring assessionable manors of Climsland and Rillaton which had remained in Duchy hands had been increased substantially (see above, pp. 159–61). The Duchy itself abandoned any upward reassessment of land values after 1434, and the assession fines and annual rents in force at this assession were to persist until well into the sixteenth century.

1 Many unfree conventionary tenants had previously been villeins holding their lands at much lower rents than those paid by conventionaries (see above, pp. 76–7).

2 Such allowances were most common in the reign of Edward IV, see above, pp. 163–5.

3 D.C.O. 475, Trematon. This holding can be traced in the hands of the same Richard Stalbat in the earliest lists of tenants: P.R.O. E.142/41; and the Caption of Seisin of 1337, P.R.O. E.120/1.

turn by reasonably uniform movements of rents of holdings of similar type and quality.

In the years immediately following the Great Plague of 1348/9 the price of much land had to be reduced, and the assessioners often tried to explain the reduction. Most frequently encountered are references to the 'lack' or 'scarcity' of tenants, or the 'poverty' of those that survived the plague. But on occasion the inadequacies of the land itself were blamed for the loss of revenues; and land for which Duchy officials were forced to sanction lower rents was sometimes termed 'worn', 'sterile' or 'boggy', and the buildings upon it 'ruinous' or 'totally destroyed'.[1] Much land did become relatively less attractive as a farming proposition after the population had been decimated, but it is evident that soil exhaustion was not the reason. Numerous examples could be given of holdings described as 'worn', 'sterile' or 'boggy' in the assessments held soon after the plague, which remained in continuous cultivation at least until the accession of Henry VII, and what is more commanded progressively higher rents on the south-eastern manors. One such example, a holding of 32 acres in Bynorthwood on Climsland manor, had its fine reduced from 25s. to 18s. at the 1364 assession, because the land was barren (*debilitas*), and yet was continuously leased at successive assessions, and in 1406 commanded a fine of 31s. 8d.

If differing trends in the rents of holdings within a single manor are to be explained some sort of a division of land according to fertility and utility is essential, however difficult it may prove. In attempting such a division the fundamental contemporary distinction between *vasta* and *terra* is most valuable, and in addition a few small holdings were termed meadow. But in the absence of any further explicit contemporary statements concerning the broad relative qualities of land it is necessary for the purposes of our analysis to resort to approximate divisions made on the basis of rent levels, however unsatisfactory they might appear at first sight. The earliest detailed information on the rents of individual conventionary holdings dates from the inauguration of the assession system in 1333. In a comparative survey of rent trends the period

[1] See the assession rolls of 1356 and 1364 (D.C.O. 472a; P.R.O. E.306/2/1; D.C.O. 473).

Appendix B

from the first assession to 1347 has much to recommend itself as the starting-point. These decades before the Black Death were times of considerable population pressure on natural resources, and contrasted strongly with the subsequent century which most certainly saw Cornwall with a much reduced population. It is the effects of these changed demand conditions upon the rents of holdings of different types and qualities which forms the subject of this Appendix.

As has been demonstrated earlier, demand for land in Cornwall in the decades before the plague of 1348/9 was greatly intensified by the pressure of population which had the effect of forcing up the rents of good and poor land alike in the quest for subsistence.[1] Consequently in the assessments held in this period the rents of all holdings were increased almost without exception. But plague by reducing the level of population brought about a drastic reappraisal of the value of all lands. The accent in the later fourteenth and the fifteenth centuries was on production for the market without the same degree of pressure on land for subsistence. Land in general became relatively abundant and it appears to have been valued according to its ability to produce foodstuffs for sale at competitive prices and support the farmer and his family efficiently.

The preparation of poor soils for cultivation was a very expensive process in the fifteenth century, with the cost of a day's unskilled labour as much as the annual rent of an acre of mediocre land. In contrast the more fertile soils could yield better returns in terms of grain and animal products with the expenditure of considerably less labour. There is an old farmers' proverb that a man cannot pay too much for good land or too little for bad, and after the Black Death with the rent of even the best land low in relation to the cost of labour and the price of agrarian products this proverb had a particular relevance. For example, if one assumes in mid-fifteenth-century Cornwall an average rent of perhaps 8d. per acre, unskilled labour at 4d. per day, and the price of a quarter of wheat in the region of 6–8s., and compares this with conditions ruling throughout England in the late eighteenth century, as described by Arthur

[1] Above, pp. 92–3.

Young, the contrast is striking. In Young's England wages were approximately four times as great as in the mid-fifteenth century, wheat prices at least five times as great, but rents at least twenty times as great. It can thus be seen that the scope for adjustments to rents was not always sufficient to make marginal land a promising farming proposition in the later middle ages, after pressure on the land for subsistence had been relaxed. And this helps to explain why vast acreages were left vacant on Helston-in-Kirrier manor, and also the low rent of waste land on most other manors, which was probably suitable for use only as rough pasture in these more spacious times.

The effects of changes in demand conditions after the Black Death which led to contrasting trends in the rents of holdings on the assessionable manors are catalogued in the assession rolls, and examples of apparently contradictory movements are not hard to find. For example, on Climsland manor substantial increases were effected to the rents of the vast majority of holdings at the assessions of 1406, 1413 and 1420, but these increases were accompanied by a growth in the acreage left untaken at each assession, which rose from approximately 150 acres to almost 300 acres, and although this unleased land was invariably all taken on temporary contracts in the years after the assessions, no fines were paid. Between 1406 and 1427 at Liskeard, also in the face of sharply rising rents on the majority of holdings, the amount of land left untaken at each assession doubled from less than 200 acres to more than 400 acres. Furthermore at the 1427 assession we find that whilst the bulk of holding were leased with small increments to their assession fines other holdings had their fines reduced. Such contrasting movements as these must be explained in terms of differing demand for differing qualities of land.

The fundamental dichotomy was between trends in the rents of *terra* and *terra vasta*. With very few exceptions on assessionable manors all over Cornwall, irrespective of whether the value of the bulk of the *terra* was rising or falling, waste and poor quality land commanded much lower rents than it had before the Black Death. On the eastern manors, upon which the rents of the majority of holdings rose steeply to new heights in the century after the Black

Appendix B

Death, the rents of waste land generally failed to recover the levels attained before 1348/9. At Liskeard between the assessions of 1347 and 1434 rents of average conventionary holdings increased by approximately one third whilst rents of waste declined sharply. For example, 30 acres of waste in Bynorthdonne, worth 4s. 1d. annually in 1347/8, was in 1421 incorporated without extra charge into a holding of 32 acres of *terra*; and some 100 acres of waste in Looden, which had been realising approximately 24s. in the thirteen-forties, was left untaken at each assession after 1420. At Climsland many small pieces of waste to be found on the pre-Black Death assession rolls are absent from those of the later fourteenth and the fifteenth centuries, and the pasture of Hengesdonne leased for 16s. annual rent and an assession fine of 3s. 4d. in 1347 realised only 12s. annual rent and 12d. fine in 1427.

The rents of holdings composed of poor quality land generally followed trends similar to those of the rents of waste land: being relatively cheap before the Black Death and difficult to lease afterwards. At Climsland the holdings situated in Thornecombe and Northdonne are excellent examples of land of this type; both hamlets were situated amongst the waste pastures on the northern extremities of the manor;[1] before 1348/9 the lands of these hamlets were, at 2d. per acre, realising little more than half the average prevailing rent, and in the course of the later fourteenth and the fifteenth centuries they averaged only 1¼d. per acre, which was little more than a quarter the rent of the vast bulk of holdings. At Liskeard the central body of land in slack demand after 1348/9 was situated in Doubleboys, Donnhouse, Dene, and the Old Deer Park, which similarly had been relatively cheap to rent in 1347 at only 2d. or 3d. per acre compared with as much as 6d. for an acre of the better quality land. Doubleboys, situated to the west of Liskeard borough in thickly-wooded country, contained lands of mixed quality, parts of the vill maintained and even increased their value after the Black Death, yet some 200 acres were left untaken at assession after assession in the fifteenth century to be subsequently rented on temporary contracts without any fines being levied. Much

[1] See the map of Climsland above, p. 20.

Appendix B

of the hamlets of Donnhouse, Dene, and the Old Deer Park reverted to waste. These lands were surely lands of indifferent
quality which had been rendered unattractive to potential farmers by
the drastically changed economic circumstances of the post-plague
era.

In the west of Cornwall, as in the east, demand for waste and
relatively infertile land was very slack after the Black Death.
Almost 2,000 acres of poor quality land on Helston-in-Kirrier was
left permanently vacant, whilst much that stayed in cultivation had
its rent slashed. At Tybesta, trends in the rent of 40 acres of waste at
Coyspost may be taken as typical: in 1347 it was demised for 20s.
annual rent and an assession fine of 13s. 4d., in the later fourteenth
century leases were made at 20s. annually, and by 1406 a rent of only
9s. was payable.

Yet, with the striking exception of Helston-in-Kirrier, even
manors which suffered a severe depression in the demand for their
lands in the fifteenth century had little land which was left idle for
any length of time. The slump which afflicted the western manors
from the first quarter of the fifteenth century, and the north-
eastern manors from the middle of the century, did not lead to
large numbers of vacant holdings, but rather to a downward
reappraisal of rents. Lands which were left unleased at assessions
were invariably taken up on yearly contracts by the following
Michaelmas when the assessional term started. None except the
poorest waste land slipped permanently out of use.

Some exceptions to the fall in demand for waste and rough
pasture from the mid-fourteenth century are afforded on the manors
of north-eastern Cornwall. On Helstone-in-Triggshire in particular,
large areas of waste were leased in the fifteenth century at rents
comparable with those ruling in pre-Black Death times. A probable
explanation may be found in the increasing pasturage of animals in
this part of Cornwall, possibly fostered by a demand for summer
pasture from Devon graziers.[1]

The rate at which the rents of holdings rose on the eastern
manors in the century after the plague of 1349 was far from uniform,

[1] Carew, *Survey of Cornwall*, p. 24 (see also above, p. 23).

273

and certain lands increased their value at a rate much faster than average. At Liskeard, where average assession fines almost doubled between 1347 and 1434 leading to an average rise in the annual charge upon holdings of almost a third, on a number of holdings frequently described as meadow, fines as much as trebled and as a consequence annual charges doubled. For example the charge imposed upon 4 acres in Whiteland rose from 3s. 9d. in 1347 to 7s. 3d. by 1413 and 7s. 7d. by 1441; whilst over the same period that on two closes comprising 15 acres in Luxiscrosse rose from 11s. 7d. to 21s. 2d. At Climsland also there were a number of holdings that seem to have been in such great demand that they increased in value by much more than the average. For whilst assession fines in 1427 were some 60 per cent higher on average than 1347, fines on holdings at Whiteforde and Hille had increased by more than 100 per cent, and at Beaulieu by more than 170 per cent.

On the other hand fines on some other holdings on these two manors increased much slower than average. For example, at Climsland the fine on a holding in Ovese which had been 15s. in 1347 was only 20s. 6d. in 1427, whilst on a holding in Boraton the fine rose from 23s. only as high as 29s. At Liskeard, the fines of a larger proportion of holdings demonstrated a below-average growth-rate, and it was predominantly these holdings that had their fines reduced at the assession of 1427, or that even remained untaken, as can be seen from the following examples.

	Assession Fine		
	1347	1420	1427
1 messuage 46 acres in Trevelmont	46s. 8d.	56s. 8d.	53s. 4d.
Annual rent 11s.			
2 messuages 22 acres in Trevelmont	30s.	32s. 8d.	26s.
Annual rent 4s.			
1 messuage 29 acres in Trevelmont	28s.	36s. 8d.	33s. 4d.
Annual rent 5s. 10d.			
1 messuage 17 acres in Treburgy	26s. 8d.	30s.	*in manu domini*
Annual rent 4s. 3d.			
1 messuage 14 acres in Hethlond	16s.	21s. 4d.	19s. 8d.
Annual rent 5s.			

(There was an average increase in assession fines of between 80 and 100 per cent between 1347 and 1427 at Liskeard.)

Appendix B

Just as there were many different rates of increase in the rents of individual holdings upon manors whose lands were appreciating in value, so were there different rates of decrease in the rents of holdings on those manors whose lands were falling in value. At Helstonin-Kirrier, where aggregate rent receipts never recovered to pre-Black Death levels, the rents of individual holdings fell at varying rates both immediately after the plague and subsequently to the boom at the start of the fifteenth century. It has already been mentioned that almost half of this manor was of no value at all to the Duchy after 1349, and as would be expected the rents of the poorer lands which remained in cultivation were drastically reduced. A typical example of such a fall is that of a hundred acres of waste in Pentyr worth 13s. 8d. in 1347 and leased for 3s. 4d. in 1486. Yet other holdings, those which had been expensive relative to other holdings before the Black Death and which were thus presumably more fertile, remained in demand at rents close to their former levels. For example, a messuage and 22 acres in Chienhale vill leased for 7s. rent and an assession fine of 12s. before 1348/9 still realised 7s. annually in Edward IV's reign; whilst 2 messuages and 80 acres in Roslyn leased for 24s. annual rent and an assession fine of 13s. 4d. in 1347 were worth 22s. annually to the Duchy in 1486. Many further examples of above-average rent levels on Helston manor in the late fifteenth century could be given from the fertile vills of Hellistoth, Pencois, Calvenath, Lisgree, and Chienhale. Thus once again, as on eastern manors, it was the rents of fertile holdings which fared better than those of poor lands.

At Tybesta, where assession fines were slashed by between a third and a half on the majority of holdings between 1434 and 1441, much smaller reductions were registered upon some holdings, as for example on a messuage and 36 acres in Carahoda, whose fine was reduced only from 50s. to 40s. and no further. At Tintagel most assession fines were less than half their pre-Black Death levels when the manor returned to the hands of the Duchy at the close of the reign of Henry VI, yet holdings in the vills of Trewarman and Tregatta had higher fines. At the same time on Tewington manor, which was also suffering from a depression in demand for land, the holdings of Tewyn vill alone had assession fines levied on them.

K

Appendix B

From the mass of rent movements catalogued in the assession rolls of the seventeen Duchy manors in the fourteenth and fifteenth centuries a central coherent theme can be grasped which might be briefly summarised thus: those lands which were cheaper and less in demand before the Black Death, and therefore presumably relatively infertile, became even less attractive relative to the other lands in the course of the later fourteenth and the fifteenth centuries.

Soil exhaustion does not appear to have been a significant factor on any of the assessionable manors, despite the rigours difficult to dissociate from short-lease farming and on land frequently not of the best quality. Holdings which fell out of cultivation were invariably poor quality lands, as difficult to lease immediately after the plague of 1348/9 as in the fifteenth century. The great mass of holdings were farmed continuously throughout the later middle ages, and what is more with sharply rising rents for much of the period on the eastern manors. The prevalence of ley farming no doubt did much to maintain the fertility of soils. There is no evidence to suggest that the qualities of any holdings changed significantly for the worse —what did change were the conditions governing demand for land.

Fluctuations in the rents of conventionary holdings in the later middle ages have so far been examined in the context of movements within individual manors: the relative movements in the value of lands of different assessionable manors over the same two hundred years is also worthy of mention. Continuous increases on the south-eastern manors raised the rent of an average acre of land on Clims-land from 3d./3½d. to 4d./5d., and on Liskeard from 4d./6d. to 7d./8d. In central Cornwall the highly priced lands of Tewington manor were some 15–30 per cent lower in Edward IV's reign than they had been in 1347, which meant perhaps an average fall per acre of from 1s. 3d. to 10d. or 1s. The value of lands on Tybesta fell from an average of 8d. or 8½d. to 6d. or 7d. between 1347 and 1441. At Tintagel, a manor with a particularly wide range of rents, falls of some 10–15 per cent were registered over the course of the fifteenth century which amounted to a decline of from perhaps 9d. to 8d. or 11d. to 9½d. per acre on some fairly typical holdings. Viewed in this context the various booms and slumps experienced in the demand for

Appendix B

land of each assessionable manor can be seen in terms of a reassessment of the value of lands in different parts of the county, with those lands in the east of the county becoming relatively more valuable and those in the central and western regions becoming less valuable.

NOTES TO TABLES 22–6

For the following tables an attempt has been made to select a representative sample of landholdings of differing types, quality, and size. As will be seen from these tables the annual rent was usually fixed and changes in the value of holdings were reflected in flexible assession fines. The rent per acre per annum of each holding has been calculated by adding one seventh of the seven-year assession fine to the annual rent and dividing by the number of acres. All leases commenced at Michaelmas, and the dates given in the tables are of the Michaelmas at which they began to the Michaelmas at which they ended.

Appendix B

TABLE 22 *Assession fine : for a seven-year period*
Rent per acre : per annum

Michaelmas/Michaelmas		1333–40 s.	d.	1340–7 s.	d.	1347–8 s.	d.	1348–57 s.	d.	1357–64 s.	d.	Clims- 1364–71 s.	d.
A messuage and 8 acres in Whiteforde	Assession fine	5	0	5	0	5	0	nil		5	0	5	0
Annual rent: 2s.	Rent per acre		4		4		4		3		4		4
A messuage and 8 acres in Whiteforde	Assession fine	5	0	5	0	5	0	nil		5	0	6	0
Annual rent: 2s.	Rent per acre		4		4		4		3		4		4¼
2 messuages and 48 acres in Whiteforde	Assession fine	30	0	30	0	30	0	nil		30	0	31	0
Annual rent: 7s. 6d.	Rent per acre		3		3		3		2		3		3
A messuage and 32 acres in Whiteforde	Assession fine	24	0	24	0	24	0	nil		24	0	24	0
Annual rent 5s. 4d.	Rent per acre		3¼		3¼		3¼		2		3¼		3¼
A messuage and 8 acres in Ovese	Assession fine	8	0	8	0	8	0	nil		8	0	8	0
Annual rent: 1s. 4d.	Rent per acre		3¾		3¾		3¾		2		3¾		3¾
A messuage and 16 acres in Ovese	Assession fine	15	0	15	0	15	0	nil		15	0	16	0
Annual rent: 2s. 8d.	Rent per acre		3½		3½		3½		2		3½		3¾
A messuage and 8 acres in Lythewille	Assession fine	7	0	7	0	7	0	nil		7	0	8	0
Annual rent: 16d.	Rent per acre		3½		3½		3½		2		3½		3¾
A messuage and 16 acres in Lythewille	Assession fine	13	4	13	4	13	4	nil		13	4		
Annual rent: 2s. 6d.	Rent per acre		3¼		3¼		3¼		2		3¼		
A messuage and 32 acres and 3 acres waste in Lythewille	Assession fine	22	0	22	0	22	0	nil		13	4[a]	22	0
Annual rent: 5s. 4½d.	Rent per acre		3¼		3¼		3¼		2		2¾		3¼
A messuage and 18 acres in Bysouthcombe	Assession fine	10	0	10	0	10	0	nil		10	0	10	0
Annual rent: 3s. 2d.	Rent per acre		3		3		3		2		3		3
A messuage and 32 acres in Bysouthcombe	Assession fine	20	0	20	0	20	0	nil		20	0	15	0
Annual rent: 3s. 10d.	Rent per acre		2½		2½		2½		1½		2½		2¼
A messuage and 36 acres in Bysouthcombe	Assession fine	25	3	25	3	25	3	nil		25	6	26	8
Annual rent: 3s. 8d.	Rent per acre		2½		2½		2½		1¼		2½		2½
A messuage and 20 acres in Boraton	Assession fine	18	0	18	0	18	0	nil		18	0	18	0
Annual rent: 3s.	Rent per acre		3¼		3¼		3¼		1¾		3¼		3¼
A messuage and 16 acres in Beaulieu	Assession fine	13	4	13	4	13	4	nil		13	4	13	4
Annual rent: 2s. until Michaelmas 1420, then 2s. 6d.	Rent per acre		3		3		3		1½		3		3
A messuage and 30 acres in Hille	Assession fine	20	0	20	0	20	0	nil		25	0	28	0
Annual rent: 3s. 10d.	Rent per acre		2½		2½		2½		1½		3		3
A messuage and 28 acres in Knocket	Assession fine	13	4	13	4	13	4	nil		13	4	13	4
Annual rent: 3s. 6d.	Rent per acre		2¼		2¼		2¼		1½		2¼		2¼
A messuage and 18 acres in Knocket	Assession fine	13	4	13	4	13	4	nil		13	4	13	4
Annual rent: 2s.	Rent per acre		2¾		2¾		2¾		1½		2¾		2¾
A messuage and 20 acres in Dounhouse	Assession fine	8	0	8	0	8	0	nil		8	0	8	0
Annual rent: 3s. 4d.	Rent per acre		2¾		2¾		2¾		2		2¾		2¾
A messuage and 16 acres in Dounhouse	Assession fine	5	0	5	0	5	0	nil		5	0	5	6
Annual rent: 2s. 8d.	Rent per acre		2½		2½		2½		2		2½		2½
2 messuages and 50 acres in Northdoun	Assession fine	18	0	18	0	18	0	nil		18	0	10	0
Annual rent: 5s. 4d.	Rent per acre		2		2		2		1¼		2		1¾
2 messuages and 64 acres in Thorncombe	Assession fine					32	0	nil		nil			
Annual rent: 6s. 8d.	Rent per acre						2		½		1¼		

[a] Fine reduced because the

land

	1371–8		1392–9		1399–1406		1406–13		1413–20		1420–7		1427–34		1434–41		1441–8		1448–69		1469–90		1490–7	
s.	d.	s.	d.	s.	d.	s.	d.	s.	d.	s.	d.	s.	d.	s.	d.	s.	d.	s.	d.	s.	d.	s.	d.
6	8	8	0	8	0	10	0	11	0	12	0	13	4	13	4	13	4	13	4	13	4	13	4
6	$\overset{4\frac12}{8}$	7	$\overset{4\frac34}{6}$	7	$\overset{4\frac34}{6}$	9	$\overset{5}{2}$	11	$\overset{5\frac14}{0}$	12	$\overset{5\frac12}{0}$	13	$\overset{6}{4}$	13	$\overset{6}{4}$	13	$\overset{6}{4}$	13	$\overset{6}{4}$	13	$\overset{6}{4}$	13	$\overset{6}{4}$
42	$\overset{4\frac12}{0}$	44	$\overset{4\frac34}{0}$	44	$\overset{4\frac34}{0}$	60	$\overset{4\frac34}{0}$	64	$\overset{5\frac14}{0}$	65	$\overset{5\frac12}{0}$	66	$\overset{6}{8}$	66	$\overset{6}{8}$	66	$\overset{6}{8}$	66	$\overset{6}{8}$	66	$\overset{6}{8}$	66	$\overset{6}{8}$
26	$\overset{3\frac12}{8}$	28	$\overset{3\frac12}{0}$	28	$\overset{3\frac12}{0}$	34	$\overset{4}{8}$	36	$\overset{4\frac14}{0}$	37	$\overset{4\frac14}{8}$	40	$\overset{4\frac14}{0}$	40	$\overset{4\frac14}{0}$	40	$\overset{4\frac14}{0}$	40	$\overset{4\frac14}{0}$	40	$\overset{4\frac14}{0}$	40	$\overset{4\frac14}{0}$
10	$\overset{3\frac12}{0}$	10	$\overset{3\frac12}{0}$	10	$\overset{3\frac12}{0}$	13	$\overset{4}{4}$	14	$\overset{4}{0}$	15	$\overset{4}{0}$	16	$\overset{4\frac14}{0}$	16	$\overset{4\frac14}{0}$	16	$\overset{4\frac14}{0}$	16	$\overset{4\frac14}{0}$	16	$\overset{4\frac14}{0}$	16	$\overset{4\frac14}{0}$
16	$\overset{4\frac14}{0}$	17	$\overset{4\frac14}{0}$	18	$\overset{4\frac14}{0}$	20	$\overset{5}{0}$	20	$\overset{5}{0}$	20	$\overset{5\frac14}{0}$	20	$\overset{5\frac14}{6}$	20	$\overset{5\frac14}{6}$	20	$\overset{5\frac14}{6}$	20	$\overset{5\frac14}{6}$	20	$\overset{5\frac14}{6}$	20	$\overset{5\frac14}{6}$
10	$\overset{3\frac34}{0}$		$3\frac34$		4	8	$\overset{4}{0}$	9	$\overset{4}{0}$	10	$\overset{4}{0}$	11	$\overset{4\frac14}{0}$	11	$\overset{4\frac14}{0}$	11	$\overset{4\frac14}{0}$	11	$\overset{4\frac14}{0}$	11	$\overset{4\frac14}{0}$	11	$\overset{4\frac14}{0}$
	4	16	0	16	0	20	$\overset{3\frac34}{0}$	22	$\overset{3\frac34}{0}$	22	$\overset{4}{6}$	24	$\overset{4\frac14}{0}$	24	$\overset{4\frac14}{0}$	24	$\overset{4\frac14}{0}$	24	$\overset{4\frac14}{0}$	24	$\overset{4\frac14}{0}$	24	$\overset{4\frac14}{0}$
22	0	23	$\overset{3\frac12}{10}$	23	$\overset{3\frac12}{10}$	30	$\overset{4}{0}$	32	$\overset{4\frac14}{0}$	34	$\overset{4\frac14}{0}$	43	$\overset{4\frac14}{4}$	43	$\overset{4\frac14}{4}$	43	$\overset{4\frac14}{4}$	43	$\overset{4\frac14}{4}$	43	$\overset{4\frac14}{4}$	43	$\overset{4\frac14}{4}$
11	$\overset{3\frac14}{0}$	12	$\overset{3\frac14}{0}$	12	$\overset{3\frac14}{0}$	13	$\overset{3\frac34}{4}$	14	$\overset{3\frac34}{4}$	15	$\overset{3\frac34}{0}$	16	$\overset{4\frac14}{0}$	16	$\overset{4\frac14}{0}$	16	$\overset{4\frac14}{0}$	16	$\overset{4\frac14}{0}$	16	$\overset{4\frac14}{0}$	16	$\overset{4\frac14}{0}$
20	$\overset{3}{0}$	23	$\overset{3\frac14}{0}$	23	$\overset{3\frac14}{0}$	30	$\overset{3\frac12}{0}$	30	$\overset{3\frac12}{8}$	32	$\overset{3\frac34}{0}$	36	$\overset{3\frac34}{0}$	36	$\overset{3\frac34}{0}$	36	$\overset{3\frac34}{0}$	36	$\overset{3\frac34}{0}$	36	$\overset{3\frac34}{0}$	36	$\overset{3\frac34}{0}$
30	$\overset{2\frac34}{0}$	31	$\overset{2\frac34}{0}$	32	$\overset{2\frac34}{0}$	38	$\overset{3}{8}$	40	$\overset{3}{0}$	41	$\overset{3\frac14}{0}$	42	$\overset{3\frac12}{0}$	42	$\overset{3\frac12}{0}$	42	$\overset{3\frac12}{0}$	42	$\overset{3\frac12}{0}$	42	$\overset{3\frac12}{0}$	42	$\overset{3\frac12}{0}$
19	$\overset{2\frac34}{0}$	19	$\overset{2\frac34}{0}$	19	$\overset{2\frac34}{0}$	24	$\overset{3}{0}$	26	$\overset{3\frac14}{8}$	26	$\overset{3\frac14}{8}$	28	$\overset{3\frac14}{0}$	28	$\overset{3\frac14}{0}$	28	$\overset{3\frac14}{0}$	28	$\overset{3\frac14}{0}$	28	$\overset{3\frac14}{0}$	28	$\overset{3\frac14}{0}$
16	$\overset{3\frac12}{0}$	22	$\overset{3\frac12}{0}$	22	$\overset{3\frac12}{0}$	30	$\overset{3\frac34}{0}$	32	$\overset{4}{0}$	33	$\overset{4}{4}$	34	$\overset{4\frac14}{4}$	34	$\overset{4\frac14}{4}$	34	$\overset{4\frac14}{4}$	34	$\overset{4\frac14}{4}$	34	$\overset{4\frac14}{4}$	34	$\overset{4\frac14}{4}$
23	$\overset{3\frac14}{0}$		4	30	$\overset{4}{6}$	37	$\overset{4\frac34}{2}$	38	$\overset{5}{6}$	40	$\overset{5}{0}$	44	$\overset{5\frac14}{0}$	44	$\overset{5\frac14}{0}$	44	$\overset{5\frac14}{0}$	44	$\overset{5\frac14}{0}$	44	$\overset{5\frac14}{0}$	44	$\overset{5\frac14}{0}$
15	$\overset{2\frac34}{0}$	16	$\overset{3\frac14}{0}$	16	$\overset{3\frac14}{0}$	20	$\overset{3\frac34}{0}$			22	$\overset{3\frac34}{0}$	23	$\overset{4}{1}$	23	$\overset{4}{1}$	23	$\overset{4}{1}$	23	$\overset{4}{1}$	23	$\overset{4}{1}$	23	$\overset{4}{1}$
14	$\overset{2\frac12}{0}$	16	$\overset{2\frac12}{0}$	16	$\overset{2\frac12}{0}$	18	$\overset{3}{0}$	20	0	20	$\overset{3\frac34}{6}$	21	$\overset{3\frac14}{0}$	21	$\overset{3\frac14}{0}$	21	$\overset{3\frac14}{0}$	21	$\overset{3\frac14}{0}$	21	$\overset{3\frac14}{0}$	21	$\overset{3\frac14}{0}$
10	$\overset{2\frac34}{0}$	10	$\overset{3}{0}$	10	$\overset{3}{0}$	11	$\overset{3}{0}$			12	$\overset{3\frac14}{2}$	13	$\overset{3\frac12}{0}$	13	$\overset{3\frac12}{0}$	13	$\overset{3\frac12}{0}$	13	$\overset{3\frac12}{0}$	13	$\overset{3\frac12}{0}$	13	$\overset{3\frac12}{0}$
6	$\overset{2\frac34}{0}$	8	$\overset{2\frac34}{0}$	8	$\overset{2\frac34}{0}$	9	$\overset{3}{0}$			9	$\overset{3}{6}$	10	$\overset{3}{0}$	10	$\overset{3}{0}$	10	$\overset{3}{0}$	10	$\overset{3}{0}$	10	$\overset{3}{0}$	10	$\overset{3}{0}$
10	$\overset{2\frac12}{0}$		$\overset{3}{\text{nil}}$		$\overset{3}{\text{nil}}$	6	$\overset{3}{8}$				$\overset{3}{\text{nil}}$		$\overset{3}{\text{nil}}$	6	$\overset{3}{8}$			6	$\overset{3}{8}$			3	
3	$\overset{1\frac34}{4}$		$\overset{1\frac14}{\text{nil}}$		$\overset{1\frac14}{\text{nil}}$		$\overset{1\frac12}{\text{nil}}$				$\overset{1\frac14}{\text{nil}}$		$\overset{1\frac14}{\text{nil}}$				$\overset{1\frac12}{\text{nil}}$		nil	10	$\overset{1\frac12}{8}$
	$1\frac14$		$1\frac14$		$1\frac14$		$1\frac12$				$1\frac14$		$1\frac14$				$1\frac14$		$1\frac14$		$1\frac12$

house had been burnt down.

Appendix B

TABLE 23 *Assession fine : for a seven-year period*
Rent per acre : per annum

Michaelmas/Michaelmas		1333–40		1340–7		1347–8		1348–57		Lis- 1357–64	
		s.	d.	s.	d.	s.	d.	s.	d.	s.	d.
15 acres in Luxiscrosse	Assession fine	53	4	53	4	53	4	nil		53	4
Annual rent: 4s.	Rent per acre		9¼		9¼		9¼		3¼		9¼
4 acres in Whiteland	Assession fine	12	0	12	0	12	0	nil		12	0
Annual rent: 2s.	Rent per acre		11¼		11¼		11¼		6		11¼
A messuage and 34 acres in Treyher	Assession fine	46	8	46	8	46	8	nil		46	8
Annual rent: 15s.	Rent per acre		7¾		7¾		7¾		5¼		7¾
A messuage and 26 acres in Treyher	Assession fine	36	8			40	0	nil		40	0
Annual rent: 11s. 6d.	Rent per acre		7¾				8		5¼		8
A messuage and 24 acres in Trewythelan	Assession fine	30	0	30	0	30	0	nil		30	0
Annual rent: 7s. 3d.	Rent per acre		5¾		5¾		5¾		3½		5¾
A messuage and 25 acres in Trewythelan	Assession fine	30	0	30	0	30	0	nil		30	0
Annual rent: 7s. 3d.	Rent per acre		5½		5½		5½		3½		5½
A messuage and 23 acres in Rosnonnan	Assession fine	33	4	33	4	33	4	nil		33	4
Annual rent: 5s.	Rent per acre		5		5		5		2¾		5
A messuage and 26 acres in Rosnonnan	Assession fine	30	0	30	0	30	0	nil		30	0
Annual rent: 8s.	Rent per acre		5¾		5¾		5¾		3¾		5¾
A messuage and 24 acres in Tympellon	Assession fine	26	8	26	8	26	8	nil		26	8
Annual rent: 6s. 8d.	Rent per acre		5¼		5¼		5¼		3¼		5¼
A messuage and 24 acres in Tympellon	Assession fine	26	8	26	8	26	8	nil		26	8
Annual rent: 6s. 4d.	Rent per acre		5		5		5		3¼		5
A messuage and 38 acres in Trevekker	Assession fine	33	4	33	4	33	4	nil		33	4
Annual rent: 5s. 4d.	Rent per acre		3		3		3		1½		3
A messuage and 40 acres in Trevekker	Assession fine	30	0	30	0	32	0	nil		32	0
Annual rent: 5s. 6d.	Rent per acre		3		3		3		1¾		3
A messuage and 33 acres in Boduel	Assession fine	32	0	32	0	32	0	nil		32	0
Annual rent: 5s.	Rent per acre		3½		3½		3½		1¾		3½
A messuage and 19 acres in Boduel	Assession fine	13	4	13	4	13	4	nil		13	4
Annual rent: 2s. 7d.	Rent per acre		2¾		2¾		2¾		1¾		2¾
33 acres in Cadusket	Assession fine	20	0	20	0	20	0	nil		20	0
Annual rent: 6s. 6d.	Rent per acre		3		3		3		2¼		3
A messuage and 40 acres (including 31 acres waste) in Newhouse	Assession fine	16	0	16	0	16	0	nil		10	0
Annual rent: 5s.	Rent per acre		2¼		2¼		2¼		1½		2
A messuage and 32 acres in Halbothek	Assession fine	35	0	35	0	35	0	nil		35	0
Annual rent: 7s.	Rent per acre		4¾		4¾		4¾		2½		4¾
A messuage and 16 acres in Halbothek	Assession fine	18	0	18	0	18	0	nil		18	0
Annual rent: 3s. 4d.	Rent per acre		4½		4½		4½		2½		4½
A messuage and 42½ acres in Doubleboys	Assession fine	26	8	26	8	26	8	nil		1	0
Annual rent: 10s.	Rent per acre		4		4		4		3		3

Appendix B

keard

1364–71		1371–8		1392–9		1399–1406		1406–13		1413–20		1420–7		1427–34		1434–41		1441–8		1448–69		1469–90	
s.	d.	s.	d.	s.	d.	s.	d.	s.	d.	s.	d.	s.	d.	s.	d.	s.	d.	s.	d	s.	d.	s.	d.
53	4	61	0	66	0	66	0	90	0	90	0	120	0	120	0	120	0	120	0	120	0	120	0
	9¼		10¼		10¾		10¾	1	1½	1	1½	1	5	1	5	1	5	1	5	1	5	1	5
15	2	17	2	26	8	26	8	30	0	36	8	38	0	38	6	39	0	39	0	39	0	39	0
1	0½	1	0½	1	5½	1	5½	1	6¾	1	9¼	1	10¼	1	10½	1	11	1	11	1	11	1	11
46	8	50	0	53	4	53	4	60	0	65	0	66	8	66	8	66	8	66	8	66	8	66	8
	7¾		7¾		8		8		8¼		8½		8½		8½		8½		8½		8½		8½
30	0	32	0	33	0	33	0	39	0	39	0	46	8	46	8	47	2	47	2	47	2		
	7¼		7½		7½		7½		8		8		8½		8½		8½		8½		8½		
30	0	40	0	44	0	44	0	54	0	54	0	62	0	63	4	63	10	63	10	63	10	63	10
	5¾		6½		6¾		6¾		7½		7½		8		8¼		8¼		8¼		8¼		8¼
30	0	40	0	40	0	40	0	50	0	50	0	60	0	62	0	62	0	62	0	62	0	62	0
	5½		6¼		6¼		6¼		7		7		7¾		7¾		7¾		7¾		7¾		7¾
34	2	36	0	36	8	36	8	40	0	40	0	66	8	67	8	68	2	68	2	68	2	68	2
	5¼		5¼		5¼		5¼		5½		5½		7½		7½		7¾		7¾		7¾		7¾
30	0	32	0	35	4	35	4	40	0	40	0	45	0	45	6	46	0	46	0	46	0	46	0
	5¾		6		6		6		6¼		6¼		6¾		6¾		6¾		6¾		6¾		6¾
26	8	28	0	32	0	32	0	35	4			47	0	47	6	48	0	48	0	48	0	48	0
	5¼		5¼		5½		5½		6				6¾		6¾		6¾		6¾		6¾		6¾
26	8	30	0	30	0	30	0	36	8	50	0	51	0	51	0	52	0	52	0	52	0	52	0
	5		5¼		5¼		5¼		5¾		6¾		6¾		6¾		6¾		6¾		6¾		6¾
33	4	35	0	36	8			40	0	40	0	50	0	52	0	52	6	52	6	52	6	52	6
	3		3¼		3¼				3½		3½		4		4		4¼		4¼		4¼		4¼
32	0	33	4	33	4	35	0	40	0	40	0	53	4	56	8	57	2	57	2	57	2	57	2
	3		3		3		3¼		3½		3½		4		4		4		4		4		4
30	0	33	4	33	4	33	4	36	8	36	8	41	8	43	0	43	6	43	6	43	6	43	6
	3½		3¾		3¾		3¾		3¾		3¾		4		4		4		4		4		4
13	4	13	4	16	0	16	0	18	0	18	0	21	0	21	8	21	11	21	11	21	11	21	11
	2¾		2¾		3		3		3¼		3¼		3½		3½		3½		3½		3½		3½
20	0	21	0	22	0	22	0	26	8			nil		26	8	26	8	21	8	nil		7	3
	3		3¼		3½		3½		3¾				2¼		3¾		3¾		3½		2¾		2¾
6	0	4	0	5	0	5	0	6	8	6	8	11	0	13	0	13	0	14	0	14	0	14	0
	1¾		1¾		1¾		1¾		1¾		1¾		2		2		2		2		2		2
35	0	35	0	35	0	35	0	40	0	40	0	46	0	46	8	46	8	46	8	46	8	46	8
	4¾		4¾		4¾		4¾		4¾		4¾		5¼		5¼		5¼		5¼		5¼		5¼
18	0	18	0	22	0	22	0	25	4	25	4	31	4	32	0	32	3	32	3	32	3	32	3
	4½		4½		4¾		4¾		5		5		6		6		6		6		6		6
nil		nil		1	0	nil				nil		nil						nil				nil	
	3		3		3		3				3		3						3				3

Appendix B

TABLE 24 *Assession fine: for a seven-year period* *Rent per acre: per annum*

Michaelmas/Michaelmas		1333–40		1340–7		1347–8		1348–56		Helstone-in- 1356–7	
		s.	d.	s.	d.	s.	d.	s.	d.	s.	d.
A messuage and 17 acres in Trevelek	Assession fine					20	0	nil		nil	
Annual rent: 10s.	Rent per acre						9		5¼		7
A messuage and 16 acres and 2 acres moor and meadow in Trevelek	Assession fine			23	0	23	4	nil		nil	
Annual rent: 12s.	Rent per acre				10		10		6		8
A messuage and 17 acres and 1 acre meadow in Trevegan	Assession fine	20	0			20	0	nil		nil	
Annual rent: 10s.	Rent per acre		8½				8½		5		7
A messuage and 20 acres in Trevegan	Assession fine	20	0			20	0	nil		nil	
Annual rent: 11s.	Rent per acre		8¼				8¼		5		6½
A messuage and 18 acres in Tregoodwalder	Assession fine	13	4			13	4	nil		nil	
Annual rent: 8s.	Rent per acre		6¾				6¾		4		5¼
A messuage and 22 acres in Trewalder	Assession fine					15	0	nil		nil	
Annual rent: 12s.	Rent per acre						8		5		6½
A messuage and 22 acres in Trewalder	Assession fine					13	4	nil		nil	
Annual rent: 12s.	Rent per acre						7¾		6		6½
A messuage and 22 acres in Trewalder	Assession fine					13	4	nil		nil	
Annual rent: 12s.	Rent per acre						7¾		5		6½
A messuage and 19 acres in Treyvthant	Assession fine			16	0	13	6	nil		nil	
Annual rent: 7s.	Rent per acre				5¾		5½		3½		4½
A messuage and 18 acres in Forda	Assession fine	25	0	25	0	25	0	nil		nil	
Annual rent: 10s.	Rent per acre		9		9		9		5		6¾
A messuage and 20 acres in Tresithen	Assession fine			20	0	20	0	nil		nil	
Annual rent: 7s.	Rent per acre				6		6		3		4½
A messuage and 19 acres in Tresithen	Assession fine			20	0	20	0	nil		nil	
Annual rent: 7s.	Rent per acre				6¼		6¼		3¼		4½
A messuage and 10½ acres in Helstone	Assession fine					6	8	nil		nil	
Annual rent: 3s. 4d.	Rent per acre						4¾		3		4
A messuage and 7½ acres in Helstone	Assession fine					5	0	nil		nil	
Annual rent: 2s. 6d.	Rent per acre						5		3		4
A messuage and 16 acres in Pencarou	Assession fine			10	0	10	0	nil		nil	
Annual rent: 7s. 3d.	Rent per acre				6½		6½		4		5½
A messuage and 13 acres in Pencarou	Assession fine			15	0	15	0	nil		nil	
Annual rent: 7s.	Rent per acre				8½		8½		5		6½
5 acres waste in Helsbury	Assession fine	2	0	2	0	2	0	nil		nil	
Annual rent: 2s. 4d.	Rent per acre		6		6		6		4		5½
3 messuages and 120 acres waste in Goosehill	Assession fine					11	0			nil	
	Annual rent					7	8			7	8
	Total charge					9	3			7	8

[a] Does not include 20s. *donum*.
[b] Does not include 10s. *donum*.
[e] Does not include 10s. *donum*.
[f] Does not include 10s. *donum*.
[i] Does not include 5s. *donum*.
[k] Does not include 6s. 8d. *donum*.

Appendix B

Triggshire

1357–64		1364–71		1371–8		1399–1406		1406–13		1420–7		1427–34		1441–62		1462–9		1469–76	
s.	d.	s.	d.	s.	d.	s.	d.	s.	d.	s.	d.	s.	d.	s.	d.	s.	d.	s.	d.
20	0	23	4	23	4	23	4	25	0	25	0[a]	25	0	25	0	25	0		
	9		9¼		9¼		9¼		9½		9½		9½		9½		9½		
23	4	23	4	23	4	13	4	23	4	23	4[b]	23	4	23	4	23	4	23	4
	10		10		10		9¼		10		10		10		10		10		10
18	0	18	0	18	0			20	0	20	0[c]	20	0	20	0	20	0	20	0
	8¼		8¼		8¼				8½		8½		8½		8½		8½		8½
12	0	19	0	20	0	20	0	22	0	22	0[d]	22	0	22	0	22	0	22	0
	7¾		8¼		8¼		8¼		8½		8½		8½		8½		8½		8½
13	4	13	4	13	4	13	4	20	0	20	0[e]	20	0	20	0	20	0	20	0
	6¾		6¾		6¾		6¾		7¼		7¼		7¼		7¼		7¼		7¼
14	0	15	0	15	0	15	0	15	0	16	0[f]	16	0	15	0	16	0	16	0
	8		8		8		8		8		8		8		8		8		8
13	4	14	0	14	0	14	0	16	0	16	0[g]	16	0	16	0	16	0	16	0
	7¾		7¾		7¾		7¾		8		8		8		8		8		8
13	4	14	0	14	0	14	0	16	0	16	0[h]	15	0	14	0	15	0	15	0
	7¾		7¾		7¾		7¾		8		8		8		7¾		8		8
nil		6	8	6	8	11	8	12	0	12	0[i]	12	0	12	0	12	0	12	0
	4½		5		5		6		6		6		6		6		6		6
18	0	18	0	20	0	20	0	23	4	23	4[k]	nil		23	4	23	4	23	4
	8¼		8¼		8½		8½		8¾		8¾		6¾		8¾		8¾		8¾
18	0	18	0	20	0	20	0	22	0			22	0	22	0	22	0	22	0
	5¾		5¾		6		6		6				6		6		6		6
16	0	16	0	20	0	20	0	22	0			22	0	22	0	22	0	22	0
	5¾		5¾		6¼		6¼		6¼				6¼		6¼		6¼		6¼
5	0	5	0	6	8	6	8	8	0	8	0	8	0	8	0	8	0	8	0
	4¾		4¾		4¾		4¾		5		5		5		5		5		5
5	0	5	0	5	0	5	0	6	8	6	8	6	8	6	8	6	8	6	8
	5		5		5		5		5½		5½		5½		5½		5½		5½
6	8	6	8	10	0	10	0	13	4	23	4	23	4	nil		6	0	6	0
	6		6		6½		6½		7		8		8		5½		6		6
8	0	8	0	13	4	13	4	13	4	26	8	nil		nil		26	8	6	8
	7½		7½		8¼		8¼		8¼		10		6½		6½		10		7½
2	0	nil		2	0			3	0			3	0	3	0				
	6		5¾		6				6½				6½		6½				
3	0	nil		23	4	nil		nil				nil		nil				nil	
7	8	7	8	7	8	9	0	13	4			13	4	13	4			13	4
8	1	7	8	11	0	9	0	13	4			13	4	13	4			13	4

[c] Does not include 10s. *donum*.
[g] Does not include 10s. *donum*.
[d] Does not include 10s. *donum*.
[h] Does not include 10s. *donum*.

Appendix B

TABLE 25 *Assession fine: for a seven-year period* *Rent per acre: per annum*

Michaelmas/Michaelmas		1333–40		1340–7		1347–8		1348–56		1356–7		Ty- 1357–64	
		s.	d.	s.	d.	s.	d.	s.	d.	s.	d.	s.	d.
A message and 12 acres in Luscoys	Assession fine	13	4	13	4	13	4	nil		nil		13	4
Annual rent: 6s.	Rent per acre		8		8		8		4½		6		8
2 messuages and 12 acres in Luscoys	Assession fine	16	0	16	0	16	0	nil		nil		16	0
Annual rent: 6s.	Rent per acre		8¼		8¼		8¼		4½		6		8¼
2 messuages and 12 acres in Pennans	Assession fine	9	0	9	0	9	0	nil		nil		9	0
Annual rent: 7s.	Rent per acre		8½		8½		8½		5¼		7		8½
A message and 24½ acres in Penbithewan	Assession fine	30	0	30	0	30	0	nil		nil		26	8
Annual rent: 10s.	Rent per acre		7		7		7		3¾		4¾		6¾
A message and 18 acres in Nanstallan	Assession fine	26	8	26	8	26	8	nil		nil		20	0
Annual rent: 9s.	Rent per acre		8½		8½		8½		4½		6		8
A message and 20 acres in Treswallan	Assession fine	20	0	20	0	20	0	nil		nil		20	0
Annual rent: 9s.	Rent per acre		7		7		7		4		5½		7
A message and 31 acres in Pengelly	Assession fine	60	0	60	0	60	0	nil		nil		60	0
Annual rent: 13s. 4d.	Rent per acre		8½		8½		8½		4		5¼		8½
A message and 18 acres in Trewynnow	Assession fine	18	0	18	0	18	0	nil		nil		10	0
Annual rent: 8s.	Rent per acre		7		7		7		4		5½		6¼
A message and 21 acres in Trevillick	Assession fine	30	0	20	0	20	0	nil		nil		20	0
Annual rent: 10s.	Rent per acre		8¼		7¼		7¼		4¼		5¾		7¼
A message and 21 acres in Trevillick	Assession fine	30	0	30	0	30	0	nil		nil		20	0
Annual rent: 10s.	Rent per acre		8¼		8¼		8¼		4¼		5¾		7¼
A message and 19 acres in Tybeste	Assession fine	26	8	26	8	26	8	nil		nil		21	8
Annual rent: 9s.	Rent per acre		8		8		8		4¼		5¾		7½
A message and 19 acres in Tybeste	Assession fine	26	8	26	8	26	8	nil		nil		26	8
Annual rent: 9s.	Rent per acre		8		8		8		4¼		5¾		8
A message and 18 acres and 2 acres waste in Nanstallan	Assession fine	27	8	27	8	27	8	nil		nil		20	0
Annual rent: 9s.	Rent per acre		8¾		8¾		8¾		4½		6		8
A message and 18 acres in Nanstallan	Assession fine	26	8	26	8	40	0	nil		nil		30	0
Annual rent: 9s.	Rent per acre		8½		8½		11[a]		4½		6		9
40 acres waste called Coispost or Coyscren	Assession fine	13	4			13	4	nil		nil		nil	
	Annual rent	20	0			20	0	6	8[b]	16	0	20	0
	Total charge	21	11			21	11	6	8[b]	16	0	20	0

[a] Leased as two separate 9-acre holdings, each

[b] An average of 6s. 8d. was received

Appendix B

besta 1364–71		1371–8		1378–85		1399–1406		1406–13		1413–20		1420–7		1427–34		1441–8		1462–9		1469–76	
s.	d.	s.	d.	s.	d.	s.	d.	s.	d.	s.	d.	s.	d.	s.	d.	s.	d.	s.	d.	s.	d.
13	4	13	4	13	4	9	0	10	0					16	8	6	8	6	8	6	8
	8		8		8		7¼		7½						8½		7		7		7
13	4	13	4	13	4	13	4	14	0	16	0	16	0	16	0	8	0	8	0	8	0
	8		8		8		8		8		8¼		8¼		8¼		7¼		7¼		7¼
0	0	9	0	9	0			9	0			nil		nil		nil		nil		nil	
	8½		8½		8½				8½				7		7		7		7		7
30	0	30	0	30	0	30	0	31	8	31	8	35	0	nil		24	0	24	0	24	0
	7		7		7		7		7		7		7¼		4¾		6½		6½		6½
24	0	26	0	26	0	27	0	27	0	25	0	31	8	31	8	10	0	10	0	10	0
	8¼		8½		8½		8½		8½		8¼		9		9		7		7		7
19	0	13	4	13	4			20	0	20	0	22	0	22	0	4	0	4	0	4	0
	7		6½		6½				7		7		7¼		7¼		5¾		5¾		5¾
60	0	60	0	60	0			60	0	60	0	66	8	66	8	nil		20	0	20	0
	8½		8½		8½				8½		8½		8¾		8¾		5¼		6¼		6¼
9	0	10	0	10	0			11	0			nil		nil		3	4	3	4	3	4
	6¼		6¼		6¼				6½				5½		5½		5¾		5¾		5¾
20	0	20	0	20	0	21	0	21	0	21	0	23	0	23	0	6	0			21	0
	7¼		7¼		7¼		7½		7½		7½		7½		7½		6¼				7½
20	0	20	0	20	0	20	0	21	8	21	8	21	8	nil		nil				17	8
	7¼		7¼		7¼		7¼		7½		7½		7½		5¾		5¾				7
24	0	26	8	26	8	26	8	28	4	28	4	28	4	28	4	11	8	11	8	11	8
	7¾		8		8		8¼		8¼		8¼		8¼		8¼		6¾		6¾		6¾
4	0	26	8	26	8	26	8	26	8	26	8	28	4	28	4	6	0			6	0
	7¾		8		8		8		8		8		8¼		8¼		6¼				6¼
24	0	26	0	26	0	27	0	27	8			nil		nil		3	4	nil		nil	
	8¼		8½		8½		8½		8¾				6		6		6¼		6		6
25	0	26	0	26	0			25	0			nil		nil		6	0	6	0	6	0
	8¼		8½		8½				8¼				6		6		6½		6½		6½
nil		nil				nil		nil		nil				nil		nil		nil		nil	
20	0	20	0			9	0	9	0	9	0				9	9	0	9	0	8	0
20	0	20	0			9	0	9	0	9	0				9	9	0	9	0	8	0

bearing 5s. 6d. annual rent and 20s. assession fine.
each year from sales of herbage

Appendix B

TABLE 26   *Assession fine: for a seven-year period*
Total charge (per annum): annual rent plus one seventh
of assession fine

Michaelmas/Michaelmas		1333–40	1347–8	Helston-in- 1348–56
		s. d.	s. d.	s. d.
100 acres waste in Pentir	Assession fine	26 8	nil	Of
	Annual rent	14 8	13 8	no
	Total charge	18 6	13 8	value[a]
100 acres waste in Nansplothek	Assession fine		6	Of
	Annual rent		5 0	in
	Total charge		5 1	value
A messuage and 50 acres in Carily	Assession fine		4 0	nil
	Annual rent		15 0	10 0
	Total charge		15 7	10 0
2 messuages and 160 acres in Forsgoi	Assession fine	6 8	12	
	Annual rent	12 0	6 0	
	Total charge	12 11	6 2	
2 messuages and 80 acres in Roslyn	Assession fine		13 4	nil
	Annual rent		24 0	16 0
	Total charge		25 11	16 0
A messuage and 33 acres in Tresperson	Assession fine	66 8	33 4	nil
	Annual rent	20 0	20 0	13 4
	Total charge	29 6	24 9	13 4
A messuage and 22 acres in Chienhale	Assession fine		12 0	nil
	Annual rent		7 0	4 8
	Total charge		8 9	4 8

[a] I.e., no revenues at all were obtained from this land.
[b] The land had remained unfarmed for so long that it had relapsed into woodland.

Appendix B

Kirrier	1356–7	1357–64	1364–71	1371–8	1378–85	1406–13	1465–72	1472–9	1479–86	1486–93
	s. d.	s. d.	s. d.	s. d.	s. d.	s. d.	s. d.	s. d.	s. d.	s. d.
	Of	Of	Of	Of	nil	Of	Of	nil		nil
	no	no	no	no	8 0	no	no	3 4		3 4
	value	value	value	value	8 0	value	value	3 4		3 4
	Of	Of	Of	Of	Of	Of	Infra	Infra	Infra	
	no	no	no	no	no	no	foresta[b]	foresta	foresta	
	value	value	value	value	value	value				
	nil	nil	nil	1 0	1 0	nil			nil	
	15 0	15 0	15 0	15 0	15 0	16 0			9 0	
	15 0	15 0	15 0	15 2	15 2	16 0			9 0	
	nil	nil	nil	nil	nil	nil	nil	nil		nil
	6 0	6 0	5 0	3 0	3 0	3 0	3 0	4 0		4 0
	6 0	6 0	5 0	3 0	3 0	3 0	3 0	4 0		4 0
	nil	nil	4 8	4 8	4 8	10 0	nil	nil	nil	nil
	24 0	24 0	24 0	24 0	24 0	24 0	24 0	24 0	24 0	24 0
	24 0	24 0	24 8	24 8	24 8	25 5	24 0	24 0	24 0	24 0
	nil	10 0	20 0	26 8	26 8	33 4		nil		nil
	20 0	20 0	20 0	20 0	20 0	20 0		16 0		16 0
	20 0	21 5	22 10	23 10	23 10	24 9		16 0		16 0
	nil	nil	nil	1 0	1 0	4 0	nil		nil	nil
	7 0	7 0	7 0	7 0	7 0	7 0	7 0		7 0	7 0
	7 0	7 0	7 0	7 2	7 2	7 9	7 0		7 0	7 0

Appendix C

TIN PRESENTED FOR COINAGE IN CORNWALL: 1300-1485

The appearance of another set of statistics throwing light on late medieval Cornish tin production needs some explanation. The following graph is composed of a total of 105 years' figures covering the period 1300-1485; of these 58 have not previously been published and 9 are significant corrections of figures already published. With such a comprehensive statistical series as now exists there is little room for speculation or controversy. The two peaks of production are plain, as are the two major troughs. In particular the 'new' figures establish without doubt the serious progressive long-term decline in output which gripped the industry for most of the fifteenth century and caused production to persist at levels almost 50 per cent below those attained in the 1330s and the early fifteenth century.

The amounts of tin presented for coinage are not synonymous with production, for there was constant evasion of duty throughout the middle ages. Nevertheless the rate of duty remained stable at 40s. per thousandweight and there is no evidence that the incidence of smuggling fluctuated significantly in the course of the fourteenth and fifteenth centuries.

All the statistics used in this graph have been checked, whether previously published or not. For statistics already published, see G. R. Lewis, *The Stannaries*, Appendix J; L. F. Salzman, 'Mines and Stannaries', p. 92; A. R. Bridbury, *Economic Growth in England in the Later Middle Ages* (1962), p. 26. For the actual amounts of tin presented each year in pounds and detailed references to all sources, see M. J. Hatcher, 'The Assessionable Manors of the Duchy of Cornwall in the Later Middle Ages' (London Ph.D. thesis, 1967), II, 487-93.

In the construction of the graph the short hundred of five score has been used (Salzman, 'Mines and Stannaries', pp. 92-3).

1300-1 = tin presented for coinage after the Michaelmas coinages of 1300 up to and including the Michaelmas coinages of 1301.

288

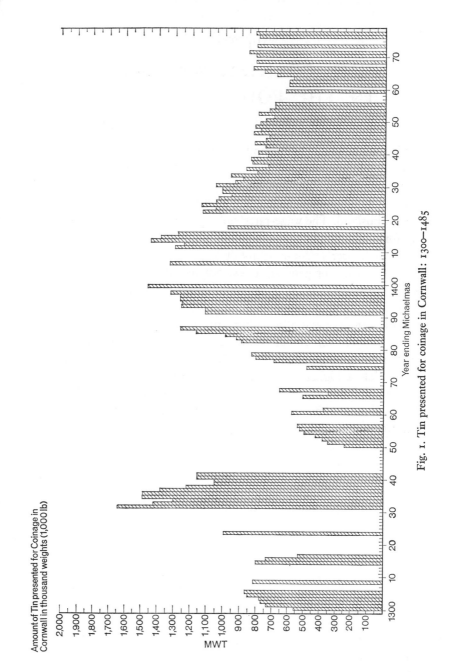

Amount of Tin presented for Coinage in Cornwall in thousand weights (1,000 lb)

MWT

Year ending Michaelmas

Fig. 1. Tin presented for coinage in Cornwall: 1300—1485

Appendix D

SOME CORNISH WAGE-RATES IN THE FOURTEENTH AND FIFTEENTH CENTURIES

This graph has been compiled almost exclusively from Duchy records of labour hired for works on the castles of Trematon, Tintagel, Launceston and Restormel, and the deer-parks of the manors of Trematon, Restormel, Liskeard, Helstone-in-Triggshire and Climsland. The wage-rates paid by the Duchy were remarkably uniform throughout the county.

The labourer's wage-rates are those paid for unskilled labour hired by the Duchy for general duties, not usually specified. The semi-skilled or craftsmen's rates are derived from those paid to thatchers, carpenters, masons and tilers, but not to plumbers who were usually remunerated at a higher rate. Different rates were paid in some periods for labour employed on manorial works, such as hedging, ditching, and fencing and for labour employed on buildings, for which a higher standard of work was presumably required, and rates could also vary according to the seasons; these differential rates have been distinguished by the use of broken and unbroken lines.

Appendix D

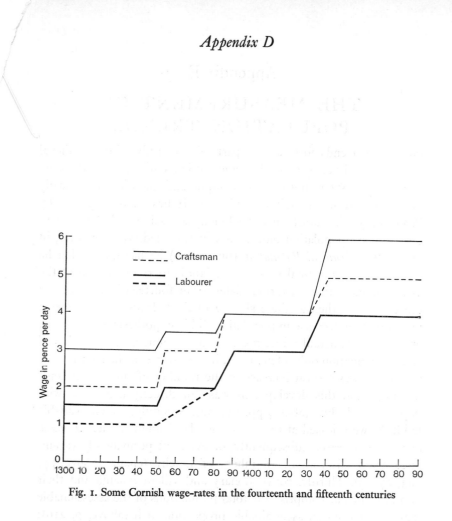

Fig. 1. Some Cornish wage-rates in the fourteenth and fifteenth centuries

Appendix E

THE MEASUREMENT OF POPULATION TRENDS

Population trends form a vital part of any study of the medieval economy, and yet worthwhile demographic statistics are extremely difficult and often impossible to compile and historians are usually forced to rely upon indirect evidences. It has been suggested by Professor J. C. Russell that the Duchy assession rolls be used to cast light on population movements in late medieval Cornwall; in his *British Medieval Population* (pp. 265–6) he has taken what he assumes to be the total numbers of landholders on certain of the assessionable manors at various dates in the fourteenth and fifteenth centuries, and then as these show a distinct decline he assumes a proportionate decrease in population. This hypothesis is, of course, open to fundamental criticisms on many grounds, of which it will suffice to mention only a few. First, in the course of the later middle ages there was a great increase in the number of substantial landholdings, and this development was not directly connected with population decline (above, pp. 225–32). Secondly, not all available holdings were leased at the assessions, land might be left *in manu domini* to be leased subsequently, or even left permanently vacant, once again affecting the numbers of Duchy tenants (above, pp. 123, 272–3). Thirdly, conventionary and villein tenants and their families did not comprise the total populations of the assessionable manors, or even an ascertainable proportion of it (above, p. 219); sub-tenants were common, and the assession rolls give no details of free tenants (above, pp. 231–5).

A more sophisticated attempt to use assession rolls for demographic purposes by recording the identity of each tenant at successive assessions might appear more promising at first, but holdings changed hands frequently, and for many reasons other than the deaths of tenants (above, pp. 98–9). Thus, despite the seductive attractions of this unique range of documents, one must eschew the temptation to compile masses of superficially impressive but patently worthless demographic statistics.

Appendix E

For a statistical approach, however dubious, we must therefore fall back on the highly unsatisfactory index—institutions of priests to benefices. The following graph is of the yearly institutions of priests to some 155 benefices in Cornwall; it has been compiled from the published registers of the medieval bishops of Exeter. Institutions created by the resignations of incumbents or an exchange of benefices have not been included. It should be borne in mind that there was frequently a delay between the death of a priest and the institution of a new one.

In this study only slight use has been made of the trends in the numbers of institutions, but they have proved useful in spotlighting periods of extremely high mortality such as 1348–50 and 1360–2.

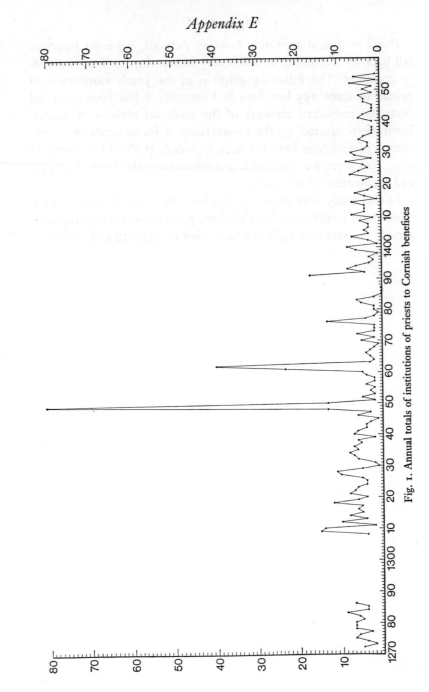

Fig. 1. Annual totals of institutions of priests to Cornish benefices

BIBLIOGRAPHY

A. MANUSCRIPT SOURCES

1. *Public Record Office*

(a) Manorial Documentation
  (i) Enrolled Manorial Accounts of the Earldom of Cornwall
      (26 Edward I–11 Edward III, 27 rolls)
      SC.6.816/9, 10; E.119/1; SC.6.811/1–812/1; E.370/5/19; SC.6.1094/
      11–1095/1.
  (ii) Enrolled Manorial Accounts of the Duchy of Cornwall
      (12 Edward III–17 Edward IV, 70 rolls)
      SC.6.816/11–822/4.
  (iii) Receivers' Accounts and the Great Rolls of Debts
      (11 Edward III–7 Edward IV, 78 rolls)
      SC.6.812/2–816/8.
  (iv) Assession Rolls
      (14 Edward III–13 Henry VII, 15 rolls)
      SC.11. Roll 153; E.306/2/1–2/16.
  (v) Rentals and Surveys
      E.142/6 and 7, E.152/8, C.133/95 (extent of possessions of the late
      Earl Edmund, 28 Edward I); E.142/41 (various surveys, 1–5 Ed-
      ward III); E.120/1 (Caption of Seisin); L.R.2.247 (fragment of
      extent of Cusancia and Berwyk, 19 Edward III); SC.12.2/27 (extent
      of Lostwithiel, 8 Edward III); SC.12.22/14 (extent of Penkneth, 35
      Edward III); SC.12.2/22 (schedule of Duchy manors and castles,
      Edward III); SC.11. Roll 968 (rental of Launceston, 3 Edward IV).
  (vi) Court Rolls (Edward III–Edward IV)
      Calstock: SC.2.158/10–158/12; Climsland: SC.2.158/32; Liskeard:
      SC.2.160/25–160/31; Moresk: SC.2.161/18; Penlyne: SC.2.161/
      62; Penkneth: SC.2.161/63; Penmayne: SC.2.161/67; Talskiddy:
      SC.2.163/17; Tewington: SC.2.163/18; Tintagel: SC.2.163/25;
      Trematon: SC.2.164/1–2.
  (vii) Miscellaneous Documents relating to the Assessionable Manors
      SC.6.1290/1–1291/3; E.370/5/11–5/22; E.306/10/1–5.
  (viii) Pipe Rolls and Foreign Accounts (E.372 and E.364)

Bibliography

These have been used extensively for details of the assessionable manors and tin coinage whilst the estates were in crown hands.
28 Edward I–8 Edward III, 18 enrolments concerning the estates of the Earldom of Cornwall.
3 Richard II–10 Edward IV, 59 enrolments concerning the Duchy of Cornwall.
See also E.306/11/1 (extracts from Foreign Accounts enrolled on Pipe Rolls, 31–35 Edward I).
(ix) Miscellaneous Cornish Manorial Accounts (Edward I–Edward IV) SC.6.822/5–823/42.

(b) Cornish Stannary Documentation
   (i) Coinage Rolls (29 Edward I–10 Edward IV)
     E.101/260/20, 21, 25; 261/1, 3, 6, 7, 8, 11, 17, 19, 20; 262/21, 22, 25, 26, 28, 29, 30; 263/1, 19, 21, 22, 23, 24, 26, 28; 264/1, 4, 5, 7, 9, 10; 265/1, 2, 4, 8, 20, 21, 22, 24, 25; 266/1, 2, 3, 6, 7, 8, 13, 14, 15, 16, 19, 22, 23, 24; 267/1.
     See also E.306/5/1.
   (ii) Court Rolls (29 Edward III–22 Edward IV)
     Blackmore: SC.2.156/26–157/12; Foweymore: SC.2.159/1–12; Penwith-and-Kirrier: SC.2.161/81–162/7; Tywarnhaile: SC.2.164/34–37.
     See also E. 101/260/1.
   (iii) Miscellaneous Stannary Documents
     E.101/263/13, 15; 264/2; 265/3; 620/33; 667/4.

(c) Customs Accounts
   (i) Plymouth and Fowey
     E.122/113/1–114/17.
   (ii) Duchy Haveners' Accounts (in addition to those enrolled with manorial accounts)
     E.122/40/13, 19; 180/4, 5; 216/19.
   (iii) Various Cornish Accounts
     E.122/17/7; 39/3–6; 70/8; 113/3; 176/3; 180/2, 3; 189/150; 193/34; 216/18; E.159/178.

(d) Subsidy Rolls, etc.
     E.179/87/5, 7, 9, 29–35, 37, 93.
     E.359/41; E.372/161, m.41.

Bibliography

(e) Miscellaneous.
  (i) Exchequer Accounts Various
    Works: E.101.461/11–461/25.
    See also E.306/11/2.
    Army, Navy and Ordnance: E.101/16/1; 603/2
    See also C.145/111/1.
    Sheriffs' Administrative Accounts, Cornwall: E.101/554/1.
  (ii) Ancient Petitions
    SC.8. Files 315, 333, 344. Petitions numbers 79, 186, 1868, 1869,
    5029, 5080, 5161, 5162, 9468, E.561.
    See also E.306/11/3, 4.
  (iii) Chancery Miscellanea
    C.47: Bundle 52, files 1–5.
  (iv) Chancery, Parliamentary and Council Proceedings (C.49)
  (v) Inquisitions *Post Mortem* (C.133–139, Edward I–Edward IV)
  (vi) Inquisitions *Ad Quod Damnum* (C.145)
  (vii) Exchequer T.R. Miscellaneous Books (E.36): vols. 57, 144, 278,
    279, 280
  (viii) Exchequer K.R. Miscellanea (E.163)
  (ix) Exchequer K.R. Parliamentary and Council Proceedings (E.175)
  (x) Exchequer L.T.R. Memoranda Rolls (E.368)
  (xi) Exchequer L.T.R. Miscellaneous Rolls (E.370)
  (xii) Ancient Correspondence (SC.1)
  (xiii) Kings Bench: Justices Itinerant and Ancient Indictments

2. *Duchy of Cornwall Office*

(a) Manorial Documentation
  (i) Enrolled Manorial Accounts of the Duchy of Cornwall
    (16 Edward III–1 Henry VII, 66 rolls)
    D.C.O. 1–75.
  (ii) Receivers' Accounts including the Great Rolls of Debts
    (29 Edward III–3 Henry VII, 16 rolls)
    D.C.O. 197–212.
  (iii) Assession Rolls
    (7 Edward III–23 Henry VII, 17 Rolls)
    D.C.O. 471–486.

(b) Miscellaneous
  Stannary Court roll, Foweymore 21 Henry VI.

297

Bibliography

Abridgement of the Extent of Cusancia and Berwyk, 19 Edward III, and a fragment of the Extent.
Book of Cornish Charters, Edward I–Edward IV.
Book of Duchy Charters, 1333–1644.

3. British Museum

Add MSS 12493, 36644, 41661.
Lansdowne MS 261.

4. Cornwall County Record Office

Fragment of the Extent of Cusancia and Berwyk, 19 Edward III (Mount Edgecumbe Records, Accession 821).
Sixteenth-century transcript of a fragment of the White Book of Cornwall (M.T.D. 31/1).

5. Royal Institution of Cornwall

The Henderson Collection; especially a transcript of a fragment of the White Rook of Cornwall.

6. Cambridge Library

Fragment of the Extent of Cusancia and Berwyk, 19 Edward III (Dd. ix–36).

For the convenience of the reader a chronological list of surviving enrolled ministers' accounts is herewith appended. These documents frequently contain the accounts of Duchy sheriffs, keepers of fees, haveners, stannary bailiffs, and borough reeves, as well as those of manorial officials.

1338/9	SC.6.816/11		1352/3	SC.6.817/3
1339/40	SC.6.816/12		1353/4	SC.6.817/4
1341/2	D.C.O. 1		1354/5	D.C.O. 7
1344/5	D.C.O. 2		1355/6	D.C.O. transcript
1346/7	D.C.O. 3		1356/7	D.C.O. 11
1348/9	D.C.O. 4		1357/8	SC.6.817/6
1349/50	D.C.O. 5		1358/9	SC.6.817/7
1350/1	SC.6.817/1		1359/60	D.C.O. 13
1351/2	D.C.O. 6		1361/2	SC.6.817/8

1362/3	D.C.O. 15	1416/17	SC.6.820/8
1363/4	SC.6.817/9, 10	1417/18	SC.6.820/9
1365/6	D.C.O. 17	1422/3	SC.6.820/11
1368/9	D.C.O. 18	1425/6	SC.6.820/12; D.C.O. 45
1369/70	SC.6.818/1, 2	1426/7	SC.6.820/13
1370/1	SC.6.818/3	1427/8	SC.6.820/14, 15
1371/2	SC.6.818/4	1428/9	D.C.O. 46
1372/3	SC.6.818/5	1431/2	SC.6.821/1, 2
1373/4	D.C.O. 15	1433/4	SC.6.821/3
1374/5	D.C.O. 20	1434/5	SC.6.821/4
1376/7	SC.6.818/6	1437/8	D.C.O. 48
1377/8	SC.6.818/7; D.C.O. 23	1439/40	D.C.O. 49
1378/9	SC.6.818/8	1441/2	SC.6.821/6
1379/80	D.C.O. 26	1444/5	D.C.O. 52
1381/2	SC.6.818/9	1448/9	D.C.O. 53
1382/3	SC.6.818/11	1451/2	SC.6.821/7
1385/6	D.C.O. 28	1453/4	SC.6.821/8; D.C.O. 54
1386/7	SC.6.818/12	1454/5	D.C.O. 55
1387/8	SC.6.819/1	1455/6	SC.6.821/9
1390/1	SC.6.819/2	1456/7	D.C.O. 56
1391/2	SC.6.819/3	1458/9	D.C.O. 57
1393/4	D.C.O. 31	1459/60	D.C.O. 58
1395/6	SC.6.819/6	1461/2	SC.6.821/11
1396/7	SC.6.819/8	1462/3	SC.6.822/1
1398/9	SC.6.819/9	1466/7	D.C.O. 59
1400/1	SC.6.819/10	1467/8	D.C.O. 60, 61
1401/2	SC.6.819/11	1471/2	D.C.O. 62, 63
1402/3	SC.6.819/12; D.C.O. 33	1472/3	D.C.O. 64
1403/4	SC.6.819/13, 14	1473/4	D.C.O. 65
1404/5	SC.6.819/15	1474/5	D.C.O. 66, 67
1405/6	D.C.O. 35	1475/6	D.C.O. 68; SC.6.822/2
1406/7	D.C.O. 36	1476/7	SC.6.822/3
1407/8	D.C.O. 37; SC.6.820/2	1477/8	D.C.O. 69
1408/9	D.C.O. 38, 39	1478/9	D.C.O. 70, 71
1409/10	D.C.O. 40	1479/80	D.C.O. 72
1410/11	SC.6.820/3	1480/1	D.C.O. 73
1411/12	D.C.O. 41	1483/4	D.C.O. 74
1414/15	D.C.O. 42	1484/5	D.C.O. 75
1415/16	D.C.O. 43		

B. PRINTED ORIGINAL SOURCES

These sources have been indexed under the title of the book. In this and the following section the place of publication is London except when stated otherwise.

Calendar of Charter Rolls Preserved in the Public Record Office (1903, etc.).

Bibliography

Calendar of Close Rolls Preserved in the Public Record Office (1892, etc.).
Calendar of Fine Rolls Preserved in the Public Record Office (1911, etc.).
Calendar of Inquisitions Miscellaneous Preserved in the Public Record Office (1916, etc.).
Calendar of Inquisitions Post Mortem Preserved in the Public Record Office (1906, etc.).
Calendar of Patent Rolls Preserved in the Public Record Office (1891, etc.).
Carte Nativorum: A Peterborough Abbey Cartulary of the Fourteenth Century, ed. C. N. L. Brooke and M. M. Postan (Northamptonshire Record Society, vol. XX; 1960).
Cartulary of St. Michael's Mount, ed. P. L. Hull (Devon and Cornwall Record Society, new ser., vol. V; 1962).
Episcopal Registers of the Diocese of Exeter, ed. F. C. Hingeston-Randolph, 10 vols (London and Exeter, 1886–1915); comprising the registers of: Walter Bronescombe (1257–80); Peter Quivil (1280–91); Thomas de Brytton (1292–1307); Walter de Stapledon (1307–26); John de Grandisson (1327–69); Thomas de Brantyngham (1370–94); Edmund Stafford (1395–1419); Edmund Lacy (1420–55). Two further volumes of Edmund Lacy's register, ed. G. R. Dunstan, have been published by the Canterbury and York Society in conjunction with the Devon and Cornwall Record Society (1961–4).
Foedera, Conventiones, Litterae, etc. ed. T. Rymer, 4 vols in 7 parts. (Record Commission, 1811–59).
The Itinerary of John Leland, 1535–43, ed. L. Toulmin-Smith, 5 vols (1907–10).
Ministers' Accounts of the Earldom of Cornwall, 1296–7, ed. L. M. Midgley, 2 vols (Camden Society, 3rd ser., vols LXVI, LXVIII; 1942–5).
Proceedings and Ordinances of the Privy Council of England, ed. Sir Harris Nicolas, 6 vols (1834–7).
Registers of Edward the Black Prince, 1348–1365, 4 vols (1930–3).
Rotuli Parliamentorum, 6 vols (1767–77).
Statutes of the Realm, 9 vols (1810–24).
Walter of Henley's Husbandry, etc., ed. E. Lamond (1890).

C. PRINTED SECONDARY SOURCES: THE DUCHY OF CORNWALL
AND THE HISTORY AND TOPOGRAPHY OF CORNWALL

Allen, J. *History of the Borough of Liskeard* (Liskeard, 1856).
Balchin, W. G. V. *The Making of the English Landscape, 2: Cornwall* (1954).

Bibliography

Beresford, M. W. 'Dispersed and Grouped Settlement in Medieval Cornwall', *Ag. H.R.*, XII (1964).

Boase, G. C. *Collectanea Cornubiensia—A collection of Biographical and Topographical Notes relating to the County of Cornwall* (Truro, 1890).

Boase, G. C. and Courteney, W. P. *Bibliotheca Cornubiensis*, 3 vols (1874–82).

Borlase, W. *Observations on the Antiquities, Historical and Monumental, of the County of Cornwall* (2nd edn, 1769).

Campbell, Stella M. 'The Haveners of the Medieval Dukes of Cornwall and the Organisation of the Duchy Ports'. *J.R.I.C.*, new ser., IV (1962).

Carew, Richard. *Survey of Cornwall* (1769 edn).

Clowes, R. L. 'On the Historical Documents in the Duchy of Cornwall Office', *Royal Cornwall Polytechnic Society Annual Report* (1930).

Coate, Mary. 'The Duchy of Cornwall: its history and administration, 1640–1660', *T.R.H.S.*, 4th ser., X (1927).

—— *Cornwall in the Great Civil War* (Oxford, 1933).

Concanen, George. *A Report of the Trial at Bar—Rowe vs. Brenton* (1830).

Cox, Thomas. *Cornwall* (1720–1).

Crawford, O. G. S. 'The Work of Giants', *Antiquity*, X (1936).

Daniell, J. J. *A Compendium of the History and Geography of Cornwall* (4th edn by Thurston C. Peter, 1906).

Denholm-Young, N. *Richard of Cornwall* (Oxford, 1947).

Devon and Cornwall Notes and Queries (in progress) Exeter, 1900– .

Doddridge, Sir John. *The History of the Ancient and Modern Estate of the Principality of Wales, Duchy of Cornwall and Earldom of Chester* (1630).

Drew, S. (ed.). *The History of Cornwall*, 2 vols (Helston, 1824).

Dudley, D. and Minter, E. M. 'The Medieval Village at Garrow Tor, Bodmin Moor', *Medieval Archaeology*, VII (1963).

Elliot-Binns, L. E. *Medieval Cornwall* (1955).

Gilbert, C. S. *Historical Survey of the County of Cornwall*, 2 vols (Plymouth, 1817–20).

Gilbert, Davies. *Parochial History of Cornwall*, 4 vols (1838).

Gover, J. B. 'Cornish Place Names', *Antiquity*, II (1928).

Halliday, F. E. *A History of Cornwall* (1959).

Hals, William. *Parochial History of Cornwall* (n.p., n.d.).

Harrington, E. *The Circle or an Historical Survey of Sixty Parishes and Towns in Cornwall* (Helston, 1819).

Hatcher, John. 'A Diversified Economy: Later Medieval Cornwall', *Ec. H.R.*, 2nd ser., XXII (1969).

Hencken, H. O'N. *The Archaeology of Cornwall and Scilly* (1932).

Bibliography

Henderson, Charles. *Essays in Cornish History*, ed. A. L. Rowse and M. I. Henderson (Oxford, 1935).

Hull, P. L. 'The Statute Merchant Seal of Lostwithiel', *Archives*, VI, 29 (1963).

Jenkin, A. K. Hamilton. *The Cornish Miner* (1927).

—— *Cornwall and its People* (1945).

Lake, William (publisher). *A Complete Parochial History of the County of Cornwall*, 4 vols (Truro, 1867–72).

Lewis, G. R. *The Stannaries* (Harvard Economic Studies, III, 1906).

Lysons, Daniel and Samuel. *Magna Britannia III Cornwall* (1814).

Maclean, Sir John. *The Parochial and Family History of the Deanery of Trigg Minor, Cornwall*, 3 vols (Bodmin, 1873–9).

Manning, James. *The Practice of the Court of Exchequer* (1827).

Marshall, William. *The Rural Economy of the West of England*, 2 vols (1796).

Nance, R. Morton. *A Guide to Cornish Place Names* (4th edn, Marazion, 1963).

Norden, J. *Speculi Britanniae Pars—A Topographical and Historical Description of Cornwall* (1728).

Pearse, R. *The Ports and Harbours of Cornwall* (St Austell, 1963).

Penaluna, W. *An Historical Survey of the County of Cornwall*, 2 vols (Helston, 1838).

Peter, R. and O. B. *Histories of Launceston and Dunheved* (Plymouth, 1885).

Pevsner, N. *The Buildings of England: Cornwall* (1951).

Polwhele, R. *The History of Cornwall*, 7 vols (1803–16).

Pounds, N. J. G. 'The Domesday Geography of Cornwall', *Royal Cornwall Polytechnic Society Annual Report* (1942).

—— 'Lanhydrock Atlas', *Antiquity*, XIX (1945).

Rawson, R. R. 'The Open-Field in Flintshire, Devonshire and Cornwall', *Ec. H.R.*, 2nd ser., VI (1953).

Robbins, A. F. *Launceston Past and Present* (Launceston, 1884).

Roddis, R. *Cornish Harbours* (1951).

Rowe, J. *Cornwall in the Age of the Industrial Revolution* (Liverpool, 1953).

Rowse, A. L. 'The Duchy of Cornwall', *The Gentleman's Magazine* (January 1937).

—— *Tudor Cornwall, Portrait of a Society* (1941).

—— (ed.), *The West in English History* (1949).

Royal Institution of Cornwall, Journals and Reports (in progress) 1862– .

Bibliography

Salzman, L. F. 'Mines and Stannaries', in *The English Government at Work, 1327–1336*, vol. III, ed. J. F. Willard, W. A. Morris, W. H. Dunham (Cambridge, Mass., 1950).

Sharp, Margaret. 'The Administrative Chancery of the Black Prince before 1362', in *Essays in Medieval History presented to T. F. Tout*, edited by A. G. Little and F. F. Powicke (Manchester, 1925).

Smirke, E. 'On Certain Obscure Words in Charters, Rentals, Accounts, etc., of Property in the West of England', *Archaeological Journal*, V (1848).

—— 'Notes on the Cornish Acre', *Royal Institution of Cornwall, 43rd Report*, Appendix II (1862).

Stanes, R. G. F. 'A Georgicall Account of Devonshire and Cornwall in Answer to some Queries concerning Agriculture. Samuel Colepresse (1667)', *Transactions of the Devon Association*, XCVI, 1964.

Toy, S. *The History of Helston* (Oxford, 1936).

Victoria History of the Counties of England: Cornwall, ed. William Page, 2 vols (1906–21).

Worgan, G. B. *General View of the Agriculture of Cornwall* (1811).

D. UNPUBLISHED SECONDARY SOURCES: THE DUCHY OF CORNWALL AND THE HISTORY AND TOPOGRAPHY OF CORNWALL

Bayley, *Report on the Earldom and subsequently Duchy of Cornwall* (Duchy of Cornwall Office, n.d.).

Clowes, R. L. *Stoke Climsland—Historical Notes* (Duchy of Cornwall Office, 1930).

Freeth, G. *Report relating to the Cornish Manors* (Duchy of Cornwall Office, c. 1836).

Illingworth, W. *Report on the Office of Havener or Keeper of the Ports of the Duchy, and the rights appertaining thereto; and on the Butlerage and Prisage of Wines* (Duchy of Cornwall Office, 1822).

Midgley, L. M. 'Edmund Earl of Cornwall and his place in History' (Manchester, M.A. thesis; 1930).

Whetter, J. C. A. 'The Economic History of Cornwall in the Seventeenth Century' (London, Ph.D. thesis; 1965).

E. PRINTED SECONDARY SOURCES: GENERAL

Agrarian History of England and Wales Vol. IV 1500–1640, ed. J. Thirsk (Cambridge, 1967).

Bibliography

Bean, J. M. W. *The Estates of the Percy Family, 1416–1537* (Oxford, 1958).

Bennett, H. S. *Life on the English Manor 1150–1400* (Cambridge, 3rd edn, 1948).

Beresford, M. W. 'Lot Acres', *Ec. H.R.*, XIII (1943).

Beresford, M. W. and St Joseph, J. K. *Medieval England: An Aerial Survey* (Cambridge, 1958).

Beveridge, W. H. 'The Yield and Price of Corn in the Middle Ages', *Economic History (a supplement to the Economic Journal)*, May 1927.

—— 'A Statistical Crime of the Seventeenth Century', *J.E.B.H.* (August 1929).

—— 'Westminster Wages in the Manorial Era', *Ec. H.R.*, 2nd ser., VIII (1955).

Bridbury, A. R. *England and the Salt Trade in the Later Middle Ages* (Oxford, 1955).

—— *Economic Growth: England in the Later Middle Ages* (1962).

Brown, E. H. Ph. and Hopkins, S. V. 'Seven Centuries of Building Wages', *Economica*, new ser., XXII (1955).

—— 'Seven Centuries of the Prices of Consumables, compared with Builders' Wage Rates', *Economica*, XXIII (1956).

Buckatzsch, E. J. 'The Geographical Distribution of Wealth in England, 1086–1843', *Ec. H.R.*, 2nd ser., III (1950).

Cambridge Economic History of Europe, vols. I–III (Cambridge, 1952–66).

Carus-Wilson, E. M. *Medieval Merchant Venturers* (1954).

—— 'Evidences of Industrial Growth on Some Fifteenth Century Manors', *Ec. H.R.*, 2nd ser., XII (1959).

—— *The Expansion of Exeter at the Close of the Middle Ages* (Exeter, 1963).

Carus-Wilson, E. M. and Coleman, O. P. *England's Export Trade, 1275–1547* (Oxford, 1962).

Chibnall, A. C. *Sherington—Fiefs and Fields of a Buckinghamshire Village* (Cambridge, 1965).

Clapham, Sir John. *A Concise Economic History of Britain from the Earliest Times to 1750* (Cambridge, 1949).

Darby, H. C. and Finn, R. Welldon. *The Domesday Geography of South-West England* (Cambridge, 1967).

Davenport, F. G. *The Economic Development of a Norfolk Manor, 1086–1565* (Cambridge, 1906).

Denholm-Young, N. *Seigneurial Administration in England* (Oxford, 1937).

Bibliography

Duby, G. *L'economie rurale et la vie des compagnes dans l'occident medieval*, 2 vols (Paris, 1962).

Dufresne, Caroli. *Glossarium ad Scriptores Mediae et Infirmae Latinitatis*, 7 vols (Paris, 1840–50).

Field, R. K. 'Worcestershire Peasant Buildings in the Later Middle Ages', *Medieval Archaeology*, IX (1965).

Finberg, H. P. R. *Tavistock Abbey—A Study in the Social and Economic History of Devon* (Cambridge, 1951).

—— 'The Open Field in Devonshire', *Antiquity*, XXIII (1949).

Finberg, H. P. R. and Hoskins, W. G. *Devonshire Studies* (1952).

Fox, L. *The Administration of the Honour of Leicester in the Fourteenth Century* (Leicester, 1940).

Gasquet, F. A. *The Great Pestilence* (1893).

Gras, N. S. B. *The Evolution of the English Corn Market*, Harvard Economic Studies, XIII (Cambridge, Mass., 1915).

—— *The Early English Customs System* (Cambridge, Mass., 1918).

Gray, H. L. *English Field Systems* (Cambridge, Mass., 1915).

Hallam, H. E. *Settlement and Society—A Study of the Early Agrarian History of South Lincolnshire* (Cambridge, 1965).

Harvey, Barbara, F. 'The Population Trend in England between 1300 and 1348', *T.R.H.S.*, 5th ser., XVI (1965).

Harvey, P. D. A. *A Medieval Oxfordshire Village: Cuxham 1240–1400* (Oxford, 1965).

Hilton, R. H. *The Economic Development of some Leicestershire Estates in the Fourteenth and Fifteenth Centuries* (Oxford, 1947).

—— 'The Social Structure of Rural Warwickshire in the Middle Ages', *Dugdale Society Occasional Papers*, IX (1950).

—— *The Decline of Serfdom in Medieval England* (Studies in Economic History, 1969).

Holmes, G. A. *The Estates of the Higher Nobility in Fourteenth Century England* (Cambridge, 1957).

Homans, G. C. *English Villagers of the Thirteenth Century* (Cambridge, Mass., 1941).

Hoskins, W. G. 'The Reclamation of the Waste in Devon', *Ec. H.R.*, XIII (1943).

—— *Devon* (1954).

—— *The Making of the English Landscape* (1955).

Kenyon, Nora. 'Labour Conditions in Essex in the Reign of Richard II', *Ec. H.R.*, IV (1934).

Kerridge, E. *The Agricultural Revolution* (1967).

Bibliography

Kingsford, C. L. *Prejudice and Promise in Fifteenth Century England* (Oxford, 1925).

Latham, R. E. *Revised Medieval Latin Word-List from British and Irish Sources* (1965).

Levett, A. E. 'The Black Death on the Estates of the See of Winchester', *Oxford Studies in Social and Legal History*, ed. P. Vinogradoff, vol. V (Oxford, 1916).

—— 'A Note on the Statute of Labourers', *Ec. H.R.*, VI (1932).

—— *Studies in Manorial History* (Oxford, 1938).

Lucas, H. S. 'The Great European Famine of 1315–1316, and 1317', *Speculum*, V (1930).

Mace, F. A. 'Devonshire Ports in the Fourteenth and Fifteenth Centuries', *T.R.N.S.*, 4th ser., VIII (1925).

Maitland, F. W. *Domesday Book and Beyond* (Cambridge, 2nd edn, 1907).

Martin, C. T. *The Record Interpreter* (2nd edn, 1910).

Morgan, M. *English Lands of the Abbey of Bec* (Oxford, 1946).

Mumford, W. F. 'Terciars on the Estates of Wenlock Priory', *Transactions of the Shropshire Archaeological Society*, LVIII (1965).

Myers, A. R. *The Household of Edward IV* (Manchester, 1959).

Neilson, N. 'Customary Rents', *Oxford Studies in Social and Legal History*, ed. P. Vinogradoff, vol. II (Oxford, 1910).

Orwin, C. S. and C. S. *The Open Fields* (2nd edn, Oxford, 1954).

Page, F. M. *The Estates of Crowland Abbey* (Cambridge, 1934).

Perroy, E. 'Les crises du XIVᵉ Siècle', *Annales*, IV (1949).

Postan, M. M. 'The Fifteenth Century', IX (1939).

—— 'Some Economic Evidence of Declining Population in the Later Middle Ages', *Ec. H.R.*, 2nd ser., II (1950).

—— 'Histoire Economique Moyen Ages'. *IXᵉ Congrès International des Sciences Historiques*, I, Rapports (Paris, 1950).

—— 'Village Livestock in the Thirteenth Century', *Ec. H.R.*, 2nd ser., XV (1962).

Postan, M. M. and Power E. (eds). *Studies in Fifteenth Century Trade* (1933).

Power, E. 'The Effects of the Black Death on Rural Organisation in England', *History*, III (1918).

Powicke, Sir M. and Fryde, E. B. (eds). *Handbook of British Chronology* (1961).

Pugh, T. B. *The Marcher Lordships of South Wales, 1415–1536* (Cardiff, 1963).

306

Putnam, B. H. *The Enforcement of the Statutes of Labourers during the first decade after the Black Death, 1349–59* (New York, 1908).

—— *Proceedings before the Justices of the Peace in the Fourteenth and Fifteenth Centuries* (Ames Foundation Publication, 1938).

—— *The Place in Legal History of Sir William Shareshull* (Cambridge, 1950).

Raftis, J. A. *The Estates of Ramsey Abbey—A Study in Economic Growth and Organisation* (Toronto, 1957).

Rogers, J. E. Thorold. *History of Agriculture and Prices in England*, 7 vols (Oxford, 1866–1902).

—— *Six Centuries of Work and Wages* (1894).

Russell, J. C. *British Medieval Population* (Albuquerque, 1948).

Saltmarsh, J. and Darby, H. C. 'The Infield-Outfield System on a Norfolk Manor', *Economic History*, III (1935).

Salzman, L. F. *English Industries of the Middle Ages* (1913).

Schofield, R. S. 'The Geographical Distribution of Wealth in England, 1334–1649', *Ec. H.R.*, 2nd ser., XVIII (1965).

Schreiner, J. 'Wages and Prices in England in the Later Middle Ages', *Scandinavian Economic History Review*, II (1954).

Seebohm, F. *The English Village Community* (4th edn, 1890).

Skeat, W. W. *An Etymological Dictionary of the English Language* (4th edn, Oxford, 1924).

Smith, R. A. L. *Canterbury Cathedral Priory—A Study in Monastic Administration* (Cambridge, 1943).

Söininen, A. M. 'Burn-beating and the Technical Basis of Colonisation in Finland in the 16th and 17th Centuries', *Scandinavian Economic History Review*, VII (1959).

Somerville, R. *History of the Duchy of Lancaster, vol. I, 1265–1603* (1953).

Steffen, G. F. *Geschichte der Englischen Lohnarbeiter*, vol. I (Stuttgart, 1901).

Tout, T. F. (ed.). *Chapters in the Administrative History of Medieval England*, 6 vols (Manchester, 1920–33).

Tupling, G. H. *The Economic History of Rossendale*, Chetham Soc., new ser., LXXXVI (Manchester, 1927).

Ugawa, K. 'The Economic Development of some Devon Manors in the Thirteenth Century', *Transactions of the Devon Association*, vol. XCIV (1962).

Willard, J. F. *Parliamentary Taxes on Personal Property, 1290–1334* (Cambridge, Mass., 1934).

L

F. UNPUBLISHED SECONDARY SOURCES: GENERAL

Kew, J. E. 'The Land Market in Tudor Devon' (Exeter, Ph.D. thesis; 1968).

Payne, R. C. 'The Agricultural Estates in Wiltshire of the Duchy of Lancaster in the 13th, 14th, and 15th Centuries' (London, Ph.D. thesis; 1939).

Sharp, M. 'Contributions to the History of the Earldom and County of Chester, 1237–1399' (Manchester, Ph.D. thesis; 1926).

Touchard, H. 'Les Douanes municipales d'Exeter (Devon): publication des rôles de 1381 à 1433' (University of Paris, Doctoral thesis, 1967).

INDEX

Abberbury, Sir Richard, 137
administration of estates, *see* assessionable manors, auditors, receiver, reeve, steward
Advent parish, 22, 23
agriculture, 8–17; and mining, 35–6, 73, 93–4, 101, 120, 143, 146, 168–9, 238–43, 249, 251; *see also* arable farming, pastoral husbandry, convertible husbandry, foodstuffs, demand for
Alren, Desiderata (Climsland), 61
Anne, queen of Richard II, 137, 138 n.
annual rents, described, 53, 87
Aquitaine, Principality of, 37
arable farming, 14–16, 270–1; stimulus to, 169–70; *see also* baticium, beat-burning, convertible husbandry
Arundell, John, 181, 198 n.
Ashburton, 172
assarting, *see* colonisation
assession fine, described, 53–4, 62, 87
assession rolls, 3, 16, 64, 67, 218, 220, 267–8, 292–3
assessionable manors: documentation, 2–3; profits, early 14th century, 90–2, 196, later 14th century, 118–19, 128, 196–8, early 15th century, 198, later 15th century, 167, 198–9, graph, 201 ; administration, Chapter 2 *passim*, post-Black Death, 116–17, later 14th century, 126–8, 136–9, general, 257–8. *See also* Calstock, Climsland, Helston-in-Kirrier, Helstone-in-Triggshire, Liskeard, Moresk, Penkneth, Penlyne, Penmayne, Restormel, Rillaton, Talskiddy, Tewington, Tintagel, Trematon, Tybesta, Tywarnhaile

assessions: described, 53–7; officials of, 54, 70, 75, 94, 130, 160
auditors of accounts, 54, 56, 96, 112, 117, 126; functions of, 46–7, 49–50
Audley, Sir Hugh, 4
auxilium, 69

bailiff-errant, 45, 46
Bakhampton, Alner and William, 71
Bakhampton, Richard, 70–1, 236–7, 248
Bandyn, Robert, 86
Bardi of Florence, 239
Barlebien, Radulph (Calstock), 232
barley, 15
Basset, John (Helston-in-Kirrier), 96, 253
baticium, 82–4; *see also* beat-burning
beadles, 40–1, 62
Beales' (Climsland), 41
beat-burning, 12–14; *see also baticium*, waste pastures, cultivation of
Beaulieu (Climsland), 274, 278–9
Beaupel, Sir Robert, 237, 238 n.
berbiage, 68–9
Berwyk, Hugo de, survey of, 95
Bestus, Roger (Climsland), 171 n.
Biagga, John (Helstone-in-Triggshire) 68 n., 100
Bile, Thomas (Climsland), 60
Bilkemore, Robert, 239
bird-snares, 59, 185
Black Death: strikes Cornwall, 102–3; mortalities during, 102–3, 105; effects on assessionable manors and landholding, Chapter 5 *passim*, 122, 229, 231, 269–70; *see also* plague
Black Prince, *see* Edward, of Woodstock
Black Rock Passage, 193
Blackmore stannary district, 6 n., 16,

Index

Index

Chagford, 172
Channel Islands, trade with, 34
Chapman, John (Tintagel), 99
Chester, Earldom of, 6, 37
chevage, 56 n., 78, 101, 221-2
Chidley, Jacob (Tewington), 42, 162
Chienhale (Helston-in-Kirrier), 275, 286-7
Church, licences to enter, 77, 256
Chyna, Henry (Tintagel borough), 244
Clemence, Thomas, 181, 209 n., 252 n.
clerics, and landholding, 68, 248
Clerk, Roger (Liskeard), 253
Clifford, William de, 138 n.
Climsland manor, 4, 17, 18, 41, 56 n., 60, 61, 62, 68, 71, 76, 77, 83, 84, 94 n., 99, 100, 108, 126, 129, 131, 134, 137, 156, 157-8, 160-1, 164 n., 172, 175, 195, 220, 221, 223, 233, 258, 268 n., 269, 271, 272, 274, 276; description of, 19-23; map, 20; economic conditions and profitability, early 14th century, 89, Black Death, 104-7, later 14th century, 122-3, 129-30, early 15th century, 150-3, later 15th century, 158-9; graphs, 202, 262; tables of rents of individual holdings, 278-9; carrying services, 66; cloth production, 171, 174, 221-2; *censar'*, 171; fulling mills, 171, 174, manorial court, 136, 195; deer park, 84, 179, 202 n., 224 (*see also* deer parks, Carrybullock park); toll-tin, 161; woodland, 185
cloth production, *see* textile production
Clyker, William, de (Liskeard), 253
Clyner (Liskeard), 185
Coate, Miss Mary, 1, 72 n.
coinage duty, *see* tin
coinage towns, 21 n., 24 n.
colonisation, 73, 82-4, 85, 92, 168-9
Colyn, John (Helstone-in-Triggshire), 230 n.
common pastures, absence on assessionable manors, 15
Controller of Works, 46, 181
conventionary system, *see* assessions

conventionary tenants: numbers and distribution, 53, 72, 76-7; size of holding, 11, 16, 99-101, 121, 139, 225-35; transfer of holdings, 57-8, 98-9, 220-1; economic status of, 218-19, 235-56; and the trade in tin, 238-43, 249, 251
conventionary tenure: conditions of, 52-7, 62-70, 86-7, 218-19; history of, 71-9; under Richard II, 138-9; under Henry VI, 156-7
convertible husbandry, 11-12, 270-1, 276
Conyngswood (Liskeard), 185
Coombe, Matthew (Lostwithiel), 244
Cornborough, Alfred, 184
Corndon waste (Helstone-in-Triggshire), 252
Cornish acre, 18, 65
Cornwall: topography and climate, 8-10, 16; agriculture, 8, 11-16, 270-1; settlement patterns, 8-9, 16-17, 20; economic structure, 29-36, 167-73, 222-5, 258; wealth of, 8-9, 172-3; reputation in middle ages, 1; exports cloth, 169-71; imports grain, 146-7; threatened with invasion, 144-5; ports, 5, 171; sheriff, 5; county courts, 5, 43; hundred courts, 5, 43; inhabitants of, 1-2; language of, 1-2; sheriffs of, 45 n.
Cornwall, John of, 138 n.
Courtenay, Thomas, Earl of Devon, and struggle for stewardship of Cornwall, 47-8
Cowythaday, Robert, 249
Coyscren (Tybesta), *see* Coyspost
Coyspost (Tybesta), 273, 284-5
Creed parish, 26
Cremabit (Liskeard), 115
Cresy, John de (Helston-in-Kirrier), 60
Crinscombe (Calstock), 19, 185
Crok, Jacob (Foweymore stannary), 234
Crostang (Helston-in-Kirrier), 28
Cumberland, 148
Curtoys, Gerard (Lostwithiel), 244

311

Index

Index

horses, 16
Hoyk, John (Liskeard), 171 n., 254
Huntingdon, John, Earl of, 149, 198
huntyngsylver, 65
Hyde, Thomas de la, 196 n.

imprisonment of debtors, 51, 94, 96, 138 n., 197
Ingepenne, Roger de, 80 n.
inheritance customs, 41, 57, 59, 63–4, 68, 72; death duties, 78, 103–4, 120, 129, 194
Inny River, 19
institutions of priests to benefices, 102–3, 292–4
inventories, 254–6
Iota, Drogo, 99
Ireland, trade with, 34
Isabella, wife of Edward II: tenure of Earldom of Cornwall, 4–5, 75; financial provision for, 4; administration of estates, 85

Jagow, William (Tybesta), 58 n., 232, 251
Joan, wife of Edward the Black Prince: dower of, 7, 47, 137, 198; administration of estates, 47, 138 n., 145, 247; death, 137–8
Johan, John (Liskeard), 255
John, of Eltham, tenure of Earldom of Cornwall, 5, 86; administration of estates, 74–6, 86–90
Jolly, Randolph (Lostwithiel), 244
Jordan, John (Tewington), 56
juries, 40–1, 63
Justices of Labourers, visits to Cornwall, 121 n., 144, 290–1
Juyl, Richard (Trematon), 40,248, 256

Kellygrey, John de (Helstone-in-Triggshire), 60
Kendale, Edward de, assession of, 125
Kendale, John de, 71, 237
Kenstock, *see* Camelford and Kenstock mills
Kenston (Climsland), 131
Kent, 148
Kernek, Nicholas (Helstone-in-Trigg-

shire), 39–40, 124, 249
King Arthur, 22
Kirrier hundred, 240
Kittowe, John and Radulph (Helstone-in-Triggshire), 230
Knocket (Climsland), 278–9
Knylly (Liskeard), 185

La Rochelle, battle of, 145
labour services, 64–7, 191
Lamenes, 243
Lanargh, John (Helston-in-Kirrier), 242–3
Landewarent, John de (Liskeard), 60
Langa, Walter (Tintagel borough), 244
Lanlivery parish, 24
Lanteglos parish, 22
Launceston, 5, 19, 21, 66, 246n.; jail, 94, 96; deer park, 179; castle, 179
lead mines, 19, 29, 223
leasehold tenure, *see* conventionary tenure
Leen, David (Liskeard), 253
Lenche, William, 62, 193
ley farming, *see* convertible husbandry
Leye, Walter de (Climsland), 55
leyrite, 67, 79, 194–5
life tenure, conditions of, 70–1, 99
Lincolnshire, 148
Linkinhorne parish, 19
Lisgree (Helston-in-Kirrier), 97, 275
Liskeard borough, 5, 19–21, 86, 245, 246 n.
Liskeard manor, 4, 17, 23, 39, 41, 45 n., 58 n., 60, 63, 65 n., 66, 68, 69, 72 n., 80, 83, 103, 137, 144, 156, 157–8, 160, 164, 173, 197, 220, 221, 224, 233, 236, 237 n., 245, 250, 253, 254, 255, 258, 271, 272, 273, 274, 276; description of, 19–21; economic conditions and profitability, early 14th century, 88–9, Black Death, 112–16, later 14th century, 124–5, 130–2, early 15th century 150–3, later 15th century, 159, graphs, 206–7, 263; tables of rents of individuals holdings, 280–1; size

Index

Polscoth mill (Penlyne), 118
Pomeray, Henry le, 86 n.
Pomeray, William (Liskeard), 231 n., 251
population: movements, 92, 100–1, 102, 105, 119, 128–9, 140, 168, 270; measurement of, 102, 292–4; mobility of, 120, 220–2
Portugal, trade with, 34
Poulestonbrigge, 60
Pouvre, Richard (Climsland), 99
prices, of grain at Exeter, 146–7; of grain from Tavistock Abbey manors, 146–7; of raw materials, 144
Primatyn, Peter (Helston-in-Kirrier), 253
Pronta, John (Tintagel borough), 244
Purlee, John de, 118, 246–7
Putte (Climsland), 153
Putte, Richard (Climsland), 55

quarrying, 29, 34, 149, 225; see also Delabole, 'hellyngstones'
Queynte, Serlo (Lostwithiel), 244
Quoynte, Thomas (Lostwithiel), 239

Randolph, John (Liskeard), 255
receiver, 54, 104, 117, 126, 127 n., 128; functions, 42–6, 50–1, 185; receiver-general, 43, 47, 48
receivers' accounts: 2, 44 n., 51, 138, 200; Great Roll of Debtors, 51
recognitio, 158, 160
Rede, Stephen (Penlyne), 60
Redruth, 26, 246 n., 249 n.
reeve: functions, 37–42, 49–50, 51, 190; election of, 38–9, 62; perquisites of office, 40; assistance given to, 162
reliefs, 6, 59–60, 72
rent collectors, 41–2, 162
'Rents of Assize', 49, 68, 81, 95, 165, 174
Reprenne bridge (near Lanhydrok), 191
Restormel manor, 4, 24, 61–2, 65, 71, 137, 138, 159, 181 n., 198, 199; description of, 24–5; economic conditions and profitability, early 14th century, 89, Black Death, 112–14,

later 14th century, 123–4, 132, later 15th century, 162; castle, 24, 62, 197; deer park, 24, 65, 179–83, 224; fishery, 24; mill, 118; woodland, 166, 185
Reynold, Nicholas (Liskeard), 164
Richard, of Cornwall, 3, 86 n.
Richard II, tenure of Duchy of Cornwall, 7, 198; inherits part of Duchy, 47, 137–8; administration of estates, 47, 49 n., 138–9, 271 n.; overthrown, 149
Rill, John de (Rillaton), 103
Rillaton manor, 4, 17, 21, 23, 40, 63, 66, 83, 94 n., 103, 108, 126, 137, 138, 156, 157, 160, 161, 172, 258, 268 n.; description of, 19, 21; economic conditions and profitability, early 14th century, 89, Black Death, 104, later 14th century, 122–3, 129–30, early 15th century, 150–3, later 15th century, 159, graphs, 203, 262; manorial court, 136, 195; suit to mill, 67; toll-tin, 161; woodland, 185
Rivers, Earl, see Woodville, Anthony
Robyn, John, 209 n.
Roche parish, 25
Roger, John (Tintagel borough), 244
Roskymmer, Richard de (Helston-in-Kirrier), 60
Roslyn (Helston-in-Kirrier), 133 n., 275, 286–7
Rosnonnan (Liskeard), 280–1
Rosnornan, Simon (Liskeard), 253
Rothe, John (Climsland), 225 n.
Rothe, William (Climsland), 233
'rounceys', 16
Rowse, Dr A. L., 1
Russell, Prof. J. C., 292
Russell, John (Liskeard), 171 n., 234, 254
Russell, Richard (Tintagel), 57
rye, 15

St Agnes parish, 27
St Austell parish, 25
St Blazey parish, 25
St Clements parish, 26

Index

St Dominic parish, 18
St Gwinear, 243
St Hermit, rector of, 68 n.
St Ives, 222
St Kewe, 222
St Minver parish, 23
St Neulina, John de (Helston-in-Kirrier), 236, 240
St Saviour, 191
St Stephens' parish, 17
St Wendron, vicar of (Helston-in-Kirrier), 68 n.
St Wendron, John, vicar of, 248
salt, import of, 32
Saltash, 5, 18, 22, 34, 40, 86, 192, 199, 221, 245, 246, 248, 256
Sampite, Andrew (Helston-in-Kirrier), 253
sanding, 13–14
Sandwich, 35
Sarnsfeld, Margaret, 155, 198
Scluys, battle of, 144
Scoria, John (Climsland), 195
Scoria, Roger (Climsland), 77
Scurra, John (Helston-in-Kirrier), 234, 253
sea, importance to Cornwall, 32–4, 168; employment provided by, 223
Segrave, Hugh de, 136
Share, William (Liskeard), 233
Shareshull, William de, 247 n.
sheep, 15, 16, 69, 170–1, 234
shipbuilding, 29, 35, 149
shipping, 29, 32, 149
silver mines, 19, 29, 120 n., 223, 239
Sken, John (Helston-in-Kirrier), 253
Sody, Richard (Tywarnhaile), 156 n.
Somerset, 148; graziers of, 23; textile production in, 169
Sorn, Matilla le (Tybesta), 74
Southampton, 33, 35
Spain, trade with, 34; war with, 144–5
stabulagium, see huntyngsylver
Stacy, William (Tavistock), 248
Stafford, Earl of, estates in Cornwall, 63
Stalbat, Richard (Trematon), 268
stannaries: 6 n., 16, 21, 43, 196, 197 n.; profits of, 5–6; courts, 143;

shortage of labour, 143; of Devon, 172, 223
Stere, Alice (Helstone-in-Triggshire), 54 n.
steward, 47, 48, 54, 104, 112, 117, 126, 128; functions of, 42–6, 185; Chief Steward, 43
Stithians parish, 27
Stoke (Trematon), 119–120
Stoke Climsland parish, 19
Stonor, Sir William, 2
Sturte (Liskeard), 152
sub-tenancies, 16, 68, 139, 219, 231–5, 237–8, 252
Surveyor of game in Cornwall, 46, 179 n.
Sussex, 148
Sutton, port of, 22, 144–5, 238
Symon, Philip (Tewington), 68 n.

tallage, described, 61–2
tallies, 50
Talskiddy manor, 4, 24, 137, 150, 199, 236; economic conditions and profitability, 89, 162
Tamar River, 17, 18, 19, 191, 192, 223; fish weir, 223; salmon in, 19, 33
Tavistock, abbey of, 237 n.; and fish weir of Calstock, 66, 191, 205 n.; grain prices on manors of, 147
Tavistock, borough of, 18, 172, 225
Tavistock, William (Tavistock), 191
tax assessments, 1327 assessment, 219, 238, 240–1, 243, 253; 1514–15 and 1523–4 assessments, 172–3; *see also under* tinners
Tewington manor, 4, 26, 39, 40, 42, 45 n., 56, 59, 68, 69, 72 n., 83, 137, 138 n., 159, 181 n., 198, 223, 226, 236, 238, 275, 276; description of, 25; economic conditions and profitability, early 14th century, 88–9, Black Death, 107–10, later 14th century, 123–4, 132, later 15th century, 162–3, graphs, 212, 265; size of holdings, 16–17, 25, 100, 168, 222; compared to Tywarnhaile, 27; influence of tin-mining on

319